PECAN-NECTARINE
LAYER CAKE
pg. 216

LADIES' HOME
JOURNAL.

Recipes
1999

Ladies' Home Journal Books
Des Moines, Iowa

Ladies' Home Journal® Books
An Imprint of Meredith® Books

LADIES' HOME JOURNAL®

Recipes 1999

Project Editor: Kristi M. Fuller
Contributing Editors: Sarah P. Basso,
    Winifred Moranville,
    Kelly Staikopoulos, Joyce Trollope

Art Director: Richard Michels

Graphic Designer: Kimberly B. Zarley

Prototype Designer: Joannah Ralston

Copy Chief: Catherine Hamrick

Copy and Production Editor: Terri Fredrickson

Copy Editor: Sheila Mauck

Proofreaders: Susie Kling, Lisa Stone

Electronic Production Coordinator:
    Paula Forest

Editorial and Design Assistants: Judy Bailey,
    Mary Lee Gavin, Karen Schirm

Production Director: Douglas M. Johnston

Book Production Managers: Pam Kvitne,
    Marjorie J. Schenkelberg

MEREDITH® BOOKS

Editor in Chief: James D. Blume

Design Director: Matt Strelecki

Managing Editor: Gregory H. Kayko

Vice President, General Manager:
    Jamie L. Martin

LADIES' HOME JOURNAL®
MAGAZINE

Editor in Chief: Myrna Blyth

Food Editor: Jan Hazard

Associate Food Editor: Carol Prager

Assistant Editor: Jane Yagoda-Goodman

Recipe Testers: Cynthia DePersio, Sarah
    Reynolds, Michele Peters

Consumer Marketing Director: Beth von Linden

Product Development Manager: Chuck Cordray

MEREDITH PUBLISHING GROUP

President, Publishing Group:
    Christopher M. Little

Vice President, Consumer Marketing &
    Development: Hal Oringer

MEREDITH CORPORATION

Chairman and Chief Executive Officer:
    William T. Kerr

Chairman of the Executive Committee:
    E. T. Meredith III

COVER PHOTOGRAPH:

Chocolate-Caramel Layer Cake
(see recipe, page 260)
Photographer: Alan Richardson

JULIA CHILD'S
DUCK ROAST WITH
POLENTA
pg. 182

All of us at Meredith® Books are dedicated to providing you with the information and ideas you need to create delicious foods. We welcome your comments and suggestions. Write to us at: Meredith® Books, Food Editorial Department, 1716 Locust St., Des Moines, IA 50309-3023.

If you would like to order additional copies of this book, call 1-800-439-4119.

First Edition. Printing Number and Year: 5 4 3 2 1   03 02 01 00 99

ISSN: 1526-0038

ISBN: 0-696-20969-1

PÂTÉ IN
SAVORY PUFFS
pg. 291

Table of Contents

Recipes
1999

GRILLED
POTATOES
WITH AIOLI
pg. 26

POT ROAST
pg. 58

Welcome inside the LHJ kitchen

Every recipe that comes from the Ladies' Home Journal® Kitchen is created to suit your needs—from our delicious and decadent desserts and no-fuss weekday family meals to our easy, elegant appetizers and entrées that help you celebrate special occasions and holidays in style.

In this, our first annual cookbook, we're proud to present more than 300 recipes from another year of great food from the LHJ® Kitchen. You'll also find innovative tips and timesaving techniques from our food pros that will give you great results and get you out of the kitchen fast. Most important, we triple-test each recipe so you can make each one with confidence. Here's to a year of great cooking in *your* kitchen!

Myrna Blyth • Editor-in-Chief

Recipes 1999

PINK MARGARITAS;
PIÑA COLADA
pg. 40
TROPICAL FRUIT
BLEND
pg. 36

great
beginnings

SHRIMP AND
JICAMA SALSA
pg. 20
MINI CRAB CAKES
pg. 21

Set the tone of your party with the first bites of the night. From appetizers and cocktails just right for an elegant *al fresco* affair to winning finger foods and super sippers to nibble as you cheer on your favorite team, these recipes will make every gathering a great one.

mediterranean bites, finger foods,

GRILLED CALAMARI SALAD
pg. 18
PANINI WITH GRILLED
MUSHROOMS
pg. 19
STUFFED GRAPE LEAVES
pg. 18

SCORING STROMBOLI;
SPICY KICKOFF STROMBOLI
pg. 32

GINGER-LIME
CHICKEN
SKEWERS
pg. 26

skewers and more....
let the fun begin

MEDITERRANEAN
SEAFOOD
pg. 22

party **foods**
invite
sociability

GRILLED
POTATOES
WITH AIOLI
pg. 26

THE PERFECT
LEMONADE
pg. 38

asian-style angels on horseback

Three simple additions make this classic appetizer different and delicious. We substitute sweet scallops for the traditional oysters, wrap them in strips of pickled Asian ginger and bacon, then douse them with teriyaki.

Prep time: 10 minutes • Broiling time: 6 to 8 minutes

- 10 thin slices bacon (about 8 oz.)
     Asian pickled ginger
- 20 large sea scallops (about 1 lb.), tough
     muscle removed
- 3 tablespoons teriyaki sauce
- 2 tablespoons brown sugar
     Wasabi paste (optional)

1. Cut bacon slices in half crosswise.

2. Line a large jelly-roll pan with foil. Cut ginger into dime-size pieces. Place one piece of ginger in center of one piece of bacon. Place a scallop on one end of bacon and roll up; secure with a round wooden toothpick and place on prepared pan. Repeat, arranging scallops $1/2$ inch apart on prepared pan.

3. Heat broiler.

4. Combine teriyaki sauce and brown sugar in a cup until sugar is dissolved; brush over bacon and scallops. Broil 4 to 5 minutes, until crisp and lightly charred. Carefully turn scallops and broil about 2 to 3 minutes more, until crisp. Transfer with a slotted spoon to a serving platter. Serve immediately with wasabi paste on the side, if desired. Makes 20 appetizers.

Per appetizer: 50 calories, 1.5 g total fat, 0.5 g saturated fat, 10 mg cholesterol, 201 mg sodium, 3 g carbohydrates, 5 g protein, 14 mg calcium, 0 g fiber

smoked salmon and horseradish dip

Here's a fantastic dip for salmon fans.

Total prep time: 5 minutes plus chilling

- 4 ounces smoked salmon, divided
- 1 cup sour cream
- 2 teaspoons chopped fresh dill
- 1 teaspoon fresh lemon juice
- ½ teaspoon prepared horseradish
- ¼ teaspoon salt
- ⅛ teaspoon freshly ground pepper
     Plain bagel chips (optional)

Chop salmon into small pieces; set aside. Combine half of the salmon with next six ingredients in a food processor or blender and pulse to combine. Transfer to a bowl and stir in remaining salmon. *(Can be made ahead. Refrigerate overnight or up to 3 days.)* Serve with bagel chips, if desired. Makes $1\frac{1}{2}$ cups.

Per tablespoon: 26 calories, 2 g total fat, 1 g saturated fat, 5 mg cholesterol, 65 mg sodium, 0 g carbohydrates, 1 g protein, 12 mg calcium, 0 g fiber

test kitchen tip

party math

Wondering how many appetizers to serve at your next party? We've figured it out for you:

For light cocktail parties of the pre-dinner variety, plan to serve about 8 hors d'oeuvres per person. For cocktail buffets that may become full meals for your guests, double that amount. For such occasions, a good rule of thumb is to plan serving something more substantial with the nibbles, such as thick slices of one of the Stromboli appetizers (page 32) or Ginger-Lime Chicken Skewers (page 26).

quiche lorraine squares

Here, the classic cheese pie from the Lorraine region in France gets an elegant, cocktail-party update. Serve these savory bite-size squares warm or at room temperature.

Prep time: 25 minutes plus chilling
Baking time: 43 to 50 minutes

PASTRY:

- 2 cups all-purpose flour
- 1 teaspoon salt
- ½ cup vegetable shortening
- ¼ cup cold butter or margarine, cut up
- 5 to 6 tablespoons cold water

FILLING:

- 2 slices bacon
- 1 cup chopped onions
- 8 large eggs
- 2 cups half-and-half or light cream
- ¼ teaspoon freshly ground pepper
  Pinch nutmeg
- 8 ounces Gruyère or Swiss cheese, shredded (2 cups)

1. *Make pastry:* Place the flour and salt in a large bowl. Cut in the shortening and butter until mixture resembles coarse crumbs. Sprinkle with water, 1 tablespoon at a time, tossing with a fork until pastry holds together.

2. On a lightly floured surface with a floured rolling pin, roll dough into a rectangle, 2 inches larger all around than a 15½×10½-inch jelly-roll pan. Fold dough into quarters and gently ease into pan, allowing dough to overhang edge. (If pastry tears, press together with fingertips.) Fold overhang in and press into side of the pan, then trim pastry even with edge of pan. Freeze about 15 minutes, until firm.

3. Meanwhile, heat oven to 425°F. Line pastry with foil and fill with dried beans or uncooked rice. Bake 15 minutes. Remove foil and beans, then bake 8 to 10 minutes more, until pastry is golden brown. Cool baked pastry crust on a wire rack. Reduce oven temperature to 350°F.

4. *Make filling:* Cook bacon in a medium skillet over medium heat until crisp. Remove bacon with a slotted spoon and transfer to paper towels to drain. Crumble bacon. Add onions to drippings in skillet and cook 6 to 8 minutes, until tender and lightly browned.

5. Whisk eggs in a medium bowl with cream, pepper and nutmeg until blended. Sprinkle bacon, cheese and onions over crust, then pour egg mixture over filling. Bake 20 to 25 minutes, until filling is just set in center. Cool 15 minutes. Cut into 1½-inch squares. (*Can be made ahead. Cover and refrigerate overnight. Uncover and reheat in heated 350°F. oven 10 to 15 minutes.*) Makes 54 squares.

Per square: 90 calories, 6 g total fat, 3 g saturated fat, 42 mg cholesterol, 82 mg sodium, 4 g carbohydrates, 3 g protein, 57 mg calcium, 0 g fiber

lobster-and-crab stuffed mushrooms

These baked mushrooms add a touch of opulence to the appetizer tray. We got the recipe from the Red Lobster restaurant in Atlanta, Georgia.

Prep time: 45 minutes • Baking time: 12 minutes

- 2 **tablespoons butter**
- 2 **tablespoons minced celery**
- 1 **tablespoon minced onion**
- 1 **tablespoon minced red bell pepper**
- 2 **pounds white mushrooms**
- 1 **cup oyster crackers, crushed**
- 6 **ounces cooked lobster meat, chopped**
- ¼ **pound cooked fresh lump crabmeat, picked over and shredded**
- ¼ **cup plus ⅔ cup shredded white cheddar cheese, divided**
- 1 **large egg**
- 2 **tablespoons water**
- ¼ **teaspoon Old Bay Seasoning**
- ⅛ **teaspoon garlic powder**
  Salt
- ⅛ **teaspoon freshly ground pepper**
- 3 **tablespoons olive oil**

1. Heat oven to 400°F. Melt butter in a small skillet over medium heat. Add celery, onion and bell pepper. Cook 2 minutes, until tender; cool.

2. Remove stems from mushrooms; finely chop half the stems (about ¾ cup). Reserve remaining stems for another use.

3. Combine celery mixture, the chopped stems, crackers, lobster meat, crabmeat, ¼ cup of the cheese, the egg, water, Old Bay Seasoning, garlic powder, ⅛ teaspoon salt and the pepper in a bowl.

4. Grease two large jelly-roll pans. Brush the caps with olive oil. Sprinkle caps with salt. Stuff caps with lobster-crab mixture. Arrange caps in prepared pans. Divide and top with remaining ⅔ cup cheese. Bake 12 minutes, until lightly browned. Makes about 50 mushrooms.

Per mushroom: 35 calories, 2.5 g total fat, 1 g saturated fat, 12 mg cholesterol, 57 mg sodium, 2 g carbohydrates, 2 g protein, 21 mg calcium, 0 g fiber

wine biscuits

Crisp and peppery, these "cocktail cookies," made from a frozen slice-and-bake dough, are a fine accompaniment to a glass of wine.

Prep time: 20 minutes plus chilling
Baking time: 12 minutes per batch

- 1 **cup white wine**
- 2 **cups all-purpose flour**
- 1 **teaspoon baking powder**
  Freshly ground pepper
- ½ **teaspoon salt**
- ½ **cup butter, softened (no substitutions)**
- ¼ **cup vegetable shortening**
- ½ **cup sugar**
- 1 **large egg white, beaten with 1 tablespoon water**

1. Bring wine to boil in a small saucepan over high heat. Boil until reduced to ¼ cup, 8 to 10 minutes. Cool to room temperature.

2. Combine flour, baking powder, ¾ teaspoon pepper and the salt in a medium bowl. Beat butter, shortening and sugar in a mixer bowl until light and fluffy. Blend in cooled wine. Add dry ingredients; beat 1 minute. (Dough will be sticky.) Divide dough in half. Spoon each half onto a sheet of plastic wrap; shape each into a 10×1-inch log. Freeze overnight.

3. Heat oven to 350°F. Cut frozen logs into ¼-inch slices and place on ungreased cookie sheets. Brush tops of biscuits with beaten egg white. Grind additional pepper on top. Bake 12 minutes, until edges are golden, switching position of pans halfway through baking. Cool completely on cookie sheets. *(Can be made ahead. Store at room temperature up to 1 month.)* Makes 80 biscuits.

Per biscuit: 30 calories, 2 g total fat, 1 g saturated fat, 3 mg cholesterol, 32 mg sodium, 4 g carbohydrates, 0 g protein, 5 mg calcium, 0 g fiber

olive oil 101

How do you go about choosing which olive oil is right for you and the dish in which it's an ingredient? Here's an olive oil primer:

extra-virgin olive oil

MADE FROM THE FIRST PRESSING OF olives, extra-virgin olive oil is cold-pressed—a chemical-free process of extracting the oil. This is the highest quality oil and has the lowest acidity, the fruitiest olive flavor, aroma and green-gold color. Not coincidentally, it's also the most expensive. Use when the olive flavor really counts, such as on grilled vegetables and breads.

olive oil

SOMETIMES CALLED PURE OLIVE OIL, this oil is made with both refined olive oil and virgin olive oil. It has a milder and mellower flavor than the virgin oils, and it is best used when other flavors would dominate, such as in pesto. Pure olive oil is excellent as a cooking oil for sautéing or stir-frying, because it has a higher smoke point than the virgin oils.

light olive oil

LIGHT OR EXTRA-LIGHT OLIVE OIL is not lighter in calories or fat, as its name might imply, but is simply lighter in color and flavor than other olive oils.

caponata

A classic eggplant relish from Sicily, caponata is Italy's answer to France's ratatouille. Enjoy it with pita triangles and crackers.

Prep time: 20 minutes • Cooking time: 65 to 70 minutes

- 1½ pounds eggplant, cut into 1-inch pieces
- 2 teaspoons kosher salt
- 6 tablespoons extra-virgin olive oil, divided
- 1 cup chopped onions
- ¼ teaspoon salt
- 1 red bell pepper, cut into 1-inch pieces
- 4 cloves garlic, thinly sliced
- 1 can (15 oz.) plum tomatoes in juice, finely chopped
- ¼ cup plus 2 tablespoons fresh basil leaves, thinly sliced
- 1 cup diced celery with leaves
- 1 cup cracked Sicilian green olives, chopped
- 5 tablespoons red wine vinegar
- 1 tablespoon sugar
- 1 tablespoon drained capers

1. Toss eggplant with kosher salt in a colander. Place colander on a plate and let stand 30 minutes. Rinse eggplant under cold water. Pat dry with paper towels. Set aside.

2. Meanwhile, heat 3 tablespoons of the oil in a large skillet over medium-low heat. Add onions and cook until softened, 8 to 10 minutes. Add salt, bell pepper and garlic. Cover and cook until peppers are just tender and still hold their shape, 8 minutes. Stir in tomatoes and basil; cook until mixture begins to thicken, 5 minutes. Cover skillet and simmer over low heat 15 minutes, stirring occasionally. Transfer vegetables to a large bowl.

3. Heat remaining 3 tablespoons oil in the same skillet over medium heat. Add celery and cook 6 minutes, until tender. Transfer celery to bowl with a slotted spoon, leaving as much oil in the skillet as possible. Increase heat to medium-high; add eggplant and cook, turning eggplant occasionally, 5 to 8 minutes, until eggplant is almost tender. Return vegetables to skillet with eggplant; stir to combine. Cover and simmer over low heat, stirring occasionally, until all vegetables are tender, 15 minutes.

4. Rinse olives in hot water in sieve. Pat dry; pit* and quarter. Add olives, vinegar, sugar and capers to vegetables. Simmer 5 minutes more, to blend flavors. Transfer to a serving bowl. *(Can be made ahead. Cover and refrigerate up to 2 days. Bring to room temperature before serving.)* Serve warm or at room temperature. Makes 5^1/$_2$ cups.

Note: To pit an olive, place the olive on a cutting board. Lay the flat side of a large knife directly over the olive. Press the blade with your fist to split the flesh of the olive. Remove the pit.

Per tablespoon: 15 calories, 1 g total fat, 0 g saturated fat, 0 mg cholesterol, 95 mg sodium, 1 g carbohydrates, 0 g protein, 4 mg calcium, 0 g fiber

mascarpone-stuffed figs

This autumn-flavored appetizer is a no-cook choice. If fresh figs are hard to find, substitute six ripe pears, cut into eighths.

Total prep time: 25 minutes

- **6** ounces thinly sliced prosciutto
- **12** fresh figs, quartered
- **¼** cup mascarpone cheese or whipped cream cheese
- **1** large fresh lime, quartered
  Freshly ground pepper

1. Cut each slice of prosciutto lengthwise in half, then crosswise in half again.

2. Top each fig quarter with ¼ teaspoon of the mascarpone, then wrap in a prosciutto strip. Arrange wrapped figs on a serving platter. Squeeze a few drops of lime juice over each fig and sprinkle with pepper. Makes 48 appetizers.

Per appetizer: 20 calories, 1 g total fat, 0 g saturated fat, 4 mg cholesterol, 66 mg sodium, 3 g carbohydrates, 1 g protein, 5 mg calcium, 1 g fiber

olive paste

Total prep time: 10 minutes

Olive paste is popular in Mediterranean cooking—here, orange peel lends extra interest.

- **1** cup pitted kalamata olives (about 40)
- **4** anchovy fillets, rinsed and patted dry
- **3** tablespoons extra-virgin olive oil
- **1** clove garlic, peeled
- **½** teaspoon grated orange peel

Combine all ingredients in a food processor or blender. Process until smooth. *(Can be made ahead. Cover and refrigerate up to 1 week. Bring to room temperature before serving.)* Makes ^{3}/$_4$ cup.

Per tablespoon: 65 calories, 6.5 g total fat, 1 g saturated fat, 1 mg cholesterol, 252 mg sodium, 2 g carbohydrates, 0 g protein, 4 mg calcium, 0 g fiber

---

test kitchen tip

fig facts...

Figs possess a soft flesh and a multitude of miniscule edible seeds. They can be oval or round, with a color ranging from dark purple or black to practically white. Among the most common types available:

CALIMYRNA FIGS OR SMYRNA FIGS, from California and Turkey respectively, are large with green skin and white flesh.

ADRIATIC FIGS have a pear shape and violet to brown skin.

MISSION FIGS have purplish-black skin and extremely tiny seeds.

Fresh figs are available from June through October. They should be used as soon as possible after purchase, as they are very perishable. Otherwise, store figs in the refrigerator up to 3 days.

---

the olive tray

Olives make for an easy, elegant and toothsome nibble to serve with before-dinner drinks.

olive varieties

Here's a sampling of widely available varieties:

GAETA OLIVES are small, wrinkled and usually reddish brown in color. They have a slightly earthy flavor.

SICILIAN OLIVES are small green ovals, intensely flavored and traditionally spiced with red pepper and oregano or fennel.

NIÇOISE OLIVES are purple-brown to black. They are small, tender and shiny and have a larger pit-to-meat ratio than most olives.

KALAMATA OLIVES are purple-black and shiny; the smallest have the most intense flavor.

great marinades

Fine on their own, olives can also benefit from a good soak with compatible flavors. Consider marinating olives in some high-quality olive oil and one or more of the following: orange or lemon peel; fresh thyme, lemon thyme, rosemary or oregano; garlic; freshly ground black pepper; red pepper flakes; fresh hot peppers (see tip, page 95); vermouth or vodka.

serving ideas

Though they can certainly stand alone served in a series of small bowls or artfully arranged on a platter, olives also are terrific with a crisp crackerbread such as lahvosh or a rustic country-style bread, and a soft, spreadable goat cheese. Another good accompaniment to an olive tray is a bowl of toasted, seasoned nuts.

taramasalata

Tarama is a pale orange cod roe that gives this dip a wonderful vibrant hue. Serve this Greek specialty with pita wedges, crackers or assorted crudités.

Prep time: 15 minutes • Cooking time: 15 minutes

- 1   **medium baking potato (8 oz.), peeled and cut into 1-inch pieces**
- 1   **package (3 oz.) cream cheese, softened**
- ⅓   **cup tarama (salted cod, carp or mullet roe) or 1 jar (2 oz.) red lumpfish caviar**
- ¼   **cup ground blanched almonds**
- ¼   **cup fresh lemon juice**
- 1   **tablespoon minced red onion**
- ½   **cup olive oil**
      Pita wedges (optional)

1. Combine potato pieces and cold water to cover in a small saucepan; bring to boil. Reduce heat and cook about 15 minutes, until very tender. Drain potatoes. Transfer to a food mill or potato ricer. Force potatoes through the mill into a large mixing bowl.

2. Beat potatoes at high speed with cream cheese, tarama, almonds, lemon juice and onion, until smooth. With mixer at low speed, gradually drizzle in the olive oil, beating constantly, until mixture is very smooth. Serve with pita wedges, if desired. Makes 2 cups.

Per tablespoon: 55 calories, 5 g total fat, 1 g saturated fat, 13 mg cholesterol, 34 mg sodium, 2 g carbohydrates, 1 g protein, 6 mg calcium, 0 g fiber

pancetta cheese breadsticks

This recipe makes more than 100 breadsticks—so you'll have plenty for a large gathering, or to give to friends.

Prep time: 1 hour
Baking time: 30 to 35 minutes per batch

- **2 packages active dry yeast**
- **2 teaspoons sugar**
- **2 teaspoons salt**
- **¼ cup plus 3 tablespoons extra-virgin olive oil, divided**
- **1½ cups warm water (105°F. to 115°F.), divided**
- **4 to 4¼ cups all-purpose flour, divided**
- **6 ounces pancetta, finely chopped**
- **1 cup freshly grated Romano cheese, divided**
- **2 teaspoons finely chopped fresh sage**
- **½ teaspoon freshly ground pepper**

1. Combine yeast, sugar, salt, ¼ cup of the oil and ¼ cup of the warm water in a large mixer bowl. Beat 3 minutes on medium speed, until yeast is dissolved. Reduce speed to low; beat in ½ cup of the flour until smooth. Beat remaining 3½ to 3¾ cups flour alternately with remaining 1¼ cups water. Beat in pancetta, ½ cup of the Romano, the sage and pepper. (Dough will be slightly sticky.) Knead dough until smooth and elastic, 10 minutes. Cover and let stand 15 minutes.

2. Heat oven to 325°F. Brush 2 large cookie sheets with oil; set aside.

3. Divide dough into quarters. Shape one quarter dough into a 15-inch log; cut into 1-inch pieces. Roll each piece into a 12-inch stick; cut each stick in half and place 1 inch apart on prepared sheets. Repeat process with another quarter of dough (keep remaining dough covered). Cover breadsticks and let stand 20 minutes.

4. Brush breadsticks with 1½ tablespoons of the oil; sprinkle with ¼ cup of the Romano cheese. Bake 30 to 35 minutes, until golden brown. Cool on wire racks. Repeat process with remaining dough, 1½ tablespoons oil and ¼ cup Romano. *(Can be made ahead. Store in brown paper bags up to 2 days.)* Makes 9 dozen breadsticks.

Per breadstick: 35 calories, 2 g total fat, 0 saturated fat, 2 mg cholesterol, 66 mg sodium, 4 g carbohydrates, 1 g protein, 9 mg calcium, 0 g fiber

test kitchen tip
caviar splurges and substitutes

Ever sophisticated—and costly—caviar is the quintessential elegant hors d'oeuvre. The Taramasalata recipe, page 14, offers a great way to stretch caviar into a recipe that can serve a crowd. However, for times when you want to splurge and go for pure, unadulterated foods, it pays to bone up on this lavish ingredient.

WHAT IS CAVIAR? Caviar is the roe (eggs) of fish. Sturgeon roe is considered premium caviar. The main types of sturgeon roe are beluga, osetra and sevruga.

WHEN ONLY THE BEST WILL DO... *Beluga,* found in the Caspian Sea, is known and appreciated for its large soft eggs, and is the most expensive caviar; its color ranges from pale silver to black.

NEXT IN LINE... *Osetra* is gray to brownish gray, with medium-size eggs, while *sevruga* caviar has smaller grayish eggs.

The less pricey varieties of caviar include *lumpfish* caviar, *whitefish* caviar and *salmon* or *red* caviar.

KEEP IN MIND... All caviar is very perishable, and needs to be kept refrigerated.

easy antipasto

An impromptu antipasto tray is a cinch to put together—particularly if you have an Italian market or import store nearby that sells antipasto elements. Select from these ingredients:

meats

PROSCIUTTO, the much-loved Italian cured ham from Parma, tastes great wrapped around thin half-moons of melon, peeled and quartered fresh figs or pear slices.

PAPER-THIN SLICES OF SALAMI add a spicy number on your tray, especially when you try a peppery or garlicky version.

cheeses

THIN SLICES OF IMPORTED CHEESES, such as Parmesan, pecorino Romano, tangy imported provolone or pepato—a spicy hard cheese studded with whole black peppercorns —are a must for the antipasto assortment.

and more...

CANNELLINI BEANS marinated in olive oil, garlic and fresh rosemary, or tossed with sliced red onions, tuna, olive oil, salt and pepper, make a nice addition to the tray.

LIGHTLY GRILLED VEGETABLES, such as red bell peppers, eggplant and zucchini, tossed with extra-virgin olive oil, sea salt and freshly ground pepper match with meat and cheese.

PINZIMONIO, a dipping sauce that consists simply of high-quality extra-virgin olive oil, sea salt and freshly ground pepper, served alongside slices of fresh fennel, bell peppers and crisp celery, is a great option, too.

three-pesto torta

This tasty three-layer torta will be a hit at every gathering. Best of all, it can be made ahead of time for smart party planning.

Total prep time: 45 minutes plus chilling
Microwave used

CHEESE LAYER:
- 1   cup whole milk ricotta cheese
- 6   ounces goat cheese
- 1   package (3 oz.) cream cheese, softened

TOMATO LAYER:
- 1   tablespoon olive oil
- ⅓   cup minced onion
- 1   ounce (about 10 dry-packed) sun-dried tomatoes

BASIL LAYER:
- ⅔   cup packed fresh basil leaves, washed and dried well
- 3   tablespoons toasted pine nuts (pignoli)
- 3   tablespoons freshly grated Parmesan cheese
- 1   teaspoon chopped garlic
- 1   tablespoon olive oil
- ¼   teaspoon salt
  -
  Toast rounds (optional)

1. *Make cheese layer:* Combine all cheese layer ingredients in a food processor. Process until smooth, scraping sides of bowl twice, about 1 minute. Transfer to a bowl; cover and refrigerate.

2. *Make tomato layer:* Meanwhile, heat oil over medium heat; add onion and cook 8 minutes until golden brown and caramelized. Cover tomatoes with water in a medium microwaveproof bowl; microwave on High 4 minutes. Remove and let stand 10 minutes. Drain tomatoes in a sieve, pressing out excess liquid. Place tomatoes in a clean processor bowl with onions, scraping oil from pan. Process until a thick paste forms. Transfer to a small bowl.

3. *Make basil layer:* Place basil leaves in a clean processor bowl; add pine nuts, Parmesan, garlic, olive oil and salt. Process until a paste forms. Transfer to a small bowl; cover surface with plastic wrap.

4. Line a 4-cup soufflé dish or bowl with plastic wrap, pressing until smooth. Spread tomato layer evenly into bottom of dish with fingertips. Gently spread a scant $^2/_3$ cup cheese mixture over tomato. Dot with half the basil pesto; lightly spread with fingertips. Repeat layering cheese, basil pesto then remaining cheese. Cover top with plastic wrap and refrigerate overnight. *(Can be made ahead. Cover top with plastic wrap and refrigerate up to 2 days.)* Remove top layer of plastic wrap. Invert mixture onto plate and remove soufflé dish. Carefully peel off plastic wrap. Serve with toast rounds, if desired. Makes 20 servings.

Per serving: 95 calories, 8 g total fat, 4 g saturated fat, 18 mg cholesterol, 113 mg sodium, 3 g carbohydrates, 5 g protein, 56 mg calcium, 0 g fiber

baked ricotta

Baked ricotta, imported from Italy, is quite a delicacy. Since it's not always available stateside, we decided to make it ourselves. It couldn't be easier. Just shape it and bake it and serve with our Red Pepper Chutney (see recipe, right), assorted breads and crudités.

Prep time: 5 minutes plus chilling • Baking time: 1 hour

1 **large container (45 oz.) whole milk ricotta cheese**

1. Line a large sieve with a double layer of cheesecloth, letting the excess overhang sides, and place over a bowl. Spoon in the ricotta. Cover and allow to drain in the refrigerator overnight.

2. Heat oven to 400°F. Discard drained liquid in the bowl. Using cheesecloth, lift ricotta and transfer to a 1½-quart ovenproof bowl, Charlotte mold or soufflé dish, letting cheesecloth overhang sides. Bake 1 hour or until top is browned. Cool on a wire rack 15 minutes. Lift ricotta and cheesecloth from bowl; drain again in sieve 30 minutes. Discard any

remaining liquid. Wrap and refrigerate at least 3 hours. *(Can be made ahead. Cover and refrigerate up to 48 hours.)* Just before serving, peel off cheesecloth. Makes 24 servings.

Per serving: 100 calories, 7 g total fat, 5 g saturated fat, 29 mg cholesterol, 48 mg sodium, 2 g carbohydrates, 6 g protein, 110 mg calcium, 0 g fiber

red pepper chutney

The key to the sweet flavor of this spread is cooking the onions very slowly over low heat. Serve it with the baked ricotta, left, and with a selection of crudités and artisan-quality breads or crackers.

Prep time: 15 minutes • Cooking time: 1 hour 10 minutes

2 **tablespoons olive oil**
4 **cups finely chopped sweet white onions (about 2 lbs.)**
3 **large red bell peppers, finely chopped (4 cups)**
1 **teaspoon salt**
½ **teaspoon red pepper flakes**
¼ **teaspoon fennel seeds**
½ **cup cider vinegar**
¼ **cup sugar**
2 **tablespoons chopped fresh parsley**
Assorted breads and crudités (optional)

1. Heat oil in a large skillet over medium-low heat. Add onions; cover and cook, stirring occasionally, about 45 minutes, until very tender and just beginning to brown.

2. Stir in bell peppers, salt, red pepper flakes and fennel seeds and cook, covered, stirring occasionally, 15 minutes.

3. Increase heat to high. Add vinegar and sugar and cook, stirring, about 10 minutes more, until almost dry. Cool. *(Can be made ahead. Cover and refrigerate up to 3 days.)* Stir in parsley, and, if desired, serve with breads and crudités. Makes 3 cups.

Per tablespoon: 20 calories, 1 g total fat, 0 g saturated fat, 0 mg cholesterol, 48 mg sodium, 3 g carbohydrates, 0 g protein, 4 mg calcium, 0 g fiber

grilled calamari salad

Here is a refreshing way for calamari fans to enjoy a salad—with a lemon-thyme dressing that complements the flavor of the calamari perfectly. Pictured on page 6.

Prep time: 25 minutes • Grilling time: 3 to 4 minutes

- **4 large celery ribs, peeled and diagonally sliced (2 cups)**

LEMON-THYME DRESSING:
- **3 tablespoons extra-virgin olive oil**
- **2 tablespoons fresh lemon juice**
- **1½ teaspoons chopped fresh thyme leaves**
- **1 teaspoon finely chopped garlic**
- **½ teaspoon salt**
- **½ teaspoon coarsely ground or cracked pepper**

- **2 pounds cleaned squid (calamari), bodies sliced into rings**
- **1 tablespoon olive oil**
- **¼ pound green olives with herbs (such as thyme, oregano, marjoram), pitted and coarsely chopped**
- **½ cup very thinly sliced red onion**
- **1 tablespoon chopped fresh flat-leaf parsley**
  Lemon wedges, for garnish (optional)

1. Heat grill with oiled grill basket on grill rack.

2. Bring a medium saucepan filled with water to boil. Add celery and cook 5 seconds, drain in colander and rinse under cold water. Set aside.

3. *Make lemon-thyme dressing:* Whisk all dressing ingredients together in a large serving bowl.

4. Toss squid with oil in a medium bowl. Spread evenly in bottom of hot grill basket. Cover basket and grill 3 to 4 minutes, until squid turns opaque. Add to dressing. Toss with celery, olives and onion. Sprinkle top with parsley. Garnish with lemon, if desired. Makes 6 cups.

Per 1 cup: 255 calories, 14 g total fat, 2 g saturated fat, 353 mg cholesterol, 750 mg sodium, 8 g carbohydrates, 25 g protein, 84 mg calcium, 2 g fiber

stuffed grape leaves

Commonly used by Greek and Middle Eastern cooks to wrap ingredients, grape leaves are the large green leaves of the grapevine. In this recipe, the leaves are stuffed with a savory combination of sautéed onion, celery, cumin, rice and pine nuts as well as fresh mint, dill and lemon juice. If desired, ground lamb also may be cooked and added to the mix. Boiling the grape leaves first makes them tender enough for wrapping, and toasting the pine nuts brings out their exceptional flavor. Pictured on page 6.

Prep time: 1½ hours plus standing
Cooking time: 30 to 40 minutes

- **1 jar (16 oz.) grape leaves, drained**
- **3 tablespoons extra-virgin olive oil, divided**
- **1½ cups chopped onions**
- **1 cup chopped celery with leaves**
- **¼ teaspoon cumin**
- **1 cup long-grain rice**
- **2 cups chicken broth**
- **½ teaspoon salt**
- **½ pound ground lamb (optional)***
- **½ cup toasted pine nuts**
- **¼ cup chopped fresh mint**
- **⅓ cup chopped fresh dill**
- **4 tablespoons fresh lemon juice, divided**
- **1 cinnamon stick, broken in half**
  Crumbled feta cheese, for garnish (optional)

1. Bring 6 quarts water to boil in a large Dutch oven. Unroll grape leaves (reserve any torn leaves and set aside). Boil leaves in 3 batches, 5 minutes per batch, until tender. Remove leaves with tongs to colander. Set aside. Discard water.

2. Heat 1 tablespoon of the oil over medium heat in a 2½- to 3-quart saucepan. Add onions and cook until softened, 5 minutes. Add celery and cumin; cook until celery begins to soften, 3 minutes. Stir in rice, broth and salt. Cook, uncovered, until liquid just evaporates, 8 to 10 minutes. Remove pan from heat; place a sheet of wax paper over top of rice. Cover pan with a tight-fitting lid and let stand 20 minutes. (If using lamb, prepare as directed in note below.)

3. Fluff rice with a fork and transfer to a large bowl. Stir in lamb (if using), pine nuts, mint, dill and 2 tablespoons of the lemon juice.

4. Place 1 grape leaf smooth side down and tip end away from you. Place 1 heaping tablespoon of the rice mixture in the middle of the leaf. Starting at the stem end, fold stem end and left and right sides over the filling to make an envelope. Then tightly roll and place tip side down on a large tray. Repeat process with remaining leaves and rice mixture.

5. Line bottom of a large Dutch oven with reserved torn leaves and broken cinnamon stick. Tightly arrange rolls in the Dutch oven, stacking them if necessary. Drizzle leaves with the remaining 2 tablespoons *each* oil and lemon juice. Add 1½ cups water; cover leaves with a sheet of wax paper and place a plate large enough to cover the leaves on top. Weigh down plate with a heat-proof bowl filled with pie weights or dried beans. Bring water to a simmer over medium-low heat and cook until rolls are tender, 30 to 40 minutes. Remove bowl, plate and wax paper. Transfer grape leaves to large serving platter. Cool 10 to 15 minutes. *(Can be made ahead. Transfer to air-tight container. Cover and refrigerate up to 3 days. Serve cold or room temperature. Lamb grape leaves should be eaten at room temperature or slightly warm.)* Serve sprinkled with feta cheese, if desired. Makes 40 to 50 leaves.

Note: For lamb filling, prepare rice as directed in step # 2. Heat a large nonstick skillet over medium-high heat 2 minutes. Add lamb, breaking up into small pieces with the back of a spoon. Stir in ¼ teaspoon *each* cumin, cinnamon and salt and ⅛ teaspoon freshly ground pepper. Cook until lamb is no longer pink, 5 to 8 minutes. Transfer to a small bowl. Proceed with recipe as directed.

Per leaf: 40 calories, 2 g total fat, 0.5 g saturated fat, 0 mg cholesterol, 276 mg sodium, 4 g carbohydrates, 5 g protein, 26 mg calcium, 0 g fiber

panini with grilled mushrooms

This sandwich can be served as an entrée or sliced and served as an appetizer. Either way, it's hearty, because the portobello, a matured version of the cremino mushroom, is so meaty and has an outstanding flavor. Here, the portobellos are grilled, teamed up with ricotta salata and topped with fresh arugula and tomatoes for just the right combination. Pictured on page 6.

Prep time: 15 minutes • Grilling time: 10 minutes

- **3** tablespoons olive oil
- **3** tablespoons red wine vinegar
- **1** tablespoon chopped garlic
- **½** teaspoon freshly ground pepper
- **¼** teaspoon salt
- **3** large portobello mushroom caps
- **6** ounces ricotta salata or mozzarella cheese, cut into 4 slices
- **4** small crusty rolls or ciabiatta rolls, split
- **1** small bunch arugula, trimmed
- **2** medium beefsteak tomatoes, sliced ¼ inch thick

1. Heat grill. Combine oil, vinegar, garlic, pepper and salt in a small bowl. With a knife or a teaspoon, gently scrape away the gills (the black portion underneath the caps) from each mushroom cap.

2. Brush both sides of mushrooms with oil mixture. Grill mushrooms, 5 minutes per side, until tender. Transfer to a cutting board and cut into ½-inch-thick slices.

3. Place one slice of ricotta on bottom half of each split roll. Divide and top each evenly with mushrooms, arugula and tomatoes. Cover with roll tops. Cut each roll into thirds. Makes 12 servings.

Per serving: 145 calories, 7.5 g total fat, 2.5 g saturated fat, 13 mg cholesterol, 398 mg sodium, 15 g carbohydrates, 5 g protein, 58 mg calcium, 1 g fiber

shrimp and jicama salsa

Jicama is a slightly sweet and crunchy tuber vegetable that is available in most produce sections. It adds a clean, crisp bite to this refreshing salad. Select jicama that is blemish-free. Pictured on page 5.

Prep time: 30 minutes • Grilling time: 10 to 13 minutes

- 1 **jalapeño chile (see tip, page 95)**
- 1 **pound medium shrimp, peeled and deveined**
- 2 **tablespoons extra-virgin olive oil, divided**
- 2 **tablespoons chopped fresh mint, divided**
- ¼ **teaspoon salt**
- ¼ **teaspoon ground red pepper**
- ⅛ **teaspoon cumin**
- 1 **medium jicama, peeled and cut into ¼-inch dice**
- 2 **tablespoons minced onion**
- ¾ **to 1 pound cherry tomatoes, cut into quarters**
- 3 **tablespoons fresh lime juice**
  Tortilla chips (optional)

1. Heat grill or grill pan.

2. Grill jalapeño until skin is evenly charred, 5 to 8 minutes. Transfer to a small plastic bag; let stand 10 minutes, until cool.

3. Meanwhile, combine shrimp, 1 tablespoon *each* of the oil and mint, the salt, ground red pepper and cumin in a small bowl. Grill shrimp until just cooked through, 2 to 2½ minutes per side. (If using grill pan, grill shrimp in two batches.) Cut each shrimp crosswise into thirds; transfer to large bowl.

4. Peel and chop jalapeño; stir into shrimp with remaining ingredients, except tortilla chips. Serve with tortilla chips, if desired. Makes 6 cups.

Per ¼ cup: 40 calories, 1.5 g total fat, 0 g saturated fat, 23 mg cholesterol, 50 mg sodium, 4 g carbohydrates, 3 g protein, 14 mg calcium, 2 g fiber

goat cheese with ancho chiles

The sweet raisin-like flavor of the chiles with a bit of heat complements the creamy, tart goat cheese. Tip: Plan ahead. The cheese needs to marinate in the refrigerator for three days for the ancho oil to work its magic.

Total prep time: 30 minutes plus marinating

- 1 **package (1¼ oz.) dried ancho chiles* (see tip, page 95)**
- 1 **cup olive oil**
- 1 **(10- or 11-oz.) log soft goat cheese**
- 1 **cup fresh cilantro leaves**
- 1 **baguette, sliced and toasted**

1. Place chiles in a large bowl. Add enough hot water to cover. Let stand 15 minutes, until softened. Remove stems and any seeds. Pat dry and toast chiles in a medium nonstick skillet over low heat for 3 to 5 minutes, until slightly darkened.

2. Add oil to skillet. Gently warm chiles in oil until softened, 15 minutes. Remove pan from heat. Cool chiles in oil to room temperature. Transfer to a clean, dry glass jar with tight-fitting lid; refrigerate overnight.

3. Let chile oil stand at room temperature, 30 minutes. Place the log of cheese in a glass 9×5-inch loaf pan.

4. Strain chile oil through a sieve over cheese. Discard any seeds. Using scissors, cut the chiles into thin strips. Add strips to oil and cheese. Cover and marinate cheese in the refrigerator 3 days.

5. Sprinkle cilantro leaves on bottom of a serving plate. Transfer cheese to top of cilantro and pour oil and ancho strips over cheese. Serve with toasted baguette. Makes 8 to 12 servings.

*Note: Can be found in ethnic sections of supermarkets, or in Spanish or Latino specialty stores.

Per serving: 400 calories, 32 g total fat, 9 g saturated fat, 24 mg cholesterol, 362 mg sodium, 20 g carbohydrates, 10 g protein, 109 mg calcium, 2 g fiber

mini crab cakes

Use top-grade chunks of lump or jumbo crabmeat for these tasty little bites. Pictured on page 5.

Prep time: 45 minutes plus chilling
Baking time: 10 to 13 minutes

7	slices firm white bread, cut up
¼	cup mayonnaise
1	large egg
1	tablespoon hot red pepper sauce
1	tablespoon fresh lemon juice
1	teaspoon Worcestershire sauce
½	teaspoon salt
½	cup finely minced celery
⅓	cup minced red bell pepper
2	tablespoons minced onion
1	pound cooked fresh lump or jumbo crabmeat or 1 can (16 oz.) refrigerated, pasteurized crabmeat, picked over
2	tablespoons chopped fresh flat-leaf parsley
6	teaspoons olive oil, divided
	Fresh parsley and lemon slices, for garnish (optional)
	Hot red pepper sauce (optional)
	Hot jalapeño sauce (optional)

1. Pulse bread in a food processor to fine crumbs. Whisk mayonnaise, egg, red pepper sauce, lemon juice, Worcestershire sauce and salt in a bowl. Stir in ³/₄ cup of the bread crumbs, the celery, bell pepper and onion. Gently stir in crab. Cover and refrigerate 2 hours.

2. Transfer remaining bread crumbs to a large shallow dish; toss with parsley. Place a 25-inch-long piece of waxed paper on flat surface. Pack a level measuring tablespoon with crab mixture and drop onto bread crumbs; gently turn to coat and shape into 1¹/₂-inch cake. Place on waxed paper. Repeat.

3. Heat oven to 350°F. Lightly coat a large cookie sheet with vegetable cooking spray. Heat 1¹/₂ teaspoons of the oil in a large nonstick skillet over medium-high heat. Add about 8 to 10 crab cakes to skillet and cook 1¹/₂ to 2 minutes per side, until golden. Transfer to prepared sheet. Repeat

with remaining oil and crab cakes. *(Can be made ahead. Cool completely. Transfer cakes to an airtight container and freeze up to 1 week. Thaw 30 minutes in the refrigerator.)*

4. Bake crab cakes 10 minutes, until cooked through and hot (12 to 13 minutes, if partially frozen). Garnish with parsley and lemon, if desired. Serve with red pepper sauce and hot jalapeño sauce. Makes about 36 crab cakes.

Per crab cake: 50 calories, 2.5 g total fat, 0 g saturated fat, 19 mg cholesterol, 121 mg sodium, 3 g carbohydrates, 3 g protein, 21 mg calcium, 0 g fiber

---

test kitchen tip

the cheese plate

Whether you choose to serve a cheese plate before dinner or during the meal, here are tips for putting together an impressive assortment:

CHOICES, CHOICES
Serve between three and five cheeses that feature different textures (soft or semisoft, semi-hard or sliceable, hard and blue), types of milk (cow, goat or sheep), sharpness and countries of origin—along with any artisan varieties. For instance, combine a soft and mild cheese—such as a fresh goat cheese or triple cream cheese—with a semisoft and full-flavored cheese, such as a blue-veined Stilton and a firm, piquant Parmesan. Figure on about two ounces of cheese per person, and you'll have plenty.

TIME IT RIGHT
Soft, fresh cheeses may be served slightly chilled, but for peak flavor and aroma, serve all other cheeses at room temperature. Remove them from the refrigerator about 1 hour before you plan to serve your cheese plate—and be sure to keep them covered.

Rewrap any leftover cheeses separately with a clean piece of plastic wrap and refrigerate.

mediterranean seafood

This delicate assortment of squid, shrimp, scallops and mussels is nothing short of spectacular. Try any combination of your favorite kinds of fish or shellfish—you just adjust the cooking time. You can even prepare this dish with just shrimp (you'll need four pounds). Pictured on page 7.

Prep time: 40 minutes • Cooking time: 7 to 11 minutes

2	lemons
	Salt
1	pound cleaned squid (calamari), bodies sliced
1½	pounds medium shrimp, peeled and deveined
1	pound bay scallops
2	pounds mussels, scrubbed and debearded*
½	teaspoon freshly ground pepper
½	cup olive oil
½	cup sliced green onions
2	tablespoons chopped fresh parsley

1. Grate 1 tablespoon peel from lemons and squeeze enough juice to equal 4 tablespoons. Set peel and juice aside.

2. Bring 2 quarts water to boil in a large Dutch oven. Stir in 1 tablespoon of the lemon juice and 1 teaspoon salt. Add squid and cook 1 to 2 minutes, until opaque. Transfer with a slotted spoon to a large bowl.

3. Return water to boil; add shrimp and cook 2 to 3 minutes, until opaque. Drain shrimp; cool.

4. Bring another 1 quart of water to boil in the same Dutch oven. Stir in 1 tablespoon lemon juice and 1 teaspoon salt. Add scallops and cook 2 to 3 minutes, just until cooked through. Remove 1 cup cooking liquid to a cup, then drain scallops. Return reserved liquid to the Dutch oven. Add mussels; cover and cook 2 to 3 minutes, until mussels open. (Discard any unopened and empty shells.) Drain and cool. Transfer 8 mussels to bowl; set aside. Remove remaining mussels from shells; discard shells.

5. Combine remaining 2 tablespoons lemon juice, reserved lemon peel, 2 teaspoons salt and the pepper in a large bowl. Whisk in oil. Add squid, shrimp, scallops, mussels, green onions and parsley; toss to coat. Garnish with reserved mussels. Makes 8 servings.

*Note: To debeard mussels: Scrub the shells with a stiff brush under cold running water; then, with a small sharp knife, cut off the "beards" (small black tufts attached to shells).

Per serving: 330 calories, 17 g total fat, 2.5 g saturated fat, 265 mg cholesterol, 1,042 mg sodium, 6 g carbohydrates, 37 g protein, 84 mg calcium, 0 g fiber

romesco sauce

This classic sauce from Catalonia makes a great dip!

Prep time: 30 minutes plus standing
Baking time: 15 to 20 minutes

3	dried ancho chiles (see tip, page 95)
2	large tomatoes
8	tablespoons olive oil, divided
1	teaspoon finely chopped jalapeño chile (see tip, page 95)
2	one-inch-thick slices white Italian-style country bread
1	tablespoon chopped garlic
¼	cup blanched almonds, toasted and finely ground
¼	cup hazelnuts, toasted, skinned and finely ground
1	tablespoon red wine vinegar
½	teaspoon salt
	Toasted bread (optional)

1. Soak ancho chiles in enough hot water to cover. Let stand until chiles have softened, 20 minutes. Drain. Remove seeds and chop.

2. Meanwhile, heat oven to 350°F. Place tomatoes and 2 tablespoons of the olive oil in an ovenproof skillet. Bake tomatoes until skins begin to peel, 15 to 20 minutes. Remove from skillet. Cool. Discard skins and coarsely chop, reserving juice. Transfer tomatoes and juice to a bowl.

3. Heat 2 tablespoons of the olive oil in the same skillet over medium heat. Add reserved anchos and jalapeño and cook until jalapeño softens, 5 minutes. Transfer chile mixture to bowl with tomatoes. Wipe out skillet and heat 2 tablespoons olive oil over medium-high heat. Add bread and cook 1 to 2 minutes per side until oil is absorbed and slices are golden. Cool slightly, then cut into small pieces.

4. Puree garlic with tomato mixture in a blender until smooth. Add nuts and bread; puree, scraping down sides of blender with rubber spatula. Add vinegar, remaining 2 tablespoons olive oil and the salt, blending until smooth. Serve with toasted bread, if desired. Makes 2 cups.

Per tablespoon: 50 calories, 4 g total fat, 0.5 g saturated fat, 0 mg cholesterol, 16 mg sodium, 3 g carbohydrates, 1 g protein, 9 mg calcium, 1 g fiber

tarator dip

Serve this garlicky dip with a hearty country-style bread.

Total prep time: 15 minutes

- **1   cup toasted, skinned hazelnuts or walnuts**
- **½   cup water**
- **1   cup fresh bread crumbs**
- **2   cloves garlic, crushed**
- **2   tablespoons white wine vinegar**
- **½   teaspoon salt**
- **½   cup olive oil**
- **1   tablespoon chopped fresh flat-leaf parsley**
       Pinch paprika

Pulse toasted hazelnuts in a food processor until finely ground. Sprinkle water over bread crumbs in medium bowl. Add moistened bread crumbs, garlic, vinegar and salt to food processor bowl and pulse until blended. With processor motor running, slowly pour oil through feed tube and process until smooth. Transfer to a small serving bowl. Sprinkle top with parsley and paprika. Makes 1½ cups.

Per tablespoon: 75 calories, 7.5 g total fat, 1 g saturated fat, 0 mg cholesterol, 58 mg sodium, 2 g carbohydrates, 1 g protein, 12 mg calcium, 0 g fiber

skordalia

Serve as a sauce with grilled vegetables, meats, poultry or fish or as a dip with crudités or bread.

Prep time: 20 minutes • Cooking time: 15 minutes

- **2   large (8 oz. each) baking potatoes, peeled and cut into 1-inch chunks**
- **2   tablespoons chopped garlic**
- **1   teaspoon salt**
- **⅓   cup slivered almonds, toasted**
- **3   slices firm white bread, crusts removed**
- **½   cup olive oil**
- **3   tablespoons fresh lemon juice**
- **2   tablespoons white wine vinegar**
- **3   tablespoons hot water**

1. Bring potato chunks and enough water to cover in a large saucepan to boil. Boil potatoes 15 minutes, until tender.

2. Meanwhile, mash garlic and salt together, pressing with flat side of a knife to form a paste; transfer paste to a large mixer bowl. Pulse cooled almonds in a food processor until finely ground; transfer to a plate and set aside. Process bread to fine crumbs; add to garlic paste in the mixer bowl.

3. Drain potatoes; press through a ricer or food mill into the mixer bowl. Combine olive oil, lemon juice and vinegar in a cup. Pour half the oil mixture into potatoes in mixer bowl and beat on medium speed. Gradually beat in remaining oil mixture until blended. Increase speed to medium-high; add 3 tablespoons very hot water and beat until fluffy, about 30 seconds. Beat in almonds just until combined. Transfer to a serving bowl; cover and refrigerate 1 hour before serving. Makes 2³/₄ cups.

Per tablespoon: 40 calories, 3 g total fat, 0.5 g saturated fat, 0 mg cholesterol, 63 mg sodium, 3 g carbohydrates, 1 g protein, 6 mg calcium, 0 g fiber

chermoula dip

Fresh herbs, lemon and garlic get a little kick from a hint of paprika and red pepper, making this dip a refreshing change of pace with veggies or tortilla chips.

Total prep time: 10 minutes

- ¾ **cup packed fresh cilantro leaves**
- ¼ **cup packed fresh flat-leaf parsley leaves**
- 4 **cloves garlic, chopped**
- ¼ **cup fresh lemon juice**
- 2 **teaspoons paprika**
- 1 **teaspoon cumin**
- ¼ **teaspoon salt**
- ¼ **teaspoon ground red pepper**
- 6 **tablespoons extra-virgin olive oil**

Process cilantro, parsley, garlic, lemon juice, paprika, cumin, salt and red pepper in a blender until combined. With blender motor running, slowly add olive oil. Blend until smooth. Makes ³/₄ cup.

Per tablespoon: 65 calories, 7 g total fat, 1 g saturated fat, 0 mg cholesterol, 46 mg sodium, 1 g carbohydrates, 0 g protein, 9 mg calcium, 0 g fiber

picante sauce

Picante (pee-KAHN-tay) in Spanish means spicy hot. Whether you serve it as a sauce or dip, this recipe will live up to its name.

Total prep time: 30 minutes

- 1 **large clove garlic, unpeeled**
- 1 **can (14½ oz.) whole tomatoes in puree**
- ⅔ **cup chopped onion**
- ¼ **cup white wine vinegar**
- 2 **tablespoons chopped jalapeño chile (see tip, page 95)**
- ½ **teaspoon salt**
- ¼ **teaspoon sugar**
- 2 **tablespoons chopped fresh cilantro**

Cook garlic in a skillet over medium-low heat, turning, until charred and soft, 12 to 15 minutes.

When cool enough to handle, peel and mash garlic. Bring garlic, tomatoes, onion, vinegar, jalapeño, salt and sugar in a saucepan to boil, stirring to break up tomatoes. Simmer 10 minutes. Cool. Add cilantro. Makes 2 cups.

Per tablespoon: 5 calories, 0 g total fat, 0 g saturated fat, 0 mg cholesterol, 57 mg sodium, 1 g carbohydrates, 0 g protein, 6 mg calcium, 0 g fiber

guacamole

This is our best guacamole. It will surely become a staple in your recipe repertoire.

Total prep time: 20 minutes

- ⅓ **cup minced fresh onion**
- 2 **ripe avocados, pitted and peeled**
- 1 **tomato, diced**
- 2 **tablespoons fresh lime juice**
- 1 **tablespoon chopped fresh cilantro**
- 1½ **teaspoons minced serrano chile (see tip, page 95)**
- 1 **teaspoon minced garlic**
- ½ **teaspoon salt**
- ¼ **teaspoon dried oregano, crushed**

Rinse onion in a sieve under cold water; drain. Mash avocados in a bowl. Add onion, tomato, lime juice, cilantro, serrano chile, garlic, salt and oregano. Makes 2 cups.

Per tablespoon: 25 calories, 1.5 g total fat, 0.5 g saturated fat, 0 mg cholesterol, 35 mg sodium, 2 g carbohydrates, 0 g protein, 4 mg calcium, 1 g fiber

pico de gallo

Our pico de gallo (PEE-koh day GI-yoh) is a perfect dip to make in summer, while fresh tomatoes are in season.

Total prep time: 20 minutes plus chilling

- ½ **pound fresh tomatoes, diced**
- 1 **green bell pepper, diced**
- ⅓ **cup chopped fresh cilantro**
- ¼ **cup finely chopped white onion**

2 jalapeño chiles, finely chopped (see tip,
     page 95)
2 tablespoons fresh lime juice
¼ teaspoon salt

Combine tomatoes, bell pepper, cilantro, onion,
jalapeño chiles, lime juice and salt in a bowl.
Refrigerate until chilled. Makes 2¼ cups.

Per tablespoon: 5 calories, 0 g total fat, 0 g saturated fat,
0 mg cholesterol, 17 mg sodium, 1 g carbohydrates,
0 g protein, 1 mg calcium, 0 g fiber

chile con queso

Serve this rich and spicy dip with tortilla chips.

Total prep time: 15 minutes

1 tablespoon oil
1 large Anaheim (New Mexico) chile, chopped
     (see tip, page 95)
½ cup minced onion
1 small tomato, chopped
½ cup chicken broth
1 package (16 oz.) shredded Monterey Jack
     and cheddar cheese

Heat oil in a saucepan over medium heat. Add
chile, onion and tomato and cook, until softened,
5 minutes. Add chicken broth; bring to boil.
Reduce heat to low. Add cheese and stir until
cheese melts. Serve immediately. Makes 1¾ cups.

Per tablespoon: 75 calories, 6 g total fat, 3.5 g saturated fat,
17 mg cholesterol, 119 mg sodium, 1 g carbohydrates,
4 g protein, 118 mg calcium, 0 g fiber

salsa verde

*There's no substitute for tomatillos (tohm-ah-TEE-ohs)
in this lively salsa.*

Total prep time: 30 minutes

¾ pound fresh tomatillos, husks removed, or
     1 can (11 oz.) tomatillos, rinsed and drained
1 poblano chile (see tip, page 95)
1 serrano chile (see tip, page 95)

1 teaspoon minced garlic
1 teaspoon salt
¼ teaspoon sugar
½ cup water
2 tablespoons chopped onion
2 tablespoons chopped fresh cilantro

Heat broiler. Arrange fresh tomatillos (if using)
and chiles on a foil-lined broiler pan. Broil,
turning, 7 to 8 minutes, until charred. Wrap; let
stand 10 minutes. Peel and seed chiles. Pulse fresh
or canned tomatillos, chiles, garlic, salt (use
½ teaspoon salt if using canned tomatillos) and
sugar in a food processor, until chopped. Stir in
water, onion and cilantro. Makes 1½ cups.

Per tablespoon: 5 calories, 0 g total fat, 0 g saturated fat,
0 mg cholesterol, 97 mg sodium, 1 g carbohydrates, 0 g protein,
2 mg calcium, 0 g fiber

test kitchen tip

the right stuff for tex-mex cooking

*Don't let unfamiliar-sounding ingredients keep
you from trying the marvelous flavors of Tex-Mex
cooking. Most Mexican ingredients called for in
our recipes in this book can easily be found in the
produce aisles or international section of the
supermarket or at Hispanic-food specialty stores.*

TOMATILLOS are Mexican green tomatoes
covered with papery skins. They offer a hint of
lemon, apple and herb flavors.

JICAMA is a root vegetable. Its crunchy white
flesh has a light, sweet apple flavor.

MASA HARINA, used in tamales or to
thicken sauces, is a type of flour made from
specially processed corn.

CHIPOTLES IN ADOBO SAUCE are actually
jalapeños that have been smoked, then canned
in tomato sauce with onions and garlic.

alfresco appetizer menu

GINGER-LIME CHICKEN SKEWERS
below

GRILLED POTATOES WITH AIOLI
below right

ANTIPASTO AND BRUSCHETTA
see tips, pages 16 and 27

ginger-lime chicken skewers

Chicken is seasoned with a host of Asian aromatics—ginger, cilantro, lime and sesame oil. We chose boneless chicken thighs because they stay moist and tender on the grill. Before skewering, lightly pound the thicker section of the thighs for even cooking. (Remember to wash your hands when handling raw poultry.) Pictured on page 7.

Prep time: 20 minutes plus marinating
Grilling time: 10 to 12 minutes

1   **pound boneless, skinless chicken thighs, cut into 1-inch pieces**
1   **tablespoon chopped fresh ginger**
3   **tablespoons chopped fresh cilantro**
2   **tablespoons Asian fish sauce (nuac mam or nam pla)**
1   **tablespoon vegetable oil**
1   **tablespoon minced green onion**
1   **teaspoon grated lime peel**
1   **teaspoon Asian sesame oil**

DIPPING SAUCE:
2   **tablespoons light soy sauce**
2   **tablespoons fresh lime juice**
1   **tablespoon vegetable oil**
2   **teaspoons honey**
¼   **teaspoon grated lime peel**
■
12   **large green onions**

Wooden skewers, soaked in water 30 minutes
Green onion tops, for garnish (optional)

1. ■ Combine chicken and next seven ingredients in a medium bowl. Cover and marinate in refrigerator for 1 hour. *(Can be made ahead. Refrigerate up to 24 hours.)*

2. ■ *Make dipping sauce:* Combine soy sauce and next four ingredients in a small bowl. Set aside. Makes ⅓ cup. *(Can be made ahead. Cover and refrigerate up to 24 hours.)*

3. ■ Prepare grill according to manufacturer's direction for direct grilling.

4. ■ Cut each green onion crosswise into 2-inch pieces. Alternately skewer four to five pieces of chicken and two pieces of green onion on each skewer. Grill kebabs over medium coals until lightly charred and cooked through, 5 to 6 minutes per side. Line a serving plate with green onion tops, if desired; arrange kebabs on top. Serve with dipping sauce. Makes 6 servings.

Per serving: 170 calories, 9 g total fat, 1.5 g saturated fat, 63 mg cholesterol, 469 mg sodium, 6 g carbohydrates, 17 g protein, 33 mg calcium, 1 g fiber

grilled potatoes with aioli

Want a great starter? Grab a potato! We offer a batch of beauties—golden, red and purple—and serve them with a fabulous garlic mayonnaise infused with saffron. (Cooking time to parboil the potatoes will vary according to size, but the grilling time will remain the same.) Pictured on page 8.

Prep time: 25 minutes
Grilling time: 16 to 18 minutes

AIOLI:
2   **medium cloves garlic, unpeeled**
2   **slices firm white bread, torn into bite-size pieces**
½   **cup mayonnaise**
1   **tablespoon fresh lemon juice**
½   **teaspoon minced shallot**

¼　teaspoon salt
⅛　teaspoon ground red pepper
　　Pinch saffron threads
3　tablespoons water
　■
1　pound small Yukon gold potatoes, halved
1　pound small red potatoes (or ½ lb. *each*
　　red potatoes and purple potatoes), halved
1　tablespoon olive oil
½　teaspoon salt
½　teaspoon freshly ground pepper
　　Metal skewers (or wooden skewers, soaked
　　in water for 30 minutes)
　　Chopped fresh parsley, for garnish (optional)

1. *Make aioli:* Heat a skillet over medium heat; add garlic and toast about 15 to 18 minutes, turning until garlic skin is charred in spots and feels soft when pressed with a spoon. Cool.

2. Gently squeeze garlic cloves from skins; transfer to a food processor. Add bread, mayonnaise, lemon juice, shallot, salt, red pepper and saffron, and process, gradually adding water through feed tube until smooth. Transfer to a small serving bowl. *(Can be made ahead. Cover and refrigerate up to 24 hours.)* Makes ³⁄₄ cup.

3. Meanwhile, prepare grill according to manufacturer's direction for direct grilling.

4. Bring potatoes and enough cold salted water to cover to boil in a large saucepan. Cook 5 to 6 minutes until potatoes are just tender; drain in a colander and cool.

5. Gently toss potatoes with oil, salt and freshly ground pepper in a large bowl. Skewer 4 to 6 potatoes on 6 skewers.

6. Oil grill. Grill, turning occasionally until browned on all sides, 16 to 18 minutes. Slide potatoes off skewers onto a serving platter. Sprinkle with parsley, if desired. Serve with aioli. Makes 12 appetizer servings or 6 side servings.

Per appetizer: 150 calories, 8.5 g total fat, 1.5 g saturated fat, 5 mg cholesterol, 226 mg sodium, 16 g carbohydrates, 2 g protein, 8 mg calcium, 1 g fiber

toast, italian style

A toast before dinner—and not just the glass-clinking kind—can really warm up a party. With the grill fired up already, bruschetta (Italians say broo-SKEH-tah)—thick slices of toasted bread crowned with fresh, savory toppings—is the perfect, no-fuss appetizer. Though it can be broiled, grilling the bread over open coals imparts it with a smoky allure.

CLASSIC BRUSCHETTA

Grill thick slices of hearty country bread. Rub the slices with a peeled, cut garlic clove and brush with fragrant extra-virgin olive oil—then top with any one (or more) of the embellishments listed below. A drizzle of extra-virgin olive oil, a little salt and a grind or two of fresh pepper is a nice addition to any of the tomato combinations.

TOPPING IDEAS

- Tomatoes and herbs
- Tomatoes and chopped red onions
- Tomatoes and chopped shallots
- Tomatoes and capers
- Tomatoes and chopped arugula
- Tomatoes, fresh mozzarella and fresh basil
- Chopped olives
- White beans marinated in olive oil, garlic and freshly ground pepper
- Chopped fresh herbs
- Soft goat cheese and strips of grilled red bell pepper
- Slivers of Parmesan cheese
- Paper-thin slices of prosciutto

Though bruschetta is traditionally served as an appetizer, a couple of slices also make a lovely light meal with a salad and a glass of wine.

zucchini fritters with chile-pistachio dip

This recipe makes 20, so double the recipe if you're planning a large gathering.

Prep time: 25 minutes • Cooking time: 22 minutes

CHILE-PISTACHIO DIP:

 2 New Mexican chiles (see tip, page 95)
 ¼ cup olive oil, divided
 2 medium tomatoes, chopped
 ½ teaspoon curry powder
 3 tablespoons toasted pistachios
 ½ teaspoon salt
 1 tablespoon water

FRITTERS:

 2 medium (¾ lb.) zucchini
 ½ cup all-purpose flour
 ¾ teaspoon baking powder
 ½ teaspoon salt
 ⅛ teaspoon curry powder
 2 large eggs, lightly beaten
 2 tablespoons heavy or whipping cream
 1 teaspoon grated onion
 4 teaspoons olive oil, divided

1. *Make chile-pistachio dip:* Heat broiler. Arrange chiles on a foil-lined cookie sheet and broil 4 inches from heat, 3 minutes per side, until charred. Wrap foil around chiles; let stand 10 minutes. Lightly scrape peel off chiles with a small knife; discard peel.

2. Meanwhile, heat 1 tablespoon of the oil in a medium nonstick skillet over medium-high heat; add tomatoes and cook 4 minutes. Add curry powder and cook 1 minute more, until very soft and thick.

3. Process pistachios in a food processor until finely ground. Add chiles, remaining 3 tablespoons oil, the tomato mixture, salt and water and process until smooth. (If the dip is too thick, add a little water, 1 teaspoon at a time, to reach desired consistency). Transfer to a bowl. (Makes 1½ cups).

4. *Make fritters:* Coarsely grate zucchini on a double-thick layer of paper towels. Let stand 5 minutes; pat top with towels.

5. Whisk flour, baking powder, salt and curry together in a medium bowl. Stir in eggs, cream, zucchini and onion.

6. Heat 1 teaspoon of the oil in a large nonstick skillet over medium heat. Drop 5 scant tablespoonfuls of zucchini mixture into skillet. Cook 2 minutes per side, until golden and cooked in center. Transfer to a platter and keep warm. Repeat 3 more times with remaining oil and batter. Serve immediately with chile-pistachio dip. Makes 20 appetizers.

Per appetizer: 70 calories, 5.5 g total fat, 1 g saturated fat, 23 mg cholesterol, 145 mg sodium, 5 g carbohydrates, 1 g protein, 26 mg calcium, 1 g fiber

tex-mex grilled scampi

Shrimp takes only minutes to grill, so have the rest of your menu ready. Then, dig in when the shrimp are done.

Prep time: 15 minutes plus marinating
Cooking time: 4 to 6 minutes

 1 pound medium shrimp in shells
 2 tablespoons fresh lime juice
 2 tablespoons tequila
 1 tablespoon vegetable oil
 2 jalapeño or serrano chiles, sliced thin*
 ½ teaspoon salt

COCKTAIL SAUCE:

 ½ cup bottled chili sauce
 2 tablespoons minced jalapeño or serrano chiles*
 1 tablespoon prepared horseradish
 1 tablespoon fresh lime juice
 1 tablespoon tequila

 ▪

 Metal skewers

1. With a small, sharp knife, cut along curved side of each shrimp to the tail, remove vein and leave shells on. Combine lime juice, tequila, oil, sliced chiles and salt in a medium bowl. Add shrimp; toss to combine. Cover and refrigerate 30 minutes.

2. *Make cocktail sauce:* Combine chili sauce, minced chiles, horseradish, lime juice and tequila in a small bowl. Makes 3/4 cup.

3. Prepare grill. Thread shrimp on 6 skewers. Grill over medium-hot heat 2 to 3 minutes per side, until shrimp turn pink and are opaque. Serve with cocktail sauce. Makes 4 servings.

Note: See tip, page 95, regarding handling hot chiles.

Per serving: 170 calories, 3 g total fat, 0.5 g saturated fat, 140 mg cholesterol, 732 mg sodium, 11 g carbohydrates, 20 g protein, 38 mg calcium, 0 g fiber

shrimp quesadillas

This peppy recipe comes from Rene Restaurant in Sedona, Arizona.

Prep time: 30 minutes • Baking time: 10 to 12 minutes

SALSA:

3	medium tomatoes, seeded and diced
1	can (6 oz.) tomato juice
1	small onion, finely chopped
3	tablespoons chopped fresh cilantro
1	tablespoon hot red pepper sauce
	Half of a jalapeño chile, seeded and minced (see tip, page 95)
1½	teaspoons minced garlic
1	teaspoon cumin
½	teaspoon salt

6	medium poblano chiles (1 lb.) (see tip, page 95)
4	tablespoons olive oil, divided
1½	pounds medium shrimp, peeled and deveined
1½	teaspoons prepared cajun spice
½	teaspoon salt
1	package (1 lb.) shredded Mexican four-cheese blend
⅓	cup chopped fresh cilantro
6	burrito-size (10-inch) flour tortillas
	Lime wedges, for garnish (optional)

1. *Make salsa:* Combine salsa ingredients in a medium bowl. Cover and refrigerate overnight.

2. Arrange oven racks on upper and lower third of oven. Heat broiler. Line broiler pan with aluminum foil. Arrange chiles on prepared pan. Broil 4 inches from heat, 10 to 12 minutes, turning chiles until evenly charred. Wrap tightly in foil and cool. Reduce oven temperature to 425°F.

3. Meanwhile, heat 2 tablespoons of the oil in a 12-inch skillet over high heat, 2 minutes. Toss shrimp, cajun spice and salt in a medium bowl. Add shrimp to skillet and cook 3 minutes, until lightly browned. Transfer to a large bowl.

4. Peel skin and discard seeds from chiles; coarsely chop. Add chiles to bowl with shrimp and toss with cheese and cilantro.

5. Brush 2 large cookie sheets with 1 tablespoon of the oil. Arrange tortillas on a flat surface. Cover half of each tortilla with some of the shrimp mixture; fold tortilla over to cover filling. Arrange on prepared sheet; brush top of each tortilla with ½ teaspoon of the remaining oil. Bake 10 to 12 minutes, switching and rotating sheets between racks halfway through baking, until lightly browned. Cut each quesadilla into 6 wedges and serve immediately with salsa and, if desired, lime wedges. Makes 36 wedges.

Per wedge: 115 calories, 6.5 g total fat, 3 g saturated fat, 34 mg cholesterol, 286 mg sodium, 7 g carbohydrates, 7 g protein, 112 mg calcium, 1 g fiber

---

test kitchen tip

cleaning shrimp

No doubt about it—shrimp is one of the best cocktail nibblers around. Don't be daunted by the job of cleaning shrimp yourself. It's a snap. With kitchen scissors, cut the shell, following the curve of the outer back, moving from the top toward the tail to expose the dark vein. Rinse under cold water while slipping off the shell and the vein. Drain and pat dry on paper towels.

party nibblers

Here are two great all-purpose starters to jump-start your next gathering.

sliced nectarines with prosciutto

SLICE 4 NECTARINES into 8 wedges each. Wrap each wedge with a slice of prosciutto (4 oz. total). Chill. Makes 32 wedges.

Per wedge: 15 calories, 5 g total fat, 0 g saturated fat, 3 mg cholesterol, 65 mg sodium, 2 g carbohydrates, 1 g protein, 1 mg calcium, 0 g fiber

eggplant caviar

HEAT OVEN to 450°F. Line a jelly-roll pan with foil; brush with 1 teaspoon olive oil. Slice 2 medium eggplants in half lengthwise. Place cut sides down on prepared pan. Wrap 3 large cloves of garlic in foil. Place garlic on pan with eggplant. Bake eggplant and garlic 20 minutes; remove garlic and set aside.

BAKE EGGPLANT 25 to 30 minutes more, until very soft and skin is slightly charred. Cool. Discard any large seeds from eggplant. Scoop eggplant pulp into a food processor bowl; discard skin.

REMOVE GARLIC FROM ITS SKIN; add to eggplant with 3 tablespoons olive oil, 1 tablespoon fresh lemon juice and ¼ teaspoon salt. Pulse, 2 to 3 times, until mixture is smooth. Transfer to a serving bowl. Garnish with 1 tablespoon thinly sliced basil. Serve with grilled pita bread, cut into triangles, if desired. Makes 1½ cups.

Per tablespoon: 30 calories, 2.5 g total fat, 0.5 g saturated fat, 0 mg cholesterol, 30 mg sodium, 1 g carbohydrates, 0 g protein, 15 mg calcium, 1 g fiber

samosas with yogurt sauce

Street vendors in India often sell these savory stuffed pastry triangles to their customers in the open air. Traditionally, these meat and/or vegetable-stuffed treats are fried. Our version is baked and stuffed with a spicy vegetable filling contrasted by a cooling mint yogurt sauce.

Prep time: 1½ hours
Baking time: 17 to 20 minutes per batch

PASTRY:
- 3 cups all-purpose flour
- ¼ teaspoon salt
- ¼ teaspoon ground red pepper
- ¾ cup vegetable shortening
- 7 to 10 tablespoons ice water

FILLING:
- ¾ pound baking potatoes, peeled and chopped
- Salt
- Water
- 2 tablespoons vegetable oil, divided
- ½ cup minced onion
- 2 teaspoons minced garlic
- 1 teaspoon minced fresh ginger
- 4 teaspoons minced jalapeño chiles (see tip, page 95)
- 1 teaspoon curry powder
- ½ teaspoon cumin
- ⅛ teaspoon ground red pepper
- ⅓ cup frozen baby peas, thawed
- 1 tablespoon minced fresh cilantro
- 1 large egg, lightly beaten

SAUCE:
- 1 container (16 oz.) plain low-fat yogurt
- 2 tablespoons minced fresh cilantro
- 2 tablespoons minced fresh mint
- ½ teaspoon cumin
- ½ teaspoon salt
- ¼ teaspoon freshly ground pepper

1. *Make pastry:* Combine flour, salt and ground red pepper in a large bowl. Cut in shortening until mixture resembles fine crumbs. Sprinkle with ice water, 1 tablespoon at a time, tossing with a fork until pastry holds together. Shape into a disk; wrap and chill while preparing filling.

2. *Make filling:* Meanwhile, bring potatoes, 1 teaspoon salt and enough cold water to cover to boil in a small saucepan. Boil 12 to 15 minutes or until tender. Drain, then transfer to a medium bowl and mash coarsely with a spoon. Set aside.

3. Heat 1 tablespoon of the oil in a large nonstick skillet over medium heat. Add onion, garlic and ginger; cook 4 minutes or until vegetables are tender. Add jalapeño, curry, cumin, $3/4$ teaspoon salt and the red pepper; cook 30 seconds, until fragrant. Stir in mashed potatoes, peas, cilantro and the remaining 1 tablespoon oil.

4. Heat oven to 400°F. Grease 2 cookie sheets. Set aside. Divide dough into quarters. On a lightly floured surface, roll one quarter of pastry (keeping remaining dough refrigerated) very thin, about $1/16$ inch thick. Cut circles with a floured, $2^{1}/_{2}$-inch round cutter. Place a level teaspoon of filling onto half of each pastry circle. Brush edge of pastry with water and fold over filling, then press edges of pastry with a fork to seal. Arrange pastries 1 inch apart on prepared cookie sheets. Combine the egg and 1 teaspoon water in a cup and brush over pastries. Repeat with remaining pastry, filling and egg mixture, rerolling scraps.

5. Bake pastries, 1 cookie sheet at a time, 17 to 20 minutes, until golden. Transfer to wire racks; cool slightly. *(Can be made ahead. Cool completely. Freeze in a single layer on jelly-roll pans. To reheat, cover frozen pastries with foil and place in a heated 375°F. oven 15 minutes.)*

6. *Make sauce:* Combine the yogurt, cilantro, mint, cumin, salt and pepper in a small bowl. Serve with warm pastries. Makes 60 appetizers.

Per appetizer: 60 calories, 3.5 g total fat, 1 g saturated fat, 4 mg cholesterol, 81 mg sodium, 6 g carbohydrates, 1 g protein, 18 mg calcium, 0 g fiber

fried calamari with creamy salsa

Prep time: 20 minutes plus chilling
Cooking time: 1 minute per batch

CREAMY SALSA:
- ½ cup mayonnaise
- 3 tablespoons prepared salsa
- 2 teaspoons minced pickled jalapeño chile (see tip, page 95)
- 1 teaspoon jalapeño chile pickle liquid

CALAMARI:
- ¼ cup all-purpose flour
- ¼ cup cornstarch
- Salt
- ¼ teaspoon freshly ground pepper
- ¼ cup beer
- 2 tablespoons butter or margarine, melted
- 1 large egg yolk
- ¼ teaspoon red pepper sauce
- Vegetable oil, for frying
- 1 pound cleaned squid (calamari), bodies sliced into ½-inch-thick rings, keeping tentacles intact

1. *Make creamy salsa:* Combine the mayonnaise, salsa, minced jalapeño and jalapeño liquid in a medium bowl until smooth. Cover and refrigerate until ready to serve.

2. Combine flour, cornstarch, $1/4$ teaspoon salt and the pepper in a large bowl. Whisk in the beer, butter, egg yolk and red pepper sauce until smooth.

3. For calamari, heat $1^{1}/_{2}$ inches of oil in a large deep pot or Dutch oven to 375°F. on a frying thermometer. Dip squid into batter, then add to pot with a slotted spoon, a few pieces at a time. Cook squid about 1 minute, until golden. Transfer with a slotted spoon to paper towels to drain. Sprinkle lightly with salt. Repeat process with remaining squid. Transfer to a serving platter and serve immediately with creamy salsa. Makes 6 servings.

Per serving: 370 calories, 29 g total fat, 6 g saturated fat, 232 mg cholesterol, 375 mg sodium, 13 g carbohydrates, 13 g protein, 35 mg calcium, 0 g fiber

spicy kickoff stromboli

These zesty slices are filled with sun-dried tomatoes, olives, garlic and red pepper flakes. Mild provolone cheese lends a mellow richness to the mix, or try sliced Swiss cheese instead. Pictured on page 6.

Prep time: 35 minutes plus rising
Baking time: 15 to 20 minutes

- **1   recipe Pizza Dough (page 33)**
- **¼   cup oil-packed sun-dried tomatoes, drained and finely chopped**
- **¼   cup kalamata olives, pitted and chopped**
- **¼   cup pimiento-stuffed green olives, chopped**
- **¼   cup chopped fresh flat-leaf parsley**
- **3   tablespoons freshly grated Parmesan cheese**
- **1   teaspoon minced garlic**
- **¼   teaspoon dried oregano**
- **¼   teaspoon red pepper flakes**
- **½   pound sliced provolone cheese**
- **1   large egg, beaten**

1. Prepare pizza dough as directed.

2. Meanwhile, combine tomatoes, kalamata olives, green olives, parsley, Parmesan, garlic, oregano and red pepper flakes in a small bowl.

3. Heat oven to 425°F. Grease a large cookie sheet. Divide pizza dough in half. On a lightly floured surface, with a floured rolling pin, roll one piece of dough to a 15×8-inch rectangle. Top with half of the provolone cheese, leaving a ½-inch border. Sprinkle cheese with half the olive mixture. Brush the border along one long edge with egg. Roll up from opposite long edge of dough not brushed with egg. Pinch seam to seal. Place roll, seam side down, on prepared cookie sheet; pinch ends and tuck under. Repeat with remaining dough and filling, arranging rolls 4 inches apart on cookie sheet. Brush tops of rolls with egg. Make 5 shallow diagonal slashes on top of each roll.

4. Bake logs 15 to 20 minutes, until browned. Cool on a wire rack. *(Can be made ahead. Cover and refrigerate up to 2 days or let stand at room temperature up to 2 hours. To reheat, bake in a 375°F. oven 5 minutes.)* Cut each log into eighteen ½-inch-thick slices. Makes 36 slices.

Per slice: 85 calories, 4 g total fat, 1.5 g saturated fat, 11 mg cholesterol, 207 mg sodium, 9 g carbohydrates, 3 g protein, 60 mg calcium, 0.5 g fiber

scoring stromboli

Stromboli, a Philadelphia specialty (Go Eagles!), is a cheese and pepperoni sandwich wrapped in pizza dough. To feed a crowd, we made ours hero-size and cut it into thin slices. This version calls for ham, fontina and Parmesan cheese. You'll find rosemary ham in the cold cuts section at the supermarket. Pictured on page 6.

Prep time: 25 minutes plus rising
Baking time: 15 to 20 minutes

- **1   recipe Pizza Dough (opposite)**
- **½   pound sliced rosemary ham or baked ham**
- **½   pound fontina cheese, shredded**
- **1   large egg, beaten**
- **2   tablespoons freshly grated Parmesan cheese**
- **¼   teaspoon chopped fresh rosemary**

1. Prepare pizza dough as directed.

2. Heat oven to 425°F. Grease a large cookie sheet. Divide dough in half. On a lightly floured surface, with a floured rolling pin, roll one piece of dough to a 15×8-inch rectangle. Top with half of the ham, overlapping slices and leaving a ¹/₂-inch border. Sprinkle ham with half of the fontina. Brush the border along one long edge with egg. Roll up from opposite long edge of dough not brushed with egg. Pinch seam to seal. Place log, seam down, on prepared cookie sheet; pinch ends and tuck under. Repeat with remaining dough and filling, arranging rolls 4 inches apart on cookie sheet. Brush tops of rolls with egg. Make 5 shallow diagonal slashes on top of each roll. Combine Parmesan and rosemary in a small bowl; sprinkle over tops of rolls.

3. Bake 15 to 20 minutes, until well browned. Cool on a wire rack. *(Can be made ahead. Cover and refrigerate up to 2 days or let stand at room temperature up to 4 hours. To reheat, bake in a 375°F. oven 5 minutes.)* Cut each roll into eighteen ¹/₂-inch-thick slices. Makes 36 slices.

Per slice: 85 calories, 3.5 g total fat, 1.5 g saturated fat, 16 mg cholesterol, 213 mg sodium, 9 g carbohydrates, 4 g protein, 43 mg calcium, 0.5 g fiber

pizza dough

Total prep time: 10 minutes plus rising

- ¼ **cup warm water (105°F. to 115°F.)**
- 1 **tablespoon honey**
- 1 **package active dry yeast**
- 3 **cups all-purpose flour**
- 1 **teaspoon salt**
- ¾ **cup cold water**
- 2 **tablespoons olive oil**

1. Stir the ¹/₄ cup warm water and honey in a 2-cup glass measure until blended. Sprinkle top of mixture with yeast and let stand 5 minutes, until yeast is bubbly.

2. Meanwhile, pulse together flour and salt in a food processor to combine.

3. Add the ³/₄ cup cold water and olive oil to yeast mixture. With motor running, pour yeast mixture through feed tube; process 1 minute until mixture forms a ball. Place dough in a greased bowl, turning to grease top. Cover and let rise in a warm place until doubled in bulk, about 1 hour. Makes enough dough for 2 pizzas or strombolis.

---

test kitchen tip

game-day plan

If you're planning to serve the game-day menu on page 32, a little do-ahead work will make the preparation much easier.

UP TO 2 WEEKS AHEAD:
- Shop for all non-perishable ingredients.
- Make and freeze Linebacker Brownies.

UP TO 2 DAYS AHEAD:
- Buy ingredients for Scoring Stromboli.
- Make and refrigerate Scoring Stromboli.

UP TO 1 DAY AHEAD:
- Shop for remaining ingredients.
- Remove brownies from freezer to thaw.

UP TO 4 HOURS AHEAD:
- Make and refrigerate Ten-Layer Touchdown Salad.

UP TO 2 HOURS AHEAD
- Make and refrigerate Go Buffalo Chicken Wraps.

UP TO 1 HOUR AHEAD:
- Bring Go Buffalo Chicken Wraps to room temperature.

10 MINUTES BEFORE SERVING:
- Bake Scoring Stromboli in 375°F. oven for 5 minutes.

To bring something new to the hors d'oeuvres tray, here's how to choose, cut and cook some up-to-date selections:

GREEN, YELLOW OR SNAP BEANS
Look for a bright color and firm texture without blemishes. Very fresh beans can be served uncooked. For blanching, trim ends of beans and cook in a large amount of boiling salted water for 1 to 2 minutes, depending on the beans' size and freshness. Immediately rinse under cold running water. Pat dry. Wrap well and refrigerate up to 24 hours.

FENNEL
Look for firm, creamy-colored bulbs with some of the stems and leaves attached. Trim the stems, then quarter the bulb and remove the core. Cut into thick slices and serve raw. Fresh is best, so once you have sliced fennel sticks, serve immediately.

ENDIVE
Heads should be firm, crisp and creamy white. Avoid heads with brown outer leaves. Cut the head at the core; carefully separate the whole leaves for serving. Whole heads can be refrigerated, covered, up to 3 days.

ASPARAGUS
Look for firm spears, $1/2$ inch thick, and at least two-thirds green. Trim any white, woody bases. For larger spears, peel the bottom portion of the stalk with a vegetable peeler. Blanch in rapidly boiling water for 2 to 3 minutes. Immediately rinse under cold running water. Pat dry. Wrap; refrigerate up to 24 hours.

quarterback dip

Cheesy and addictive, this concoction gets its kick from diced tomatoes with green chiles and pickled jalapeños.

Prep time: 25 minutes · Cooking time: 15 minutes

    2   tablespoons olive oil
    4   green onions, chopped
    3   tablespoons flour
    1   teaspoon cumin
    1   pint (16 oz.) half-and-half cream
    1   package (8 oz.) cream cheese, softened
    1   cup shredded cheddar cheese
    1   cup shredded Monterey Jack cheese
    1   can (10 oz.) diced tomatoes with green
        chiles
    4   pickled jalapeños, minced (see tip, page 95)
        Chili powder and sliced green onion, for
        garnish (optional)
        Tortilla chips and raw vegetables, for dipping
        (optional)

1. Heat oil in a medium saucepan over medium-low heat. Add green onions and cook 2 minutes. Stir in flour and cumin; cook 1 minute, stirring. Gradually stir in half-and-half. Bring to a simmer, stirring frequently. Simmer 1 minute. Remove pan from heat. Add cream cheese, stirring until cream cheese melts.

2. Return pan to low heat. Gradually add cheddar and Monterey Jack cheeses, stirring until melted. Stir in tomatoes with green chiles, and jalapeños. Cook until heated through (do not boil). Transfer to a serving bowl. Sprinkle with chili powder and sliced green onion, and serve warm with chips and vegetables, if desired. *(Can be made ahead. Cool. Transfer dip to a medium microwaveproof bowl. Cover with plastic wrap and refrigerate up to 24 hours. Microwave on High 3 to 4 minutes, stirring every minute, until heated through.)* Makes 5 cups.

Per 2 tablespoons: 70 calories, 6 g total fat, 3.5 g saturated fat, 17 mg cholesterol, 105 mg sodium, 2 g carbohydrates, 2 g protein, 62 mg calcium, 0 g fiber

snowflake snack mix

Every bite of this white chocolate-coated mix is so satisfying and most definitely impossible to resist.

Prep time: 15 minutes plus standing
Baking time: 1 hour
Microwave used

- 3 cups bite-size crispy corn squares cereal
- 3 cups bite-size crispy wheat squares cereal
- 1 can (11.5 oz.) peanuts or mixed nuts
- 1 package (8 to 10 oz.) thin pretzel twists
- ½ cup butter or margarine
- ½ cup firmly packed brown sugar
- ½ cup light corn syrup
- 1 teaspoon ground ginger
- 1 teaspoon red pepper sauce
- ¼ teaspoon salt
- 9 ounces white chocolate squares

1. Heat oven to 250°F.

2. Combine cereal, nuts and pretzels in a large roasting pan.

3. Combine butter, sugar, syrup, ginger, red pepper sauce and salt in a medium saucepan. Bring mixture to boil, stirring. Pour over cereal mixture; stir well until evenly coated.

4. Bake mixture 1 hour, stirring every 20 minutes until nuts are lightly toasted. Arrange two overlapping 24-inch-long sheets of wax paper on the counter. Spoon cereal mixture over sheets; spread evenly. Cool.

5. Melt chocolate in a medium-size microwaveproof bowl on High 1½ to 2 minutes until softened; stir until smooth. Drizzle over cereal mixture. Let stand until chocolate hardens, 1 hour. *(Can be made ahead. Store in airtight container up to 2 weeks.)* Makes 16 cups.

Per ½ cup: 210 calories, 11 g total fat, 4 g saturated fat, 9 mg cholesterol, 302 mg sodium, 26 g carbohydrates, 4 g protein, 33 mg calcium, 1 g fiber

---

test kitchen tip
great apéritifs

Served with appetizers, apéritifs whet the appetite and refresh the palate for the main event—and they're a lovely way to get a party going. Here are just a few:

a splash of wine

Try the following combinations with well-chilled Chardonnay, Riesling, Chenin Blanc, Sauvignon Blanc, Pinot Grigio or Vouvray:
Stir a spoonful of eau de vie, such as framboise, Mirabelle or pear brandy, into a glass of chilled white wine. Embellish with a raspberry or a thin slice of plum or pear to fit the appropriate fruit essence.
Add crème de cassis (black currant liqueur) to white wine to make a classic kir.
Add a dash of cranberry or orange juice and a bit of seltzer to white wine. Garnish with a sprig of fresh mint.

a bit of bubbly

Like white wine, champagne can serve as the base for a number of interesting apéritifs. Try it combined with slightly chilled dry sherry, or with a dash of port.
Or, for a kir royale, combine the crème de cassis with cold champagne.

the classics

For a classic apéritif, garnish vermouth with a twist of orange or lemon. Or, serve sherry, either alone, on the rocks or with a little soda.
For pure refreshment on a warm summer evening, it's hard to beat a bit of Campari—the brilliant red and slightly bitter Italian apéritif—with a splash of tonic or soda and a squeeze of fresh citrus over ice.

banana-mango smoothie ❤LOW FAT EASY

Shake up your morning routine with this delicious blend of yogurt, calcium-fortified orange juice, fresh mango and banana. One smoothie a day accounts for almost a third of your daily calcium requirement—and can start your mornings with real fruity fervor.

Total prep time: 10 minutes

- 1   small ripe banana, peeled and cut in half
- 1   container (6 or 8 oz.) low-fat maple-vanilla or vanilla yogurt
- 1   small ripe mango, peeled, seeded and chopped
- ½   cup calcium-fortified orange juice
- 1   teaspoon sugar
- ½   cup ice cubes

Puree banana, yogurt, mango, orange juice and sugar in a blender. With machine on, add ice cubes, one at a time, through feed tube, until mixture is smooth and thick. Makes 2 servings.

Per serving: 210 calories, 1.5 g total fat, 1 g saturated fat, 5 mg cholesterol, 68 mg sodium, 46 g carbohydrates, 6 g protein, 268 mg calcium, 2 g fiber

tropical fruit blend ❤LOW FAT EASY

Here's a jazzy concoction that's easy to whip up for a crowd. It's just the ticket when a festive—yet nonalcoholic—beverage is in order. Pictured on page 5.

Prep time: 15 minutes plus freezing

- 2   ripe mangoes, peeled, seeded and cubed
- 4   cups fresh or frozen strawberries, cut up
- 2   bananas, peeled and cut up
- 1½ cups pineapple juice, divided
- 2   cups ice cubes

1. Puree half the mango, strawberries, banana and ½ cup of the pineapple juice in a blender. Pour

mixture into a container with a tight-fitting lid. Repeat with remaining fruit and ½ cup of the juice. Cover and freeze puree until firm, 5 hours.

2. Let mixture stand at room temperature 10 to 15 minutes, until slightly softened.

3. Chop 1 cup of ice in a blender. Add 1 container of the fruit puree and ¼ cup of the remaining pineapple juice. Blend on medium-high speed until smooth. Pour into serving glasses. Repeat. Makes 8 cups.

Per 1 cup: 105 calories, 0.5 g total fat, 0 g saturated fat, 0 mg cholesterol, 3 mg sodium, 27 g carbohydrates, 1 g protein, 23 mg calcium, 3 g fiber

nectarine-orange smoothie EASY

Protein-rich soy milk provides the base for this vitamin-packed drink. A cup of orange juice balances out the wonderful sweet flavor of the fresh nectarines.

Total prep time: 15 minutes

- ½   pound fresh nectarines or peaches, peeled and cut up
- 1   cup soy milk, chilled
- ⅓   cup orange juice
- 1   tablespoon sugar
      Ice cubes
      Sliced nectarines or peaches and mint sprigs, for garnish (optional)

Puree nectarines, soy milk, juice and sugar in a blender. Blend until mixture is thick and smooth. Serve over ice. Garnish with sliced nectarines and mint sprigs, if desired. Makes 2½ cups.

Per 1¼ cups: 160 calories, 2.5 g total fat, 0 g saturated fat, 0 mg cholesterol, 57 mg sodium, 30 g carbohydrates, 6 g protein, 47 mg calcium, 2 g fiber

honeydew-grape smoothie

Pretty to look at and just as tasty to savor, this low-calorie drink is a great way to start the day.

Total prep time: 10 minutes

- **2 cups (8 oz.) peeled and cubed honeydew melon or cantaloupe**
- **2 cups green or red seedless grapes**
- **⅔ cup white grape juice, chilled**
- **4 ice cubes**

Puree honeydew melon, grapes and white grape juice in a blender on high speed. With machine running, add ice through feed tube, one cube at a time, until mixture is thick and smooth. Serve immediately. Makes 3 cups.

Per 1 cup: 140 calories, 1 g total fat, 0 g saturated fat, 0 mg cholesterol, 14 g sodium, 35 g carbohydrates, 1 g protein, 16 mg calcium, 2 g fiber

strawberry-apple smoothie

A combination of frozen strawberries, low-fat strawberry yogurt and a sweet apple makes this a favorite for all age groups.

Total prep time: 10 minutes

- **1 cup strawberry low-fat yogurt**
- **1 bag (6 oz.) frozen strawberries**
- **1 Gala, Fuji or Golden Delicious apple, peeled, cored and cut up**
- **1 tablespoon sugar**
- **1 cup ice cubes**

Puree yogurt, strawberries, apple and sugar in a blender on high speed. With machine running, add ice through feed tube one cube at a time, until mixture is thick and smooth. Makes 3 cups.

Per 1 cup: 135 calories, 1 g total fat, 1 g saturated fat, 3 mg cholesterol, 44 mg sodium, 29 g carbohydrates, 4 g protein, 125 mg calcium, 3 g fiber

---

test kitchen tip

snack savvy

Satisfying munchies that—at 100 calories or less—won't bust your waistline!

MIDMORNING SNACKS
- 1 slice raisin bread: 90 calories.
- Half of one cantaloupe: 80 calories.
- 3 bagel chips: 70 calories.

MIDAFTERNOON SNACKS
- 38 goldfish pretzels: 100 calories.
- 2 Lorna Doone cookies: 70 calories.
- 1 small bunch red grapes: 80 calories.

FOR HIGH ENERGY
- 1 tablespoon creamy peanut butter: 95 calories.
- 1 ounce part-skim mozzarella cheese with 2 melba toast rounds: 100 calories.

WARMING SNACKS
- Half of one baked potato topped with 2 tablespoons salsa: 84 calories.
- 1 envelope Lipton Chicken Noodle Cup-A-Soup made with water: 50 calories.

TV SNACKS
- 18 pistachio nuts: 100 calories.
- 2 tablespoons dry-roasted sunflower seeds: 95 calories.

three-berry shake

This strawberry, blueberry and raspberry shake is an energizing pick-me-up for any time of the day.

Total prep time: 5 minutes

- **1** pint fresh strawberries, hulled and halved
- **½** cup skim milk
- **¼** cup fresh blueberries
- **¼** cup fresh raspberries
- **½** small ripe banana, sliced
- **2** tablespoons honey
- **1** cup ice cubes
  Mint sprigs, for garnish (optional)

Combine strawberries, milk, blueberries, raspberries, banana, honey and ice cubes in a blender; puree until smooth. Garnish with mint, if desired. Makes 2 servings.

Per serving: 170 calories, 1 g total fat, 0 g saturated fat, 1 mg cholesterol, 36 mg sodium, 41 g carbohydrates, 4 g protein, 105 mg calcium, 4 g fiber

watermelon agua fresca

Here's another superb nonalcoholic choice. It's the perfect refresher for a warm summer day—and a wonderful way to enjoy watermelon!

Total prep time: 15 minutes

- **4** cups watermelon, cut into ¾-inch cubes and seeded
- **1** cup water
- **¼** cup sugar
  Lime slices, for garnish (optional)

Combine watermelon, water and sugar in a blender. Puree until smooth. Pour into a 1½-quart pitcher. Serve over ice in glasses. Garnish with lime slices, if desired. Makes 6 servings.

Per serving: 65 calories, 0.5 g total fat, 0 g saturated fat, 0 mg cholesterol, 2 mg sodium, 16 g carbohydrates, 1 g protein, 9 mg calcium, 0 g fiber

the perfect lemonade

This is it! The all-time-great summertime cooler. Sure, you can make it from an instant mix. But when the dog days of summer are upon you, try this fresh-squeezed version, in all its tart yet sweet lemony glory. To get more juices from the lemons, microwave them for about a minute. Pictured on page 8.

Prep time: 20 minutes plus chilling and freezing
Cooking time: 5 minutes
Microwave used

SUGAR SYRUP:
- **1** cup water
- **1½** cups sugar
  ■

- **15** to 18 medium lemons (3 cups juice)
- **5** cups cold water
- **1** lemon, washed and thinly sliced
- **14** small fresh mint sprigs

1. ■ *Make sugar syrup:* Bring water and sugar to boil in a small saucepan, stirring occasionally, until sugar dissolves. Pour into a bowl. Cool.

2. ■ Microwave 5 or 6 lemons at a time on High 1 to 1½ minutes, just until warm to the touch. Roll whole lemons between palms to soften. Cut lemons in half and squeeze juice. Discard seeds and transfer juice and pulp to a large pitcher. Repeat with remaining lemons. Stir in cooled syrup and water.

3. ■ Measure 1½ cups lemonade mixture in a 2-cup glass measure. (Stir sliced lemon into remaining lemonade mixture; cover and refrigerate.) Arrange one sprig of mint per cube in an ice-cube tray; pour in the 1½ cups lemonade mixture. Freeze the lemonade ice-cube tray 4 hours, until firm.

4. ■ Pour lemonade into tall glasses over lemonade ice cubes. Makes about 8 cups.

Per 1 cup: 170 calories, 0 g total fat, 0 g saturated fat, 0 mg cholesterol, 2 mg sodium, 47 g carbohydrates, 1 g protein, 17 mg calcium, 0 g fiber

ginger-orange iced tea LOW FAT EASY

Iced tea has never been so refreshing! Just as ginger adds a refreshing bite to foods, it adds zing to drinks, as well. This brewed tea is also flavored with sugar syrup and lemon slices, then served with a splash of bubbly seltzer and plenty of ice.

Prep time: 10 minutes plus standing
Cooking time: 10 minutes

SYRUP:

- 1 **cup water**
- ½ **cup sugar**
- **Peel from half an orange**
- 2 **thin slices of fresh ginger**

- 3 **cups boiling water**
- 8 **black-tea bags**
- 2 **cups cold seltzer**
- 1 **dozen ice cubes**
- 3 **thin lemon slices, for garnish (optional)**

1. *Make syrup:* Combine water, sugar, orange peel and ginger in a small saucepan. Bring to boil; reduce heat and simmer 10 minutes. Remove peel and ginger; let stand 20 minutes. *(Can be made ahead. Cool. Refrigerate overnight.)*

2. Meanwhile, pour boiling water over tea bags in a large heatproof pitcher or saucepan; steep tea 2 minutes. Remove tea bags; let stand 10 minutes.

3. Stir syrup into tea; add seltzer, ice cubes and, if desired, lemon slices. Makes 6 to 8 servings.

Per serving: 50 calories, 0 g total fat, 0 g saturated fat, 0 mg cholesterol, 7 mg sodium, 13 g carbohydrates, 0 g protein, 4 mg calcium, 0 g fiber

---

test kitchen tip

a well-stocked bar

Hosting the perfect party may hinge on many things—great food, good weather and a compatible mix of people—but your guests will be especially pleased if you can serve them their favorite beverage. With these supplies on hand, you or your bartender will be able to pour the most requested libations:

SPIRITS
A basic bar should include vodka, gin, scotch and bourbon.
How much to buy: A 1-liter bottle yields twenty-two $1\frac{1}{2}$-ounce drinks.

MIXERS AND SODAS
Seltzer, club soda, sparkling mineral water and tonic; orange juice, cranberry juice, grapefruit juice, pineapple juice and tomato juice; a variety of soft drinks
How much to buy: For mixers, plan on three liters of mixer for every liter of liquor. Mineral water and seltzer: $\frac{1}{2}$ liter per person (1 liter per person if many guests prefer nonalcoholic beverages). Soft drinks: 2 cans (or 24 ounces) per person; for adults, at least half should be diet drinks.

ETC.
Lemons and limes
Coffee (regular and decaffeinated)
Beer and wine
How much to buy: Beer: 2 cans or bottles per person. Wine: $\frac{2}{3}$ bottle per person for a long party (2 glasses with hors d'oeuvres, 2 glasses with dinner). Because most people prefer white wine, buy in a ratio of 4 bottles of white to 1 of red.

pink margaritas

Think pink! This lavish version of a favorite party drink gets its festive color from cactus pears, though frozen cranberry concentrate can be used, too. Our recipe also calls on Cointreau, that heavenly orange-flavored liqueur from France. Pictured on page 5.

Total prep time: 20 minutes plus freezing

SUGAR SYRUP:

- 1 cup sugar
- ½ cup water
- ▪

- 4 cactus pears, peeled and quartered, or 1 cup frozen cranberry concentrate, thawed
- 1 cup fresh lime juice (6 to 8 limes)
- 2 cups ice cubes, divided
- 1½ cups chilled tequila, divided
- 4 tablespoons Cointreau, divided

1. *Make sugar syrup:* Bring sugar and water to boil in a small saucepan; reduce heat and simmer until sugar is dissolved, about 5 minutes. Refrigerate until cold.

2. Puree cactus pears in a blender. Strain mixture through a sieve into a bowl; discard seeds (or pour cranberry concentrate into bowl). Stir in lime juice and sugar syrup. Divide mixture between two containers with tight-fitting lids. Cover and freeze overnight.

3. Let mixture stand at room temperature 10 to 15 minutes, until slightly softened.

4. Chop 1 cup of the ice in blender until well crushed. Add 1 container of cactus pear puree, ³/₄ cup of the tequila and 2 tablespoons of the Cointreau. Blend until smooth. Pour into serving glasses. Repeat. Makes 8 cups.

Per 1 cup: 260 calories, 0 g total fat, 0 g saturated fat, 0 mg cholesterol, 3 mg sodium, 35 g carbohydrates, 1 g protein, 32 mg calcium, 2 g fiber

piña colada

Cool, creamy and refreshing—this is the pick when it's summertime—and you want the living to be easy. Pictured on page 5.

Total prep time: 15 minutes plus freezing

- 2 cans (20 oz. each) pineapple chunks in own juice
- 2 cans (15 oz. each) cream of coconut
- 3½ cups cold pineapple juice, divided
- 6 tablespoons fresh lemon juice
- 1½ cups chilled light rum, divided

1. Measure pineapple chunks with juice from can to equal 4 cups; set aside. Puree cream of coconut, reserved pineapple chunks, 2 cups of the pineapple juice and the lemon juice in a blender until smooth, scraping sides if necessary. Divide mixture between two airtight containers with tight-fitting lids. Freeze mixture 5 hours.

2. Let mixture stand at room temperature 10 to 15 minutes, until slightly softened.

3. Puree 1 container of frozen pineapple mixture, ³/₄ cup of the pineapple juice and ³/₄ cup of the chilled rum in blender. Pour into serving glasses. Repeat with remaining frozen pineapple mixture, pineapple juice and rum. Makes 10 cups.

Per 1 cup: 370 calories, 20 g total fat, 17.5 g saturated fat, 0 mg cholesterol, 57 mg sodium, 29 g carbohydrates, 4 g protein, 16 mg calcium, 1 g fiber

---

test kitchen tip

cool it!

Don't try to keep your party beverages cold in the fridge—when it's party time you'll need the space. Instead, look for large tin buckets (they're inexpensive) and fill them with ice and drinks. The easily accessible buckets will save your guests from having to crowd into the kitchen to refresh their beverages.

MEAT LOAF WITH
ROASTED-PEPPER
SAUCE
pg. 60

daily dinner inspirations

Family dinners aren't just for weekends. Easy, breezy recipes for perfect roast chicken, pastas, kebabs, savory meat loaf and more, are far from tired, they're inspired—with loads of fresh veggies and flavors from around the world.

HERB-COATED
EYE ROUND
ROAST
pg. 57

ITALIAN PINWHEEL
STEAKS
pg. 56

wake up

SPINACH-ORANGE SALAD
WITH STRAWBERRY
DRESSING
pg. 52

ASIAN
STEAK-AND-
NOODLE BOWL
pg. 63

SAVORY SIRLOIN
BURGERS
pg. 60

soups, **salads**–even
the all-American burger–
to a world of **flavors**

TEQUILA SHRIMP AND
PEPPER KEBABS
pg. 73

roasted, grilled or pan-fried,

FLOUNDER WITH
ZUCCHINI RELISH
pg. 70

ROAST CHICKEN
WITH HERBS AND
GARLIC
pg. 51

PASTA ALLA
MARINARA
pg. 68

CHICKEN-NUT
SALAD
pg. 52

chicken's

always a favorite

CHICKEN
DRUMETTE
KEBABS
pg. 74

FOOLPROOF
CHICKEN CUTLETS
pg. 54

from
Mexican-style
pork...to Turkish

SAUSAGE KEBABS
ON GREENS
pg. 72

PORK AND
SALSA
VERDE
pg. 72

lamb kebabs,

fresh ideas make
family **dinners** fun
to cook and eat

TURKISH LAMB
KEBABS
pg. 74

a sandwich supper is simple and satisfying

REUBEN
SANDWICH
pg. 76

THE MIGHTY
EGGLESS SALAD
SANDWICH
pg. 76

ranch chicken with potatoes and gravy

A salad dressing mix makes this recipe doubly delicious, both sprinkled over the chicken, and in the savory gravy.

Prep time: 30 minutes • Baking time: 20 to 23 minutes

- 1 **package (1 oz.) Hidden Valley Original Ranch Salad Dressing and recipe mix, divided**
- ¼ **teaspoon freshly ground pepper**
- 4 **whole chicken legs, cut at joint**

MASHED POTATOES AND GRAVY:

- 1½ **pounds medium all-purpose potatoes, peeled and quartered**
- ⅔ **cup hot milk**
- 1 **tablespoon butter or margarine**
- ¼ **teaspoon salt**
- ⅛ **teaspoon freshly ground pepper**
- ¼ **cup water**
- ⅓ **cup sour cream**

1. Heat oven to 350°F. Set aside 1 tablespoon of the salad dressing and recipe mix. Combine remaining mix with pepper; sprinkle over chicken. Heat a 12-inch ovenproof skillet over medium-high heat. Add chicken and cook, turning occasionally, 10 to 12 minutes, until browned. Drain excess fat from skillet. Transfer skillet to oven and bake chicken 20 to 23 minutes, until cooked through.

2. Meanwhile, bring potatoes with enough water to cover in a 3-quart saucepan to boil; reduce heat. Cook 13 to 15 minutes, until fork-tender. Drain. Beat in milk, butter, salt and pepper until smooth.

3. Transfer chicken to 4 serving plates. Combine reserved 1 tablespoon ranch salad dressing and recipe mix and water in cup; whisk into drippings in skillet. Heat over medium heat; whisk in sour cream. Bring to boil and boil 1 minute. Serve gravy with chicken and mashed potatoes. Serves 4.

Per serving: 475 calories, 23.5 g total fat, 9.5 g saturated fat, 127 mg cholesterol, 830 mg sodium, 30 g carbohydrates, 34 g protein, 95 mg calcium, 2 g fiber

spicy orange chicken *EASY* *LOW FAT*

This super-quick weeknight dinner bursts with lively Asian flavors. Be sure your pan is hot before adding the chicken; the trick is to brown it quickly for best flavor, texture and color.

Total prep and cooking time: 20 minutes

- 3 **teaspoons Asian chili oil, divided**
- 2 **bags (10 oz. each) fresh spinach, rinsed well**
- 2 **oranges**
- 1 **tablespoon lite soy sauce**
- 1 **teaspoon honey**
- 1 **teaspoon grated fresh ginger**
- ¾ **teaspoon salt, divided**
- 1 **pound chicken tenders**
- ¼ **teaspoon freshly ground pepper**
- 2 **teaspoons finely chopped garlic**
   Hot cooked rice (optional)

1. Heat 1 teaspoon of the chili oil in a 12-inch nonstick skillet over medium-high heat. Add spinach; cover and cook until just wilted, 4 to 5 minutes. Arrange on a platter; cover with plastic wrap to keep warm.

2. Meanwhile, cut peel and pith (the white membrane) off one orange. Slice orange crosswise, then halve slices. Squeeze enough juice from the remaining orange to equal ⅓ cup. Combine juice, soy sauce, honey, ginger and ¼ teaspoon of the salt in a cup.

3. Sprinkle chicken with remaining ½ teaspoon salt and the pepper. Wipe out skillet. Add remaining 2 teaspoons chili oil and heat over medium-high heat. Add chicken and cook 3 minutes, until cooked through, turning as it browns. Add garlic, and cook, stirring 1 minute more. Add orange juice mixture and sliced orange; bring to boil and boil 1 minute. Pour over spinach and serve immediately with rice, if desired. Makes 4 servings.

Per serving: 225 calories, 5.5 g total fat, 1 g saturated fat, 66 mg cholesterol, 772 mg sodium, 14 g carbohydrates, 31 g protein, 176 mg calcium, 5 g fiber

chicken with zesty tomatoes

Capers add intrigue to this extra-easy one-skillet entrée.

Total prep and cooking time: 20 minutes

- **12 ounces gnocchetti or cavatelli**
- **4 boneless, skinless chicken breast halves (5 oz. to 7 oz. each)**
- **½ teaspoon salt**
- **¼ teaspoon freshly ground pepper**
- **1 tablespoon butter or margarine**

SAUCE:
- **2 tablespoons butter or margarine**
- **2 teaspoons finely chopped garlic**
- **1 teaspoon chopped fresh rosemary or ½ teaspoon dried rosemary**
- **¾ cup chicken broth**
- **1 medium tomato, diced**
- **1 tablespoon capers**
- **¼ teaspoon salt**
- **⅛ teaspoon freshly ground pepper**
- **Crusty bread (optional)**

1. Start to cook pasta according to package directions. Meanwhile, sprinkle chicken with salt and pepper. Melt the 1 tablespoon butter in a 12-inch skillet over medium-high heat. Add chicken and cook 5 to 6 minutes per side, until cooked through. Remove chicken; wrap in a large piece of foil and seal tightly. Let stand 3 to 4 minutes.

2. *Make sauce:* Melt the 2 tablespoons butter in same skillet over medium heat. Add garlic and rosemary and cook 30 seconds to 1 minute, stirring, until fragrant. Add remaining sauce ingredients; bring to boil, reduce heat and cook 5 minutes until sauce is slightly reduced.

3. Drain pasta; divide among 4 serving plates. Top each with a chicken breast, then spoon sauce over tops. Serve with bread, if desired. Serves 4.

Per serving: 595 calories, 12.5 g total fat, 6 g saturated fat, 122 mg cholesterol, 927 mg sodium, 66 g carbohydrates, 51 g protein, 43 mg calcium, 3 g fiber

chicken and polenta

Ever wonder what to do with those tubes of refrigerated polenta you've spotted in the supermarket produce section? Here's a great way to use this convenient (and popular!) ingredient.

Total prep and cooking time: 20 minutes

- **1½ pounds boneless, skinless chicken thighs**
- **¾ teaspoon salt, divided**
- **2 green bell peppers, coarsely chopped**
- **1 medium onion, coarsely chopped**
- **2 teaspoons cumin**
- **1 can (10 oz.) diced tomatoes and green chiles**
- **1 tablespoon olive oil**
- **1 tube (1 lb.) prepared refrigerated polenta, cut crosswise into 8 equal slices**
- **2 tablespoons chopped fresh cilantro**

1. Sprinkle chicken with ½ teaspoon of the salt.

2. Heat a 12-inch nonstick skillet over high heat 2 minutes. Add chicken and cook, turning as it browns, 3 minutes. Add peppers and onion; cook 3 minutes. Add cumin and cook, stirring, 30 seconds. Add diced tomatoes and chiles and remaining ¼ teaspoon salt. Reduce heat to medium-high, cover and cook 6 to 7 minutes more, until chicken is cooked through.

3. Meanwhile, heat oil in a large nonstick skillet, over medium-high heat. Add polenta slices; cook 2 minutes per side until golden.

4. Arrange 2 slices polenta in each of 4 shallow serving bowls. Divide and spoon hot chicken mixture over polenta. Sprinkle each serving with cilantro. Makes 4 servings.

Per serving: 355 calories, 10.5 g total fat, 2 g saturated fat, 141 mg cholesterol, 1,071 mg sodium, 25 g carbohydrates, 37 g protein, 53 mg calcium, 5 g fiber

roast chicken with herbs and garlic

You'll be surprised at how flavorful a chicken can be when you tuck some fresh seasonings under the skin before it's roasted. Pictured on page 44.

Prep time: 15 minutes plus standing
Roasting time: 1 hour 15 to 20 minutes

1	whole chicken (3½ lbs.)
1¼	teaspoons kosher salt, divided
¾	teaspoon freshly ground pepper, divided
½	lemon
4	cloves garlic, divided
3	large sprigs rosemary, divided
6	teaspoons butter, softened (no substitutions)

1. Heat oven to 425°F. Arrange a metal folding rack in a 13×9-inch roasting pan. Set aside.

2. Rinse chicken under cold running water; pat skin and cavity dry with paper towels. Discard excess fat. Sprinkle cavity with ¼ teaspoon each of the salt and pepper. Place lemon half, 1 garlic clove and 1 of the rosemary sprigs inside cavity. Thinly slice remaining 3 cloves of garlic and remove leaves from remaining 2 rosemary sprigs.

3. Carefully lift skin away from chicken breast with fingers or the handle of a wooden spoon. Place 2 teaspoons butter, sliced garlic and rosemary leaves under skin. Rub remaining 4 teaspoons butter over entire chicken. Sprinkle with remaining 1 teaspoon salt and ½ teaspoon pepper. Tie legs together with kitchen string. Place chicken, breast side down, on rack.

4. Roast 30 minutes. Reduce oven temperature to 350°F. Turn chicken to one side, roast 15 minutes. Turn chicken to other side and roast 15 minutes. Turn chicken breast side up and roast 15 to 20 minutes more, until a meat thermometer inserted in chicken thigh registers (without touching bone) 180°F.

5. Transfer chicken, breast side up, to a cutting board. Cover loosely with foil; let stand 10 minutes before carving. Makes 4 servings.

Per serving: 450 calories, 26.5 g total fat, 8.5 g saturated fat, 162 mg cholesterol, 633 mg sodium, 1 g carbohydrates, 48 g protein, 39 mg calcium, 0 g fiber

test kitchen tip
chicken safety

Here are some tips for handling raw chicken:

WHEN BUYING CHICKEN, check the "sell-by" date on the package and keep it separated from other foods in your grocery cart. At the checkout, have it packed in a separate plastic bag.

UPON ARRIVING HOME, immediately refrigerate the packaged chicken in the coldest section, placing it on a tray to catch drips. Freeze the chicken if you won't be cooking it within a day or two.

THAW FROZEN, wrapped chicken in the refrigerator—never on the countertop.

KEEP WORK SURFACES, hands, cutting boards and utensils scrupulously clean, washing them with hot, soapy water after working with raw chicken. Use a dishwasher-safe cutting board so that it can be sanitized after use and use disinfectant cleansers on work surfaces for extra protection. Designate one cutting board for raw poultry and meats and a separate one for chopping veggies.

AVOID CROSS-CONTAMINATING between raw and cooked poultry. Never put cooked meat on the same plate that held raw poultry unless the plate has been sanitized.

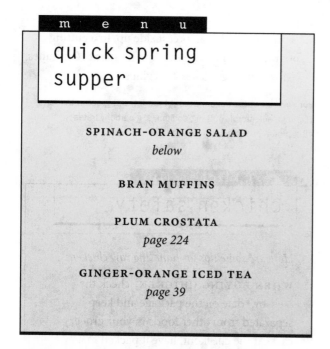

m e n u

quick spring supper

SPINACH-ORANGE SALAD
below

BRAN MUFFINS

PLUM CROSTATA
page 224

GINGER-ORANGE ICED TEA
page 39

spinach-orange salad L O W F A T   E A S Y

Plan your meal around a main-dish salad that's packed full of good nutrition. Pictured on page 42.

Prep time: 15 minutes • Cooking time: 10 to 12 minutes

- ½ **teaspoon salt**
- ¼ **teaspoon freshly ground pepper**
- 4 **boneless, skinless chicken breast halves (about 1 lb.)**
- 2 **bags (6 oz. each) baby spinach, rinsed**
- 2 **oranges, peeled and sectioned**
     Strawberry Dressing (recipe follows)
- ¼ **cup sliced natural almonds, toasted**

1. Sprinkle salt and pepper over both sides of chicken. Lightly coat a heavy grill pan or cast-iron skillet with vegetable cooking spray. Heat 1 to 2 minutes over medium-high heat. Add chicken and cook 5 to 6 minutes per side, until cooked through. Transfer to a cutting board.

2. Toss spinach and oranges with 3 tablespoons Strawberry Dressing. Slice each chicken breast. Divide spinach among 4 serving plates.

3. Top each serving of spinach mixture with a sliced chicken breast, then sprinkle 1 tablespoon almonds over each salad. Serve with remaining Strawberry Dressing. Makes 4 servings.

Per serving: 220 calories, 5 g total fat, 0.5 g saturated fat, 65 mg cholesterol, 141 mg sodium, 13 g carbohydrates, 1 g protein, 145 mg calcium, 4 g fiber

strawberry dressing E A S Y

Add plenty of flavor to the main-dish chicken salad with this fruity dressing. Pictured on page 42.

Total prep time: 15 minutes

- 1 **cup quartered strawberries**
- 1½ **tablespoons balsamic vinegar**
- 1 **tablespoon hazelnut* or sunflower oil**
- 2 **teaspoons honey**
- ¼ **teaspoon salt**
- ⅛ **teaspoon freshly ground pepper**

Puree all ingredients in blender. Makes ³⁄₄ cup.

*Note: Available in specialty food stores or gourmet section of the supermarket.

Per serving: 55 calories, 4 g total fat, 0 g saturated fat, 0 mg cholesterol, 433 mg sodium, 6 g carbohydrates, 1 g protein, 6 mg calcium, 1 g fiber

chicken-nut salad

Provide a creamy avocado dressing for just the right finish to a warm chicken salad. Pictured on page 45.

Prep time: 15 minutes • Baking time: 12 to 15 minutes

- ⅓ **cup shelled pistachio nuts, finely ground**
- ¾ **teaspoon salt, divided**
- ¼ **teaspoon freshly ground pepper, divided**
- 4 **boneless, skinless chicken breast halves (1½ lbs.)**
- 2 **tablespoons olive oil, divided**

1 medium sweet white onion
1 can (8½ oz.) whole kernel corn, drained
AVOCADO DRESSING:
1 large ripe avocado, pitted and peeled
3 tablespoons olive oil
3 tablespoons fresh lime juice
1 tablespoon water
½ teaspoon salt
⅛ teaspoon freshly ground pepper
▪
1 head romaine lettuce, sliced

1. Heat oven to 375°F. Combine nuts with ½ teaspoon of the salt and ⅛ teaspoon of the pepper in pie plate. Press smooth side of chicken breasts into nut mixture to coat. Heat 1 tablespoon of the oil in a large ovenproof skillet over medium-high heat. Add chicken, nut side down, and cook 2 minutes per side. Transfer to oven and bake 12 to 15 minutes, until cooked through.

2. Meanwhile, dice enough onion to equal ½ cup; set remaining onion aside for dressing. Heat remaining 1 tablespoon oil in another large nonstick skillet over high heat. Add diced onion and remaining ¼ teaspoon salt and ⅛ teaspoon pepper. Cook 3 minutes, until onion is lightly charred. Add corn and cook 2 minutes.

3. *Make avocado dressing:* Grate 1 teaspoon from the remaining onion on the large hole of a grater. Puree grated onion and remaining dressing ingredients in blender. Makes 1 cup.

4. Line 4 serving plates with romaine. Slice chicken and arrange one sliced breast half over romaine on each plate. Top with corn mixture. Serve with avocado dressing. Makes 4 servings.

Per serving: 565 calories, 34.5 g total fat, 5 g saturated fat, 99 mg cholesterol, 944 mg sodium, 21 g carbohydrates, 46 g protein, 101 mg calcium, 6 g fiber

chicken with herbs

Talk about convenient—just grab a can of chicken broth with herbs and you've got a jump start on a tempting chicken dinner tonight. For this recipe, we've used chicken breasts with the wing attached. Fresh tomatoes, garlic and chopped olives are added along with the broth to round out the sauce.

Prep time: 15 minutes • Cooking time: 36 to 43 minutes

1 tablespoon olive oil
4 chicken breast halves with wing attached (12 oz. each)
¾ teaspoon salt
¼ teaspoon freshly ground pepper
2 teaspoons finely chopped garlic
2 medium ripe tomatoes, chopped
1 can (15 oz.) chicken broth with Italian herbs
½ cup pitted kalamata olives, chopped
1 box (10 oz.) couscous, cooked according to package directions
1 tablespoon chopped fresh flat-leaf parsley

1. Heat oil in a large skillet over medium-high heat. Sprinkle chicken with salt and pepper; arrange chicken, skin side down, in a skillet. Cook 8 to 10 minutes until browned. Turn chicken and cook 5 minutes, until cooked through.

2. Add garlic to skillet; cook, stirring, 30 seconds. Add tomatoes and cook 2 minutes, until thickened. Add broth and olives; bring to boil. Reduce heat and simmer 20 to 25 minutes, covered, turning chicken once, until cooked through. Serve chicken with sauce over couscous. Sprinkle with parsley. Makes 4 servings.

Per serving: 740 calories, 27.5 g total fat, 7 g saturated fat, 146 mg cholesterol, 1,303 mg sodium, 62 g carbohydrates, 58 g protein, 59 mg calcium, 3 g fiber

foolproof chicken cutlets

Make sure the coating sticks by dipping cutlets in egg, instead of milk or water, before coating with crumbs. Pictured on page 46.

Prep time: 15 minutes • Cooking time: 10 to 12 minutes

- 4   boneless, skinless chicken breast halves (about 4 oz. to 5 oz. each)
- ¾   teaspoon salt, divided
- ½   teaspoon freshly ground pepper
- 1   cup fresh bread crumbs (2 or 3 slices)
- 2   tablespoons freshly grated Parmesan cheese
- 1   tablespoon chopped fresh flat-leaf parsley
- 1   teaspoon chopped fresh rosemary (no substitutions)
- 1   large egg
- 1   large egg white
- 3   tablespoons olive oil
     Lemon wedges and coleslaw (optional)

1. Place chicken breasts, smooth side down, on a large sheet of plastic wrap. Cover with a second sheet of plastic wrap and pound gently with bottom of a small saucepan to ¹/₂-inch thickness. Remove plastic and sprinkle both sides with ¹/₂ teaspoon of the salt and the pepper.

2. Combine bread crumbs, cheese, parsley, rosemary and remaining ¹/₄ teaspoon salt on a piece of waxed paper. Beat whole egg and egg white in a pie plate. Dip both sides of each cutlet in egg, then in bread crumb mixture, to lightly coat.

3. Heat a 12-inch skillet over medium-high heat 1 minute. Add oil; when it starts to ripple, add cutlets and cook until golden brown on each side and cooked through, about 5 to 6 minutes. Transfer cutlets to 4 serving plates. Serve with lemon wedges and coleslaw, if desired. Makes 4 servings.

Per serving: 300 calories, 14.5 g total fat, 3 g saturated fat, 130 mg cholesterol, 658 mg sodium, 6 g carbohydrates, 34 g protein, 76 mg calcium, 0 g fiber

turkey nuggets with pineapple-soy dipping sauce

Looking for a kid-friendly supper to serve on a busy weeknight? This is it! Tip: Marinate the turkey in the morning, then, after work, dinner will be on the table that much sooner.

Prep time: 20 minutes plus marinating
Cooking time: 13 minutes
Microwave used

MARINADE:
- 2   tablespoons soy sauce
- 1   tablespoon vegetable oil
- 2   teaspoons minced garlic
- 1   teaspoon grated fresh ginger

- 1½   pounds turkey tenderloins, cut into 1½-inch chunks
- 1   tablespoon cornstarch
- 1   jar (2.6 oz.) sesame seeds
- 2   tablespoons vegetable oil

DIPPING SAUCE:
- 1   jar (12 oz.) pineapple preserves or orange marmalade
- 2   tablespoons soy sauce
- ½   teaspoon red pepper flakes (optional)
- 1   teaspoon distilled white vinegar

     Steamed broccoli (optional)
     Cooked rice (optional)

1. *Make marinade:* Combine all marinade ingredients in a large bowl. Add turkey; toss to coat. Cover and marinate in the refrigerator 20 minutes. *(Can be made ahead. Refrigerate up to 24 hours.)* Stir cornstarch into turkey mixture until well blended; sprinkle with sesame seeds, turning to coat all sides.

2. Heat the 2 tablespoons oil in a 12-inch nonstick skillet over medium-high heat. Add turkey and cook 11 to 13 minutes, turning as it browns, until golden and cooked through.

3. *Make dipping sauce:* Meanwhile, combine preserves, soy sauce and pepper flakes, if using, in microwaveproof bowl. Microwave on High 2 minutes until preserves are melted; stir in vinegar. Serve turkey nuggets with sauce, and, if desired, broccoli and rice. Makes 4 servings.

Per serving: 610 calories, 20.5 g total fat, 3 g saturated fat, 106 mg cholesterol, 720 mg sodium, 63 g carbohydrates, 47 g protein, 220 mg calcium, 3 g fiber

italian pot pie

Our homemade Parmesan pastry is a snap to make, and adds extra richness to this pie. However, if you prefer, you can substitute your pastry recipe for a double crust pie, or use refrigerated pie crusts. And with our freezing instructions, you can eat one pie now and save another for a busy night.

Prep time: 45 minutes plus chilling
Baking time: 40 to 45 minutes

PARMESAN PASTRY:

- 2 **cups all-purpose flour**
- ⅔ **cup freshly grated Parmesan cheese**
- ¾ **teaspoon salt**
- ¾ **cup butter or margarine, cut up**
- 6 **to 7 tablespoons cold water**

- 1 **pound Italian sausage links, sliced**
- 1½ **pounds boneless, skinless chicken breasts, cut into ¾-inch chunks**
- 1 **medium onion, chopped**
- 1 **can (35 oz.) whole tomatoes in juice**
- 3 **pounds Swiss chard**
- 2 **to 4 tablespoons freshly grated Parmesan cheese**
   Cooked zucchini (optional)

1. *Make Parmesan pastry:* Pulse flour, Parmesan and salt in a food processor to blend. Add butter; pulse until mixture resembles coarse crumbs. Sprinkle 5 tablespoons of the water over mixture. Pulse, adding remaining 1 to 2 tablespoons water if necessary, just until mixture is moistened and begins to hold together (dough should still be crumbly). Gather dough into a ball; cut in half and shape into two disks. Wrap disks and refrigerate 30 minutes.

2. Meanwhile, heat a 12-inch nonstick skillet over medium-high heat. Add sausage; cook 3 to 5 minutes until browned. Transfer to a bowl with a slotted spoon. Discard excess drippings. Increase heat to high; add chicken to skillet and cook 3 to 5 minutes, turning chicken occasionally until lightly browned. Add onion; cook 3 to 4 minutes until tender. Add tomatoes and juice; bring to boil, breaking up tomatoes with a spoon. Reduce heat; simmer 7 to 8 minutes more. Add sausage and cool.

3. Meanwhile, heat oven to 375°F. Trim stems from chard and coarsely slice leaves and stems. Bring ½ cup water, chard stems and leaves to boil in a large pot. Cover and cook 9 to 10 minutes, until stems are tender. Drain in a colander, pressing out excess liquid with a spoon.

4. Stir chard into cooled chicken-sausage mixture; divide mixture between two 2-quart baking dishes. Divide and sprinkle 2 tablespoons Parmesan over tops (4 tablespoons if using prepared or refrigerated pastry).

5. Roll each pastry disk so it extends 1 inch beyond edge of each baking dish. Place pastry on top of each dish, pressing pastry against side of dish to seal in filling. Cut 2 slits in center of each. *(Can be made ahead. Tightly wrap dishes and freeze up to 2 weeks.)* Bake pot pies 40 to 45 minutes, until tops are golden and filling is bubbly. (For frozen pies, unwrap dishes and let stand at room temperature 30 minutes. Bake in a 350° F. oven 30 minutes. Increase oven temperature to 375° F. and bake 45 minutes more.) Serve with zucchini, if desired. Makes 6 servings per pot pie.

Per serving: 405 calories, 22 g total fat, 11 g saturated fat, 91 mg cholesterol, 1,042 mg sodium, 25 g carbohydrates, 27 g protein, 193 mg calcium, 3 g fiber

from flank steak to pinwheels

Place flank steak on a cutting board. Use a long knife and hold it horizontal to board; slice steak in half lengthwise without cutting all the way through, starting at one of the long sides of the meat. Use your other hand to steady the meat. Open steak like a book. Spread with the filling, then roll following recipe directions.

italian pinwheel steaks

How many pinwheels this recipe makes depends on the shape of the steak. Pictured on page 42.

Prep time: 30 minutes plus chilling
Broiling time: 10 to 12 minutes

FILLING:

- 1 **bunch fresh spinach (1¼ lbs.), trimmed, or**
     1 bag (10 oz.) fresh spinach, rinsed
- ¾ **cup fresh bread crumbs**
- ¼ **cup freshly grated Parmesan cheese**
- 2 **tablespoons chopped sun-dried tomatoes in oil**
- 2 **tablespoons toasted pine nuts**
- 1 **tablespoon chopped garlic**
  ■
- 1 **beef flank steak (1½ lbs.)**
- ¼ **teaspoon salt**
- ¼ **teaspoon freshly ground pepper**
- 2 **cups orzo, cooked according to package**
     directions
- 2 **teaspoons grated lemon peel**
     Tossed greens (optional)

1. *Make filling:* Place spinach with water clinging to its leaves in a large saucepan. Cook over high heat, stirring once, just until wilted, 2 to 3 minutes; drain. When cool enough to handle, squeeze dry, then coarsely chop. Combine spinach and next five ingredients in a small bowl until well blended.

2. Cut flank steak open (see tip, left). Spread filling over cut sides of steak, leaving a 1-inch border along the 2 long sides. Roll steak up tightly from one long side. Wrap tightly in plastic wrap and refrigerate 20 minutes.

3. Lightly brush a broiler pan with oil. Heat broiler. Unwrap steak. Cut roll into ¾-inch-thick pieces. Secure seam of each piece with a toothpick. Sprinkle both sides of each piece with salt and pepper. Place rolls on prepared broiler pan. Broil 4 inches from heat, 10 to 12 minutes, turning once halfway through, until cooked through. Remove toothpicks before serving.

4. Toss cooked orzo with lemon peel. Divide orzo among 6 serving plates. Divide and top each serving with pinwheel steaks and, if desired, tossed greens. Makes 6 servings.

Per serving: 480 calories, 15.5 g total fat, 5.5 g saturated fat, 60 mg cholesterol, 345 mg sodium, 50 g carbohydrates, 35 g protein, 150 mg calcium, 4 g fiber

mahogany beef with eggplant and peppers

Slice the beef paper-thin and cook it for less than a minute so that it will be tender. Serve it with roasted vegetables.

Total prep and cook time: 35 minutes

- 4 **Asian eggplants (1¼ lbs. total)**
- 2 **large red bell peppers**
- 1 **tablespoon olive oil**
- 1 **tablespoon chopped garlic**
- 1½ **teaspoons grated fresh ginger**

1½ **pounds boneless beef bottom round roast, thinly sliced**

¼ **teaspoon salt**

¼ **cup dark corn syrup**

3 **tablespoons mirin***

2 **tablespoons tamari sauce***

3 **teaspoons olive oil**

3 **tablespoons thinly sliced green onions**
   Cooked rice (optional)

1. Heat oven to 425°F. Line a large jelly-roll pan with foil. Brush eggplant and bell peppers with oil; arrange on prepared pan. Roast 20 to 25 minutes, until eggplant is tender and peppers are lightly charred. When cool, cut peppers in half and seed.

2. Meanwhile, finely chop garlic and ginger together on a cutting board. Toss 1 teaspoon of the garlic-ginger mixture with beef and salt in a medium bowl.

3. Combine remaining garlic-ginger mixture, corn syrup, mirin and tamari sauce in a cup for glaze.

4. Heat 1 teaspoon of the oil in a large nonstick skillet over high heat. Add one-third of the beef and stir-fry 1 minute; transfer to a medium bowl. (If beef is pink in spots, that's okay; it will continue to cook as it stands.) Repeat process with remaining 2 teaspoons oil and beef.

5. Add glaze to skillet; boil 1 minute. Divide beef and vegetables among 6 serving plates. Drizzle servings with glaze and top with green onions. Serve with rice, if desired. Makes 6 servings.

*Note: Can be found in spice aisle or ethnic sections of supermarkets, or in Asian specialty stores.

Per serving: 375 calories, 20 g total fat, 6.5 g saturated fat, 73 mg cholesterol, 519 mg sodium, 22 g carbohydrates, 25 g protein, 52 mg calcium, 2 g fiber

herb-coated eye round roast

Roasting times for the beef can vary, so always use a meat thermometer to test for doneness. Pictured on page 41.

Prep time: 20 minutes plus standing
Baking time: 1 hour to 1 hour 20 minutes

HERB PASTE:

1 **teaspoon cumin seeds**

⅓ **cup packed fresh cilantro leaves**

⅓ **cup packed fresh parsley leaves**

¼ **cup olive oil**

4 **cloves garlic, crushed**

1 **tablespoon grated fresh ginger**

1½ **teaspoons salt**

¼ **teaspoon freshly ground pepper**

2 **teaspoons olive oil**

1 **(2½ to 3 lbs.) eye round beef roast**
   Baked sliced sweet potatoes (optional)

1. *Make herb paste:* Toast cumin in a small skillet over low heat until fragrant, 1 to 2 minutes. Transfer cumin to blender. Add remaining paste ingredients and puree until smooth.

2. Heat oven to 350°F. Brush a 13×9-inch roasting pan with the oil. Rub herb paste over entire roast. Place roast in prepared pan. Insert ovenproof-dial meat thermometer so tip is centered in thickest part of roast. (This thermometer will remain in roast during entire roasting time.) Roast 1 hour to 1 hour 20 minutes, or until temperature registers 145°F. for medium-rare. (If using an instant-read thermometer, insert the metal shaft into the center of roast. Let stand 20 seconds, then remove.) Cover roast loosely with foil; let stand 10 to 15 minutes before slicing. Serve with sweet potatoes, if desired. Serves 6.

Per serving: 385 calories, 26.5 g total fat, 7.5 g saturated fat, 89 mg cholesterol, 658 mg sodium, 2 g carbohydrates, 33 g protein, 26 mg calcium, 0.5 g fiber

no more lumpy gravy!

A great way to dress up an everyday roast is to prepare gravy to accompany the meat (or poultry), using some of the pan drippings. If gravy making is not your forte and it sometimes ends with lumps, here are ways to repair or prevent lumps from forming in the future:

Pour the prepared lumpy gravy through a sieve to remove any lumps. Or, whirl the gravy in a blender until it is smooth.

Next time, avoid the lump problem by combining flour or cornstarch with a little cold water to form a paste. Using a wire whisk, gradually stir the paste into the hot liquid. Cook and stir, until gravy is thickened and bubbly, and the starch or flour is thoroughly cooked.

pot roast

Cook once, eat twice! That's our plan with the recipes on these two pages. Enjoy this pot roast—perhaps as a warming Sunday night supper. Then, during the week, stir up the luscious Pasta with Ragout (page 59), using leftovers from the pot roast.

Prep time: 30 minutes · Baking time: 2¹/₂ hours to 3 hours

1	teaspoon salt, divided
½	teaspoon freshly ground pepper
1	(4½ to 5 lbs.) beef round bottom round rump roast
1	tablespoon olive oil
3	cups chopped onions
4	cloves garlic
2	large carrots, cut into 2-inch pieces
2	celery ribs, cut into 2-inch pieces
½	pound parsnips, peeled and cut into 2-inch pieces
2	bay leaves
2	large sprigs fresh thyme or 1 teaspoon dried thyme
1	can (16 oz.) whole tomatoes in juice, drained and chopped (about 1 cup)
2	cans (14½ oz. each) chicken broth
1	tablespoon chopped fresh flat-leaf parsley
	Egg noodles and peas (optional)

1. Heat oven to 325°F. Sprinkle ½ teaspoon of the salt and the pepper on all sides of beef. Heat oil in a large Dutch oven over medium heat. Add roast; brown on all sides, 4 minutes per side. Transfer to a large plate.

2. Add onions to Dutch oven and cook until softened, 5 minutes. Stir in garlic, carrots, celery, parsnips, bay leaves and thyme. Cook 5 to 8 minutes, until vegetables soften. Add tomatoes and remaining ½ teaspoon salt; cook 2 minutes. Add chicken broth; bring mixture to boil. Return roast and any accumulated juices to pot.

3. Tightly cover top of Dutch oven with foil, then with a lid. Bake roast 45 minutes. Gently turn roast over. Cover and bake 1 hour 45 minutes to 2 hours more; turn roast every 45 minutes until fork-tender.

4. Carefully transfer roast to a large cutting board. Cover roast loosely with foil and keep warm. Discard bay leaves.

5. *Make sauce:* Skim fat from vegetables and broth. Place a large strainer over a large bowl. Working in batches, strain vegetables and broth in strainer, gently pressing vegetables with a large spoon to extract as much liquid as possible. Scrape vegetable puree from the underside of strainer into sauce. Repeat with remaining broth and vegetables. (For Pasta with Ragout [page 59], if desired: Transfer 1¹/₂ cups sauce and 1 pound meat to two separate airtight containers. Cover and refrigerate up to 3 days.)

6. Reheat sauce over low heat. Thinly slice meat. Arrange meat on a large serving plate. Spoon sauce over top. Sprinkle top of pot roast with parsley. Serve with egg noodles and peas, if desired. Serves 6.

Per serving: 450 calories, 24 g total fat, 8.5 g saturated fat, 12.5 mg cholesterol, 743 mg sodium, 12 g carbohydrates, 43 g protein, 46 mg calcium, 0 g fiber

pasta with ragout

Transform extra Pot Roast (page 58) into this luscious pasta dish. The herb topping (known as a "gremolata") adds a dose of freshness to the stew.

Prep time: 30 minutes • Cooking time: 30 minutes

RAGOUT:

- 1 tablespoon olive oil
- 1 cup chopped onions
- 1 cup chopped celery with leaves
- 1 teaspoon fresh thyme leaves or ¼ teaspoon dried thyme
- 1 can (28 oz.) whole tomatoes, drained and chopped
- 1½ cups sauce from Pot Roast (page 58)
- ½ teaspoon salt
- 1 pound cooked Pot Roast meat (page 58), cut into bite-size pieces
- ¼ teaspoon freshly ground pepper

HERB TOPPING:

- ½ cup finely chopped fresh flat-leaf parsley
- 2 teaspoons grated lemon or orange peel
- ¾ teaspoon minced garlic
  Pinch salt

- 1 pound penne, cooked according to package directions

1. *Make ragout:* Heat oil in a medium Dutch oven over medium heat. Add onions and cook until softened, 5 minutes. Stir in celery and thyme; cook 5 minutes until celery softens. Add tomatoes and puree; simmer 5 minutes. Stir in sauce from Pot Roast and salt. Return to a simmer and cook 10 minutes. Add Pot Roast meat and pepper; bring to boil. Reduce heat; cover and simmer 20 minutes.

2. *Make herb topping:* Meanwhile, combine all herb topping ingredients in a small bowl.

3. Toss ragout and hot pasta together in a large serving bowl; sprinkle top with herb topping. Makes 4 to 6 servings.

Per serving: 685 calories, 19 g total fat, 6 g saturated fat, 79 mg cholesterol, 902 mg sodium, 85 g carbohydrates, 40 g protein, 104 mg calcium, 4 g fiber

test kitchen tip
pastabilities

The versatility of pasta—most commonly a simple concoction of flour and water—is rivaled only by the many forms it takes.

NAMES AND SHAPES

The names of many—but not all—end in either "ini" or "oni." In Italian, "ini" is a diminutive. Tripolini, for instance, is a small bow-tie shaped pasta. Quadrettini are small squares of pasta. The "oni" on the end of the name of a type of pasta means it is generally larger in size. Rigatoni, for example, is a large, tubular pasta. Cannelloni is larger still, meant to be filled with seasoned meats, vegetables or cheeses.

The nomenclature of pasta is the poetry of the Italian kitchen, but reflects the larger world around it. For instance:

—*Acini de pepe* is Italian for "peppercorns," referring to the pasta's tiny round shape.

—*Agnolotti,* a small, crescent-shaped stuffed pasta, is Italian for "priest's caps."

—*Creste de galli,* Italian for "cockscombs," refers to a medium macaroni with a ruffled crest on the outside edge.

—*Orecchiette* are "little ears," named for their small, slightly concave, disk-like shape.

savory sirloin burgers

Take the burger to the next level of gourmet enjoyment! Pictured on page 43.

Prep time: 30 minutes • Baking time: 35 minutes

- 1½ pounds ground sirloin
- 1 tablespoon olive oil
- 2 teaspoons coarsely ground pepper or cracked pepper
- ½ teaspoon salt, divided

LEEK SAUCE:
- 1 tablespoon butter (no substitutions)
- ½ cup finely chopped leeks (white part only)
- 2 tablespoons chopped fresh flat-leaf parsley
- ¼ teaspoon salt
  Pinch ground cloves (optional)
- ¾ cup white wine
- 1 cup half-and-half cream

FRIED LEEKS:
- ¼ cup olive oil
- 1 cup thinly sliced leeks, cut into 2-inch-long strips (white part only)

1. Divide and shape sirloin into four 1¼-inch-thick oval patties. Brush both sides with oil and sprinkle evenly with pepper.

2. Heat oven to 350°F. Heat a 12-inch nonstick ovenproof skillet over medium-high heat, 2 minutes. Add patties and cook 3 to 4 minutes. Turn and sprinkle with ¼ teaspoon of the salt. Cook 3 to 4 minutes more, until both sides are well seared. Turn patties again and sprinkle tops with remaining ¼ teaspoon salt. Place skillet in oven. Bake burgers 35 minutes, or until an instant-read thermometer registers 160°F., for medium, when inserted 1 inch from edge of each burger.

3. *Make leek sauce:* Meanwhile, melt butter in a small saucepan over medium-low heat. Add leeks; cover and cook until leeks soften, 5 minutes. Increase heat to medium. Stir in parsley, salt and, if desired, cloves. Cook, uncovered, 1 minute. Add wine and gently boil, until mixture is reduced to ½ cup. Gradually whisk in cream and boil, stirring, until sauce is reduced to 1 cup, about 10 minutes. Remove from heat. Set aside.

4. *Make fried leeks:* Line a large plate with paper towels. Heat oil in a medium saucepan over medium-high heat just until oil begins to smoke. Carefully add half of leeks and cook 3 minutes, until golden brown. Remove leeks with tongs or slotted spoon and drain on paper towels. Repeat the frying with remaining leeks.

5. Reheat leek sauce over low heat, just until heated through. Divide sauce among 4 serving plates. Arrange burgers on top of each. Divide and mound fried leeks atop burgers. Makes 4 servings.

Per serving: 610 calories, 46.5 g total fat, 16 g saturated fat, 145 mg cholesterol, 696 mg sodium, 9 g carbohydrates, 38 g protein, 112 mg calcium, 1 g fiber

meat loaf with roasted-pepper sauce

This up-to-date meat loaf has outstanding moistness and flavor! Pictured on page 41.

Prep time: 35 minutes plus 5 minutes standing time
Baking time: 1 hour to 1 hour 15 minutes

- 3 red bell peppers
- 2 large cloves garlic, unpeeled

MEAT LOAF:
- 1 tablespoon olive oil
- 1 medium zucchini, shredded
- 1 medium onion, chopped
- 1 teaspoon salt, divided
- 1 tablespoon finely chopped garlic
- 3 slices firm white bread, cut into pieces
- 2 large eggs
- 2 tablespoons chopped fresh parsley
- 2 teaspoons chopped fresh thyme or
  ½ teaspoon dried thyme
- ¼ teaspoon freshly ground pepper
- 1 pound lean ground chuck

1 pound ground sirloin

ROASTED-PEPPER SAUCE:

½ cup chicken broth

2 teaspoons chopped fresh parsley

½ teaspoon chopped fresh thyme

½ teaspoon salt

¼ teaspoon freshly ground pepper

∎

**Mashed potatoes, steamed zucchini and
yellow squash (optional)**

1. ∎ Heat broiler. Place bell peppers and garlic on a foil-lined cookie sheet. Broil 6 inches from heat, 14 to 18 minutes, turning occasionally, until evenly charred. Wrap foil around vegetables; let stand until cool. Peel garlic and peppers. Remove seeds from peppers. Meanwhile, turn off broiler and heat oven to 350°F.

2. ∎ *Make meat loaf:* Heat oil in a large skillet over medium-high heat. Add zucchini and onion; cook 2 to 3 minutes, until browned. Sprinkle vegetables with ½ teaspoon of the salt; add chopped garlic and cook, stirring, 1 minute more. Cool.

3. ∎ Process bread in a food processor until crumbs form; transfer to a large bowl. Process 1 roasted pepper and eggs until smooth; add to bowl with crumbs. Stir in zucchini mixture, parsley, thyme, remaining ½ teaspoon salt and the pepper. Add chuck and sirloin. Toss lightly until combined. Transfer mixture to a 9×5-inch loaf pan; smooth top. Bake 1 hour to 1 hour 15 minutes, until an instant-read thermometer inserted in center of loaf registers 160°F.

4. ∎ *Make roasted-pepper sauce:* Meanwhile, process remaining 2 roasted bell peppers, the roasted garlic, broth and remaining sauce ingredients in food processor, until smooth. Makes 1 cup.

5. ∎ Let meat loaf stand 5 minutes, then carefully unmold onto a cutting board. Slice; serve with roasted-pepper sauce, and, if desired, mashed potatoes, zucchini and yellow squash. Serves 6.

Per serving: 440 calories, 28 g total fat, 10 g saturated fat, 167 mg cholesterol, 849 mg sodium, 14 g carbohydrates, 32 g protein, 57 mg calcium, 2 g fiber

---

test kitchen tip

in an emergency

Don't get caught short without something to prepare for fast weeknight meals. If you keep a variety of ingredients on hand, you'll be able to fix something for dinner in short order.

IN THE CABINET...
grains and grain products: various pastas, rices, couscous, quick-cooking barley.

canned and jarred foods: sun-dried tomatoes; beans; tomato products; roasted red peppers; chicken, beef and vegetable broths; tuna; salmon; anchovies and clams.

fresh foods: onions, potatoes, garlic.

sauces and seasonings: vinegars, oil (olive and vegetable), soy sauce, teriyaki sauce, marinara sauce, salsa, salad dressings, chutney, dry mustard, herbs and spices.

baking supplies: flour, sugars, cornmeal, cornstarch, baking powder and baking soda.

IN THE FRIDGE...
dairy products: eggs, milk, butter or margarine, cheeses, yogurt or sour cream.

other items: bacon, olives, mayonnaise, parsley, mustard, hot pepper sauce, salad greens and other fresh vegetables and fruits—lemons, green onions, carrots, apples and oranges.

IN THE FREEZER...
miscellaneous: frozen vegetables, nuts, ice cream and sorbet.

mini meat loaves with tomato sauce

Quick and comforting, this meat loaf recipe takes on an Italian accent with a little marinara sauce in the mix.

Prep time: 20 minutes • Baking time: 30 minutes

- **2   teaspoons olive oil**
- **1   cup chopped onions**
- **1¾ pounds unseasoned meat loaf mix (one-third each of ground veal, pork and beef) or ground round**
- **⅔   cup prepared marinara sauce**
- **⅔   cup fresh bread crumbs (2 slices)**
- **1   large egg**
- **2   tablespoons chopped fresh parsley**
- **2½ teaspoons minced garlic**
- **1   teaspoon salt**
- **¼   teaspoon freshly ground pepper**
- **Chopped fresh parsley, for garnish (optional)**
- **Steamed baby carrots (optional)**
- **Cooked couscous (optional)**
- **Additional warm marinara sauce (optional)**

1. Heat oven to 375°F. Heat oil in a large nonstick skillet over medium-high heat. Add onions and cook 5 minutes, until lightly browned; cool. Combine onions and next 8 ingredients in a large bowl, tossing meat loaf mix lightly with fingertips.

2. Divide mixture among six ungreased 4-inch (1 cup) individual fluted cake mold pans or one 8½×4½-inch loaf pan. Arrange pans on a large jelly-roll pan. Bake 30 minutes (or 60 to 70 minutes for loaf pan), until meat thermometer inserted into center of meat loaves reaches 160°F. Remove pans from oven and immediately unmold onto a jelly-roll pan. If desired, garnish with chopped parsley and serve with baby carrots, couscous and additional marinara sauce. Makes 6 servings.

Per serving: 375 calories, 26.5 g total fat, 10 g saturated fat, 140 mg cholesterol, 681 mg sodium, 7 g carbohydrates, 25 g protein, 39 mg calcium, 1 g fiber

steak fajitas

This recipe pairs skirt steak (a flavorful, yet less tender cut of beef) with citrus, garlic and chile—all piled into a soft flour tortilla. The garnishes are up to you: We topped ours with Pico de Gallo, but also try with grilled onions and bell peppers.

Prep time: 15 minutes plus marinating
Grilling time: 8 to 10 minutes

MARINADE:
- **1   tablespoon grated orange peel**
- **1   tablespoon grated lemon peel**
- **⅓   cup fresh orange juice**
- **¼   cup fresh lemon juice**
- **1   tablespoon chopped garlic**
- **1   tablespoon ground chile de arbol or chili powder**
- **½   teaspoon salt**

- **2   pounds beef skirt or flank steak**
- **6   soft flour tortillas, warmed**
- **Pico de Gallo (page 24) and sour cream, for garnish (optional)**

1. *Make marinade:* Combine all marinade ingredients in a large shallow baking dish. Add steak, turning to coat. Cover and marinate steak in the refrigerator, 45 minutes.

2. Meanwhile, heat grill. Remove steak from refrigerator and let stand at room temperature, 15 minutes. Remove steak from marinade; discard marinade. Grill steak 5 minutes. Turn and grill steak 3 to 5 minutes more, or until an instant-read thermometer inserted in center of steak reaches 135°F. for medium-rare. Transfer to a cutting board and slice. Divide and fill warm tortillas with steak, and, if desired, Pico de Gallo and sour cream. Makes 6 servings.

Per serving: 370 calories, 16.5 g total fat, 6.5 g saturated fat, 75 mg cholesterol, 359 mg sodium, 21 g carbohydrates, 32 g protein, 57 mg calcium, 1 g fiber

asian steak-and-noodle bowl

An Asian take on the one-dish meal. Pictured on page 42.

Total prep and cooking time: 35 minutes

SPICE BROTH:

- 1 **New Mexican dried chile* (see tip, page 95)**
- 1 **can (14½ oz.) chicken broth**
- 1 **can (14½ oz.) beef broth**
- 1 **piece (1 inch) ginger, sliced**
- ½ **cinnamon stick**
- 2 **star anise***
  ■
- ¼ **teaspoon Szechwan peppercorns* or coarsely ground pepper**
- ¼ **teaspoon salt**
- 2 **beef tenderloin or boneless top loin steaks, 1¾ inch thick (1 lb. total)**
- 1 **teaspoon olive oil**
- ½ **pound broad rice or wheat-flour stick noodles, such as Chinese lo mein or Vietnamese banh pho**
- 1 **tablespoon tamari sauce***
- 1 **teaspoon finely chopped garlic**
- 1 **bunch (4 to 6 oz.) watercress, trimmed**

1. *Make spice broth:* Heat a large ovenproof nonstick skillet over medium-high heat. Add chile and toast about 1 minute, pressing lightly, until slightly darkened. Transfer to a medium saucepan; add remaining spice broth ingredients. Bring to boil; reduce heat and simmer 30 minutes.

2. Meanwhile, bring 3 quarts water to boil in a large saucepan. Heat oven to 350°F.

3. Crush Szechwan peppercorns with a rolling pin. Combine with salt in a cup and rub on both sides of steaks. Heat oil in same skillet over high heat; add steaks and brown, 1 minute per side. Transfer skillet to oven and bake steaks 9 to 12 minutes, until an instant-read thermometer inserted in each steak registers 142°F. for medium-rare. Transfer meat to a cutting board.

4. Add noodles to boiling water; boil 4 minutes, just until tender. Drain in colander; rinse quickly.

5. Line a fine strainer with double-thickness cheesecloth set over a large glass measure. Strain broth through strainer, then return to saucepan. Stir in tamari and garlic. Bring just to boil. Slice steaks. Divide noodles and watercress among 4 large soup bowls. Divide and add broth to each bowl. Top with steak. Makes 4 servings.

*Note: Can be found in spice aisle or ethnic sections of supermarkets, or in ethnic specialty stores.

Per serving: 565 calories, 29 g total fat, 11 g saturated fat, 81 mg cholesterol, 1,477 mg sodium, 52 g carbohydrates, 23 g protein, 58 mg calcium, 2 g fiber

---

test kitchen tip

using your noodles

Here's a rundown of some of the Asian noodles available. Dried noodles keep indefinitely and fresh ones can be refrigerated for up to 3 days.

EGG NOODLES: Made from wheat flour and egg. Varieties include dan mian and hokkien mee from China; ba mee from Thailand and Indonesia; and mee from Malaysia. Substitute: linguine, fettuccine or spaghettini.

WHEAT-FLOUR NOODLES: Made from wheat flour, water and salt. Varieties include lo mein from China. Substitute: fettuccine or thin linguine. Also included in this category is the broader udon from Japan. Substitute: any ribbon-shaped pasta.

RICE NOODLES: Made from finely ground rice and water. Available in two forms—the crisp, threadlike, rice stick noodles, such as py mee fun from China, and banh pho from Vietnam. Substitute: vermicelli or capellini. And, for broad rice stick noodles, such as ho fun from China, substitute linguine or fettuccine.

beef and chorizo burritos

Our version of the original Tex-Mex wrap sandwich pairs ground beef with chorizo (chor-EE-zoh), a garlicky Mexican sausage made with pork and flavored with herbs, spices and chiles, available fresh or smoked.

Prep time: 30 minutes • Cooking time: 18 to 24 minutes

- ¾ **pound lean ground beef**
- ½ **pound fresh or smoked chorizo, diced**
- 2 **small Anaheim (New Mexico) chiles, seeded and chopped (see tip, page 95)**
- 1 **medium onion, chopped**
- 1½ **teaspoons olive oil**
- ½ **pound potatoes, diced**
- 2 **cloves garlic, finely chopped**
- 3 **plum tomatoes, diced**
- ½ **teaspoon dried oregano, crumbled**
- ¼ **teaspoon salt**
- 4 **burrito-size soft flour tortillas, warmed**
  Salsa Verde (page 25) and sour cream (optional)

1. Heat a 12-inch nonstick skillet over medium-high heat. Add beef and chorizo; cook 3 to 4 minutes, until meat is no longer pink. Transfer with a slotted spoon to a medium bowl.

2. Drain all but 1 tablespoon drippings from skillet. Add chiles, onion and oil; cook 3 minutes. Add potatoes; continue cooking 4 to 5 minutes, until potatoes start to brown. Reduce heat to medium and cook about 4 minutes, until potatoes are tender. Add garlic and cook 30 seconds, then add tomatoes, oregano and salt. Cook 3 to 5 minutes more, until thick.

3. Return beef mixture to skillet and heat through, 1 to 2 minutes more. Divide and spoon filling down center of each tortilla. Fold in sides and roll up. Serve burritos with Salsa Verde and sour cream, if desired. Makes 4 burritos.

Per burrito: 725 calories, 42.5 g total fat, 15 g saturated fat, 105 mg cholesterol, 1,162 mg sodium, 48 g carbohydrates, 36 g protein, 19 mg calcium, 4 g fiber

cheese enchiladas

Filled with Mexican Queso Blanco (a firm-textured mild fresh cheese) and slathered in red chile sauce (or "gravy," as they say in Texas), these are delicious and easy to make. You'll find soft corn tortillas in the refrigerated section of the supermarket.

Prep time: 1 hour plus standing • Baking time: 15 minutes

RED CHILE SAUCE:

- 1 **teaspoon cumin**
- 1 **package (2 oz.) ancho chiles (see tip, page 95)**
- 1 **tablespoon vegetable oil**
- 1 **cup chopped white onions**
- 1 **tablespoon chopped garlic**
- 1 **tablespoon chopped serrano or jalapeño chile (see tip, page 95)**
- ½ **teaspoon dried oregano, crumbled**
- 2 **cans (14½ oz. each) chicken broth**
- ¼ **cup brewed coffee**
- ½ **teaspoon salt**
- 1 **tablespoon masa harina (see tip, page 25)**
  ▪

- 8 **soft corn tortillas, warmed**
- 2 **cups shredded Queso Blanco or Monterey Jack cheese**
- ⅓ **cup thinly sliced white onion (optional)**

1. *Make red chile sauce:* Toast cumin in a large skillet over low heat, until fragrant, 2 minutes. Transfer to a cup; set aside. Add ancho chiles to skillet and heat over low heat until chiles become pliable and fragrant, 3 to 5 minutes. Transfer to a large bowl and cover with hot tap water; let stand 15 minutes, until very soft. Drain liquid from chiles. Discard stems and seeds; chop chiles.

2. Heat oil in a small Dutch oven or medium saucepan over medium heat. Add cumin and onions, garlic, serrano chile and oregano and cook until vegetables soften, 5 minutes. Stir in chopped ancho chiles, broth, coffee and salt. Bring mixture to boil; sprinkle in masa harina. Reduce heat to medium-low and simmer mixture, partially covered, 1 hour. Transfer mixture to a blender and puree. Return sauce to Dutch oven and keep warm on low heat. Makes 3 cups. *(Can be made ahead. Cool. Cover and refrigerate up to 2 days. Reheat in a saucepan to a simmer.)*

3. Heat oven to 350°F. Wrap warm tortillas in foil. Spoon 1 cup warm sauce into the bottom of a 13×9-inch baking dish. Place ¼ cup cheese in center of one warm tortilla and roll up (keep remaining tortillas wrapped). Place enchilada, seam side down, in prepared dish. Repeat with remaining tortillas and cheese. Pour remaining 2 cups sauce over enchiladas. Cover dish with foil and bake until cheese has melted and sauce is hot, about 15 minutes. Garnish top with onion, if desired. Serve immediately. Makes 4 servings.

Per serving: 420 calories, 24.5 g total fat, 11.5 g saturated fat, 50 mg cholesterol, 1,818 mg sodium, 39 g carbohydrates, 19 g protein, 538 mg calcium, 7 g fiber

soft tacos with pork

Not all tacos go crunch! Soft tacos like these use soft flour or corn tortillas.

Prep time: 30 minutes • Cooking time: 22 to 25 minutes

ROASTED TOMATOES:

- 3 **small tomatoes, cored**
- 2 **large cloves garlic, unpeeled**
- 1 **canned chipotle chile in adobo sauce* (see tip, page 95)**

- 3 **tablespoons olive oil, divided**
- ¾ **pound boneless pork loin, diced**
- 1 **pound mushrooms, chopped**
- 1 **medium onion, chopped**
- 2 **medium (½ lb.) zucchini, diced**
- ¾ **teaspoon salt**
- ¾ **teaspoon dried oregano, crumbled**
- ½ **teaspoon cumin seed, crushed**
- ½ **cup crumbled Queso Fresco* or mild feta cheese**
- 12 **soft corn tortillas, warmed**

test kitchen tip

tex-mex night

GUACAMOLE
page 24

BEEF AND CHORIZO BURRITOS
page 64

FRIJOLES
page 79

JICAMA AND ORANGE SALAD
page 78

CHOCOLATE ICE CREAM

1. *Make roasted tomatoes:* Heat broiler. Line a jelly-roll pan with foil. Broil tomatoes and garlic 6 to 8 minutes, turning once, until charred. Cool. Peel tomatoes and garlic; pulse in a blender with chipotle until almost smooth.

2. Heat 1 tablespoon of the oil in a 12-inch nonstick skillet over high heat. Add pork; cook 1½ minutes, stirring once, until brown. Transfer to a medium bowl. Add 1 tablespoon of the oil to the skillet. Add mushrooms and onion and cook 8 minutes, stirring occasionally, until browned. Add zucchini, salt, oregano and cumin; cook 3 to 4 minutes more, until zucchini is tender. Add to bowl with the pork.

3. Reduce heat to medium-high and heat remaining 1 tablespoon oil. Add roasted tomato mixture; cook 2 minutes, just until thickened. Add pork mixture to tomatoes and cook 1 minute more, until heated through. Stir in cheese. Fill each tortilla with a generous ⅓ cup filling and roll up. Makes 12 tacos.

*Note: Can be found in ethnic section of supermarkets, or in Spanish or Latino specialty stores.

Per taco: 240 calories, 11 g total fat, 3 g saturated fat, 21 mg cholesterol, 379 mg sodium, 25 g carbohydrates, 11 g protein, 87 mg calcium, 2 g fiber

pork chops with cider and onion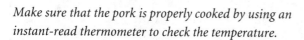

Make sure that the pork is properly cooked by using an instant-read thermometer to check the temperature.

Prep time: 10 minutes • Cooking time: 27 to 31 minutes

- **1** tablespoon plus 2 teaspoons butter or margarine, divided
- **1** medium Spanish onion (¾ lb.), thinly sliced
- **1** teaspoon salt, divided
- **½** cup chicken broth
- **¼** cup cider vinegar
- **1** tablespoon firmly packed brown sugar
- **1** tablespoon whole-grain mustard
- **4** rib pork chops, about 1 inch thick (2½ lbs.)
- **¼** teaspoon freshly ground pepper
- **1** tablespoon olive oil
- Cooked fettuccine (optional)

1. ■ Heat 1 tablespoon butter in a 12-inch nonstick skillet over medium-high heat. Add onion; cover and cook 10 to 12 minutes, until golden, stirring once. Sprinkle onion with ½ teaspoon of the salt. Cook 3 to 4 minutes more, until caramelized. Add broth, vinegar, brown sugar and mustard; bring to boil. Reduce heat slightly; cook 3 minutes. Transfer to a bowl; wipe out skillet with paper towels.

2. ■ Sprinkle chops with remaining ½ teaspoon salt and pepper. Heat oil in same skillet 1 to 2 minutes over medium-high heat. Add pork and brown 1 minute per side. Cover and cook 4 minutes, then turn chops and cook 4 to 5 minutes more, until an instant-read thermometer inserted 1½ inches deep into side of each chop registers 145°F. Spoon onion sauce over pork. Cover and cook 1 minute more. Dot onion with remaining 2 teaspoons butter. Remove skillet from heat; cover and let stand 2 minutes. (Temperature should register 155°F.) Transfer chops to a serving platter. Serve with fettuccine, if desired. Makes 4 servings.

Per serving: 515 calories, 33.5 g total fat, 12 g saturated fat, 124 mg cholesterol, 893 mg sodium, 12 g carbohydrates, 39 g protein, 75 mg calcium, 1 g fiber

pork tenderloin with tomatoes

If you wish, choose a larger piece of pork tenderloin, and you'll have plenty of leftovers, which are great in the Asian Pork and Noodle Bowl (page 67), or simply for sandwiches to pack for a delicious lunch. See the note on page 67 about preparing the extra meat.

Prep time: 1 hour plus marinating
Grilling time: 20 minutes

- **2** tablespoons extra-virgin olive oil
- **1** teaspoon salt
- **¼** teaspoon jalapeño flakes or red pepper flakes
- Grated peel of 1 orange
- Grated peel of 1 lemon
- **1½** pounds pork tenderloin*

TOMATOES:
- **1½** pounds plum tomatoes, halved
- **5** cloves garlic, unpeeled
- **2** tablespoons extra-virgin olive oil
- **¼** teaspoon salt
- **¼** teaspoon balsamic vinegar
  ■
- Cooked green beans and mashed potatoes (optional)
- Sliced lemon and fresh thyme sprigs, for garnish (optional)

1. ■ Combine oil, salt, jalapeño flakes, and orange and lemon peels in a small bowl. Spread mixture over pork; wrap and marinate in the refrigerator 1 hour. (*Can be made ahead. Refrigerate overnight.*)

2. ■ *Make tomatoes:* Meanwhile, heat oven to 350° F. Arrange tomato halves, cut sides up, and garlic on a jelly-roll pan. Drizzle tomatoes with oil. Bake until tomatoes and garlic are very soft and tomatoes are lightly brown on bottoms, 1 hour. Cool tomatoes and garlic slightly; peel garlic. Transfer tomatoes and garlic to a cutting board and coarsely chop. (*Can be made ahead. Transfer tomatoes with juice and garlic to a bowl. Cover and refrigerate overnight.*) Transfer tomatoes, their juices and garlic to a small saucepan. Stir in salt and vinegar. Set aside.

3. Heat and oil grill or grill pan. Grill pork 20 minutes, turning several times, until a meat thermometer inserted in the thickest part of each tenderloin registers 155°F.

4. Meanwhile, 10 minutes before pork is done, cook tomatoes over low heat just until heated through. Transfer pork to a cutting board. Cool 5 minutes. Slice tenderloin and serve with tomatoes and, if desired, green beans and mashed potatoes. Garnish with sliced lemon and thyme sprigs, if desired. Makes 4 to 6 servings.

Note: To make extra pork for Asian Pork and Noodle Bowl, below: Prepare pork as directed except increase pork tenderloin to 3 pounds. Marinate pork in the refrigerator with $^1/_4$ cup extra-virgin olive oil, 2 teaspoons salt, $^1/_2$ teaspoon jalapeño flakes and the grated peel of 2 oranges and 2 lemons. Cool $^3/_4$ pound grilled pork for Asian Pork and Noodle Bowl; cover and refrigerate overnight. Serve remaining grilled pork with tomatoes as directed.

Per serving: 375 calories, 22.5 g total fat, 5 g saturated fat, 106 mg cholesterol, 780 mg sodium, 8 g carbohydrates, 35 g protein, 24 mg calcium, 2 g fiber

asian pork and noodle bowl EASY

You can make this a meatless main dish, or, if desired, add some leftover pork tenderloin from the preceding recipe. Either way, you'll enjoy this homemade version of a comforting soup that's becoming increasingly popular in Asian restaurants.

Prep time: 30 minutes • Cooking time: 25 to 28 minutes

- 2 **tablespoons vegetable oil, divided**
- 1 **package (8 oz.) sliced white mushrooms**
- ½ **cup finely chopped onion**
- 1 **tablespoon finely chopped garlic**
- 1 **tablespoon grated fresh ginger**
- 3 **carrots, peeled and cut on the diagonal into ½-inch-thick pieces**
- 4 **cans (14½ oz. each) chicken broth or 4 cans (14½ oz. each) vegetable broth**
- 2 **tablespoons soy sauce**
- 1 **tablespoon rice wine vinegar**
- 1 **bunch bok choy, chopped**
- 1 **package (16 oz.) firm tofu, drained and diced**
- 4 **ounces perciatelli or bucatini pasta**
- ¾ **pound cooked pork tenderloin (see Pork Tenderloin with Tomatoes, page 66), cut into strips (optional)**
- 1 **bunch green onions, sliced**
- ½ **cup fresh cilantro leaves**

1. Heat 1 tablespoon of the oil in a medium Dutch oven over medium-high heat. Add mushrooms; cook until edges begin to brown, 3 to 5 minutes.

2. Transfer with a slotted spoon to a plate. Heat remaining 1 tablespoon oil. Add onion, garlic, ginger and carrots and cook 2 to 3 minutes, until onion begins to soften. Add chicken broth, soy sauce and rice wine vinegar. Bring to boil, reduce heat and simmer broth 10 minutes.

3. Stir in bok choy, tofu, pasta, mushrooms and, if desired, pork. Gently boil until pasta is just cooked through, 10 minutes. Stir in green onions and cilantro. Makes 4 servings.

Per serving: 690 calories, 33 g total fat, 7 g saturated fat, 80 mg cholesterol, 2,950 mg sodium, 47 g carbohydrates, 56 g protein, 535 mg calcium, 7 g fiber

cooking perfect pasta

Here are some simple solutions for cooking pasta:

NO MORE STICKING
Use enough water (4 to 6 quarts per pound of pasta) and add pasta all at once to the boiling water. When adding pasta, stir with a long-handled spoon. After the pasta is cooked, drain it and toss with sauce, if desired.

SEASONED JUST RIGHT
Pasta needs to cook in salted water for best seasoning. Add about 1 teaspoon salt per 3 quarts of boiling water.

WHEN IS PASTA DONE?
The best way to check for doneness is to remove a piece of pasta from the pot and cut in half. If there is a white line or ring in the center of the pasta, it needs further cooking. Cook pasta until it is al dente (firm to the tooth).

pasta alla marinara

To add herb flavor to the pasta sauce, add chopped fresh herbs, such as basil or oregano, the last 10 minutes of simmering for fresh-tasting flavor. Pictured on page 44.

Prep time: 15 minutes • Cooking time: 1 hour

- 3 tablespoons olive oil
- ½ cup chopped onion
- ½ cup chopped celery
- ½ cup chopped carrots
- 2 cans (28 oz. each) plum tomatoes, chopped, juice reserved
- ½ teaspoon salt
- ¼ teaspoon freshly ground pepper
- 1 pound spaghetti or penne, cooked according to package directions (see tip, above)

- ½ cup freshly grated Parmesan cheese
  Crusty bread (optional)

1. Heat oil in a large Dutch oven over medium heat. Add onion and cook until lightly browned, about 5 minutes. Add celery and carrots and cook, stirring, 5 to 8 minutes more, until vegetables are softened.

2. Slowly add tomatoes and juice, breaking up tomatoes with a spoon; add salt and pepper. Reduce heat and simmer sauce 1 hour, stirring occasionally, until thickened. Makes 4¾ cups.

3. Toss hot pasta with 3 cups marinara sauce. Divide into 6 shallow serving bowls. Serve with remaining sauce, Parmesan cheese and, if desired, crusty bread. Makes 6 servings.

Per serving: 440 calories, 11 g total fat, 2.5 g saturated fat, 6 mg cholesterol, 600 mg sodium, 70 g carbohydrates, 16 g protein, 203 mg calcium, 5 g fiber

fettucine alfredo

Low-fat milk helps to keep the calories under control.

Prep time: 15 minutes • Cooking time: 10 to 12 minutes

- 12 ounces fettucine noodles
- 2 cups (1%) low-fat milk
- ⅓ cup all-purpose flour
- 1 bay leaf
- 2 cloves garlic, peeled and crushed
- ½ cup freshly grated Romano cheese
- ¼ teaspoon salt
- ¼ teaspoon freshly ground pepper
  Pinch nutmeg
- 2 teaspoons butter or margarine
- ¼ cup chopped fresh flat-leaf parsley
- ¼ cup freshly grated Parmesan cheese
  Fresh parsley sprigs, for garnish (optional)

1. Start to cook pasta according to package directions. Meanwhile, whisk together milk and flour in a medium saucepan until flour is blended. Add bay leaf and garlic and cook over medium heat

8 minutes, stirring often with a wooden spoon, until mixture becomes slightly thickened. With a slotted spoon, remove bay leaf and garlic; discard. Add Romano cheese, salt, pepper and nutmeg, stirring, until cheese melts.

2. Drain pasta; transfer to a bowl. Toss pasta with butter and parsley, then stir in the cheese mixture and toss again. Divide pasta among 4 serving bowls; sprinkle with Parmesan cheese. Garnish with parsley sprigs, if desired. Makes 4 servings.

Per serving: 490 calories, 9 g total fat, 5 g saturated fat, 25 mg cholesterol, 465 mg sodium, 79 g carbohydrates, 22 g protein, 368 mg calcium, 3 g fiber

shrimp and peppers

A trio of bell peppers, sautéed with hints of fresh thyme and garlic, perfectly complements the sweetness of the shrimp.

Prep time: 10 minutes • Cooking time: 20 minutes

- 3 tablespoons olive oil, divided
- 4 assorted bell peppers (red, yellow and green), cut into thin strips
- 2 teaspoons chopped fresh thyme or ½ teaspoon dried thyme
- 1 teaspoon salt, divided
- 1 tablespoon chopped garlic
- 1¼ pounds medium shelled and deveined shrimp
- ¼ teaspoon freshly ground pepper
- 2 tablespoons all-purpose flour
- 2 tablespoons fresh lemon juice

1. Heat 2 tablespoons of the oil in a 12-inch non-stick skillet over medium-high heat; add peppers and cook 10 minutes. Add thyme and ½ teaspoon of the salt; cook 6 minutes more, until peppers are very tender. Stir in garlic; cook 30 seconds. Transfer to a serving platter.

2. Sprinkle shrimp with remaining ½ teaspoon salt and the pepper. Toss in a bowl with flour. Heat remaining 1 tablespoon oil in same skillet over high

heat. Add shrimp to skillet; cook 3 minutes, until pink, turning once. Sprinkle shrimp with lemon juice and serve immediately over peppers. Serves 4.

Per serving: 280 calories, 12.5 g total fat, 2 g saturated fat, 216 mg cholesterol, 795 mg sodium, 11 g carbohydrates, 36 g protein, 89 mg calcium, 1 g fiber

simple shrimp curry

Enjoy this satisfying dish spiked with curry and ginger. Serve with plenty of rice to soak up every bit of the sauce. Use regular, not lite, coconut milk for best results.

Prep time: 20 minutes • Cooking time: 6 minutes

- 2 large green onions
- 1 pound medium shelled and deveined shrimp
- 1 teaspoon salt, divided
- ⅛ teaspoon freshly ground pepper
- 2 tablespoons olive oil, divided
- 2 teaspoons grated fresh ginger
- 2 teaspoons curry powder
- 1 large (12 oz.) tomato, chopped
- 1 cup coconut milk
- 2 cups cooked rice

1. Cut off dark green tops from onions; thinly slice. Chop remaining white portion of onions; set aside.

2. Sprinkle shrimp with ½ teaspoon of the salt and the pepper. Heat 1 tablespoon of the oil in a 12-inch skillet over high heat; add shrimp and cook 1 minute, until pink, turning once. Transfer to a bowl.

3. Add remaining 1 tablespoon oil to skillet. Reduce heat; add chopped white portion of onions, ginger and curry and cook, stirring, 1 minute. Add tomato; boil 3 minutes, until mixture has slightly thickened. Add coconut milk and remaining ½ teaspoon salt; boil 1 minute. Stir in shrimp. Divide shrimp and rice among 4 serving bowls. Sprinkle top of each serving with sliced green onion tops. Makes 4 servings.

Per serving: 420 calories, 20 g total fat, 12 g saturated fat, 173 mg cholesterol, 766 mg sodium, 30 g carbohydrates, 27 g protein, 94 mg calcium, 2 g fiber

flounder with zucchini relish

This quick entrée is pictured on page 44.

Prep time: 10 minutes • Cooking time: 7 to 8 minutes

ZUCCHINI RELISH:

- ¼ cup finely chopped onion
- 1 medium zucchini (6 oz.), cut into ½-inch dice
- 1 carrot, cut into ½-inch dice
- 1 small jalapeño chile, finely chopped
  (see tip, page 95)
- 1 tablespoon white wine vinegar
- 2 tablespoons olive oil
- ½ teaspoon sugar
- ¼ teaspoon salt

- 4 skinless flounder fillets (6 oz. to 8 oz. each)
- ½ teaspoon salt
- ¼ teaspoon freshly ground pepper
- ¼ teaspoon cumin
- 4 teaspoons olive oil, divided
  Fresh tomato wedges, for garnish (optional)

1. Heat oven to 350°F. For zucchini relish, place onion in a small strainer and rinse under cold running water. Drain. Transfer to a medium bowl. Stir in remaining relish ingredients until well combined. Set aside. Makes 2 cups.

2. Cut each flounder fillet crosswise in half. Combine salt, pepper and cumin in a cup. Sprinkle on both sides of fish. Heat two large nonstick, ovenproof skillets over medium-high heat 2 minutes. Add 2 teaspoons of the oil to each skillet and swirl to coat. Place 4 pieces of flounder, skinned side down, in each skillet. Cook 3 minutes; transfer skillets to oven. Bake fish just until cooked through, 4 to 5 minutes.

3. Carefully transfer fish with 2 flexible metal spatulas to 4 dinner plates. Serve with Zucchini Relish and, if desired, tomato wedges. Serves 4.

Per serving: 300 calories, 13.5 g total fat, 2 g saturated fat, 95 mg cholesterol, 602 mg sodium, 5 g carbohydrates, 38 g protein, 51 mg calcium, 1 g fiber

salmon with couscous and kale

Serve this nutrient-packed and colorful main dish for dinner tonight. Lemon wedges spark the flavor of both the couscous and the fish.

Prep time: 20 minutes • Cooking time: 6 to 8 minutes

COUSCOUS:

- 1 tablespoon olive oil
- 2 teaspoons finely chopped garlic
- 2 cups coarsely chopped kale leaves
- 1 cup water
- ½ teaspoon salt
- ¾ cup couscous
- 1 tablespoon white wine
- 1 teaspoon butter or margarine

SALMON:

- 1¼ pounds center-cut salmon fillets
- 1 teaspoon olive oil
- ½ teaspoon salt
- ¼ teaspoon freshly ground pepper

  Lemon wedges (optional)
  Steamed green beans (optional)

1. *Make couscous:* Heat oil in a 2-quart saucepan over medium heat. Add garlic and cook 30 seconds. Add kale and stir. Cover and cook 3 to 5 minutes, until kale is almost tender. Add water and salt to kale; bring to boil. Stir in couscous; remove from heat and let stand 5 minutes. Stir in wine and butter.

2. Meanwhile, cut salmon crosswise into 4 equal strips. Heat oil in a large skillet over medium-high heat. Sprinkle fish with salt and pepper; place in skillet, skin side down. Cover and cook 6 to 8 minutes, until just cooked through.

3. Divide couscous among 4 serving plates. Top each with a salmon fillet. Serve with lemon wedges and green beans, if desired. Makes 4 servings.

Per serving: 460 calories, 21.5 g total fat, 4.5 g saturated fat, 86 mg cholesterol, 691 mg sodium, 31 g carbohydrates, 34 g protein, 76 mg calcium, 3 g fiber

salmon and potatoes with lemon vinaigrette

Prepare this meal in less than 30 minutes from start to finish. The lemon and garlic dressing enhances both the potatoes and the salmon steaks, and the salad greens turn this into a main-dish salad.

Prep time: 15 minutes • Cooking time: 11 to 13 minutes
Microwave used

- 1½ **pounds red potatoes, scrubbed and cut into 1-inch chunks**

DRESSING:
- 2 **tablespoons olive oil**
- 2 **teaspoons minced garlic**
- 2 **tablespoons fresh lemon juice**
- 1 **tablespoon white wine vinegar**
- ¼ **teaspoon salt**
- ⅛ **teaspoon freshly ground pepper**
  ■
- 4 **(1-inch-thick) salmon steaks (1½ lbs.)**
- ½ **teaspoon salt**
- ¼ **teaspoon freshly ground pepper**
- 2 **tablespoons chopped fresh flat-leaf parsley**
- 1 **teaspoon olive oil**
  Salad greens
  Lemon wedges, for garnish (optional)

1. Heat oven to 375°F.

2. Combine potatoes and enough water to cover in a 3-quart saucepan; bring to boil. Cook 12 to 13 minutes until potatoes are tender. Drain well; transfer to a bowl.

3. *Make dressing:* Meanwhile, combine the 2 tablespoons oil and the garlic in a microwave-proof 1-cup measure. Microwave on High 1 minute. Stir in remaining dressing ingredients.

4. Sprinkle both sides of salmon steaks with salt and pepper. Arrange salmon on a cookie sheet and bake 11 to 13 minutes, until just cooked through.

5. Gently toss drained potatoes with 2½ tablespoons of the dressing, the parsley and the 1 teaspoon oil.

6. Transfer a salmon steak to each of 4 serving plates. Divide potatoes among plates. Drizzle salmon with remaining dressing and serve immediately or at room temperature with salad greens. Garnish with lemon wedges, if desired. Makes 4 servings.

Per serving: 490 calories, 25 g total fat, 4.5 g saturated fat, 88 mg cholesterol, 535 mg sodium, 32 g carbohydrates, 33 g protein, 25 mg calcium, 3 g fiber

stuffed peppers

A packaged Spanish rice mix makes quick work of the vegetarian entrée.

Prep time: 15 minutes • Baking time: 25 to 30 minutes

- 4 **large yellow bell peppers, halved lengthwise and seeded**
- 1 **tablespoon olive oil**
- 1 **box (6¾ oz.) Spanish rice pilaf mix**
- 1 **cup diced zucchini**
- 1 **cup canned black beans, rinsed and drained**
- 1 **bag (8 oz.) 4-cheese Mexican shredded cheese blend, divided**

1. Arrange oven racks in top and bottom third of oven. Heat oven to 450°F. Line a jelly-roll pan with foil. Brush outside of peppers with oil. Arrange peppers cut side up on prepared pan; bake on lower oven rack 15 to 20 minutes.

2. Meanwhile, prepare Spanish rice pilaf according to package directions except add zucchini to top of rice (do not stir), during the last 5 minutes of cooking time. When rice is done, stir beans and 1½ cups of the cheese into rice. Spoon rice mixture evenly into pepper halves; divide and sprinkle remaining ½ cup cheese over tops. Bake on top oven rack 10 minutes until cheese is melted and filling is heated through. Serves 4.

Per serving: 535 calories, 28 g total fat, 13.5 g saturated fat, 50 mg cholesterol, 1,391 mg sodium, 50 g carbohydrates, 20 g protein, 484 mg calcium, 5 g fiber

pork and salsa verde

Pork with salsa verde—a zesty green sauce—is a classic Mexican dish. Pictured on page 47.

Prep time: 20 minutes plus marinating
Grilling time: 10 minutes

BRINE:

2	cups hot water
¼	cup kosher salt
¼	cup sugar
4	cloves garlic, crushed
1	serrano or jalapeño chile, minced (see tip, page 95)
1	teaspoon whole black peppercorns
¼	teaspoon red pepper flakes
2	cups cold water

■

1¾ **pounds boneless pork shoulder**

SALSA VERDE:

1	cup fresh cilantro leaves
1	cup fresh flat-leaf parsley leaves
½	cup fresh mint leaves
⅓	cup chopped onion
2	tablespoons white wine vinegar
1	tablespoon warm water
1	teaspoon capers, drained
2	cloves garlic, chopped
½	cup olive oil

■

Metal skewers (or wooden skewers soaked in water 30 minutes)

1. ■ *Make brine:* Stir hot water, salt, sugar, garlic, chile, peppercorns and red pepper flakes together in a medium bowl, until sugar has almost dissolved. Add cold water. Let cool to room temperature. Pour brine into a large heavy-duty resealable plastic storage bag. Add pork shoulder. Seal bag and turn pork to coat. Marinate pork in the refrigerator 24 hours, turning bag several times.

2. ■ *Make salsa verde:* Process all salsa ingredients except oil in a blender or food processor, until

blended. With machine on, gradually add oil through feed tube, until salsa is smooth. Divide salsa between 2 small bowls. Set aside. Makes 1 cup.

3. ■ Prepare grill according to manufacturer's directions for direct grilling.

4. ■ Drain pork in a colander. Discard brine and rinse pork under cold running water. Pat dry. Transfer pork to a cutting board and cut into 1-inch pieces. Skewer 4 or 5 pieces of pork on each of 6 skewers. Brush with salsa verde from one bowl; discard any remaining salsa verde in this bowl.

5. ■ Oil grill. Grill kebabs 10 minutes, turning several times, until cooked through. Transfer kebabs to a large serving plate. Serve with second bowl of salsa verde. Makes 6 servings.

Per serving: 505 calories, 44.5 g total fat, 12 g saturated fat, 96 mg cholesterol, 590 mg sodium, 4 g carbohydrates, 21 g protein, 43 mg calcium, 1 g fiber

sausage kebabs on greens

This main-dish salad gets extra kick from a refreshing lemon-basil dressing. Pictured on page 46.

Prep time: 45 minutes • Grilling time: 8 to 10 minutes
Microwave used

2	medium red onions
3	tablespoons olive oil
2	tablespoons fresh lemon juice
2	tablespoons chopped fresh basil
¼	teaspoon salt
¼	teaspoon freshly ground pepper
	Metal skewers
1	package (13 oz.) fully cooked sausage or 1 pound kielbasa, cut into 24 pieces
2	yellow bell peppers, cut into 6 pieces each
	One-half loaf sourdough baguette, cut into twelve ½-inch-thick pieces

DRESSING:

3	tablespoons fresh lemon juice
2	tablespoons olive oil

2 tablespoons chopped fresh basil

½ teaspoon salt

¼ teaspoon freshly ground pepper

■

8 cups assorted salad greens

1. Prepare grill according to manufacturer's directions for direct grilling. Leaving stem end attached, cut each onion into 6 wedges, being sure to include part of the stem end (this will keep onion together). Arrange onions in a single layer on a large microwaveproof plate. Cover with waxed paper; microwave on High 2 minutes.

2. Whisk together oil, lemon juice, basil, salt and pepper in a small bowl. Alternately skewer two pieces of sausage, yellow pepper, onion and bread on each of 6 skewers. Brush with half of the lemon mixture. Oil grill. Grill kebabs 4 to 5 minutes per side, brushing with remaining lemon mixture, until vegetables are softened and lightly charred.

3. *Make dressing:* Meanwhile, whisk together all dressing ingredients in a large bowl; add greens and toss. Divide greens among 6 serving plates; top each serving with a kebab. Makes 6 servings.

Per serving: 380 calories, 22 g total fat, 4.5 g saturated fat, 55 mg cholesterol, 973 mg sodium, 32 g carbohydrates, 15 g protein, 90 mg calcium, 3 g fiber

tequila shrimp and pepper kebabs ♥ LOW FAT

To skewer orange slices, thread the skewers through the peel. Pictured on page 43.

Prep time: 30 minutes plus marinating
Grilling time: 6 minutes • Microwave used

MARINADE:

⅓ cup fresh orange juice

2 tablespoons olive oil

2 tablespoons fresh lime juice

1 tablespoon grated onion

1 tablespoon coriander seeds, crushed

1 teaspoon cumin seed

1 teaspoon salt

1 teaspoon sugar

■

1 pound (about 24) large shrimp with shells

GLAZE:

1 cup orange marmalade

¼ cup tequila

2 medium jalapeño chiles, seeded and chopped (see tip, page 95)

■

2 green bell peppers, each cut into 6 squares or triangles

Metal skewers

2 oranges, each cut into six ¼-inch-thick slices

1. *Make marinade:* Combine all marinade ingredients in a large bowl.

2. With a small knife, cut slit through shell along curved side of each shrimp and devein (leave shells on). Add to marinade; marinate in the refrigerator 1 hour. Prepare grill according to manufacturer's directions for direct grilling.

3. *Make glaze:* Meanwhile, melt marmalade in a medium microwaveproof bowl on High, 30 to 40 seconds. Stir in tequila and jalapeños. Transfer half of mixture to another bowl for dipping sauce. Makes ⅔ cup.

4. Arrange bell peppers in a single layer on a large microwaveproof plate. Microwave on High, 2½ to 3 minutes, just until tender-crisp. Skewer one piece of bell pepper on one of 6 skewers. Fold orange slice in half and skewer through peel. Skewer 4 shrimp through head and tail; alternate with an orange slice and bell pepper piece. Repeat. Discard marinade.

5. Oil grill. Brush kebabs with glaze. Grill kebabs over medium coals, 3 minutes, or until shrimp turn pink, brushing with more glaze. Turn and grill 3 minutes more; brush with remaining glaze. Serve immediately, with reserved dipping sauce. Makes 6 servings.

Per serving: 305 calories, 6 g total fat, 1 g saturated fat, 93 mg cholesterol, 511 mg sodium, 47 g carbohydrates, 14 g protein, 88 mg calcium, 2 g fiber

turkish lamb kebabs

These Middle Eastern gems are pictured on page 47.

Prep time: 50 minutes · Grilling time: 11 to 13 minutes
Microwave used

TOMATO-POBLANO PUREE:
- **2** pounds plum tomatoes, halved lengthwise
- **6** poblano chiles (about 1 lb.) (see tip, page 95)
- **3** tablespoons olive oil, divided
- **1** tablespoon red wine vinegar
- **½** teaspoon minced garlic
- **½** teaspoon salt
- ■
- **1** tablespoon chopped garlic
- **1** teaspoon salt
- **2** pounds boneless leg of lamb, trimmed and cut in 1½-inch cubes (about 24 pieces)

RUB:
- **1** tablespoon paprika
- **1** teaspoon cumin
- **¼** teaspoon ground red pepper
- ■
- **3** onions
  Metal skewers
- **1** package (14 oz.) Middle Eastern bread, torn into 6 pieces, or 6 pocketless pitas
- **2** tablespoons butter, melted (no substitutions)
  Yogurt, for garnish (optional)

1. Heat oven to 450°F. Line jelly-roll pan with foil.

2. *Make tomato-poblano puree:* Toss tomatoes and chiles in a large bowl with 1 tablespoon of the oil. Arrange chiles and tomatoes, cut side up, on prepared pan. Bake 30 minutes, until tomatoes and chiles are lightly charred. Wrap vegetables in foil. Let stand to cool, 15 minutes. Unwrap vegetables. Separate chiles from tomatoes. Remove skin and seeds from chiles, and chop enough to equal 1 tablespoon. Cut remaining chiles into thin strips; set aside. Remove skin from tomatoes. Cook tomatoes in a large nonstick skillet over medium-high heat, mashing with a wooden spoon until slightly thickened, about 5 minutes. Stir in chopped chiles, vinegar, garlic and salt. Makes 1½ cups.

3. Mash garlic and salt on a cutting board with side of knife to form a paste. Rub onto lamb in a bowl, then toss with 1 tablespoon oil. For rub, combine paprika, cumin and ground red pepper in a cup; sprinkle over lamb and toss. Prepare grill according to manufacturer's direction for direct grilling.

4. Leaving stem end attached, cut each onion into 6 wedges, being sure to include part of the stem end (this will keep onion together). Arrange onions in a single layer on a large microwaveproof plate. Cover with waxed paper and microwave on High 2 minutes. Skewer 4 pieces of lamb, alternating with 3 onion wedges on each of 6 skewers. Brush remaining 1 tablespoon oil over onion wedges.

5. Oil grill. Grill lamb 10 to 12 minutes, turning skewers every 3 to 4 minutes, for medium-rare. Grill bread about 1 minute per side and arrange one piece on each serving plate. Spread top of each bread piece with 2 tablespoons tomato-poblano puree. Remove lamb from skewers; divide and place onto prepared bread. Top with poblano strips and remaining puree. Drizzle butter over each serving. Serve with yogurt, if desired. Makes 6 servings.

Per serving: 545 calories, 18.5 g total fat, 6.5 g saturated fat, 111 mg cholesterol, 1,039 mg sodium, 54 g carbohydrates, 41 g protein, 105 mg calcium, 5 g fiber

chicken drumette kebabs

Chicken drumettes are the meaty first section of the poultry wing. They cook quickly. Pictured on page 45.

Prep time: 30 minutes plus marinating
Grilling time: 20 minutes

- **2** pounds chicken drumettes (about 20)
- **½** teaspoon salt
- **¼** teaspoon freshly ground pepper
- **3** tablespoons fresh lemon juice
- **2** tablespoons extra-virgin olive oil
- **1** tablespoon chopped garlic

1 tablespoon fresh thyme leaves or
 1 teaspoon dried thyme

RED-PEPPER SAUCE:

4 red bell peppers
1 tablespoon extra-virgin olive oil
1 teaspoon sugar
1 teaspoon fresh thyme leaves or
 ¼ teaspoon dried thyme
2 teaspoons balsamic vinegar
2 teaspoons red wine vinegar
¾ teaspoon salt

 ■

Metal skewers
Fresh thyme sprigs, for garnish (optional)

1. Sprinkle chicken with salt and pepper. Combine lemon juice, oil, garlic and thyme in a large bowl or large resealable plastic storage bag. Add chicken and stir to coat. Cover and marinate in the refrigerator 2 hours or overnight.

2. *Make red-pepper sauce:* Meanwhile, heat broiler. Cut peppers in half; remove and discard ribs and seeds. Broil pepper halves, cut side down, until skin is evenly charred, 10 minutes. Wrap peppers in foil and let stand 15 to 20 minutes, until cool enough to handle. Remove skin. Puree peppers and remaining sauce ingredients in blender until smooth. Transfer sauce to a small bowl. Makes 1⅓ cups. *(Can be made ahead. Cover and refrigerate overnight.)*

3. Prepare grill according to manufacturer's instructions for direct grilling. Remove chicken (and red pepper sauce, if refrigerated) from refrigerator 30 minutes before grilling.

4. Remove chicken from marinade. Transfer marinade to a small bowl. Skewer 3 or 4 drumettes ½ inch apart on each of 4 skewers.

5. Oil grill. Grill chicken over medium coals 10 minutes, turning occasionally. Brush with remaining marinade. Discard marinade, then continue to grill drumettes 10 minutes more, until cooked through. Transfer kebabs to a large plate and, if desired, garnish with thyme sprigs. Serve with red-pepper sauce. Makes 4 servings.

Per serving: 320 calories, 19 g total fat, 4.5 g saturated fat, 98 mg cholesterol, 678 mg sodium, 7 g carbohydrates, 30 g protein, 25 mg calcium, 1 g fiber

test kitchen tip
great grilling

Even a grilling aficionado can use a few pointers now and then.

TO ENSURE THOROUGH, EVEN COOKING be sure your coals are hot enough before you place food on the grill. Allow between 25 and 30 minutes for the coals to burn evenly and develop a coating of grey ash. Gas grills need to be heated for 10 to 15 minutes.

AVOID USING LIQUID FUEL TO LIGHT COALS. Fuel that's squirted on seemingly idle coals can explode and cause serious injury. Instead, use a chimney cylinder, available at most hardware stores. The briquettes are simply poured into the cylinder and lit at the bottom, which ignites all of the coals in the cylinder in about 20 minutes. When they're red-hot in the center and ash-grey on the outside, spread them into a single layer.

DO NOT ENCOURAGE FLARE-UPS OR cook your food over a flame, which can burn food and make it taste bitter. Covering the grill will help tame the flame. If you don't have a cover, move food to another part of the grill.

BRUSH THICK, SUGARY OR OILY SAUCES on meats only during the final 10 minutes of cooking. If the sauce is put on too soon, it will burn. Blot marinated foods with paper towels.

DO NOT CROWD THE GRILL. Grilled foods need a good air flow to cook quickly and evenly. Leave at least a half-inch between food.

USE AN INSTANT-READ MEAT THERMOMETER to determine when meat, poultry and fish are properly cooked.

reuben sandwich

A lower-calorie version of the classic. Pictured on page 48.

Prep time: 10 minutes · Baking time: 2 minutes

RUSSIAN DRESSING:
- ¼ **cup light mayonnaise**
- 1½ **tablespoons ketchup**
- 1 **tablespoon sweet pickle relish**

- 2 **cups sauerkraut, rinsed and squeezed dry**
- 2 **cups shredded coleslaw mix**
- 4 **slices rye bread, toasted**
- 4 **slices Swiss cheese, cut crosswise in half (2 oz.)**
- 8 **thin slices lean corned beef (4 oz.)**

1. Heat oven to 350°F.

2. *Make Russian dressing:* Combine all dressing ingredients in a bowl. Toss sauerkraut and coleslaw mix with dressing to coat.

3. Arrange bread on a cookie sheet. On each slice, layer ½ slice of cheese, then 2 slices corned beef. Mound a generous ½ cup coleslaw mixture and top with second slice of cheese. Bake 2 minutes, until cheese melts. Makes 4 servings.

Per serving: 300 calories, 15 g total fat, 4 g saturated fat, 45 mg cholesterol, 1,065 mg sodium, 28 g carbohydrates, 13 g protein, 213 mg calcium, 4 g fiber

the mighty eggless salad sandwich

This mighty flavorful sandwich is pictured on page 48.

Total prep time: 25 minutes plus standing and chilling

- 1 **pound firm regular tofu**
- ¼ **cup chopped celery**
- ¼ **cup light mayonnaise**
- 2 **tablespoons finely chopped onion**
- 4 **teaspoons fresh lemon juice**
- 2 **teaspoons dried mustard**
- 1 **teaspoon turmeric**
- ½ **teaspoon salt**
- 8 **slices whole-wheat bread**
- 1 **cup watercress leaves**

1. To drain, press tofu to remove excess liquid as follows: Slice tofu in half horizontally into two 1-inch-thick pieces. Invert a plate onto a jelly-roll pan and cover with plastic wrap. Arrange tofu pieces side by side in the center of the plate. Cover tofu with plastic wrap, then top with another dinner plate. Weigh the plate down with a can. Let stand 30 minutes, until tofu is firm and most of the water has drained.

2. Combine pressed tofu, celery, mayonnaise, onion, lemon juice, mustard, turmeric and salt in a bowl; mash tofu mixture with a fork until smooth. Cover and refrigerate 1 hour, to blend flavors.

3. Spread tofu mixture on 4 slices of bread; top with watercress and remaining bread slices. Makes 4 servings.

Per serving: 285 calories, 13 g total fat, 2.5 g saturated fat, 5 mg cholesterol, 722 mg sodium, 31 g carbohydrates, 15 g protein, 178 mg calcium, 6 g fiber

new tuna salad

This lightened version of the creamy salad shaves fat and calories off the day's tally.

Total prep time: 15 minutes

TUNA SALAD:
- 2 **tablespoons light mayonnaise**
- 1 **tablespoon red wine vinegar**
- 1 **teaspoon extra-virgin olive oil**
- ¼ **teaspoon freshly ground pepper**
- 2 **cans (6 oz. each) solid white tuna in water, drained and flaked**
- ¾ **cup diced plum tomatoes**
- ½ **cup diced celery**
- ¼ **cup diced onion, rinsed under cold water in sieve and drained**

- 4 **cups assorted lettuce**

4 thin slices multi-grain bread, toasted and cut in halves

1 pound steamed green beans

Make tuna salad: Combine mayonnaise, vinegar, oil and pepper in a medium bowl. Stir in tuna, tomatoes, celery, and onion. Arrange 1 cup lettuce on each of 4 serving plates. Divide and spoon tuna over each. Serve each with 2 toast halves and one-fourth of the beans. Makes 4 servings.

Per serving: 220 calories, 6.5 g total fat, 1.5 g saturated fat, 23 mg cholesterol, 387 mg sodium, 25 g carbohydrates, 17 g protein, 93 mg calcium, 7 g fiber

the perfect blt

Just the right ingredients—including peak-season tomatoes and thick-cut slices of bacon—make this the sandwich of choice when fresh tomatoes are ripe for the picking.

Prep time: 10 minutes • Cooking time: 10 to 12 minutes

8 slices thick-cut bacon (about 6 oz.), divided

¼ cup mayonnaise

1 teaspoon grated lemon peel

½ teaspoon freshly ground pepper

4 (½-inch-thick) slices sourdough bread, lightly toasted

2 large green-leaf lettuce leaves, torn in half

1 medium (6 oz.) ripe beefsteak tomato, sliced ½ inch thick

Potato chips (optional)

1. Heat a large heavy-duty skillet over medium-high heat 2 minutes. Add 4 slices of the bacon; cook 2 to 3 minutes, until golden brown. Turn bacon with tongs and cook until just crisp, about 2 minutes more. Transfer bacon to a plate lined with paper towels. Repeat with remaining 4 slices bacon.

2. Combine mayonnaise, lemon peel and pepper in a small bowl. Spread 1 tablespoon on each slice of bread. Divide and arrange bacon on 2 slices of bread; layer with lettuce and tomato slices. Place

the remaining bread on the top of the tomato. Serve with potato chips, if desired. Makes 2 servings.

Per serving: 495 calories, 35.5 g total fat, 7.5 g saturated fat, 36 mg cholesterol, 849 mg sodium, 32 g carbohydrates, 13 g protein, 61 mg calcium, 3 g fiber

grilled burger deluxe

Extra touches make this version extra-inspired.

Prep time: 15 minutes • Grilling time: 15 to 16 minutes

1½ pounds ground chuck

2 teaspoons chopped fresh rosemary

½ teaspoon salt

¼ teaspoon freshly ground pepper

TARTAR SAUCE:

½ cup mayonnaise

⅓ cup chopped dill pickles

2 tablespoons finely chopped shallots

4 kaiser rolls, split

1 large bunch (6 oz.) watercress, tough stems removed

2 medium tomatoes, sliced

Potato chips (optional)

1. Heat grill. Gently combine ground chuck and rosemary in a medium bowl. Divide beef into quarters, then gently shape each piece to a $^1/_2$- to $^3/_4$-inch-thick patty. Sprinkle both sides of burgers with salt and pepper. Grill burgers 7 to 8 minutes. Turn and grill 7 minutes more, or until an instant-read meat thermometer reaches 160°F., for medium, when inserted 1 inch from edge of each burger.

2. *Make tartar sauce:* Meanwhile, combine tartar sauce ingredients in a small bowl. Divide and spread sauce on bottoms of rolls. Top with watercress, burgers, tomato and tops of rolls. Serve with potato chips, if desired. Makes 4 servings.

Per serving: 715 calories, 47 g total fat, 12.5 g saturated fat, 121 mg cholesterol, 1,035 mg sodium, 36 g carbohydrates, 37 g protein, 127 mg calcium, 3 g fiber

falafel with yogurt sauce

These falafel patties get a quick start with a mix.

Prep time: 15 minutes • Cooking time: 4 minutes per batch

- **1   box (6 oz.) falafel mix**
- **3   tablespoons chopped fresh mint, divided**
- **1   container (16 oz.) plain low-fat yogurt**
- **1   medium cucumber, peeled, seeded and cut into ½-inch pieces**
- **½   cup cherry tomatoes, quartered**
- **2   green onions, chopped**
- **⅛   teaspoon salt**
- **½   cup vegetable oil**
- **6   warm pita breads**

1. Prepare falafel according to package directions, *except* stir 2 tablespoons of the mint into mixture and let mixture stand until firm, about 8 minutes.

2. Meanwhile, heat oven to 300°F. Combine yogurt, cucumber, tomatoes, green onions, remaining 1 tablespoon mint and salt in a medium bowl. Set aside.

3. Heat oil in a large skillet over medium heat. Shape falafel mixture into twelve 2×¹/₂-inch-thick patties. Cook half of the patties until golden brown, 2 minutes per side. Transfer to a cookie sheet; keep warm in oven while cooking remaining falafel. Repeat.

4. Cut 1 inch from the top of each pita bread. For each serving, place 2 falafels in pita and spoon ¹/₃ cup yogurt mixture on top. Serve with remaining yogurt mixture. Makes 6 servings.

Per serving: 470 calories, 21 g total fat, 3.5 g saturated fat, 5 mg cholesterol, 894 mg sodium, 56 g carbohydrates, 18 g protein, 246 mg calcium, 6 g fiber

jicama and orange salad

Jicama (HEE-kah-mah) is used in many Mexican salads like this one, with oranges, red onion and cumin seed.

Total prep time: 20 minutes

- **½   cup thinly sliced red onion**
- **3   oranges, peeled and white pith removed, cut into segments**
- **2   cups peeled and diced jicama (see tip, page 25)**
- **3   tablespoons fresh lime juice**
- **1   tablespoon fresh orange juice**
- **¾   teaspoon salt**
- **¼   teaspoon freshly ground pepper**
- **⅛   teaspoon cumin seed**
- **Chopped fresh cilantro, for garnish (optional)**

Place onion in a sieve and rinse under cold water; drain, pat dry and transfer to a large serving bowl. Stir in remaining ingredients and toss until well combined. Sprinkle with cilantro, if desired. Makes 3¹/₂ cups.

Per ½ cup: 50 calories, 0 g total fat, 0 g saturated fat, 0 mg cholesterol, 252 mg sodium, 12 g carbohydrates, 1 g protein, 37 mg calcium, 3 g fiber

the perfect onion rings

Treat the family to a classic American favorite.

Prep time: 30 minutes • Cooking time: 20 minutes

- **2   cups buttermilk**
- **½   teaspoon hot red pepper sauce**
- **3   cups all-purpose flour**
- **1½ teaspoons baking powder**
- **1¼ teaspoons salt, divided**
- **¼   teaspoon freshly ground pepper**
- **1   bottle (48 oz.) vegetable oil**
- **1½ to 2 pounds sweet onions, such as Vidalia**
- **¼   teaspoon ground red pepper**

1. Heat oven to 250°F. Line a jelly-roll pan with waxed paper. Combine buttermilk and red pepper sauce in a large bowl. Combine flour, baking powder, 1 teaspoon of the salt and the freshly ground pepper in a shallow pan.

2. Heat oil in a large Dutch oven over medium-high heat to 350°F. on deep-fat thermometer. Slice onion rings crosswise into ½-inch-thick rings. Separate slices into rings.

3. Working in batches, dip onion rings in buttermilk mixture, letting excess drip off. Toss rings in flour mixture until well coated, gently shaking off excess. Place onion rings on prepared jelly-roll pan. Repeat process with remaining onions, buttermilk mixture and flour mixture.

4. With long-handled tongs, carefully place one-quarter of the onion rings in hot oil. Cook 3 to 4 minutes, turning rings a few times until onions are golden brown and cooked through. Drain on paper towels. Transfer to another jelly-roll pan or cookie sheet and keep warm in oven. Repeat process with remaining onions.

5. Arrange fried onion rings on a large serving dish. Sprinkle with remaining ¼ teaspoon salt and the ground red pepper. Serve immediately. Serves 4 to 6.

Per serving: 415 calories, 23 g total fat, 3 g saturated fat, 2 mg cholesterol, 442 mg sodium, 46 g carbohydrates, 8 g protein, 149 mg calcium, 4 g fiber

frijoles

In the Southwest, frijoles (free-HOH-les) are served either soupy in broth or mashed and fried (frijoles refritos). This recipe features both versions. If you want the beans extra spicy, do not remove seeds from the chiles.

Prep time: 20 minutes plus soaking
Cooking time: 62 to 72 minutes

- 1 **pound dry pinto beans**
- 1 **tablespoon olive oil**
- ¼ **pound salt pork, rind removed, or sliced bacon, finely chopped**
- 1 **cup chopped onions**
- 1 **serrano or jalapeño chile, finely chopped (see tip, page 95)**
- 1 **tablespoon finely chopped garlic**
- 6 **cups water**
- ¼ **teaspoon cumin seed**
- 2½ **teaspoons salt**

1. Soak beans according to package directions; drain beans.

2. Heat oil in a Dutch oven over medium-high heat. Add salt pork; cook 2 minutes, until browned. Reduce heat to medium; add onions and chile and cook 4 minutes. Add garlic and cook 1 minute. Add drained beans, water and cumin seed. Bring to boil; reduce heat to medium-low. Cover and simmer 30 minutes. Add salt and continue to cook 25 to 35 minutes more, until tender. *(Can be made ahead. Cool. Transfer to a large microwaveproof container. Cover and refrigerate overnight. To reheat: Microwave on High 10 minutes, stirring once after 5 minutes, until heated through.)* Makes 7 cups.

REFRIED BEANS (FRIJOLES REFRITOS)

Heat *1 tablespoon olive oil* or *lard* in a large skillet over medium-high heat. Add *½ cup finely chopped onion* and cook 2 to 3 minutes, until browned. Add *2 teaspoons finely chopped garlic* and cook 30 seconds. Add *2 cups cooked beans* (from recipe, above) and *⅓ to ½ cup bean liquid* to skillet. (Or, if beans have been refrigerated, microwave *2 cups refrigerated beans* and *⅓ to ½ cup bean liquid* on High, 2 to 3 minutes, until room temperature, and add to skillet.) Mash beans and liquid coarsely with back of a wooden spoon or potato masher. Cook 1 to 2 minutes more, until heated through, adding more bean liquid or water if needed. Transfer beans to a food processor. Process just until smooth. Makes 2 cups (4 servings).

Per ½-cup serving for Frijoles: 130 calories, 6 g total fat, 2 g saturated fat, 5 mg cholesterol, 382 mg sodium, 16 g carbohydrates, 5 g protein, 31 mg calcium, 3 g fiber

Per ½-cup serving for refried beans: 225 calories, 11 g total fat, 3 g saturated fat, 7 mg cholesterol, 536 mg sodium, 24 g carbohydrates, 8 g protein, 51 mg calcium, 5 g fiber

weeknight dinner

RANCH CHICKEN WITH POTATOES
AND GRAVY
page 49

SPICED CARROTS
below

FRESH FRUIT SALAD

FLAN
page 156

spiced carrots

Coating carrots with the typical flavors of Morocco (cumin, cinnamon, lemon and honey) brings out their natural sweetness.

Prep time: 10 minutes • Cooking time: 8 minutes

1	pound carrots, sliced on the diagonal ¼ inch thick
1¼	teaspoons salt, divided
1	clove garlic, crushed
1	bay leaf
1	teaspoon cumin seeds
¼	teaspoon cinnamon
2	tablespoons fresh lemon juice
2	tablespoons chopped fresh flat-leaf parsley
1	tablespoon olive oil
1	tablespoon honey

1. Bring 2 quarts water to boil in a medium saucepan. Add carrots, 1 teaspoon of the salt, garlic and bay leaf. Cook over medium-high heat, until carrots are tender, 5 minutes. Drain in colander and rinse under cold running water. Discard garlic and bay leaf.

2. Toast cumin seeds and cinnamon in a small skillet over medium-low heat until seeds become fragrant, 3 minutes. Transfer spices to a large serving bowl and whisk in remaining ingredients. Add carrots and toss to coat. *(Can be made ahead. Refrigerate overnight. Let stand at room temperature 1 hour before serving.)* Makes 6 servings.

Per serving: 65 calories, 2.5 g total fat, 0.5 g saturated fat, 0 mg cholesterol, 319 g sodium, 12 g carbohydrates, 1 g protein, 29 mg calcium, 3 g fiber

green beans and broccoli

A simple side dish revived with shallots and sherry vinegar. (It makes a great leftover, too!)

Prep time: 15 minutes • Cooking time: 8 to 9 minutes
Microwave used

1¾	teaspoons salt, divided
1	pound green beans, trimmed
1	pound broccoli florettes, cut in half
2	tablespoons extra-virgin olive oil
2	tablespoons minced shallots
¼	teaspoon freshly ground pepper
1	teaspoon sherry vinegar

1. Bring 5 quarts water and 1 teaspoon of the salt to boil in a large Dutch oven. Add green beans and broccoli; cook 5 minutes. Transfer to a colander and drain under cold running water until cool.

2. Combine oil and shallots in a large microwaveproof bowl. Microwave on High 2 minutes. Stir in remaining ³/₄ teaspoon salt, the pepper and vinegar. Add vegetables. *(Can be made ahead. Cover with plastic wrap and refrigerate up to 24 hours.)* Turn back one corner of wrap to vent and microwave on High 3 to 4 minutes, or until heated through. Toss to blend. Makes 12 servings (10¹/₂ cups).

Per serving: 40 calories, 2.5 g total fat, 0 g saturated fat, 0 mg cholesterol, 194 mg sodium, 5 g carbohydrates, 2 g protein, 31 mg calcium, 2 g fiber

SESAME SEARED
SCALLOPS
pg. 104

VEGETABLE
LASAGNE
pg. 108

market fresh and fabulous

There's a world of great produce out there, so dig in! These ultra-fresh recipes—full of fruits, vegetables and flavor, will keep you light on your feet. Whether they're the main event or served on the side, they mean dinner's in season—and in style.

GLAZED HAM
STEAK WITH
PAPAYA SALSA
pg. 102

WARM POTATO AND
SHRIMP SALAD
pg. 106

no longer sidelined,
veggies
mingle with lean meats

BEEF RIBS WITH
SWISS CHARD
pg. 96

TURKEY CUTLETS
WITH GREEN
MOLE
pg. 90

ASPARAGUS
WITH BARLEY
AND
WHEAT BERRIES
pg. 112

MUSHROOMS
AND BARLEY
OVER GREENS
pg. 106

ASIAN NOODLE
AND BEEF
SALAD
pg. 99

poultry

and seafood

MULTI-BEAN
RAGOUT
pg. 107

ASIAN BEEF AND
VEGETABLES
pg. 100

greens,
beans
and grains

SPICY PORK AND
BEAN BURRITOS
pg. 94

TRITICALE
RISOTTO
pg. 112

pack flavor and good-for-you nutrients, too

CAPONATA WITH
PORTOBELLO
MUSHROOMS
pg. 111

GREEK
VEGETABLE
GRATIN
pg. 110

RISI E BISI
pg. 120

now when you say
"eat your vegetables,"
two responses will be...

CHICKEN SALAD
WITH BASIL
pg. 91

ROASTED ASPARAGUS
pg. 115

THREE-PEA
SAUTÉ
pg. 120

"with pleasure!"

and "please, may I have
some more?"

ROAST BEEF
AND
AVOCADO
WRAP
pg. 95

to market to market to inspire great meals

SOUTHERN CORN
SALAD
pg. 118

CORN AND CRAB
PUDDING
pg. 119

oven southern "fried" chicken with crispy slaw

Prep time: 15 minutes • Baking time: 20 minutes

CHICKEN:
- ½ cup buttermilk
- 1 tablespoon Dijon mustard
- ½ teaspoon minced garlic
- ¾ teaspoon salt, divided
- ½ teaspoon hot red pepper sauce
- 4 large boneless, skinless chicken breast halves (1¼ to 1½ lbs.)
- ½ cup plain dry bread crumbs
- 3 tablespoons cornmeal
- ⅛ teaspoon freshly ground pepper

SLAW:
- 1 bag (16 oz.) coleslaw mix (or 6 cups shredded white cabbage and 2 carrots, peeled and shredded)
- 2 tablespoons cider vinegar
- 1 tablespoon sugar
- 2 teaspoons vegetable oil
- ½ teaspoon salt
- ¼ teaspoon celery seed

1. *Make chicken:* Heat oven to 400°F. Lightly coat a cookie sheet with vegetable cooking spray. Combine buttermilk, mustard, garlic, ½ teaspoon of the salt and the hot red pepper sauce in a small bowl. Pour into a 1-gallon resealable plastic bag. Add chicken; seal and refrigerate. Meanwhile, combine crumbs, cornmeal, pepper and remaining ¼ teaspoon salt in a shallow bowl. Dip both sides of chicken in crumb mixture to coat. Transfer to prepared cookie sheet; lightly coat with vegetable cooking spray. Bake 20 minutes, until golden and cooked through.

2. *Make slaw:* Place coleslaw mix in a large bowl. Combine vinegar, sugar, oil, salt and celery seed in a small saucepan. Bring to boil, pour over slaw and toss to coat. Serve with chicken. Makes 4 servings.

Per serving: 380 calories, 8.5 g total fat, 1.5 g saturated fat, 101 mg cholesterol, 1,069 mg sodium, 34 g carbohydrates, 41 g protein, 124 mg calcium, 3 g fiber

chicken salad

Although there are many spin-offs of the basic chicken salad, ours is guaranteed to satisfy—it's rich and creamy, but it's also slimmed down so it won't bust your fat and calorie budget. Sweet mango, peppery arugula and fiery chile update the flavor.

Total prep time: 30 minutes

- ⅓ cup plain low-fat yogurt
- ¼ cup light mayonnaise
- 1 tablespoon lemon juice
- 1 teaspoon Dijon mustard
- ½ teaspoon salt
- ¼ teaspoon freshly ground pepper
- 4 cups cubed cooked chicken
- 1 cup thinly sliced celery
- 1 cup peeled, seeded and sliced cucumber
- ½ cup shredded radish
- ½ cup shredded carrot
- ¼ cup chopped green onions
- 1 to 2 tablespoons seeded, minced jalapeño chile (see tip, page 95)
- 1½ cups cubed mango
- 2 tablespoons chopped fresh mint
- 1 bunch arugula or watercress

1. Whisk yogurt, mayonnaise, lemon juice, mustard, salt and pepper together in a bowl. Add chicken, celery, cucumber, radish, carrot, green onions and jalapeño. Stir until blended.

2. Just before serving, stir in mango and mint. Serve over arugula. Makes 6 servings.

Per serving: 265 calories, 11 g total fat, 2.5 g saturated fat, 87 mg cholesterol, 409 mg sodium, 13 g carbohydrates, 29 g protein, 88 mg calcium, 2 g fiber

teriyaki chicken wrap with ginger slaw LOW FAT

Chicken tenders—sometimes called chicken tenderloins—are the tender muscle of the chicken breast meat. Find them alongside other chicken products at the supermarket.

Prep time: 20 minutes • Cooking time: 5 to 7 minutes

- 1 **pound chicken tenders**
- ¼ **cup teriyaki sauce**
- 1 **tablespoon chopped garlic**

GINGER SLAW:

- 3 **tablespoons white vinegar**
- 2 **tablespoons vegetable oil**
- 1 **tablespoon sugar**
- 2 **teaspoons teriyaki sauce**
- 2 **teaspoons minced jalapeño chile (see tip, page 95)**
- 1 **teaspoon grated fresh ginger**
- 1 **teaspoon salt**
- 1 **bag (16 oz.) coleslaw mix**
  ■
- 1 **tablespoon vegetable oil**
- 4 **(10-inch) burrito-size tortillas**
- 2 **cups cooked rice**
- 1 **cup fresh cilantro leaves**

1. ■ Combine chicken, teriyaki sauce and garlic in a bowl. Refrigerate 10 minutes.

2. ■ *Make ginger slaw:* Meanwhile, combine vinegar, oil, sugar, teriyaki sauce, jalapeño, ginger and salt in a large bowl. Stir in coleslaw mix.

3. ■ Remove chicken from marinade with a slotted spoon and pat dry with paper towels; discard marinade. Heat oil in a large skillet over medium-high heat, 1 minute. Add chicken and cook, turning pieces, 5 to 7 minutes, until browned and cooked through.

4. ■ *To assemble:* Heat tortillas according to package directions. Spoon one-quarter of the rice down the center of each tortilla. Divide slaw and arrange on one side of rice. Divide cilantro and chicken and arrange next to slaw. Fold in sides of tortillas. Roll up tightly. Cut wraps in half. Makes 4 servings.

Per serving: 580 calories, 15.5 g total fat, 2.5 g saturated fat, 66 mg cholesterol, 1,660 mg sodium, 74 g carbohydrates, 36 g protein, 149 mg calcium, 3 g fiber

turkey cutlets with green mole LOW FAT EASY

Lean turkey cutlets put this in the low-fat category, while the green "mole" sauce makes it spicy. Pictured on page 82.

Prep time: 10 minutes • Cooking time: 9 minutes

- ⅓ **cup shelled pumpkin seeds, chopped**
- ½ **teaspoon cumin**
- ½ **teaspoon salt**
- ¼ **teaspoon freshly ground pepper**
- 1 **pound turkey cutlets**
- 4 **teaspoons olive oil, divided**
- ½ **cup chopped onion**
- 1 **can (4½ oz.) chopped green chiles (see tip, page 95)**
- ¼ **cup water**
- 1 **tablespoon fresh lime juice**
- 2 **tablespoons chopped fresh cilantro**
  Cooked rice (optional)

1. ■ Toast pumpkin seeds in a skillet over medium-high heat, about 2 minutes. Cool. Combine half of the seeds, the cumin, salt and pepper on waxed paper. Dip cutlets into seed mixture.

2. ■ Heat 2 teaspoons of the oil in a large nonstick skillet over medium-high heat. Add cutlets and cook 5 minutes, turning once, until cooked through. Transfer cutlets to a plate; cover and keep warm.

3. ■ Heat remaining 2 teaspoons oil in same skillet over medium heat. Add onion, chiles, water, and remaining pumpkin seeds. Cook until heated through, about 2 minutes. Remove from heat; stir in lime juice and cilantro.

4. Divide turkey cutlets among 4 serving plates. Spoon sauce evenly over turkey. Serve with rice, if desired. Makes 4 servings.

Per serving: 205 calories, 6.5 g total fat, 1 g saturated fat, 70 mg cholesterol, 543 mg sodium, 7 g carbohydrates, 29 g protein, 24 mg calcium, 1 g fiber

chicken salad with basil *EASY*

This is the chicken salad of choice when the farmers' markets are overflowing with fresh basil and beefy ripe tomatoes. To save time, shred the meat from a whole cooked deli chicken. Pictured on page 86.

Total prep time: 25 minutes

DRESSING:

- 1 yellow bell pepper, cut up
- 2 tablespoons white balsamic or white wine vinegar
- 1 tablespoon olive oil
- ¾ teaspoon salt
- ⅛ teaspoon freshly ground pepper

- 1 (2-lb.) cooked whole chicken
- ½ cup thinly sliced onion
- 2 medium ripe tomatoes, sliced
- 1 tablespoon olive oil
- ½ teaspoon salt
- ¼ teaspoon freshly ground pepper
- 1 cup whole fresh basil leaves

1. *Make dressing:* Puree all dressing ingredients in a blender until smooth.

2. Remove meat from chicken, tear into large shreds. Toss chicken and onion with half the dressing in a medium bowl; let stand 10 minutes.

3. Meanwhile, arrange tomatoes on a large serving platter and drizzle with oil; sprinkle with salt and pepper.

4. Add basil to chicken; toss. Arrange on top of tomatoes. Drizzle with remaining dressing. Makes 4 servings.

Per serving: 270 calories, 17 g total fat, 3 g saturated fat, 106 mg cholesterol, 1,442 mg sodium, 8 g carbohydrates, 25 g protein, 43 mg calcium, 2 g fiber

ham and cheese stack *EASY*

The concept—meats, cheeses and greens—is much like a chef's salad. But high-quality Westphalian ham, watercress, apples and Brie make this anything but ordinary.

Total prep time: 20 minutes

DRESSING:

- ½ teaspoon grated lime peel
- ¼ cup fresh lime juice
- 1 tablespoon honey

- 1 large bunch (6 oz.) watercress, trimmed
- 3 Gala apples, cored and sliced crosswise into rings
- ½ pound Brie cheese, cut into ⅛-inch-thick slices
- 1 pound thinly sliced Westphalian ham Whole-grain bread (optional)

1. *Make dressing:* Stir lime peel, juice and honey in a large bowl until blended. Transfer half the dressing to a cup; set aside.

2. Add watercress to bowl and toss with dressing. Layer one-quarter of the watercress, apple, Brie and ham on each of four serving plates. Repeat. Divide and drizzle reserved dressing on each serving. Serve with bread, if desired. Makes 4 servings.

Per serving: 495 calories, 25.5 g total fat, 3 g saturated fat, 136 mg cholesterol, 3,432 mg sodium, 23 g carbohydrates, 44 g protein, 172 mg calcium, 3 g fiber

trimming meat loaf fat

It's all in the ingredients. A serving of traditional meat loaf typically has about 400 calories and a whopping 20 grams of fat. The new and improved version, below, has just 275 calories and only 7 grams of fat.

So how did we cut the calories without losing flavor? In place of the traditional meat loaf ingredients—ground beef, ground pork and ground veal—we used lean, ground white turkey meat. And, we added a red curry base for zippy taste and zucchini for moisture. To top it off? Our cool and creamy yogurt sauce is a refreshing alternative to traditional ketchup.

not your mama's meat loaf LOW FAT EASY

The traditional loaf shape is about all that's similar to the meaty classic. However, this one is comfort food in its own right—it's just healthier and more waistline-friendly.

Prep time: 20 minutes • Baking time: 50 minutes

- 1 tablespoon olive oil
- 1 cup chopped onions
- 1 tablespoon red curry base*
- 2 tablespoons water

YOGURT SAUCE:
- ½ cup shredded zucchini
- 1 container (8 oz.) plain low-fat yogurt
- 1 tablespoon finely chopped onion
- ½ teaspoon salt
- ½ teaspoon sugar

- 1½ pounds ground white turkey meat
- 1 cup shredded zucchini
- 1 cup fresh bread crumbs (2 to 3 slices firm white bread)
- 1 large egg
- ¾ teaspoon salt
- Cooked broccoli and red potatoes (optional)

1. Heat oil in a medium skillet over medium-high heat. Add onions and cook 3 to 4 minutes, until lightly browned. Remove skillet from heat. Stir in curry base and water until smooth. Cool.

2. *Make yogurt sauce:* Combine zucchini, yogurt, onion, salt and sugar in a medium bowl; cover with plastic wrap and refrigerate.

3. Heat oven to 375°F. Combine turkey, zucchini, bread crumbs, egg, salt and onion mixture in a large bowl until just mixed. Line a 13×9-inch pan with foil; lightly coat foil with vegetable cooking spray. Shape turkey mixture into an 8×4-inch-wide loaf in center of prepared pan. Bake 50 minutes, or until no longer pink.

4. Remove meat loaf from oven; cover with foil and let stand 10 minutes. Slice loaf and serve with yogurt sauce and, if desired, broccoli and red potatoes. Makes 4 to 6 servings.

*Note: Can be found in spice aisle or ethnic sections of supermarkets, or in Asian specialty stores.

Per serving: 275 calories, 7 g total fat, 2 g saturated fat, 130 mg cholesterol, 996 mg sodium, 13 g carbohydrates, 39 g protein, 123 mg calcium, 2 g fiber

grilled tomato pasta, basil and shaved parmesan cheese

Grilled veggies are great on their own—but they also lend fabulous flavor to pasta for a complete meal. Plum tomatoes are a good choice to grill, since they tend to hold up well over the heat.

Total prep time: 20 minutes

- 1½ pounds plum tomatoes, cut into ½-inch-thick slices
- 1 tablespoon olive oil
- ½ teaspoon salt
- ½ teaspoon dried oregano
- ¼ teaspoon freshly ground pepper

- ½ cup packed fresh basil leaves, coarsely chopped
- 1 tablespoon olive oil
- 1 tablespoon chopped capers, drained
- 1 tablespoon red wine vinegar
- ½ teaspoon salt
- ¼ teaspoon freshly ground pepper
- 1 pound pasta, cooked
- 2 ounces freshly shaved Parmesan cheese (about ¾ cup)

1. Toss tomatoes, olive oil, salt, oregano and pepper in a large bowl. Grill tomatoes 2 to 4 minutes over medium-hot heat, turning as necessary; return to bowl.

2. Add basil, olive oil, capers, vinegar, salt and pepper. Toss with hot pasta and Parmesan cheese. Makes 6 servings.

Per serving: 395 calories, 9 g total fat, 1 g saturated fat, 7 mg cholesterol, 499 mg sodium, 65 g carbohydrates, 15 g protein, 110 mg calcium, 4 g fiber

---

test kitchen tip
what a tomato!

You say tomato...we say...go for it. Rich in lycopene, they're not only delicious, but good for you, too. Tomatoes are plentiful all year-round, though the peak season is June through September. Here are some pointers on how to select, store, ripen and peel these favorites:

TAKE YOUR PICK
Choose tomatoes that are firm and plump and have proper color for their type (there are several types of tomatoes, including the most common beefsteak, plum, green and cherry). They should also be blemish-free, yield slightly from pressure and feel heavy for their size.

THE STORY ON STORING
Tomatoes, contrary to popular belief, should never be refrigerated, as this destroys their flavor and makes the flesh too pulpy. When purchasing tomatoes from the supermarket, purchase ones that are kept at room temperature. If unripe tomatoes drop below 55°F., their texture will be mealy and they'll never ripen to maximum flavor.

PEEL OUT
Peeling tomatoes is much easier than you may think. Bring 2 quarts of water to a boil in a medium saucepan. With the point of a small knife, cut a shallow X opposite the stem end of ripe tomatoes. Add one or two tomatoes at a time to the boiling water with a slotted spoon; boil for about 30 seconds. Transfer tomatoes to a bowl filled with ice water. The skins will slip off easily.

softening tortillas

To make a roll, foldover, enchilada or burrito, you'll need to start with a warm tortilla that's soft and pliable. There are three options for softening—in the oven, microwave or skillet.

IN THE OVEN: Heat oven to 350°F. Stack four to six tortillas and wrap them in foil. Bake 8 to 10 minutes.

IN THE MICROWAVE: Stack four tortillas between two damp paper towels on a microwaveproof plate. Microwave on High, 45 seconds to 1 minute.

IN THE SKILLET: Heat a skillet over medium heat. Add one tortilla and heat, turning frequently, 30 to 45 seconds.

spicy pork and bean burritos LOW FAT

To cut the fat and calories from traditional burritos, we replaced fatty ground chuck roast with lean boneless pork chops and used low-fat flour tortillas. All this was accomplished without sacrificing flavor. Pictured on page 84.

Prep time: 30 minutes • Cooking time: 45 to 50 minutes
Microwave used

- 1   jalapeño chile (see tip, page 95)
- 1   teaspoon cumin, divided
- 1   teaspoon salt, divided
- ¾   pound boneless pork chops (about 2), trimmed

- 1   tablespoon olive oil
- 1   cup chopped onions
- 1   carrot, chopped
- 2   celery ribs, chopped
- 1   tablespoon chopped garlic
- ⅛   teaspoon cinnamon
       Pinch ground red pepper
- 1   cup chopped canned tomatoes
- 1¼   cups chicken broth
- 1   can (15 or 15½ oz.) pinto beans, drained and rinsed
- ¼   cup chopped fresh cilantro
- 1   package (20 oz.) low-fat burrito-size flour tortillas
- 2   cups cooked white rice
- ½   cup shredded Monterey Jack cheese
- 1   cup shredded iceberg lettuce
- 1   cup chopped fresh tomatoes
       Lime wedges (optional)
       Salsa (optional)

1. Heat broiler. Line a small cookie sheet with foil. Broil jalapeño 2 inches from heat, turning once, 8 to 10 minutes, until skin is charred on all sides. Wrap jalapeño in foil and let stand until cool enough to handle, 10 minutes. Remove stem, peel and seeds from jalapeño, then chop jalapeño.

2. On a sheet of waxed paper, rub ¹/₂ teaspoon of the cumin and ¹/₂ teaspoon of the salt on both sides of pork. Heat a 3-quart saucepan or small Dutch oven over medium-high heat 1 minute. Add oil and and brown pork, 2 minutes per side. Transfer pork to a cutting board; cut into ¹/₂-inch pieces and add to a bowl. Set aside.

3. Reduce heat to medium; add chopped jalapeño, onions, carrot, celery, garlic, remaining ¹/₂ teaspoon *each* cumin and salt, the cinnamon and ground red pepper. Cook vegetables, stirring until onions soften, 5 to 8 minutes. Add canned tomatoes and cook 3 minutes, until heated through. Stir in broth, beans, pork and any juices. Bring to boil; cover and simmer 30 minutes. Uncover and cook until mixture thickens slightly, 15 to 20 minutes more. Stir in cilantro.

4. Meanwhile, heat oven to 350 F°. Transfer 1½ cups bean mixture without pork to a food processor or blender and puree. (Return any pieces of pork to saucepan.) Return pureed bean mixture to saucepan and simmer over medium-low heat, just until heated through; be careful not to burn.

5. Soften tortillas according to package directions (or see tip, page 94). Spoon ¼ cup of the rice down center of one tortilla. Spoon ½ cup of bean mixture on top of rice; sprinkle with 1 tablespoon of the cheese. Arrange ⅛ cup of the lettuce and 2 tablespoons of the fresh tomatoes over cheese. Fold in sides of tortilla and roll up. Place burrito, seam side down, on prepared cookie sheet. Cover loosely with foil and keep warm in oven. Repeat with remaining tortillas, rice, bean mixture, cheese, lettuce and fresh tomatoes. Serve with lime wedges and salsa, if desired. Makes 8 burritos.

Per burrito: 385 calories, 7.5 g total fat, 2.5 g saturated fat, 33 mg cholesterol, 1,145 mg sodium, 57 g carbohydrates, 22 g protein, 170 mg calcium, 6 g fiber

roast beef and avocado wrap (EASY)

Deli roast beef gets added spark from a hit of green pepper sauce and crisp cilantro leaves, while the cucumber serves to cool things down a bit. It all wraps up to a tasty do-ahead sandwich. Pictured on page 87.

Total prep time: 25 minutes

- 1 avocado, pitted, peeled and cut into ½-inch-thick wedges
- 2 tablespoons fresh lime juice
- ¾ teaspoon salt, divided
- 4 burrito-size tortillas, warmed according to package directions, if desired
- ¾ pound sliced roast beef
- 1 cup shredded iceberg lettuce, divided
- ½ seedless cucumber, cut into 6-inch strips
- 1 cup fresh cilantro leaves
- ¼ cup green pepper sauce, divided

1. Toss avocado with lime juice and ¼ teaspoon of the salt in a small bowl.

2. Cover tortillas with roast beef; sprinkle with remaining ½ teaspoon salt. Top with lettuce, then top with cucumber and avocado down the center of each tortilla. Add cilantro leaves, then drizzle 1 tablespoon green pepper sauce over each. Fold in sides and roll up. Makes 4 servings.

Per serving: 375 calories, 15 g total fat, 3 g saturated fat, 37 mg cholesterol, 1,782 mg sodium, 39 g carbohydrates, 23 g protein, 102 mg calcium, 4 g fiber

---

test kitchen tip

chile pepper know-how

Chile peppers add extra spark to many dishes, but they require extra precautions.

HANDLING: Because chile peppers, such as jalapeños, contain volatile oils that can burn your skin and eyes, avoid direct contact with them as much as possible. When working with chile peppers, wear plastic or rubber gloves. If your bare hands do touch the chile peppers, wash your hands well with soap and warm water.

COOKING: As they cook, chile peppers release fumes that can irritate breathing passages and cause coughing. Avoid breathing these fumes.

winter-fresh supper

BEEF RIBS WITH SWISS CHARD
below

CRUSTY FRENCH BREAD

**BIBB LETTUCE WITH
VINAIGRETTE DRESSING**

LEMON MOUSSE
page 240

beef ribs with swiss chard

Slow-cooked and paired with Swiss chard, winter squash and pasta, these bite-size riblets melt off the bone—the perfect casual winter meal. Pictured on page 82.

Prep time: 40 minutes
Cooking time: 1 hour 55 minutes to 2 hours 20 minutes

3½	pounds beef chuck flanken-style ribs, well trimmed of fat
¼	teaspoon salt
¼	teaspoon freshly ground pepper
1	bunch (½ lb.) Swiss chard
4	teaspoons olive oil, divided
3	leeks, white part only, chopped
3	cloves garlic, crushed
1	teaspoon fresh thyme leaves or ½ teaspoon dried thyme
½	cup white wine
1	carrot, chopped
1	tablespoon tomato paste
4	cans (14½ oz. each) chicken broth
1	acorn or butternut squash (1½ lbs.) peeled, seeded and cut into ½-inch pieces
½	cup tubetti pasta (elbow macaroni)
	Fresh thyme sprigs, for garnish (optional)

1. Between the bones of each rib rack, cut single ribs. Sprinkle ribs with salt and pepper.

2. Strip the green leaves from the white stalks of the Swiss chard. Separately chop the leaves and the white stalks. Set both aside.

3. Heat a large Dutch oven over medium heat, 2 minutes. Add 2 teaspoons of the oil and cook half the beef until well browned on both sides, 5 to 8 minutes. Transfer beef with a slotted spoon to a large plate. Repeat process with remaining beef and drippings.

4. Discard drippings. Wipe out bottom of Dutch oven with paper towels. Heat remaining 2 teaspoons oil over medium heat. Add leeks, garlic and thyme. Cook until leeks soften, 3 to 5 minutes. Stir in wine and cook until wine just evaporates, 2 minutes. Add carrot and chard stalks and cook until vegetables begin to soften, 3 minutes. Stir in tomato paste, broth and beef; bring to boil. Reduce heat and simmer, partially covered, skimming any fat from top of broth, until meat is fork tender, 1½ to 2 hours.

5. Remove beef with slotted spoon; set aside. Strain broth through a large strainer lined with cheesecloth over a large bowl. Discard vegetables. In batches, remove fat from broth with a gravy separator, then carefully return broth to Dutch oven. Add squash and simmer until just tender, 15 to 20 minutes. Add tubetti and chard leaves. Cook 5 minutes, stirring occasionally. Return beef to Dutch oven and cook 5 minutes more, until meat is heated through. Spoon into 4 shallow serving bowls. Garnish with fresh thyme sprigs, if desired. Makes 4 servings.

Per serving: 550 calories, 25 g total fat, 8.5 g saturated fat, 96 mg cholesterol, 2,184 mg sodium, 43 g carbohydrates, 39 g protein, 152 mg calcium, 8 g fiber

polenta with beef ragout LOW FAT

Extra-lean beef, low-fat milk and defatted broth join forces to make this hearty stew a low-fat version of the Italian favorite.

Prep time: 15 minutes • Cooking time: 30 to 35 minutes

RAGOUT:
- ½ pound extra-lean ground beef
- 1 cup chopped onions
- 1 tablespoon chopped garlic
- 1 can (14 oz.) plum tomatoes, drained and chopped, juice reserved
- 1 large red bell pepper, cut up
- 1 large zucchini, chopped
- ½ cup chopped carrots
- 1 tablespoon tomato paste
- ½ teaspoon dried oregano
- ¾ teaspoon salt
- ¼ teaspoon freshly ground pepper

POLENTA:
- 1 can (14½ oz.) chicken broth, defatted
- ¼ teaspoon salt
- ½ cup yellow cornmeal
- ½ cup 1% low-fat milk
- ¼ cup chopped fresh flat-leaf parsley

1. *Make ragout:* Brown beef in a large nonstick skillet over medium-high heat. Transfer with a slotted spoon to a bowl.

2. Cook onions and garlic in skillet over medium heat until softened. Stir in reserved juice from tomatoes; cook 1 minute. Add beef and remaining ragout ingredients. Bring to boil. Cover and simmer 25 to 30 minutes.

3. *Make polenta:* Combine the broth and enough water to equal 2½ cups. Add salt. Bring to boil in a saucepan. Whisk in cornmeal. Cook, stirring,

15 minutes, until thickened. Stir in milk and parsley; cook 5 minutes. Divide polenta and ragout among 4 bowls. Makes 4 servings.

Per serving: 245 calories, 7 g total fat, 2.5 g saturated fat, 36 mg cholesterol, 1,054 mg sodium, 29 g carbohydrates, 18 g protein, 107 mg calcium, 4 g fiber

test kitchen tip

the skinny on beef vs. the rest

How do the top five leanest beef cuts rate compared with fish, chicken, turkey or other meats when it comes to fat and calories? The results may surprise you. (Note: All portions listed below are for 3 ounces, trimmed of fat and cooked.)

	FAT	CALORIES
Skinless turkey breast	0.6	115
Shrimp	0.9	84
Boneless, skinless chicken breast	3	140
Eye-round roast (beef)	4	143
Top round (beef)	4	153
Round tip (beef)	6	157
Salmon, coho*	6	157
Top sirloin (beef)	6	165
Top loin (beef)	8	176
Loin lamb chop	8	184
Center rib pork chop	8	186
Bone-in, skinless chicken thigh	9	178

Note: Salmon varieties vary greatly in fat content and therefore in calories.

low-fat beef borscht

All the veggies—onions, carrots, parsnips, beets and potatoes—stretch one pound of beef from four servings to eight.

Prep time: 1 hour • Cooking time: 2 hours 10 minutes

- 1 pound lean boneless beef chuck, cut into 1-inch cubes, trimmed
- 1 teaspoon salt
- ¼ teaspoon freshly ground pepper
- 1 tablespoon vegetable oil
- 3½ cups chopped red onions
- 1 pound carrots, sliced
- 2 cups diced parsnips
- 3 cans (13¾ oz. each) beef broth
- 3 cups water
- 1 small bay leaf
   Pinch each nutmeg and cloves
- 5 cups peeled, diced beets
- 1 pound red potatoes, scrubbed, cut into 1-inch pieces
- 1 small red cabbage, chopped (5 cups)
- 1 cup diced celery
- 2 teaspoons dillweed, divided
- ⅓ cup red wine vinegar
- 1 cup plain low-fat yogurt
   Crusty bread (optional)

1. Pat beef with paper towels. Season with salt and pepper. Heat oil in a large Dutch oven over medium-high heat. Add beef and cook until browned on all sides, 4 minutes. Transfer to a bowl with a slotted spoon. Add onions to Dutch oven and cook until translucent, 5 to 7 minutes.

2. Return beef to Dutch oven, adding carrots, parsnips, broth, water, bay leaf, nutmeg and cloves. Bring to boil. Reduce heat; cover and simmer 1½ hours.

3. Add beets, potatoes, cabbage, celery and 1 teaspoon of the dillweed. Bring to boil. Reduce heat and simmer 30 minutes until beef and vegetables are tender. Discard bay leaf. Stir in vinegar.

4. Stir remaining 1 teaspoon dillweed into yogurt in a bowl. If desired, garnish soup with a dollop of yogurt and serve with crusty bread. Makes 8 servings.

Per serving: 390 calories, 8 g total fat, 2 g saturated fat, 39 mg cholesterol, 1,363 mg sodium, 58 g carbohydrates, 23 g protein, 173 mg calcium, 12 g fiber

quick and healthy vegetable-noodle stir-fry

Just a handful of ingredients, including Asian sesame oil, Napa cabbage, carrots, green onions and soy sauce, pack incredible flavor into this very satisfying, low-fat and low-calorie meal.

Prep time: 30 minutes • Cooking time: 10 minutes

- 2 teaspoons vegetable oil
- ¼ teaspoon Asian sesame oil
- 1½ pounds Napa cabbage, sliced thin (8 cups)
- 1 bag (10 oz.) shredded carrots
- 1 bunch green onions, cut into ½-inch pieces
- 4 cups cooked spaghetti or linguine
- 3 tablespoons low-sodium soy sauce
   Rice vinegar (optional)

Heat vegetable oil and sesame oil in a large skillet over medium-high heat. Stir in cabbage, carrots and green onions. Cook, stirring, for 5 minutes, until tender-crisp. Stir in cooked pasta and soy sauce; heat through. Serve with rice vinegar, if desired. Makes 4 servings.

Per serving: 295 calories, 4 g total fat, 0.5 g saturated fat, 0 mg cholesterol, 496 mg sodium, 56 g carbohydrates, 11 g protein, 166 mg calcium, 6 g fiber

asian noodle and
beef salad *EASY*

See tip, page 59, for ideas on substituting other noodles for the Asian varieties in this recipe. Pictured on page 83.

Prep time: 30 minutes • Cooking time: 14 to 16 minutes

CURRY MARINADE:

1	tablespoon finely chopped garlic
2	tablespoons Asian fish sauce (nuac mam or nam pla)
2	teaspoons curry powder
¼	teaspoon sugar
¾	pound beef round (bottom round rump roast), cut into strips

DRESSING:

½	cup rice wine vinegar
¼	cup Asian fish sauce (nuac mam or nam pla)
¼	cup fresh lime juice
¼	cup finely shredded carrot
3	tablespoons sugar
1	whole Thai chile pepper, finely chopped (see tip, page 95), or ½ teaspoon red pepper flakes
2	teaspoons chopped garlic

4	ounces wheat-flour noodles
4	ounces Japanese soba (buckwheat) noodles
4	ounces rice noodles
2	stalks lemongrass, outer peel removed, or 1 teaspoon grated lemon peel
1	head Boston lettuce, coarsely chopped
1	cucumber, peeled, seeded and shredded
2	teaspoons vegetable oil, divided
2	tablespoons sliced green onions

1. *Make marinade:* Combine all marinade ingredients on a plate. Rub marinade onto beef strips; let stand 30 minutes.

2. *Make dressing:* Combine dressing ingredients.

3. Bring a large stockpot of water to boil. Add wheat noodles and cook 4 minutes, until tender.

Scoop noodles out with a fine-mesh sieve; rinse under cold water and transfer to a bowl. Repeat process with soba and rice noodles, transferring each batch to a separate bowl. *(Can be made ahead. Refrigerate individually in airtight containers up to 24 hours. Rinse with warm water before using.)*

4. Thinly slice lemongrass just up to where single stalk divides (discard remaining stalk). Toss lettuce and cucumber in a bowl; set aside. Heat 1 teaspoon of the oil in a 12-inch nonstick skillet over high heat. Add half the beef and half the lemongrass (or lemon peel, if using). Stir-fry 1 to 2 minutes, then transfer to a plate. Repeat. Divide and arrange lettuce mixture on 4 serving plates. Divide noodles on top, then drizzle salads with half the dressing. Divide beef on top of noodles; sprinkle with green onions. Serve with remaining dressing. Serves 4.

Per serving: 630 calories, 18.5 g total fat, 5.5 g saturated fat, 54 mg cholesterol, 1,230 mg sodium, 89 g carbohydrates, 31 g protein, 94 mg calcium, 6 g fiber

---

test kitchen tip

lean cooking equipment

Sure, it's essential to have the right ingredients for healthful cooking, but having the right kitchen equipment is important, too. The following utensils can help trim the fat from your cooking:

NONSTICK SKILLETS: Use a 10- or 12-inch skillet for searing, sautéing, simmering and stir-frying with the least amount of fat.

NONSTICK GRILL PAN: Use this stovetop pan with a built-in grooved bottom for grilling meat and poultry all year long.

VEGETABLE STEAMER BASKET: Use this handy gadget to transform a standard saucepan into a vegetable steamer. Steaming is the best method to eliminate the need for fat while cooking vegetables, yet preserving their good-for-you properties.

asian beef and vegetables

Serve minute steak strips on top of a medley of fresh vegetables tossed with spaghetti for a family-style dish. Pictured on page 84.

Prep time: 25 minutes plus marinating
Cooking time: 20 minutes

- ⅓ cup reduced-sodium soy sauce
- ¼ teaspoon red pepper flakes
- 4 boneless top round steaks (minute steaks) ½ inch thick (3 oz. each)
- 3 ounces thin spaghetti
- 3 teaspoons olive oil, divided
- 1 medium red onion (6 oz.), halved and sliced
- 1 red bell pepper, chopped
- 5 green onions, thinly sliced
- 1 tablespoon minced fresh ginger
- 2 teaspoons minced garlic
- ½ pound savoy or green cabbage, finely shredded (5 cups)
- ¼ pound cremini or white mushrooms, sliced
- ½ cup water
- ½ teaspoon salt
- ¼ teaspoon freshly ground pepper

1. Stir together soy sauce and red pepper flakes in a shallow glass baking dish. Add minute steaks; turn to coat and marinate at room temperature 30 minutes, turning once.

2. Meanwhile, cook spaghetti according to package directions; drain and rinse with cold water.

3. Heat a 12-inch nonstick skillet over medium heat. Add 2 teaspoons of the oil, the onion and bell pepper. Cook 5 minutes, until onion softens. Add green onions, ginger and garlic. Cook 1 minute, stirring. Add cabbage, mushrooms, water, salt and pepper. Bring to boil over high heat. Cook 3 minutes, stirring, until vegetables are tender-crisp.

4. Add pasta to skillet, tossing with vegetables until pasta is heated through. Transfer to a plate; cover and keep warm.

5. Wipe out skillet. Add remaining 1 teaspoon oil and heat over high heat. Add steaks. Cook 1 minute per side, until well browned and medium-rare. Place on a cutting board and thinly slice on the diagonal. Divide pasta and vegetables among 4 serving plates; top with steak. Makes 4 servings.

Per serving: 350 calories, 15 g total fat, 5 g saturated fat, 54 mg cholesterol, 1,153 mg sodium, 30 g carbohydrates, 24 g protein, 64 mg calcium, 2 g fiber

thai noodles with vegetables and tofu *LOW FAT*

If you're looking for meatless main dishes, try this tofu and noodle dish. Tofu picks up flavor from the marinade.

Prep time: 25 minutes · Cooking time: 15 minutes

- 1½ tablespoons soy sauce
- 1 teaspoon chopped fresh ginger
- ½ teaspoon minced garlic
- 1 pound firm tofu, cut into small cubes
- 1 package (8 oz.) udon noodles or whole-wheat spaghetti
- 1 can (14½ oz.) vegetable broth
- ½ cup lite coconut milk
- 2 carrots, cut into matchsticks
- 4 slices fresh ginger
- 1 large clove garlic, sliced
- 2 tablespoons fresh lime juice
- 1½ tablespoons Asian fish sauce (nuac mam or nam pla)
- 1 Thai red chile, thinly sliced (see tip, page 95)
- 1 jalapeño chile, thinly sliced (see tip, page 95)
- 4 ounces snow peas, sliced
- ¼ cup sliced green onions
- ¼ cup chopped fresh cilantro

1. Combine soy sauce, chopped ginger and garlic in a medium bowl. Add tofu cubes and toss to coat; set aside.

2. Start to cook noodles according to the package directions.

3. Meanwhile, bring broth, coconut milk, carrots, ginger slices, garlic, lime juice, fish sauce and chiles to a simmer in a Dutch oven. Simmer 8 minutes. Stir in snow peas and tofu mixture; cook just until heated through. Remove ginger slices. Drain noodles. Add noodles to Dutch oven with green onions and cilantro. Makes 4 servings.

Per serving: 450 calories, 14 g total fat, 2.5 g saturated fat, 0 mg cholesterol, 1,215 mg sodium, 55 g carbohydrates, 29 g protein, 286 mg calcium, 6 g fiber

teriyaki beef and lettuce wraps

We use iceberg lettuce leaves instead of tortillas for these tasty wraps. To simplify preparations, use a store-bought roasted garlic teriyaki sauce.

Prep time: 15 minutes • Cooking time: 10 minutes

- 1 **head iceberg lettuce**
- 2 **large carrots, shredded**
- 1 **large green bell pepper, cut into thin strips**
- 4 **tablespoons rice wine vinegar, divided**
- ¼ **teaspoon salt**
- 1 **pound lean ground beef**
- 4 **tablespoons roasted garlic teriyaki marinade and sauce, divided**
- 1 **to 2 red Thai chiles or 1 jalapeño chile, seeded and minced (see tip, page 95)**
- 1 **tablespoon water**

1. Core lettuce. Carefully remove at least 8 whole leaves; set aside. Slice enough of remaining lettuce to equal 1 cup. Toss sliced lettuce, carrots, pepper, 3 tablespoons of the rice wine vinegar and the salt in a bowl.

2. Toss beef with 3 tablespoons of the roasted garlic teriyaki sauce in a medium bowl with fingertips. Heat a large nonstick skillet over

medium-high heat. Shape beef into ½-inch balls. Add half the pieces to skillet. Cook, turning, until browned on all sides, 3 minutes; transfer to bowl. Repeat with remaining beef.

3. Return beef to skillet. Add minced chiles, water and remaining 1 tablespoon *each* vinegar and teriyaki sauce. Bring to a simmer. Cover and cook 3 minutes.

4. Spoon beef and vegetable mixture into lettuce leaves. Roll up. Makes 4 servings.

Per serving: 335 calories, 19.5 g total fat, 8 g saturated fat, 78 mg cholesterol, 975 mg sodium, 15 g carbohydrates, 24 g protein, 84 mg calcium, 3 g fiber

---

test kitchen tip

fresh sides and desserts

Keep a supply of fresh produce on hand for easy mealtime accompaniments.

SALAD GREENS: For quick salads, wash salad greens when you get home from the market, then dry them thoroughly. Store the prewashed greens in a sealed plastic bag or airtight container for up to three days. Just before serving, add sliced cucumbers, zucchini, green onions, chopped fresh herbs or tomatoes for variety, and toss with your favorite dressing.

FRESH FRUIT: For low-fat, low-sugar and speedy desserts, keep seasonal fruit selections available. Make an extra-special dessert treat with ripe bananas by peeling, freezing and turning them into thick, luscious, calorie-trimmed shakes. Just blend one fresh banana, one frozen banana and a handful of strawberries with a cup of orange juice or nonfat yogurt for a terrific fruit combination.

glazed ham steak with papaya salsa

LOW FAT *EASY*

When selecting the papaya for the salsa, look for one that is golden yellow and yields slightly to pressure. Pictured on page 81.

Prep time: 10 minutes • Cooking time: 6 minutes

PAPAYA SALSA:
- ½ cup orange juice
- 1 medium papaya, seeded, peeled and chopped
- ¼ cup chopped red onion
- ¼ teaspoon salt
- ⅛ teaspoon ground red pepper

- ¼ cup pineapple preserves
- 1 tablespoon fresh lime juice
- 2 teaspoons Dijon mustard
- 1 pound reduced-sodium boneless ham steak
  Mixed green salad (optional)

1. *Make papaya salsa:* Combine all salsa ingredients in a small bowl; set aside.

2. Heat grill pan or large nonstick skillet. Combine pineapple preserves, lime juice and mustard in a small bowl; brush over both sides of ham. Cook ham over medium-high heat until browned, about 3 minutes per side.

3. Cut ham steak into serving pieces. Serve with papaya salsa and, if desired, salad. Makes 4 servings.

Per serving: 225 calories, 4 g total fat, 1.5 g saturated fat, 54 mg cholesterol, 1,155 mg sodium, 28 g carbohydrates, 21 g protein, 33 mg calcium, 1 g fiber

soy-ginger salmon

LOW FAT

Asian flavors star in this recipe. After marinating in a soy-ginger sauce, the salmon gets a nutty flavor boost with toasted sesame and aromatic sesame oil.

Prep time: 15 minutes plus standing
Cooking time: 8 to 10 minutes

- 3 tablespoons soy sauce
- 2 tablespoons water
- 1 tablespoon sugar
- ½ teaspoon grated fresh ginger
- 1 (1 lb.) salmon fillet, cut into 4 pieces
- ½ teaspoon sesame seeds
- 2 teaspoons vegetable oil
  Vegetable cooking spray
- ½ teaspoon minced garlic
- 3 bags (10 oz. each) fresh spinach, stems removed
- 2 tablespoons water
- ½ teaspoon salt
- ¼ teaspoon Asian sesame oil
- 2 cups cooked orzo
- 4 green onions, for garnish (optional)

1. Combine soy sauce, 2 tablespoons water, the sugar and ginger in a baking dish. Add salmon, turning to coat, and let stand 15 minutes.

2. Meanwhile, heat a large nonstick skillet over medium heat 1 minute. Add sesame seeds and toast 2½ to 3 minutes. Transfer to a plate.

3. Add vegetable oil to same skillet and heat 1 minute over medium-high heat. Add salmon, skin side up; cook 3 to 4 minutes. Reduce heat to medium; turn salmon, cover and cook 3 minutes more, until cooked through. Transfer salmon to plate; discard skin. Add remaining marinade to skillet and boil 1 to 2 minutes, until syrupy.

4. Meanwhile, lightly coat a Dutch oven with vegetable cooking spray. Heat 1 minute over medium heat. Add garlic, spinach and 2 tablespoons water. Cover and cook 3 to 4 minutes, stirring occasionally until spinach is wilted. Stir in salt and sesame oil. Top salmon with soy glaze and sesame seeds. Serve with spinach and orzo. Garnish with onions, if desired. Makes 4 servings.

Per serving: 405 calories, 11.5 g total fat, 1.5 g saturated fat, 62 mg cholesterol, 1,079 mg sodium, 43 g carbohydrates, 33 g protein, 181 mg calcium, 5 g fiber

bubba's shrimp boil LOW FAT

Here's a hassle-free way to serve shrimp—cook them in their shells, then let everyone peel their own.

Prep time: 20 minutes • Cooking time: 25 minutes

- 1½ **pounds large shrimp in shells**
- 4 **large cloves garlic**
- 1 **small onion, chopped**
- 1 **lemon, halved**
- ¼ **cup pickled jalapeño chile slices (see tip, page 95)**
- 2 **tablespoons kosher salt**
- 2 **bay leaves**
- 2 **teaspoons coriander seeds**
- 2 **teaspoons mustard seeds**
- 2 **teaspoons black peppercorns**
- 1 **teaspoon celery seed**
- 1 **teaspoon hot red pepper sauce**
  Lemon wedges (optional)
  Prepared creamy potato salad (optional)

1. Make a slit through shell down center of each curved side of shrimp to the tail. Remove vein. Refrigerate shrimp in a bowl.

2. Meanwhile, bring 2 quarts water and remaining ingredients (except lemon wedges and potato salad) to boil in a medium Dutch oven or large

saucepan over medium-high heat. Boil 20 minutes. Add shrimp. Return to boil and remove from heat. Cover and let stand 5 minutes, until shrimp are pink.

3. Drain shrimp in a large colander. Discard bay leaves. Transfer shrimp and any remaining spices to 4 serving bowls. Serve with lemon wedges and potato salad, if desired. Makes 4 servings.

Per serving: 155 calories, 2.5 g total fat, 0.5 g saturated fat, 210 mg cholesterol, 797 mg sodium, 4 g carbohydrates, 29 g protein, 92 mg calcium, 0 g fiber

---

test kitchen tip
fish tips

Fresh fish makes a healthy and satisfying meal. To best store and thaw it, follow these guidelines:

KEEPING FISH FRESH
To store fresh fish steaks and fillets, wrap each piece tightly in plastic wrap or in a sealed plastic storage bag. Place the wrapped fish in a colander set in a shallow dish. Fill the dish around colander with ice. Place in the refrigerator and refrigerate (between 32°F. and 38°F.) up to 2 days, adding more ice if it melts. Do not allow the fish to have direct contact with the ice or water, as this can affect its texture and flavor.

THE DEEP FREEZE
If your fish is frozen, thaw it in the refrigerator, not at room temperature. (The same holds true for meat and poultry.)

shrimp skewers with fresh fruit salsa

Here's a deliciously fun way to enjoy shrimp that features a combination of citrus-sweet and spice.

Prep time: 25 minutes • Grilling time: 3 to 5 minutes

- 8 (8-inch) bamboo skewers
- 1 tablespoon olive oil
- 1 teaspoon grated lime peel
- ½ teaspoon chili powder
- ¼ teaspoon salt
- ⅛ teaspoon ground red pepper
- 1 pound medium shrimp, shelled and deveined

FRUIT SALSA:

- 1 cup fresh strawberries, hulled
- 1 ripe nectarine, pitted and finely chopped
- ¼ cup fresh raspberries
- 1 green onion, finely chopped
- 1 small jalapeño chile, seeded and minced (see tip, page 95)
- 2 tablespoons fresh lime juice
- 1 tablespoon minced fresh cilantro
- ¼ teaspoon salt

1. Place skewers in a pie plate and cover with cold water. Stir oil, lime peel, chili powder, salt and red pepper in a medium bowl until blended. Add shrimp and toss until evenly coated. Let stand 15 minutes.

2. *Make fruit salsa:* Meanwhile, mash 2 of the strawberries with a fork in a medium bowl. Finely dice remaining strawberries and add to bowl with remaining ingredients; stir to combine.

3. Lightly coat grill or a broiler pan with vegetable cooking spray. Heat grill pan or broiler. Drain skewers. Thread 2 shrimp on each skewer. Cook or broil shrimp, 1½ to 2 minutes per side, until cooked through. Serve immediately with salsa. Makes 4 servings.

Per serving: 132 calories, 4.5 g total fat, 0.5 g saturated fat, 131 mg cholesterol, 420 mg sodium, 9 g carbohydrates, 15 g protein, 40 mg calcium, 2 g fiber

sesame seared scallops

Smart ingredient combinations yield great taste and minimum calories and fat. Be sure not to overcook the scallops or they'll get tough. Pictured on page 81.

Prep time: 10 minutes • Cooking time: 11 minutes

- 3 tablespoons soy sauce
- 1 tablespoon rice wine vinegar
- 1 tablespoon grated fresh ginger
- ¼ cup water
- 1 pound sea scallops
- 3 tablespoons sesame seeds
- 3 teaspoons vegetable oil, divided
- 2 bell peppers (red and yellow), cut into strips
- 1 cup snow peas, trimmed

1. Combine soy sauce, vinegar, ginger and water in a small bowl.

2. Place scallops in a medium bowl with half the soy sauce mixture. Let stand 15 minutes.

3. Meanwhile, heat a large nonstick skillet over medium-high heat. Toast sesame seeds 1 minute. Transfer to a plate.

4. Heat 1 teaspoon of the oil in same skillet. Add vegetables and cook 2 minutes. Stir in remaining soy sauce mixture and cook until vegetables are tender, 3 minutes. Transfer to a plate; cover and keep warm.

5. Wipe out skillet. Heat remaining 2 teaspoons oil over high heat. Add scallops; cook 5 minutes, turning halfway through, until golden. (Scallops should feel firm to the touch.) Divide vegetables among 4 serving plates; top with scallops and sprinkle with sesame seeds. Makes 4 servings.

Per serving: 200 calories, 7.5 g total fat, 1 g saturated fat, 37 mg cholesterol, 957 mg sodium, 11 g carbohydrates, 22 g protein, 114 mg calcium, 2 g fiber

fish and chips LOW FAT

To cut fat from the British classic, we gave the fish a crispy cornflake crumb coating and skipped the deep-fat frying. To make the chips skinnier, we baked potato wedges with just a dab of olive oil.

Prep time: 15 minutes • Cooking time: 29 to 35 minutes

CHIPS:

Olive oil cooking spray or vegetable
cooking spray

2 pounds russet or baking potatoes, scrubbed
and sliced into ¼-inch-thick wedges

1 tablespoon olive oil

½ teaspoon salt

¼ teaspoon freshly ground pepper

FISH:

4 small sole fillets (about 1 pound)

½ cup buttermilk

⅛ teaspoon ground red pepper

1 cup cornflake crumbs

2 tablespoons chopped fresh parsley

Olive oil or vegetable cooking spray

Malt vinegar (optional)

Fresh flat-leaf parsley sprigs, for
garnish (optional)

1. *Make chips:* Adjust oven racks to center and lower third of oven. Heat oven to 475°F. Lightly coat two large cookie sheets with cooking spray. Pat sliced potatoes with paper towels. Toss potatoes, oil, salt and pepper in a bowl until well coated. Divide potatoes and spread in a single layer on prepared sheets. Bake potatoes 25 to 30 minutes, switching pans once halfway through, until lightly browned. Cover loosely with foil and keep warm.

2. *Make fish:* Reduce oven temperature to 200°F. Cut each fillet crosswise in half. Combine buttermilk and red pepper in a pie plate. Combine cornflake crumbs and parsley on a sheet of waxed paper. Dip each piece of fish in buttermilk mixture and coat with crumbs. Place on a cookie sheet or large plate.

3. Coat a large nonstick skillet with cooking spray. Heat over medium-high heat 1 minute. Add half of the fish. Cook 4 to 5 minutes, turning once halfway through, until fish is crisp and golden and opaque in center when tested with a small knife. Transfer cooked fish to cookie sheet and place in oven to keep warm. Repeat process with cooking spray and remaining fish.

4. Divide potatoes and fish among 4 serving plates. Serve fish and chips with malt vinegar and garnish with parsley sprigs, if desired. Makes 4 servings.

Per serving: 440 calories, 5.5 g total fat, 1 g saturated fat, 56 mg cholesterol, 782 mg sodium, 67 g carbohydrates, 29 g protein, 60 mg calcium, 4 g fiber

---

test kitchen tip

fish and chips made lighter

Ingredients and method make all the difference in cutting down on fat and calories for our version of Fish and Chips, left.

SELECT THE BEST
Choose a firm, white-fleshed fish—flounder, snapper, pollock or grouper can be substituted for the sole used in the recipe. All are equally delicious and low in fat.

FOR A CRISPY CRUST
Coat the fish with cornflake crumbs for crispness. The crumbs are typically located in the bread or flour aisle of the supermarket.

SPRAY IT
Use cooking spray to brown fish without excess fat, and to ensure that the potatoes won't stick to the pan.

warm potato and shrimp salad

Rich-flavored Yukon gold potatoes make a memorable potato salad, and the addition of shrimp takes it to an extra-opulent level. Pictured on page 82.

Prep time: 10 minutes • Cooking time: 20 minutes

- 1½ pounds medium Yukon gold or red potatoes
- 2 teaspoons salt
- 1 pound medium shrimp, shelled and deveined

DRESSING:

- 1 medium red onion
- ¼ cup whole-grain mustard
- 3 tablespoons extra-virgin olive oil
- 3 tablespoons sherry vinegar
- 1 tablespoon water
- 2 teaspoons sugar
- ¾ teaspoon salt

- 1 bag (10 oz.) European blend or spring mix salad greens

1. Bring potatoes, 2 teaspoons salt and enough cold water to cover to boil in a large saucepan. Boil 20 minutes, just until fork tender. Add shrimp to potatoes and cook just until shrimp are pink. Drain potatoes and shrimp.

2. *Make dressing:* Meanwhile, finely chop 1 tablespoon onion. (Thinly slice remaining onion for the salad.) Combine chopped onion and remaining dressing ingredients in a bowl. Chop ½ cup cooked potato. Add to dressing.

3. Toss greens and sliced onions with ⅓ cup of the dressing. Slice remaining potatoes. Divide greens among 4 serving plates. Top with potatoes and shrimp; drizzle with remaining dressing. Makes 4 servings.

Per serving: 375 calories, 12.5 g total fat, 2 g saturated fat, 140 mg cholesterol, 1,647 mg sodium, 39 g carbohydrates, 23 g protein, 109 mg calcium, 4 g fiber

mushrooms and barley over greens

If your market doesn't have frisée (also known as French endive), chicory will work just as well. Pictured on page 83.

Prep time: 15 minutes • Baking time: 15 minutes

DRESSING:

- ½ cup balsamic vinegar
- 2 teaspoons brown sugar
- 3 tablespoons extra-virgin olive oil
- ¾ teaspoon salt
- ½ teaspoon minced garlic
- ¼ teaspoon freshly ground pepper

- 4 large portobello mushroom caps (about 1¼ lbs.)
- 1 cup quick-cook barley
- ½ cup diced carrots
- 1 pound frisée or chicory salad greens

1. *Make dressing:* Bring vinegar and sugar to boil in a small saucepan. Boil 3 minutes until mixture is reduced to ⅓ cup. Whisk in remaining dressing ingredients.

2. Heat oven to 425°F. Scrape gills from mushroom caps and discard. Arrange mushrooms, smooth side up, on a cookie sheet. Transfer 2 tablespoons dressing to a cup and brush over tops of mushrooms. Bake 15 minutes. Cover with foil.

3. Meanwhile, cook barley according to package directions. Add the carrots during the last 3 minutes of cooking time. Slice mushrooms; toss with barley and ¼ cup of the dressing.

4. Toss frisée with remaining dressing. Divide among 4 serving plates. Top with barley-and-mushroom mixture. Makes 4 servings.

Per serving: 300 calories, 12 g total fat, 1.5 g saturated fat, 0 mg cholesterol, 500 mg sodium, 44 g carbohydrates, 9 g protein, 136 mg calcium, 8 g fiber

multi-bean ragout

We used heirloom beans (see tip, right), but any combination of beans can be used. Pictured on page 83.

Prep time: 30 minutes plus soaking
Baking time: 2 to 2½ hours

1½	cups assorted heirloom beans, rinsed and picked over
2	tablespoons olive oil
5	carrots, cut into thin strips
3	celery ribs, diced
1	onion, sliced
1	tablespoon chopped garlic
4	ounces pancetta (Italian bacon) or 4 slices bacon, chopped
1	can (14½ oz.) chicken broth
1	teaspoon dried oregano
1	bay leaf
½	teaspoon salt
¼	teaspoon freshly ground pepper
1	can (14½ oz.) plum tomatoes
½	cup red wine
12	ounces pappardelle or other wide noodle
¾	cup freshly grated Parmesan cheese

1. Combine assorted beans in a large bowl. Cover with 2 inches of cold water and let stand overnight. (To quick soak: Combine beans with water to cover by 2 inches in a medium Dutch oven. Bring to boil; boil 2 minutes. Cover and let stand 1 hour.) Drain beans in a colander. Set aside.

2. Heat oven to 350°F. Heat oil in a medium Dutch oven over medium heat. (If using bacon, omit oil. Cook bacon until crisp; remove with a slotted spoon. Heat drippings in Dutch oven.) Add carrots, celery, onion and garlic. Cook 5 minutes, until vegetables are softened. Stir in pancetta, if using. Cook until lightly browned, about 1 minute. Add beans, chicken broth, oregano, bay leaf, salt and pepper (and bacon, if using); bring to boil. Cover and bake 1 hour. Stir in tomatoes and red wine; bake, covered, 1 to 1½ hours more until beans are tender. Discard bay leaf.

3. To serve, cook pasta according to package directions, reserving ½ cup pasta water. When beans are tender, add enough pasta water to beans until mixture is saucy.

4. Divide pasta among 6 serving plates. Top with bean mixture and sprinkle with Parmesan cheese. Serve immediately. Makes 6 servings.

Per serving: 605 calories, 16.5 g total fat, 5.5 g saturated fat, 21 mg cholesterol, 1,072 mg sodium, 88 g carbohydrates, 28 g protein, 303 mg calcium, 10 g fiber

---

test kitchen tip

heirloom beans

As their name suggests, heirloom beans are treasured seeds passed down through generations. Many have great beauty, all have great flavor, several have evocative names, such as Wren's Egg and Tongues of Fire. Like all beans, heirloom varieties are high in protein and are good sources of calcium, potassium, iron, zinc, fiber and several B vitamins, including folate. And like all beans, these varieties can stress your digestive system—a problem that can be avoided with the proper cooking technique:

METHOD MATTERS

- Soak beans before cooking (this activates the enzymes that make the beans more digestible).
- Do not add acidic ingredients (tomatoes, citrus fruit or wine) to a pot of cooking beans until the beans have softened.
- After cooking them in boiling water for about 10 to 15 minutes with the lid off, add a small amount of salt (¼ teaspoon per cup of dry beans). This helps speed the softening process along, and also enhances flavor.
- Don't try to soften beans by adding baking soda, as your grandmother may have. Doing so destroys nutrients.

vegetable lasagne ♡ LOW FAT

Our slimmed-down version substitutes 4% milkfat cottage cheese for the ricotta. Add to that a low-fat tomato sauce and part-skim mozzarella, and this dish weighs in at just 385 calories and 11.5 grams of fat. Pictured on page 81.

Prep time: 1 hour
Baking time: 45 to 50 minutes plus standing

TOMATO SAUCE:
- 2 teaspoons olive oil
- 2 teaspoons chopped garlic
- 2 cans (28 oz. each) crushed tomatoes
- ¼ cup fresh basil leaves, chopped
- 1 teaspoon fennel seed, chopped
- ¼ teaspoon red pepper flakes

CHEESE FILLING:
- 1 large container (32 oz.) 4% milkfat cottage cheese, drained
- ⅓ cup freshly grated Parmesan cheese
- ¼ cup chopped fresh parsley
- ½ teaspoon salt
- ¼ teaspoon freshly ground pepper

- 2 teaspoons olive oil
- 1 cup chopped onions
- ½ pound sliced mushrooms
- 4 tablespoons chicken broth, divided
- 1 large bunch fresh spinach (1 lb.), trimmed and chopped, or 1 box (10 oz.) frozen chopped spinach, thawed and squeezed dry
- 12 lasagne noodles, cooked
- 1 cup shredded part-skim mozzarella cheese

1. *Make tomato sauce:* Heat oil in a medium saucepan. Add garlic and cook 30 seconds. Add remaining sauce ingredients and bring to boil. Reduce heat and simmer 15 minutes. *(Can be made ahead. Cool, transfer to airtight container and refrigerate up to 2 days. Reheat before serving.)* Makes 6 cups.

2. *Make cheese filling:* Meanwhile, process cottage cheese and Parmesan cheese in a food processor until smooth. Transfer to a medium bowl. Stir in parsley, salt and pepper.

3. Heat oil in a 12-inch skillet over medium heat. Add onions and cook, stirring, 5 minutes. Add mushrooms and cook until golden, adding 2 tablespoons of the chicken broth to prevent sticking. Transfer onion mixture to a bowl; set aside.

4. Add fresh spinach, if using, and remaining 2 tablespoons broth to same skillet. Cook, stirring, 4 to 5 minutes. Transfer spinach to a colander and squeeze until excess liquid is removed. Add to onion mixture. If using frozen spinach, add at this time.

5. *To assemble:* Heat oven to 375°F. Pour 1 cup tomato sauce on bottom of a 13×9-inch baking dish. Top with 4 lasagne noodles (they may overlap slightly). Spread half of the cheese filling over noodles. Top with half of the vegetables. Repeat layering one more time. Arrange remaining noodles over vegetables. Top with 1 cup tomato sauce and the mozzarella. (Reserve remaining 2 cups sauce for another use.) Lightly coat a piece of foil with vegetable cooking spray; cover dish with foil, coated side down, and bake 30 minutes. Uncover and bake 15 to 20 minutes more, until lasagne is bubbly. Let stand 15 minutes. Serves 8.

Per serving: 385 calories, 11.5 g total fat, 6 g saturated fat, 28 mg cholesterol, 1,031 mg sodium, 43 g carbohydrates, 28 g protein, 311 mg calcium, 4 g fiber

zucchini-leek tart

Use two medium zucchini rather than one large one so that the slices will fit snugly when arranged in the crust.

Prep time: 1 hour plus chilling
Baking time: 64 to 71 minutes

PASTRY:
- 1¼ cups all-purpose flour
- ¼ teaspoon salt

6 tablespoons cold butter (no substitutions), cut up

4 tablespoons ice water

FILLING:

1 teaspoon extra-virgin olive oil

2 medium (¾ lb.) zucchini, cut lengthwise into ¼-inch-thick slices

⅛ teaspoon salt

1 tablespoon butter (no substitutions)

1 pound leeks, chopped, white part only

1 teaspoon fresh thyme leaves

½ teaspoon salt

1 cup heavy or whipping cream

2 large eggs, lightly beaten

¼ teaspoon freshly ground pepper

½ cup shredded Gruyère or Swiss cheese

4 sprigs fresh thyme

1. *Make pastry:* Combine flour and salt in a large bowl. With a pastry blender or 2 knives, cut in butter, until mixture resembles coarse crumbs. Add water, 1 tablespoon at a time, tossing with a fork until mixture begins to hold together. Gather into a ball. Flatten into a disk; wrap and refrigerate 30 minutes or overnight.

2. Heat oven to 425°F. On a lightly floured surface, roll out pastry into a 12-inch circle. Fit into a 9-inch tart pan with removable bottom. Fold in edge of pastry. Press against side of pan and trim. Prick bottom of pastry shell with fork. Freeze 15 minutes. Line pastry shell with foil and fill with dried beans or rice. Bake 12 minutes. Remove foil and beans. Bake 15 to 17 minutes more, until crust is golden. Cool completely on a wire rack.

3. *Make filling:* Meanwhile, brush a large cookie sheet with oil. Arrange zucchini slices on prepared sheet in a single layer; sprinkle tops with the ⅛ teaspoon salt. Bake 6 minutes. Turn slices and bake 6 minutes more, until just softened. Cool on pan.

4. Melt butter in a large skillet over medium heat. Add leeks, thyme leaves and the ½ teaspoon salt. Cover and cook over medium-low heat until leeks have softened, 5 to 6 minutes.

5. Mix heavy cream, eggs, leeks and pepper in a medium bowl. Pour into crust. Arrange overlapping slices of zucchini on top of cream mixture. Sprinkle top with cheese and thyme sprigs. Bake 25 to 30 minutes, until filling is set and golden on top. Cool on a wire rack 30 minutes. Serve warm or at room temperature. Makes 6 to 8 servings.

Per serving: 415 calories, 30 g total fat, 17 g saturated fat, 147 mg cholesterol, 481 mg sodium, 30 g carbohydrates, 9 g protein, 164 mg calcium, 2 g fiber

test kitchen tip

the lowdown on leeks

Leeks may take a little extra prep time, but their mellow, earthy flavor makes the extra effort worthwhile.

WASHING LEEKS

Leeks' tightly packed leaves easily collect soil and grit, so it's important to clean them thoroughly. Here's the best way to go about it: Remove any wilted outer leaves. Cut off the green upper leaves down to where the dark green color begins to pale, then remove the root end. Next, halve them lengthwise; slice thinly and transfer to the basket of a salad spinner filled with water. Let the leeks soak for 5 minutes to allow the dirt to sink to the bottom of the spinner. Lift up the basket and rinse leeks under cold running water; spin dry. Repeat this process if the leeks are still gritty. If you don't have a salad spinner, rinse the leeks under cold running water, lifting and separating leaves as you rinse.

SELECTING AND STORING

Choose leeks with crisp, vibrantly colored leaves and a blemish-free white portion. Store them in the refrigerator in a plastic bag for up to 5 days.

power foods

Science has shown that certain nutrients have tremendous health payoffs. Here are some of the sources for these healthful nutrients.

ANTIOXIDANTS: Good sources of these potential disease-fighting nutrients include red, yellow and orange vegetables, leafy dark greens and green cruciferous vegetables.

HEART-HEALTHY FATS: All oils have different proportions of fatty acids. The healthiest oils are those that are low in saturated fats and high in monounsaturated or polyunsaturated fats, like olive, canola, peanut, corn and safflower oils.

OMEGA-3S: Found mostly in higher-fat, cold-water varieties of seafood—mackerel, tuna, salmon, sardines—it has been established that Omega-3s are vital to body development and maintenance. They also can be found in plant foods such as flaxseeds and walnuts.

CALCIUM: To help maintain strong bones, enjoy calcium in dairy products, calcium-fortified orange juice, kale and tofu.

FOLATE: Great sources of folate are beans, spinach, oranges, orange juice and strawberries. This B vitamin may help prevent birth defects and reduce the risk of heart attacks and stroke.

LYCOPENE: This antioxidant may help reduce the risk of cancers of the prostate and digestive tract. The best sources are cooked tomatoes and tomato products. Other sources include pink grapefruit and watermelon.

SOY: Evidence suggests that soy foods such as tofu may protect against heart disease, breast cancer, osteoporosis and help reduce hot flashes that may accompany menopause. Other good sources include soy milk and soy burger.

greek vegetable gratin ♥ LOW FAT

Vegetables like carrots, tomatoes, zucchini and peppers, which are rich in vitamins A, C and E, make up an alphabet stew of antioxidants and a healthy, possibly cancer-fighting meal. We start this dish with a quick homemade tomato sauce, spread it over layers of vegetables and feta cheese, top it all off with a sprinkling of Parmesan cheese, then bake to savory perfection. Pictured on page 85.

Prep time: 40 minutes plus standing
Baking time: 1 hour 30 to 40 minutes

- 1 tablespoon olive oil
- 2 medium onions, thinly sliced
- 1 large red bell pepper, thinly sliced
- ½ teaspoon salt, divided
- ½ teaspoon freshly ground pepper, divided
- 1 tablespoon minced garlic
- 1 can (14½ oz.) diced tomatoes in juice (do not drain)
- 2 pounds baking potatoes (4 medium), cut crosswise into ¼-inch-thick slices
- 1 pound carrots, thinly sliced diagonally
- 4 tablespoons freshly grated Parmesan cheese, divided
- 2 large zucchini (1 lb.), cut lengthwise into ¼-inch-thick slices
- ½ cup crumbled feta cheese, divided
- ¾ cup vegetable broth
- 2 tablespoons chopped fresh dill
  Tossed green salad (optional)

1. Heat oven to 375°F. Lightly grease a 3½- to 4-quart baking dish. Heat oil in a 12-inch skillet over medium-low heat. Add onions, bell pepper and ¼ teaspoon *each* of the salt and pepper. Cook 10 to 15 minutes, until vegetables soften and begin to brown. Add garlic and cook 1 minute, stirring. Add tomatoes and juice and bring to boil; reduce heat and simmer 5 minutes more. Set aside.

2. Arrange one-third of potato and carrot slices in the bottom of the prepared dish. Sprinkle with

1 tablespoon of the Parmesan cheese. Arrange half the zucchini slices over potatoes. Sprinkle with $\frac{1}{8}$ teaspoon *each* of the salt and pepper. Spread one-third of the tomato sauce (1 cup) over zucchini. Sprinkle with $\frac{1}{4}$ cup of the feta cheese. Repeat layering. Arrange remaining potatoes and carrots on top and spread with remaining sauce. Pour broth over vegetables then sprinkle with remaining 2 tablespoons Parmesan cheese.

3. Cover dish with greased foil. Bake 40 minutes. Uncover and bake 50 to 60 minutes more, until potatoes are tender and a small knife inserted in center of dish comes out easily. Sprinkle gratin with dill. Let gratin stand 15 minutes before serving. Serve with tossed green salad, if desired. Serves 6.

Per serving: 280 calories, 8 g total fat, 3 g saturated fat, 13 mg cholesterol, 673 mg sodium, 46 g carbohydrates, 10 g protein, 197 mg calcium, 7 g fiber

caponata with portobello mushrooms

To turn caponata into a meal, we serve it with baked portobello mushroom caps, which have a great meaty taste. Then we top it with fontina cheese and savory herbs. Pictured on page 85.

Prep time: 25 minutes • Cooking time: 40 to 45 minutes

- 1 **tablespoon olive oil**
- 1 **medium onion, chopped**
- 1 **cup chopped fennel**
- 2 **teaspoons finely chopped garlic**
- 1 **small (1 lb.) eggplant, peeled and cut into ½-inch dice**
- ⅓ **cup white wine**

MUSHROOMS:
- 8 **small portobello caps (1½ lbs.)**
- 2 **tablespoons olive oil**
- 2 **teaspoons balsamic vinegar**
- ½ **teaspoon salt**
- ½ **teaspoon freshly ground pepper**
- ∎
- 3 **tablespoons tomato paste**
- 1 **tablespoon balsamic vinegar**
- 1 **can (16 oz.) whole tomatoes in juice, chopped (do not drain)**
- 2 **tablespoons water**
- 2 **tablespoons chopped fresh parsley**
- 1 **teaspoon chopped fresh thyme**
- ½ **teaspoon chopped fresh rosemary**
- 1 **teaspoon sugar**
- ½ **teaspoon salt**
- ¼ **teaspoon freshly ground pepper**
- ¼ **pound fontina cheese, shredded**

1. Heat oil in a large nonstick skillet over medium-high heat. Add onion and fennel and cook 3 to 4 minutes until lightly browned. Add garlic and cook, stirring, 1 minute. Add eggplant and wine. Reduce heat to medium, cover and cook 15 to 25 minutes until eggplant is tender.

2. *Make mushrooms:* Meanwhile, heat oven to 425°F. Line a large cookie sheet with foil. Turn mushrooms top side down and remove dark gills with side of spoon; discard gills. Transfer caps to prepared sheet, top side up. Combine olive oil, vinegar, salt and pepper in a cup; brush on caps. Bake 15 minutes until mushrooms are tender. Cover and keep warm.

3. Stir tomato paste and vinegar into eggplant; cook 1 minute. Add tomatoes and juice, water, parsley, thyme, rosemary, sugar, salt and pepper. Cover and simmer 10 minutes, until thick.

4. *To assemble:* Turn mushroom caps over. Evenly top with cheese. Transfer to oven and bake just until cheese melts, 2 minutes. Divide caponata among 4 serving plates. Arrange 2 mushrooms on each plate. Makes 4 servings.

Per serving: 320 calories, 20 g total fat, 7 g saturated fat, 33 mg cholesterol, 1,128 mg sodium, 27 g carbohydrates, 14 g protein, 261 mg calcium, 6 g fiber

good-for-you grains

Grains make up the base of the healthy food pyramid for good reason. Loaded with fiber and nutrients, they can help lower cholesterol and make you feel full while you're dieting. For variety, try a few of the newly rediscovered grains arriving in supermarkets and specialty shops. Quinoa, amaranth, faro (spelt) and kamut are among the more intriguing grains now available.

asparagus with barley and wheat berries
LOW FAT

Asparagus teams up beautifully with grains in this soothing pilaf seasoned with pancetta. You'll need to allow some simmering time for the wheat berries, but their deep nutty flavor and chewy texture is definitely worth the wait. The asparagus is stirred in just before serving to keep it fresh and green, then a sprinkling of parsley adds a final flourish to the dish. Pictured on page 83.

Prep time: 20 minutes
Cooking time: 45 minutes plus standing

- ⅓ cup wheat berries
- ¾ teaspoon salt, divided
- 2 pounds fresh asparagus, trimmed
- 1 tablespoon olive oil
- 2 ounces pancetta (Italian bacon), chopped
- ½ cup finely chopped onion
- 1 cup pearl barley
- 1 can (14½ oz.) chicken broth
- 1 tablespoon chopped fresh parsley

1. Rinse and drain wheat berries. Bring wheat berries and 4 cups water to boil in a saucepan. Simmer wheat berries until softened but still chewy, 45 minutes. Remove from heat, cover and let stand 15 minutes.

2. Bring 2 inches of water to boil in a small Dutch oven. Add ½ teaspoon of the salt and half the asparagus; simmer until stalks are just tender, 5 to 8 minutes. Remove asparagus with tongs to a plate. Repeat; discard water.

3. Heat oil in Dutch oven over medium heat. Add pancetta and cook 2 minutes; stir in onion. Cook until onion softens. Stir in barley, broth and 1½ cups water. Bring to boil, then reduce heat. Cover and simmer until most of the liquid is absorbed, 30 to 35 minutes. Drain.

4. Cut asparagus into 2-inch pieces. Stir into barley with wheat berries and remaining ¼ teaspoon salt. Stir in parsley. Makes 6 servings.

Per serving: 265 calories, 9 g total fat, 2.5 g saturated fat, 6 mg cholesterol, 556 mg sodium, 39 g carbohydrates, 10 g protein, 48 mg calcium, 8 g fiber

triticale risotto
LOW FAT

Risotto isn't normally what we'd call a power-packed dish. But we replace arborio rice with a super-grain called triticale (triht-ih-KAY-lee), which is loaded with fiber and protein. Then we toss in Swiss chard and butternut squash for vitamins A and C, as well as for flavor. You'd never guess that increasing your fiber and whole-grain intake could taste so good. Pictured on page 84.

Prep time: 40 minutes • Cooking time: 46 to 54 minutes

- 2 cups triticale berries
- 1 butternut squash (2½ lbs.), peeled, seeded and diced
- 1 tablespoon butter, melted
- 2 cans (14½ oz. each) chicken broth
- ¼ cup water
- 1 tablespoon olive oil
- 1½ cups chopped onions
- 1 tablespoon finely chopped garlic

½ cup white wine

¾ pound Swiss chard, trimmed and leaves
    chopped (5½ cups)

1 teaspoon chopped fresh thyme

½ teaspoon salt

¼ teaspoon freshly ground pepper

⅛ teaspoon freshly ground nutmeg

⅓ cup freshly grated Parmesan cheese
    Freshly shaved* Parmesan cheese, for
    garnish (optional)

1. Heat oven to 425°F.

2. Bring triticale and water to cover by 1 inch to boil in a Dutch oven. Cook 20 minutes. Drain and transfer to a bowl. Wipe out Dutch oven.

3. Meanwhile, toss squash with melted butter on a jelly-roll pan. Bake 25 to 35 minutes until tender and browned.

4. Bring broth and water to a simmer in a large saucepan. Heat oil over medium-high heat in the Dutch oven. Add onions and cook 4 to 6 minutes, until tender and lightly browned. Add garlic and cook 1 minute. Add wine; cook 1 minute more. Stir in drained triticale and cook until wine is absorbed. Reduce heat to medium and gradually add broth mixture, ½ cup at a time, stirring, until liquid is absorbed and triticale is tender, 12 to 17 minutes. Stir in the squash, chard, thyme, salt, pepper and nutmeg; cook 4 to 5 minutes, stirring until chard is tender. Stir in grated Parmesan cheese, and garnish with Parmesan shavings, if desired. Serve immediately. Makes 6 servings.

Note: To make Parmesan shavings, use a swivel blade vegetable peeler.

Per serving: 405 calories, 8.5 g total fat, 3 g saturated fat, 9 mg cholesterol, 1,020 mg sodium, 72 g carbohydrates, 15 g protein, 215 mg calcium, 16 g fiber

---

test kitchen tip

iron for everyone

Iron carries oxygen through the body and helps provide energy. Here are some good things to know about this important nutrient:

IRON AND WOMEN:
Deficiency is a common problem among women, especially during childbearing years. To boost your iron intake, keep in mind that the body most easily absorbs iron in meat, poultry and fish (heme iron), though some vegetables and grains have iron, too.

IRON FOR VEGETARIANS:
Iron from vegetables and grains (non-heme iron) is less easily absorbed than the iron from meat, poultry and fish. (Only 2 to 20 percent of non-heme iron makes its way into the bloodstream as opposed to the 25 to 35 percent absorption rate of heme iron.) Not to worry! Keep in mind that pairing it with food rich in vitamin C helps in the absorption of iron. Experts recommend 15 milligrams of iron a day. Those who enjoy meatless meals can still gain iron's benefits. Top sources for non-heme iron are:

- 1 cup fortified breakfast cereal: 1.4 to 18 mg
- ½ cup soybean nuts: 4 mg
- 1 tablespoon blackstrap molasses: 3.5 mg
- ½ cup fresh spinach: 3.2 mg
- ½ cup kidney beans: 2.6 mg
- ¾ cup prune juice: 2.3 mg

fall vegetable couscous

This easy and hearty one-pot vegetable stew features some great flavors of fall, including winter squash and apples.

Prep time: 20 minutes • Baking time: 55 minutes

- 2 tablespoons olive oil
- 2 medium red onions, sliced
- 1 tablespoon minced garlic
- 2 teaspoons coriander
- 2 teaspoons cumin
- ⅛ teaspoon ground red pepper
- 1 medium rutabaga, peeled and diced
- 1 pound carrots, diced
- 1 medium winter squash, peeled and diced
- ½ pound potatoes, sliced
- 2 Granny Smith apples, peeled and diced
- 1 can (15 or 19 oz.) chickpeas, drained
- 1 can (13¾ or 14½ oz.) chicken broth
- 2 cups thinly sliced kale
- 1 box (10 oz.) couscous
- 1 container (8 oz.) plain low-fat yogurt

1. Heat oven to 400°F. Heat a Dutch oven over medium heat 2 minutes. Add oil and onions; cook 5 minutes, until softened. Stir in garlic, coriander, cumin and red pepper and cook, stirring, 1 to 2 minutes. Add remaining ingredients except kale, couscous and yogurt. Cover and bake until vegetables are tender, 45 minutes.

2. Stir in kale. Cover and bake 10 minutes more. Meanwhile, prepare couscous according to package directions. Serve with vegetables and yogurt. Makes 6 servings.

Per serving: 470 calories, 8 g total fat, 1 g saturated fat, 2 mg cholesterol, 520 mg sodium, 85 g carbohydrates, 16 g protein, 244 mg calcium, 18 g fiber

fresh mozzarella and tomato salad

In summer, celebrate home-grown tomatoes and the fistfuls of basil sprouting up at markets everywhere with this take on "caprese," the classic Italian salad.

Total prep time: 10 minutes

- 1 tablespoon balsamic vinegar
- 1 tablespoon minced shallots
- ½ teaspoon salt
- ½ teaspoon Dijon mustard
- ¼ teaspoon sugar
- ¼ teaspoon freshly ground pepper
- 3 tablespoons olive oil
- 1¾ pounds tomatoes, sliced ¼ inch thick
- 1 pound fresh mozzarella cheese, sliced ¼ inch thick
- ¼ cup shredded fresh basil leaves
  Cracked black pepper

1. Combine balsamic vinegar, shallots, salt, mustard, sugar and ground pepper in a small bowl. Gradually whisk in olive oil until blended.

2. Arrange sliced tomatoes and mozzarella on a large platter; drizzle with dressing. Sprinkle with basil leaves and cracked pepper. Makes 8 servings.

Per serving: 230 calories, 17.5 g total fat, 8 g saturated fat, 40 mg cholesterol, 194 mg sodium, 7 g carbohydrates, 11 g protein, 302 mg calcium, 1 g fiber

pita bread salad

To make use of day-old bread, the Italians have panzanella—bread-and-tomato salad. Here's a similar concept, known as fattoush, that hails from Egypt.

Total prep time: 25 minutes

- 2 (5- to 6-inch) day-old pita breads, split
- 1 clove garlic

½ teaspoon salt

¼ cup fresh lemon juice

¼ cup extra-virgin olive oil

3 medium red or yellow tomatoes, chopped

1 red bell pepper, diced

1 cup fresh parsley, chopped

¼ cup fresh mint, chopped

1. Cut pita in half, then cut each half into 6 pieces.

2. With flat side of a large knife, crush the garlic and salt with a knife to form paste. Combine paste with lemon juice and oil in a large serving bowl. Stir in pitas and remaining ingredients. Let stand at least 15 minutes before serving. Makes 6 servings (5 cups).

Per serving: 160 calories, 10 g total fat, 1.5 g saturated fat, 0 mg cholesterol, 313 mg sodium, 16 g carbohydrates, 3 g protein, 42 mg calcium, 2 g fiber

roasted asparagus

Roasting brings out the fullest flavor of vegetables, and asparagus is no exception. Pictured on page 86.

Prep time: 10 minutes • Baking time: 20 minutes

2 pounds fresh asparagus, trimmed

2 tablespoons olive oil

Pinch salt

Shaved Parmesan cheese (optional)

¼ teaspoon freshly ground pepper

Arrange oven racks to middle and lower third of oven. Heat oven to 400°F. Divide asparagus and spread on two jelly-roll pans. Toss each with 1 tablespoon of the oil and the salt. Roast 10 minutes. Switch pans between the racks and roast 10 minutes more, until stalks are tender. Sprinkle top with cheese, if desired, and pepper. Makes 4 to 6 servings.

Per serving: 80 calories, 6 g total fat, 1 g saturated fat, 0 mg cholesterol, 31 mg sodium, 5 g carbohydrates, 5 g protein, 32 mg calcium, 1 g fiber

test kitchen tip

sweet sweet balsamic

Balsamic vinegar, a hallmark of Mediterranean cooking, is a heady and complex ingredient with many uses.

THE FLAVOR FACTOR: Balsamic vinegar is made of gently crushed wine grapes, which are eventually fermented and aged in wooden barrels. It is a vulnerable combination of sweet and sharp. Its deep complex flavor is a result of its aging process, which can range from months to several years. Over time, the crushed grape concentrate actually becomes vinegar in the wooden barrels as the maturing vinegar slowly evaporates and gets transferred into smaller and smaller barrels. The variety of wood for the barrels, such as chestnut and cherry, also contributes to the flavor of the vinegar. This intensive time-consuming process, as well as the amount of grapes needed, puts a high price tag on balsamic vinegar. Commercially produced varieties, which don't take as many years to produce, are the most readily available in supermarkets.

USAGE: The extraordinary flavor of the finest balsamic vinegars leaves a lasting impression on one's palate. Its power should not be underestimated, however, as every drop packs intense flavor. Here are a few ways to enjoy experimenting with this distinctive ingredient:

- Add a touch to your favorite vinaigrette, or sprinkle over mixed greens with grated or shredded fresh Parmesan cheese.
- Dip a piece of plain crusty bread into a small amount of balsamic vinegar.
- Drizzle some lightly over fresh berries or ice cream.
- Try in sauces or pan juices for meats such as veal or pork.
- Add a few drops to sparkling tonic water.

fennel orange salad

This intriguing salad with thinly sliced fennel, radishes and fresh lemon and orange juice makes a refreshing light lunch or a side salad to serve with supper.

Total prep time: 15 minutes

- 2 bulbs fennel
- ¾ cup sliced radishes
- ¼ cup chopped fresh parsley
- 1 tablespoon fresh lemon juice
- 1 teaspoon grated orange peel
- 3 tablespoons fresh orange juice
- ½ teaspoon salt
- ¼ teaspoon freshly ground pepper
- 2 tablespoons olive oil

1. In a food processor, thinly slice fennel. Toss fennel, radishes and parsley together in a large bowl.

2. Combine remaining ingredients in a small saucepan, bring to boil and boil 1 minute over high heat. Pour over fennel mixture and toss to coat. Serve immediately. Makes 6 cups.

Per 1 cup: 65 calories, 4.5 g total fat, 0.5 g saturated fat, 0 mg cholesterol, 277 mg sodium, 4 g carbohydrates, 1 g protein, 30 mg calcium, 12 g fiber

creamy blush potato salad

It's not red potatoes but pan-roasted tomatoes that give this salad its pinkish hue and great taste.

Prep time: 13 minutes • Cooking time: 15 to 17 minutes

- 2½ pounds white potatoes, scrubbed
- 3 teaspoons salt, divided
- 2 large plum tomatoes (6 oz.), diced
- 3 tablespoons finely chopped onion
- ½ cup mayonnaise
- 2 tablespoons white balsamic or white wine vinegar
- ½ teaspoon freshly ground pepper
- 5 large fresh basil leaves, thinly sliced, divided

1. Cut potatoes into 1-inch pieces. Bring potatoes, 2 teaspoons of the salt and enough cold water to cover by 2 inches to boil in a large saucepan. Cook 15 to 17 minutes, until fork-tender. Drain potatoes in colander. Rinse under cold running water just until cooled to room temperature. Drain again.

2. Meanwhile, cook tomatoes in a nonstick skillet over medium-high heat 3 to 4 minutes or until thick; cool.

3. Combine tomatoes, onion, mayonnaise, vinegar, remaining 1 teaspoon salt and pepper in a food processor. Puree until smooth. Transfer to a medium bowl.

4. Set aside 1 tablespoon of the basil strips. Add potatoes and remaining basil to dressing. Toss to coat. Sprinkle top with reserved basil. Makes 6 servings.

Per serving: 270 calories, 15 g total fat, 2 g saturated fat, 11 mg cholesterol, 896 mg sodium, 31 g carbohydrates, 4 g protein, 30 mg calcium, 4 g fiber

wilted spinach with roasted potatoes and mushrooms

Love the traditional wilted spinach salad with bacon? Try this version with meaty shiitake mushrooms.

Prep time: 30 minutes • Roasting time: 20 to 25 minutes

- ¾ **pound small red potatoes, scrubbed, cut into 1-inch pieces**
- 2 **teaspoons plus 4 tablespoons olive oil, divided**
- 1 **teaspoon salt, divided**
- ½ **teaspoon freshly ground pepper, divided**
- 2 **tablespoons fresh lemon juice**
- 1 **teaspoon grated lemon peel**
- ¼ **teaspoon sugar**
- 8 **ounces white mushrooms, sliced**
- 4 **ounces shiitake mushrooms, stems removed, sliced**
- 2 **tablespoons minced shallots**
- 2 **bunches spinach, trimmed (about 1½ lbs.)**

1. Heat oven to 450°F. Place potatoes in a 9-inch square baking pan. Toss with 2 teaspoons of the oil, ¼ teaspoon of the salt and ¼ teaspoon of the pepper. Roast potatoes 20 to 25 minutes, turning occasionally, until tender and golden.

2. Meanwhile, for lemon dressing, whisk 2 tablespoons of the oil, lemon juice and peel, ½ teaspoon of the salt, remaining ¼ teaspoon pepper and sugar in a bowl; set aside.

3. Heat remaining 2 tablespoons oil in a large skillet over high heat. Add mushrooms, shallots and remaining ¼ teaspoon salt. Cook, stirring, until mushrooms are golden brown. Transfer to a bowl; add spinach.

4. Add lemon dressing to skillet. Cook over high heat until heated through, stirring to loosen any browned bits. Add hot dressing and roasted potatoes to spinach mixture. Toss and serve immediately. Makes 6 servings.

Per serving: 175 calories, 11 g total fat, 1.5 g saturated fat, 0 mg cholesterol, 439 mg sodium, 17 g carbohydrates, 5 g protein, 110 mg calcium, 4 g fiber

tarragon coleslaw salad

Fresh tarragon and orange juice add a flavor spike to this traditional picnic favorite, and white balsamic vinegar replaces the usual mayonnaise.

Total prep time: 30 minutes

- ⅓ **cup fresh orange juice**
- ¼ **cup white balsamic vinegar (or white wine vinegar with 1½ teaspoons sugar)**
- 3 **tablespoons olive oil**
- 2 **tablespoons chopped fresh tarragon**
- 2 **teaspoons salt**
- 1 **teaspoon sugar**
- ½ **teaspoon freshly ground pepper**
- 1 **head (3 lbs.) green cabbage, thinly sliced**
- 2 **cups shredded carrots**

Whisk together orange juice, vinegar, oil, tarragon, salt, sugar and pepper in a large bowl. Add cabbage and carrots; toss and serve. *(Can be made ahead. Cover and refrigerate up to 4 hours.)* Makes 10 cups.

Per ½ cup: 40 calories, 2 g total fat, 0 g saturated fat, 0 mg cholesterol, 249 mg sodium, 6 g carbohydrates, 1 g protein, 37 mg calcium, 2 g fiber

test kitchen tip
it's a wash

To clean spinach, soak leaves in a bowl of water to allow the grit to sink to the bottom. Drain and repeat until no grit is left in the bowl, then dry the leaves thoroughly in a salad spinner.

cranberry beans

White with wine-colored speckles, fresh cranberry beans are similar to pinto beans in shape, with a creamy texture and a wonderful nutty flavor. A popular summer bean eaten throughout the Mediterranean, they adapt easily to a wide variety of seasonings.

Prep time: 25 minutes • Cooking time: 67 to 69 minutes

- 1½ pounds fresh cranberry beans, shelled (2 cups)
- 3 tablespoons olive oil, divided
- 1 cup chopped onions
- 1 medium green bell pepper, chopped
- 1 small jalapeño chile, finely chopped (see tip, page 95)
- 1 large tomato (1 lb.), chopped
- 2 teaspoons sugar
- 1 teaspoon salt
- 1 tablespoon fresh lemon juice
- 1 tablespoon chopped fresh flat-leaf parsley
  Lemon wedges, for garnish (optional)

1. Bring beans and enough water to cover to boil in a 3-quart saucepan. Boil 5 minutes and drain in a colander. Set aside.

2. Wipe saucepan dry. Add 2 tablespoons of the oil and heat over medium-high heat. Add onions, bell pepper and jalapeño and cook 7 to 9 minutes, until vegetables are lightly browned. Add tomato; cover and cook 5 minutes. Add beans, just enough water to cover beans, sugar and salt. Cover and simmer 50 minutes or until beans are tender. Cool.

3. Stir remaining 1 tablespoon oil and the lemon juice into beans. Transfer to a serving dish and sprinkle with parsley. Serve at room temperature with lemon wedges, if desired. Makes 6 servings.

Per serving: 315 calories, 8 g total fat, 1 g saturated fat, 0 mg cholesterol, 401 mg sodium, 47 g carbohydrates, 16 g protein, 94 mg calcium, 8 g fiber

southern corn salad

Be sure to select bright green okra that is blemish free. See tip, page 119, for removing corn from the cob. Pictured on page 88.

Prep time: 20 minutes • Cooking time: 28 to 30 minutes

- 2 slices thick-cut bacon
- 2 tablespoons olive oil, divided
- 1 cup chopped onions
- 2 celery ribs, chopped
- ¼ teaspoon ground cumin
- ½ pound okra, sliced
- 1 cup cherry tomatoes, quartered
- ½ cup chicken broth
- 6 ears corn, kernels removed
- 1 tablespoon red wine vinegar
- ½ teaspoon salt
- ½ teaspoon freshly ground pepper

1. Cook bacon in a large nonstick skillet until crisp. Drain and crumble; discard drippings.

2. Heat 1 tablespoon of the oil in same skillet. Add onions and celery and cook until softened. Add cumin and cook 1 minute. Add okra and tomatoes; cook 5 minutes. Add broth and cook until okra is tender, 5 minutes. Transfer vegetables to a large serving bowl.

3. Heat remaining 1 tablespoon oil in skillet. Add half of the corn, increase heat to high, and cook, stirring, until lightly browned. Transfer corn with a slotted spoon to the bowl with vegetables. Repeat, cooking remaining corn.

4. Add vinegar, salt, pepper and bacon to corn mixture; stir to combine. Makes about 5 cups.

Per 1 cup: 215 calories, 9.5 g total fat, 2 g saturated fat, 4 mg cholesterol, 440 mg sodium, 31 g carbohydrates, 7 g protein, 56 mg calcium, 6 g fiber

corn and crab pudding

We've made an old-fashioned corn pudding extraordinary by adding fresh lump crabmeat that will delight with every spoonful. "Corn milk" is the hidden ingredient that makes this pudding extra creamy and luscious. It's made from pureeing fresh corn and then pressing the kernels to extract as much liquid as possible. Pictured on page 88.

Prep time: 15 minutes
Baking time: 1 hour 15 to 20 minutes

- 1 teaspoon plus 1 tablespoon butter
  or margarine, divided
- ¼ cup chopped shallots
- 6 ears corn, kernels removed (about 4 cups)
- 1 cup heavy or whipping cream
- 4 large eggs
- ¾ teaspoon hot red pepper sauce
- 2 tablespoons chopped fresh flat-leaf parsley
- ¾ teaspoon salt
- ½ pound fresh lump or jumbo or pasteurized
  canned crabmeat, picked over
- 1 tablespoon all-purpose flour
  Fresh chives (optional)

1. Heat oven to 350°F. Brush a 6-cup shallow baking dish with the 1 teaspoon butter. Place baking dish in a slightly larger roasting pan. Set aside.

2. Melt remaining 1 tablespoon butter in a small skillet over medium-low heat. Add shallots and cook until golden, 5 to 8 minutes. Set aside to cool.

3. Puree half of corn kernels (2 cups) in a food processor. Place a large sieve over a large bowl. Pour corn mixture into sieve and press with back of spoon to extract liquid from corn. Discard skins.

4. Whisk heavy cream, eggs, hot red pepper sauce, parsley and salt in bowl with corn liquid. Stir in shallots and remaining 2 cups corn kernels. Fold crabmeat and flour into mixture with a rubber spatula. Pour into prepared baking dish. Cover baking dish loosely with foil. Place baking dish in a roasting pan, making sure there is at least an inch of space between edges of pans. Pour enough hot water into roasting pan to come halfway up side of baking dish. Bake 1 hour and 5 minutes. Remove foil and bake 10 to 15 minutes more, until center of pudding is just set. Carefully remove pudding from hot water. Cool slightly. (Pudding will continue to cook while it stands.) Sprinkle top with chives, if desired. Serve warm. Makes 6 servings.

Per serving: 340 calories, 22 g total fat, 12 g saturated fat, 241 mg cholesterol, 472 mg sodium, 23 g carbohydrates, 16 g protein, 90 mg calcium, 3 g fiber

---

test kitchen tip

crazy for corn

Here are some tips for enjoying corn at its market-fresh best:

WHAT TO LOOK FOR: Fresh ears of corn should have bright green, tight-fitting husks and golden brown silk. Look for milky and plump kernels that reach all the way up to the tip of the ear, and the rows of kernels should not have any gaps. Corn is best consumed the day it's purchased.

CUTTING CORN OFF THE COB: Remove the husk and silk from an ear of corn. Cut off the top and bottom ends of the cob. Stand one ear of corn on its end on a cutting board, holding the ear near the top. With a large knife parallel to the cob, cut the kernels off with a sawing motion.

COOKING FRESH CORN ON THE COB: Remove the husks and silk from the ears of corn; rinse. Cook, covered, in enough boiling water to cover for 5 to 7 minutes, or until tender.

risi e bisi

Why say rice and peas when you can say it like the Italians—Risi e Bisi? This classic Venetian dish, similar to a risotto, makes a wonderful summertime meal. (Oh, by the way, it's pronounced "reesy-eh-beesy.") Pictured on page 86.

Prep time: 25 minutes • Cooking time: 28 minutes

- 2 **tablespoons olive oil**
- 2 **ounces sliced pancetta (Italian bacon), chopped**
- ½ **cup finely chopped onion**
- ⅓ **cup finely chopped celery**
- 1½ **cups arborio rice**
- 2 **cans (14½ oz. each) chicken broth**
- 2 **cups water**
- ¼ **teaspoon freshly ground pepper**
- 2 **cups fresh or frozen peas**
- ½ **cup finely shredded Parmesan cheese**
- 2 **tablespoons chopped fresh flat-leaf parsley**
- 1 **tablespoon butter**
  Parmesan cheese (optional)

1. Heat oil in a 6-quart Dutch oven over medium heat. Add pancetta, onion and celery. Cook, stirring, 5 minutes. Add rice and cook, stirring, 3 minutes.

2. Add broth, water and pepper; bring to boil. Reduce heat and simmer 10 minutes, stirring occasionally. Stir in peas. Simmer, 10 minutes more, stirring frequently, until peas and rice are tender.

3. Remove pan from heat. Stir in Parmesan cheese, parsley and butter. Cover and let stand 1 minute. Serve with additional Parmesan cheese, if desired. Makes 6 servings.

Per serving: 360 calories, 16 g total fat, 5.5 g saturated fat, 18 mg cholesterol, 829 mg sodium, 42 g carbohydrates, 11 g protein, 133 mg calcium, 5 g fiber

three-pea sauté

Fresh peas, sugar snaps and snow peas get a burst of flavor from orange peel. If you chop up everything ahead, the dish will be ready in less than 10 minutes. (If you're using frozen peas, start at Step 2, below.) Pictured on page 87.

Prep time: 15 minutes • Cooking time: 7 to 8 minutes

- ⅓ **cup water**
- 2 **cups fresh or frozen peas**
- 1 **tablespoon olive oil**
- 1 **cup (4 oz.) fresh sugar snap peas**
- 1 **cup (4 oz.) fresh snow peas**
- 1 **medium carrot, chopped**
- ½ **teaspoon grated orange peel**
- ¼ **teaspoon salt**
- ⅛ **teaspoon freshly ground pepper**

1. Boil water in a 12-inch nonstick skillet. Add fresh peas and cook over medium-high heat 2 to 3 minutes.

2. Add oil, frozen peas (if using), sugar snaps, snow peas, carrot, orange peel, salt and pepper.

3. Cook, stirring, until tender-crisp, 3 minutes (5 minutes if using frozen peas). Makes 6 servings.

Per serving: 155 calories, 3 g total fat, 0 g saturated fat, 0 mg cholesterol, 107 mg sodium, 25 g carbohydrates, 9 g protein, 56 mg calcium, 7 g fiber

---

test kitchen tip

peas, please

Whether you harvest peas at a farmers' market or the produce aisle, look for pea pods that snap crisply and are blemish-free. Shell green peas before using. For sugar snap peas, break off stem end and pull string away.

POD COUNT: For fresh green peas, remember that one pound of unshelled pods equals one cup shelled peas.

CHAMPION CHILI
WITH THE WORKS
pg. 136

gathering for good times

Whether it's a football Sunday bash for a bunch of buddies or a stylish soiree for six, it's always fun to get together with good friends over great food. With our hassle-free recipes and festive yet casual menus, you can enjoy your guests—and revel in their raves!

HALFTIME
MUSHROOM-AND-
PEPPER PIZZAS
pg. 132

ALL-PRO PASTA
WITH MEATBALLS
pg. 135

guests love options!

ALL-BEEF CHILI
pg. 134

FIRST YARDLINE
FRUIT SALAD
WITH TEQUILA
AND LIME
pg. 133

and **buffets** make

serving a crowd

easy on you

LINEBACKER
BROWNIES
pg. 137

TROUT WITH
PEPPER
SALAD
pg. 147

watch out!

colorful and

TOSSED GREENS
WITH BLUE CHEESE
DRESSING
pg. 130

BARBECUED BEEF
TENDERLOIN
pg. 140

BLACK-EYED PEA SALAD
pg. 151

ASIAN-STYLE GREEN
BEANS WITH CASHEWS
pg. 152

creative side dishes

might just

steal the show

TEN-LAYER
TOUCHDOWN SALAD
pg. 133

GRILLED TURKEY
BREAST WITH
PEPPERS AND CHILE
MAYONNAISE
pg. 138

CORN AND
ZUCCHINI SALAD
pg. 153

seasonally inspired
soups

SPRING PEA
SOUP
pg. 131

MATZO BALL
SOUP
pg. 131

THE ULTIMATE
SCALLOPED
POTATOES
pg. 154

and goof-proof
serve-alongs
complete the menu

PRIMAVERA
SOUP
pg. 132

the **perfect** brunch with friends makes **weekends** memorable

THE PERFECT
WAFFLES
pg. 160

mesclun salad with roasted pears

In this winter salad, pears are roasted to intensify their flavor. Select Bosc pears—they hold their shape best.

Prep time: 15 minutes • Roasting time: 30 minutes

- **3 tablespoons olive oil, divided**
- **4 large Bosc pears (2 lbs.), peeled, cored and sliced ¼ inch thick**
- **½ teaspoon kosher salt**
- **¼ teaspoon freshly ground pepper**

DRESSING:

- **¼ cup sherry vinegar**
- **1 tablespoon finely chopped shallots**
- **2 teaspoons honey**
- **½ teaspoon salt**
- **¼ teaspoon freshly ground pepper**
- **½ cup olive oil**

  ■

- **2 bags (10 to 12 oz. each) mesclun salad greens or spring salad mix**
- **6 ounces Roquefort or Saga blue cheese, crumbled**

1. Arrange oven racks on center and upper third of oven. Heat oven to 425°F. Line two large jelly-roll pans with foil; brush each with ½ tablespoon of the oil. Arrange pear slices in a single layer on prepared pans. Brush both sides of slices with remaining 2 tablespoons oil. Combine salt and pepper in a cup; sprinkle evenly over slices. Roast slices 30 minutes, switching pans between racks halfway through until pears are golden and edges are brown. Cool on pans on wire racks. *(Can be made ahead. Arrange in single layers in an airtight container. Cover and refrigerate up to 2 days. To serve, let stand at room temperature 1 hour.)*

2. *Make dressing:* Whisk together vinegar, shallots, honey, salt and pepper in a medium bowl. Gradually whisk in oil to blend. Makes ¾ cup. *(Can be made ahead. Cover and refrigerate up to 2 days. To serve, let stand at room temperature 1 hour.)*

3. Arrange greens in a large bowl. Add pear slices and cheese. Toss salad with ½ cup dressing. Serve with remaining ¼ cup dressing on the side. Serves 12.

Per serving: 220 calories, 17 g total fat, 4.5 g saturated fat, 13 mg cholesterol, 420 mg sodium, 14 g carbohydrates, 4 g protein, 126 mg calcium, 3 g fiber

sangria

Here's a quenching sipper to serve alongside spicy foods.

Total prep time: 15 minutes plus chilling

- **1 bottle (750 ml.) dry red wine (such as a hearty Burgundy)**
- **1 cup fresh orange juice**
- **½ cup fresh lime juice**
- **½ cup superfine sugar**
- **¼ cup Triple Sec (orange-flavored liqueur)**
- **2 oranges, sliced**
- **2 limes, sliced**

1. Combine all ingredients except sliced fruit in a large bowl or pitcher. Cover and refrigerate until well chilled, about 2 hours.

2. Fill a large pitcher with ice; add sliced fruit, then pour in sangria over fruit and ice. Makes 5 cups without ice.

Per 1 cup: 280 calories, 0.5 g total fat, 0 g saturated fat, 0 mg cholesterol, 10 mg sodium, 46 g carbohydrates, 2 g protein, 73 mg calcium, 1 g fiber

---

test kitchen tip
timing is everything

When planning a dinner party, allow time for a leisurely round of cocktails and hors d'oeuvres. It's best to serve dinner at least an hour later than the invitation indicates, but the "cocktail hour" should actually last no longer than an hour and a half—you don't want your guests to become famished while waiting for dinner.

tossed greens with blue cheese dressing

Serving a menu with hot and spicy flavors? For a contrast, try this salad—its buttermilk blue cheese dressing will help tame the heat. Pictured on page 124.

Total prep time: 15 minutes plus chilling

DRESSING:
- ¼ cup mayonnaise
- ¼ cup sour cream
- 1½ tablespoons cider vinegar
- 1½ tablespoons fresh lemon juice
- ¼ teaspoon hot red pepper sauce
- ¼ teaspoon minced garlic
- ¾ teaspoon salt
- ¼ teaspoon freshly ground pepper
- 1½ cups buttermilk
- 1 cup (6 oz.) crumbled Roquefort or blue cheese

- 1 large head chicory, torn
- 1 large head romaine lettuce, torn
- ¾ cup thinly sliced Vidalia or Spanish onion

1. *Make dressing:* Whisk together mayonnaise, sour cream, vinegar, lemon juice, hot red pepper sauce, garlic, salt and pepper in a bowl. Whisk in buttermilk; stir in cheese. *(Can be made ahead. Cover and refrigerate up to 6 hours.)*

2. Toss chicory, romaine and onion in a large bowl; add dressing and toss to coat. Serve immediately. Makes 8 to 10 servings.

Per serving: 170 calories, 12.5 g total fat, 5.5 g saturated fat, 25 mg cholesterol, 639 mg sodium, 7 g carbohydrates, 8 g protein, 238 mg calcium, 2 g fiber

vinaigrette dressing

Anyone who entertains needs a classic and reliable all-purpose vinaigrette. This is our perfected version. The secret? Lowering the proportion of vinegar to oil, and gradually whisking in the oil in a slow, steady stream to prevent it from separating. We also substitute chopped shallot for the more typical (and harsh) garlic.

Total prep time: 10 minutes

VINAIGRETTE:
- 2 tablespoons white wine vinegar
- 1 tablespoon red wine vinegar
- 1 tablespoon warm water
- 1 teaspoon finely chopped shallot
- 1 teaspoon Dijon mustard
- ½ teaspoon salt
- ¼ teaspoon freshly ground pepper
  Pinch sugar
- ½ cup olive oil

- 8 cups (8 oz.) assorted salad greens

1. *Make vinaigrette:* Whisk together all vinaigrette ingredients *except* oil in a medium bowl, until well combined. Slowly whisk in oil, until well blended. Makes ³/₄ cup. *(Can be made ahead. Cover and refrigerate up to 3 days.)*

2. Toss salad greens with ¹/₄ cup vinaigrette in a large serving bowl. (Reserve remaining vinaigrette for other salads.) Makes 6 servings.

Per serving: 170 calories, 18 g total fat, 2.5 g saturated fat, 0 mg cholesterol, 221 mg sodium, 2 g carbohydrates, 0 g protein, 17 mg calcium, 0 g fiber

spring pea soup

This snazzy soup is a snap to make. Just simmer water and fresh fennel for the broth, puree it with frozen peas and voilà—you've got an elegant first course. (Tip: If you don't have enough fennel stalks to make the broth, use part of the bulb.) Pictured on page 126.

Total prep time: 18 minutes plus chilling

- 1 large bulb fennel (¾ lb.), with stalks and fronds
- 4 cups water
- 1 package (10 oz.) frozen peas, thawed
- ¼ cup heavy or whipping cream
- 1 tablespoon Liquore di Limoni (lemon liqueur)
- 1 teaspoon minced shallot
- 1 teaspoon salt
- 1 tablespoon chopped fresh mint, for garnish (optional)

1. Coarsely chop enough stalks and fronds from fennel to equal 3 cups. (Reserve remaining fennel bulb.) Transfer stalks and fronds to a saucepan; add the 4 cups water and bring to boil. Simmer 10 minutes.

2. Cut ²/₃ cup matchstick-size strips from the fennel bulb.

3. Strain fennel broth; discard solids. Puree peas, cream, liqueur, shallot and salt in a blender. Add broth and blend until smooth. Strain soup through a sieve into a metal bowl. Place in a larger bowl and fill with ice and water to reach halfway up side of soup. Stir until soup is cold.

4. Divide soup among 5 serving bowls. Divide and top each serving with fennel strips. Garnish with mint, if desired. Makes 5 servings.

Per serving: 85 calories, 4.5 g total fat, 3 g saturated fat, 16 mg cholesterol, 566 mg sodium, 9 g carbohydrates, 3 g protein, 40 mg calcium, 0 g fiber

matzo ball soup

Treat guests to a home-style Old World soup. We trimmed the time by using prepared soup mix, and added fresh flavor to the matzo balls with chopped fresh dill. Pictured on page 126.

Prep time: 12 minutes • Cooking time: 15 to 18 minutes

- 2 large eggs
- 3 tablespoons vegetable oil, divided
- 1 package matzo ball mix (from a 5-oz. box)
- 1 medium onion, chopped
- 1 medium carrot, thinly sliced
- ½ cup thinly sliced celery
- 4 cans (14½ oz. each) chicken broth
  Pinch freshly ground pepper
- 1 tablespoon finely chopped fresh dill

1. Beat eggs and 2 tablespoons of the oil in a bowl with a fork; add matzo ball mix, stirring with fork until smooth. Refrigerate 10 minutes.

2. Heat remaining 1 tablespoon oil in a large saucepan over medium heat. Add onion, carrot and celery; cook 3 to 4 minutes, until tender. Add broth and pepper; bring to boil.

3. Stir dill into matzo mixture; shape by level tablespoons into 18 walnut-size balls, dropping each into hot broth during shaping. When broth returns to boil, reduce heat and simmer 15 to 18 minutes, until matzo balls have doubled in size and are cooked through. Makes 4 servings.

Per serving: 310 calories, 16 g total fat, 3 g saturated fat, 106 mg cholesterol, 3,355 mg sodium, 32 g carbohydrates, 9 g protein, 121 mg calcium, 4 g fiber

primavera soup

Primavera is Italian for spring, and true to its name, this light and pretty soup boasts the season's freshest flavors. Pictured on page 127.

Prep time: 15 minutes • Cooking time: 10 to 13 minutes

- 1 tablespoon butter (no substitutions)
- ⅓ cup minced shallots
- ½ cup diced carrots
- 1 small yellow squash, quartered and thinly sliced
- 2 cans (14½ oz. each) chicken broth
- 1 teaspoon chopped fresh thyme or tarragon
- ⅛ teaspoon freshly ground pepper
- ½ pound asparagus, trimmed and cut into ½-inch pieces
- 4 thin slices fresh lemon

Melt butter in a medium saucepan over medium-high heat. Add shallots and cook 3 minutes, until they begin to brown. Add carrots and squash; cook 3 to 4 minutes, until tender. Add broth, thyme and pepper; bring to boil. Add asparagus, reduce heat slightly and cook 3 to 5 minutes, until asparagus is tender. Divide soup among 4 serving bowls; top each with a lemon slice. Makes 4 servings.

Per serving: 80 calories, 4.5 g total fat, 2.5 g saturated fat, 8 mg cholesterol, 913 mg sodium, 8 g carbohydrates, 4 g protein, 31 mg calcium, 1 g fiber

halftime mushroom-and-pepper pizzas

Pizza perfecto! The topping is a combo of red bell peppers, shiitake mushrooms, green onions, tomatoes and three kinds of cheese. Pictured on page 121.

Prep time: 45 minutes plus rising • Baking time: 15 minutes

- 1 recipe Pizza Dough (page 33)
- 3 large portobello mushrooms
- 2 tablespoons olive oil
- 2 red bell peppers, sliced
- ½ pound shiitake mushrooms, stems removed
- 4 green onions, sliced
- ¼ teaspoon salt
- 2 tablespoons cornmeal
- 1 cup shredded mozzarella cheese
- 1 cup shredded Monterey Jack cheese with jalapeño chiles
- 3 plum tomatoes, thinly sliced
- ¼ teaspoon freshly ground pepper
- 3 tablespoons grated Parmesan cheese
- ¼ cup chopped fresh cilantro

1. Prepare pizza dough as directed.

2. Meanwhile, remove and discard stems from the portobello mushrooms; turn mushrooms top side down and remove dark gills with side of a spoon; discard gills. Slice mushroom caps. Set aside.

3. Heat oil over medium-high heat in a large nonstick skillet. Add bell peppers; cook 4 minutes, until softened. Add portobello and shiitake mushrooms; cook 5 to 7 minutes more, until softened and liquid evaporates. Stir in green onions and salt. Spread on a cookie sheet to cool.

4. Meanwhile, arrange oven racks in center and upper third of oven. Heat oven to 450°F. Grease two 14-inch pizza pans or large cookie sheets; sprinkle each pan with 1 tablespoon cornmeal. Divide pizza dough in half. On a lightly floured surface with a floured rolling pin, roll each piece into a 14-inch circle and place one on each prepared pan.

5. Combine mozzarella and Monterey Jack in a small bowl. Sprinkle dough circles with half the cheese. Divide mushroom mixture between pizzas. Sprinkle with remaining cheese mixture. Divide tomatoes, pepper and Parmesan cheese between pizzas. Bake 15 minutes, rotating pans halfway through, until cheese is browned and bubbly. Cool 5 minutes before serving. Sprinkle with cilantro. Cut into wedges. Makes 2 pies (8 slices per pie).

Per slice: 200 calories, 8.5 g total fat, 3 g saturated fat, 14 mg cholesterol, 279 mg sodium, 24 g carbohydrates, 7 g protein, 112 mg calcium, 1 g fiber

ten-layer
touchdown salad

If preparing ahead, cover the serving dish with damp paper towels to keep vegetables crisp. Pictured on page 125.

Total prep time: 40 minutes

DRESSING:

- 1   clove garlic, peeled
- ½   cup olive oil
- ¼   cup Dijon mustard
- ¼   cup water
- 2   tablespoons balsamic vinegar
- ½   teaspoon salt
- ½   teaspoon freshly ground pepper
- ½   cup fresh flat-leaf parsley leaves

- ½   pound sugar snap peas, strings removed
- 1   large head romaine lettuce, torn into bite-size pieces
- 2   large carrots, shredded
- 3   celery ribs, sliced
- 4   tomatoes, cut into chunks, or 2 pints cherry tomatoes, halved
- 1   medium cucumber, peeled, halved lengthwise and sliced
- 2   yellow bell peppers, diced
- 2   cups finely shredded red cabbage
- 1   bunch radishes, thinly sliced
- ½   cup chopped red onion
    Fresh flat-leaf parsley, for garnish (optional)

1. *Make dressing:* Press garlic through a garlic press. Puree garlic, oil, mustard, water, vinegar, salt and pepper in a blender until smooth. Add parsley and blend until chopped. Transfer to a bowl.

2. Bring a small pot of water to boil. Add sugar snap peas; cook 1 minute. Drain and rinse with cold water until cool; pat dry. In a large straight-sided glass bowl, layer lettuce, carrots, celery, tomatoes, cucumber, bell peppers, cabbage, sugar snap peas, radishes and onion. *(Can be made*

ahead. Cover and refrigerate salad and dressing separately up to 4 hours.) Garnish with parsley, if desired. Serve dressing on the side. Serves 12.

Per serving: 135 calories, 9.5 g total fat, 1 g saturated fat, 0 mg cholesterol, 245 mg sodium, 10 g carbohydrates, 3 g protein, 58 mg calcium, 3 g fiber

first yardline
fruit salad with
tequila and lime

This refreshing salad is pictured on page 123.

Prep time: 30 minutes plus chilling · Cooking time: 10 minutes

SYRUP:

- ¾   cup sugar
- ¼   cup water
- ¼   cup fresh lime juice
- 2   to 3 tablespoons tequila

- 3   cups fresh pineapple chunks
- 2   pints fresh strawberries, halved
- ½   pound green seedless grapes
- 2   pink grapefruits, sectioned
- 2   navel oranges, sectioned
- 4   kiwis, peeled and cut into chunks
- 2   ripe mangoes, peeled, seeded and cut into chunks
- 1   teaspoon grated lime peel

1. *Make syrup:* Bring sugar and water to boil in a small saucepan. Reduce heat and simmer until sugar dissolves, about 2 minutes. Remove from heat and stir in lime juice and tequila. Cool to room temperature; cover and refrigerate 2 hours, until cold.

2. Meanwhile, combine pineapple, strawberries, grapes, grapefruit, oranges, kiwis and mangoes in a large serving bowl; stir gently to combine. *(Can be made ahead. Refrigerate up to 2 hours.)* Just before serving, stir lime peel into syrup and drizzle syrup over fruit. Makes 10 servings (12 cups).

Per serving: 200 calories, 1 g total fat, 0 g saturated fat, 0 mg cholesterol, 4 mg sodium, 48 g carbohydrates, 2 g protein, 46 mg calcium, 5 g fiber

all-beef chili

Masa harina (a flour made from specially processed corn) thickens the chili and gives it a subtle roasted-corn flavor. Pictured on page 122.

Prep time: 20 minutes • Cooking time: 1 hour 15 minutes

- **3** **ancho chiles* (see tip, page 95)**
- **4** **teaspoons olive oil, divided**
- **2½** **pounds ground round (or 2 lbs. beef chuck shoulder, cut into ¾-inch cubes†)**
- **2** **cups chopped onions**
- **4** **cloves garlic, chopped**
- **1** **tablespoon cumin**
- **¾** **teaspoon salt**
- **2** **tablespoons chopped jalapeño chile (see tip, page 95)**
- **1** **tablespoon tomato paste**
- **2** **cans (14½ oz. each) chicken broth**
- **¼** **cup masa harina***
- **Sour cream, lime wedges, warm flour or corn tortillas, sliced green onions, red pepper flakes and shredded cheese (optional)**

1. Place anchos in a medium bowl; add enough hot water to cover. Let stand until softened, 15 to 20 minutes. Drain chiles; discard seeds and stems. Finely chop and set aside.

2. Meanwhile, heat 2 teaspoons of the oil in a medium Dutch oven over high heat. Brown half the beef, about 5 minutes. Transfer to a plate with a slotted spoon. Discard all but 2 teaspoons drippings, then brown remaining beef.

3. Discard drippings; wipe out bottom of pan with paper towels. Add remaining 2 teaspoons oil to Dutch oven. Cook onions, garlic, cumin and salt over medium heat until onions soften, 8 to 10 minutes. Stir in chopped anchos and jalapeño; cook 1 minute, until jalapeño softens. Add beef, tomato paste and broth. Add masa harina and stir well. Bring to boil. Reduce heat; cover and simmer 1 hour 15 minutes, until chili has thickened. Serve with sour cream, lime wedges, tortillas, green onions, red pepper flakes and shredded cheese, if desired. Makes 8 servings.

†*To make chili with cubed beef:* Follow directions above, *except* brown half the beef, 5 minutes. Transfer to a plate with a slotted spoon. Add *1 teaspoon olive oil* to drippings and brown remaining beef. Simmer chili, partially covered, 1½ to 2 hours, until beef is fork-tender.

**Note:* Can be found in ethnic section of supermarkets, or in Spanish or Latino specialty stores.

Per serving with ground beef: 365 calories, 23 g total fat, 8 g saturated fat, 87 mg cholesterol, 751 mg sodium, 11 g carbohydrates, 29 g protein, 40 mg calcium, 2.5 g fiber

Per serving with cubed beef: 245 calories, 11 g total fat, 3 g saturated fat, 69 mg cholesterol, 753 mg sodium, 11 g carbohydrates, 27 g protein, 40 mg calcium, 2.5 g fiber

all-pro pasta with meatballs

Baked pasta is a surefire crowd pleaser, especially when it's chock-full of spicy meatballs. Pictured on page 122.

Prep time: 1 hour • Baking time: 35 minutes

- 1½ **pounds lean ground beef**
- 1 **pound hot Italian sausage links, casings removed**
- 1 **clove garlic, peeled**
- 1 **box (10 oz.) frozen chopped spinach, thawed**
- ½ **cup plain dry bread crumbs**
- 1 **cup freshly grated Parmesan cheese, divided**
- 2 **large eggs**
- ½ **teaspoon salt**
- ½ **teaspoon freshly ground pepper**
- 6 **cups prepared marinara or pasta sauce**
- 1 **pound ziti**
- 1 **container (15 oz.) part-skim ricotta cheese**
- ½ **pound part-skim mozzarella cheese, cut into ½-inch cubes**
- 2 **tablespoons chopped fresh parsley**

1. Crumble ground beef and sausage into a large bowl. Press garlic through a garlic press. Add garlic to beef mixture with spinach (do not squeeze dry), bread crumbs, ½ cup of the Parmesan cheese, the eggs, salt and pepper. Mix and shape by rounded tablespoons into 5 dozen meatballs. Arrange meatballs on a cookie sheet.

2. Bring marinara or pasta sauce to a simmer, stirring occasionally, in a large Dutch oven. Carefully drop meatballs, one at a time, into sauce. Cover and simmer until meatballs are cooked through, 30 minutes, stirring occasionally to prevent meatballs from sticking. *(Can be made ahead. Transfer to a storage container. Cover and refrigerate up to 24 hours.)*

3. Meanwhile, heat oven to 375°F. Cook pasta according to package directions just until al dente, about 8 minutes. Drain. Transfer pasta to a shallow 4-quart baking dish. Add sauce and meatballs, then stir to combine. Cover dish loosely with foil and bake 20 minutes.

4. Combine ricotta and remaining ½ cup Parmesan cheese in a bowl. Uncover dish and sprinkle with mozzarella cheese; stir to combine. Spoon rounded tablespoonfuls of ricotta mixture over pasta. Cover loosely; bake 15 minutes more. Sprinkle with parsley. Makes 12 servings.

Per serving: 675 calories, 38 g total fat, 15 g saturated fat, 135 mg cholesterol, 1,681 mg sodium, 48 g carbohydrates, 37 g protein, 413 mg calcium, 4 g fiber

---

test kitchen tip

touchdown celebration planner

Follow this do-ahead timetable for the menu on page 134, and you won't miss the action on the day of the game.

UP TO 2 WEEKS AHEAD:
- Shop for all non-perishable items.

UP TO 1 DAY AHEAD:
- Shop for remaining ingredients.
- Make and refrigerate Quarterback Dip.
- Make and refrigerate meatballs for All-Pro Pasta with Meatballs.
- Make chocolate chip cookies (use your favorite recipe).

UP TO 4 HOURS AHEAD:
- Make and refrigerate Ten-Layer Touchdown Salad.

UP TO 2 HOURS AHEAD:
- Finish making All-Pro Pasta with Meatballs and keep warm while serving.

JUST BEFORE SERVING:
- Transfer Quarterback Dip to microwaveproof bowl and microwave on High 3 to 4 minutes, stirring once per minute until heated through.
- Make garlic bread (use your favorite recipe).

champion chili with the works

To tame the heat from the chipotle chile, serve the chili with sour cream, plain yogurt or shredded cheese. Pictured on page 121.

Prep time: 55 to 60 minutes • Cooking time: 1 hour

- 4 tablespoons olive oil, divided
- 1 large butternut squash (2½ lbs.), peeled, seeded and cut into ¾-inch chunks
- 3 medium onions, chopped
- 1 pound carrots, sliced
- 2 green bell peppers, coarsely chopped
- 1 package (10 oz.) frozen corn
- 2 tablespoons chili powder, divided
- 1 tablespoon cumin, divided
- 3 teaspoons salt, divided
- ½ teaspoon dried oregano
- 2 tablespoons minced garlic
- ½ teaspoon freshly ground pepper
- 2 cans (28 oz. each) plum tomatoes in juice
- 2 cans (12 oz. each) beer
- 1 chipotle chile in adobo,* minced (see tip, page 95)
- 1 can (15 to 16 oz.) black beans, drained and rinsed
- 1 can (15 to 16 oz.) kidney beans, drained and rinsed
- 1 can (15 to 16 oz.) pinto beans, drained and rinsed
- 1 large zucchini, diced
  Fresh thyme sprigs, for garnish (optional)

1. Adjust oven racks to center and upper third of oven. Heat oven to 425°F. Toss 2 tablespoons of the oil, the squash, onions, carrots, green peppers, corn and ½ teaspoon *each* of the chili powder, cumin and salt together in a large bowl. Divide and spread on 2 large jelly-roll pans. Roast 40 to 45 minutes, stirring vegetables and rotating pans halfway through roasting, until tender. Set aside.

2. Meanwhile, toast remaining chili powder, cumin, 2 teaspoons of the salt and the oregano in a nonstick skillet over medium heat, stirring constantly until spices are fragrant, about 2 minutes.

3. Heat remaining 2 tablespoons oil in a large Dutch oven over medium heat. Add garlic and cook, stirring, just until garlic begins to turn golden, about 1 minute. Stir in toasted spices and remaining ½ teaspoon salt and the pepper. Add tomatoes, beer and chipotle. Bring to boil, stirring to break up tomatoes. Add beans; return to boil. Reduce heat; cover and simmer 30 minutes, stirring frequently. Add roasted vegetables and zucchini; simmer 15 minutes more, stirring occasionally. Spoon into serving bowls; garnish with thyme, if desired. Makes 12 servings (18 cups).

*Note: Can be found in ethnic section of supermarkets, or in Spanish or Latino specialty stores.

Per serving: 245 calories, 6 g total fat, 0.5 g saturated fat, 0 mg cholesterol, 900 mg sodium, 43 g carbohydrates, 9 g protein, 135 mg calcium, 9 g fiber

go buffalo chicken wraps

These tortilla rolls pack all the great taste of the classic wings—chicken slathered in hot pepper sauce, served with crunchy celery and creamy blue cheese dressing.

Prep time: 40 minutes plus marinating
Broiling time: 6 to 8 minutes

- ½ cup hot red pepper sauce, divided
- 2 tablespoons olive oil
- 1 teaspoon minced garlic
- ¼ teaspoon freshly ground pepper, divided
- 2 pounds chicken tenders

DRESSING:
- ⅓ cup sour cream
- ⅓ cup mayonnaise
- ¾ cup crumbled Gorgonzola or other blue cheese
- 1 teaspoon fresh lemon juice

8 (10-inch) burrito-size flour tortillas

3 cups finely shredded iceberg lettuce

3 celery ribs, tough strings removed, cut into thin strips

1. Whisk ¼ cup of the pepper sauce, the oil, garlic and ⅛ teaspoon of the pepper in a large bowl until blended. Add chicken and toss to coat. Cover and marinate in the refrigerator 30 minutes.

2. *Make dressing:* Meanwhile, stir all dressing ingredients together in a small bowl.

3. Heat broiler. Place chicken on a jelly-roll pan in a single layer. Broil 6 to 8 minutes, turning once, until cooked through.

4. Spread each tortilla with 2 tablespoons dressing, leaving a 1½-inch border. Divide and arrange a line of lettuce, chicken and celery about 1 inch from the bottom edge of each tortilla. Combine remaining ¼ cup red pepper sauce and ⅛ teaspoon pepper in a small bowl; drizzle over celery. Tightly roll up tortillas; wrap in waxed paper. *(Can be made ahead. Refrigerate up to 2 hours.)* Cut in half through paper to serve. Makes 8 servings.

Per serving: 465 calories, 21.5 g total fat, 6 g saturated fat, 85 mg cholesterol, 948 mg sodium, 33 g carbohydrates, 34 g protein, 171 mg calcium, 2 g fiber

linebacker brownies

Decorate the top of brownies with chocolate candies while they are still hot. This way the candies won't fall off when the brownie is cut into bars. Pictured on page 123.

Prep time: 20 minutes plus chilling
Baking time: 25 to 30 minutes

8 ounces unsweetened chocolate squares

1 cup butter or margarine, softened

2½ cups sugar

8 large eggs

1 tablespoon vanilla extract

1½ cups all-purpose flour

¼ cup unsweetened cocoa

¼ teaspoon salt

8 foil-wrapped solid milk-chocolate candies

7 foil-wrapped solid milk- and white-chocolate candies

1. Melt chocolate squares according to package directions; cool. Meanwhile, heat oven to 325°F. Line a 15×10×1-inch jelly-roll pan with foil. Grease foil. Set aside.

2. Beat butter and sugar in a large mixer bowl at low speed until creamy, about 2 minutes. Beat in eggs, one at a time, until well mixed. Beat in cooled chocolate and vanilla. Stir in flour, cocoa and salt. Spoon batter into prepared pan and spread evenly.

3. Bake 25 to 30 minutes, until a toothpick inserted in center comes out with a few moist crumbs (toothpick should not be too wet).

4. Unwrap candies. Cut each in half lengthwise. Turn oven off. Remove pan from oven. Arrange candies on top of brownies, cut sides down, in 6 rows (5 candies across per row). Return brownies to turned-off oven; let stand 5 minutes. Completely cool brownies in pan on wire rack. Refrigerate 30 minutes. Cut into squares. *(Can be made ahead. Wrap well and freeze up to 2 weeks.)* Makes 30 brownies.

Per brownie: 220 calories, 12.5 g total fat, 7 g saturated fat, 74 mg cholesterol, 102 mg sodium, 26 g carbohydrates, 3 g protein, 21 mg calcium, 2 g fiber

test kitchen tip

clever cuts

Next time you make brownies or any bar cookies, try cutting them into different shapes for a change of pace.

TANTALIZING TRIANGLES:
Cut 2- or 2½-inch squares, then cut each one in half diagonally. Or, make rectangular bars and cut each one diagonally.

DELICIOUS DIAMONDS:
Cut parallel lines lengthwise to pan, then cut lines diagonally 1 to 1½ inches apart crosswise, making diamond shapes.

moroccan chicken

For a Mediterranean take on skillet chicken, quick-cook chicken thighs, then simmer with olives, spices, nuts and preserved lemon.

Prep time: 15 minutes • Cooking time: 28 to 30 minutes

8	chicken thighs, backbone removed if attached (2½ to 3 lbs.)
2	tablespoons grated onion
1	teaspoon grated fresh ginger
1	teaspoon chopped garlic
½	teaspoon salt
¼	cup pitted kalamata olives, coarsely chopped
2	tablespoons chopped preserved lemon*
2	tablespoons pine nuts (pignoli)
⅛	teaspoon red pepper flakes
⅔	cup chicken broth
2	teaspoons honey
1	tablespoon chopped fresh cilantro
	Flatbread (optional)

1. Heat a 12-inch nonstick skillet over medium-high heat. Add chicken, skin side down, and cook 8 minutes, turning once halfway through, until well browned. Transfer to a double layer of paper towels.

2. Discard all but 2 tablespoons drippings in skillet; reduce heat to medium. Add onion, ginger, garlic and salt and cook 1 minute, stirring, just until onion begins to brown. Add olives, preserved lemon, pine nuts and red pepper flakes; cook 1 minute. Add broth, honey and chicken; cover and simmer 10 minutes. Turn chicken and continue simmering, uncovered, 8 to 10 minutes more, until sauce is reduced and chicken is cooked through. Transfer to a platter and sprinkle with cilantro. Serve with flatbread, if desired. Makes 4 servings.

*Note: To make preserved lemons, bring *1 or 2 large lemons, rinsed and cut into eight wedges,* and *2 quarts of water* to boil in a large saucepan; boil 5 minutes. Drain. Bring *3 cups water, ½ cup sugar* and *2 tablespoons kosher salt* to boil in same saucepan, stirring to dissolve sugar and salt. Add precooked lemons; cover and simmer until lemon

is tender, 1 hour. *(Can be made ahead. Refrigerate up to two weeks.)* To use, drain and chop lemons.

Per serving: 330 calories, 15 g total fat, 3.5 g saturated fat, 98 mg cholesterol, 1,107 mg sodium, 21 g carbohydrates, 30 g protein, 41 mg calcium, 1 g fiber

grilled turkey breast with peppers and chile mayonnaise

Discover how great a whole turkey breast is to grill. The turkey is rubbed with a pasilla chile paste (which also flavors the mayonnaise), then grilled over indirect heat for an incredible smoky flavor. Tip: Buy a boneless, not skinless, turkey breast. The skin will help keep the turkey moist and juicy. Pictured on page 125.

Prep time: 45 minutes plus standing and marinating
Grilling time: 70 to 75 minutes

PASILLA PASTE:

1	package (2 oz.) pasilla chiles (see tip, page 95)*
3	tablespoons olive oil
½	cup chicken broth or water
¼	cup fresh cilantro leaves
1	tablespoon chopped garlic
1	tablespoon honey
1	teaspoon salt
1	whole boneless turkey breast (6 to 8 lbs.), halved
1	teaspoon salt

ROASTED PEPPERS:

2	poblano or Anaheim chiles, halved (see tip, page 95)
2	yellow bell peppers, halved
2	red bell peppers, halved
1	tablespoon olive oil
½	teaspoon salt
1	tablespoon olive oil

½ **cup mayonnaise**
2 **tablespoons fresh lime juice**
   Warm flour or corn tortillas

1. *Make pasilla paste:* Combine chiles in a bowl with hot water to cover by 2 to 3 inches. Let stand until softened, 15 to 20 minutes. Discard water. Remove seeds and stems. Puree chiles, oil and remaining pasilla paste ingredients in a blender or food processor.

2. Arrange turkey breast halves in a baking dish. Sprinkle with salt. Remove ½ cup of the pasilla paste to a small bowl and cover. Spread remaining paste over turkey breast halves. Cover and refrigerate turkey and paste overnight.

3. *Make roasted peppers:* Heat broiler. Line a broiler pan with foil. Place poblanos and bell peppers, cut side down, on prepared pan. Broil until skins are evenly charred, 8 to 15 minutes. Wrap in foil; cool 20 minutes. Peel and discard skins. Finely chop poblanos and peppers. Transfer to a medium bowl. Stir in oil and salt. *(Can be made ahead. Cover and refrigerate overnight.)*

4. Remove turkey, poblanos and peppers from refrigerator 30 minutes before grilling. Prepare grill for indirect grilling (see "Indirect Grilling," right).

5. Meanwhile, remove 1 tablespoon of the reserved ½ cup pasilla paste to a small bowl; stir in oil. Set aside. Combine remaining pasilla paste, mayonnaise and lime juice in a bowl. Cover and refrigerate.

6. Arrange turkey breasts, skin side up, on area of grill directly over drip pan. Cover and grill over medium fire (300°F. to 325°F.) 30 minutes; brush turkey halves with half the pasilla oil. Cover and grill 30 minutes. Brush with remaining pasilla oil. Cover and grill 10 to 15 minutes more, until an instant-read thermometer inserted in center of breast reaches 165°F. Transfer turkey to cutting board. Let stand 10 minutes. Serve turkey with pasilla mayonnaise, roasted poblanos and peppers and tortillas. Makes 8 to 10 servings.

*Note: Can be found in ethnic section of supermarkets, or in Spanish or Latino specialty stores.

Per serving: 710 calories, 38 g total fat, 8 g saturated fat, 206 mg cholesterol, 946 mg sodium, 10 g carbohydrates, 79 g protein, 76 mg calcium, 2 g fiber

---

test kitchen tip

indirect grilling

To grill larger pieces of meat, use this technique, called indirect grilling. Refer to your owner's manual for directions specific to your grill.

FOR GAS
Open the lid. Check that all burner control knobs are turned OFF and that there is plenty of fuel in the tank. Remove cooking grate. Place disposable foil drip pan over one burner (if you have a three-burner gas grill, place pan over center burner).* Replace cooking grate. Turn on the gas. Light grill according to manufacturer's instructions. Close lid; heat burners on High, until thermometer registers 500°F. to 550°F., about 10 to 15 minutes. Turn off burner under the drip pan. Reduce heat to medium or medium-low on remaining burner(s). Proceed as recipe directs. *Note: If there is not enough room between the heat source and the cooking grate for a drip pan, position a large disposable foil pan on top of the cooking grate over the unlit burner. Place a small rack inside the pan; arrange food on top of rack.

FOR CHARCOAL
Remove lid; open all vents. Remove cooking grate. Build two equal piles of charcoal (30 to 60 total, depending on grill size) opposite each other on charcoal grate near grate's edge. Ignite charcoal; burn 25 to 30 minutes, until coals are covered with a light coating of ash (if one side seems hotter than the other, use long-handled tongs to rearrange coals). Place a large foil pan in center of grate, between piles of coals. Replace cooking grate; place food over drip pan.

menu

best-of-the-beef barbecue

GOAT CHEESE WITH ANCHO CHILES
page 20

BARBECUED BEEF TENDERLOIN
below

TOSSED GREENS WITH BLUE CHEESE DRESSING
page 130

BLACK-EYED PEA SALAD
page 151

ASSORTED FRESH BERRIES

barbecued beef tenderloin

Our down-home tenderloin, served with a lip-smacking bourbon barbecue sauce, is a cinch. Pictured on page 124.

Prep time: 30 minutes plus standing
Grilling time: 60 to 65 minutes

BOURBON SAUCE:

- 3 tablespoons butter (no substitutions)
- 2 large shallots, minced
- ⅔ cup bourbon
- ½ cup ketchup
- ½ cup distilled white vinegar
- ⅓ cup pure maple syrup
- ⅓ cup unsulphured molasses
- 1 tablespoon Worcestershire sauce
- ½ teaspoon salt
- ½ teaspoon freshly ground pepper

DRY RUB:

- 2 tablespoons paprika
- 1 tablespoon sugar
- 1½ teaspoons chili powder

- 1 teaspoon salt
- ½ teaspoon freshly ground pepper
- 4 pounds center-cut beef tenderloin

1. *Make bourbon sauce:* Melt butter in a 2-quart saucepan over medium-high heat; add shallots and cook 4 minutes, until they begin to brown. Add remaining sauce ingredients; bring to boil, then reduce heat and simmer 20 minutes. *(Can be made ahead. Cover; refrigerate up to 2 days.)*

2. Heat grill.

3. *Make dry rub:* Combine all dry rub ingredients in a cup. Using your fingers, coat beef with rub.

4. Remove ⅔ cup of the bourbon sauce for basting. Cover and grill beef 30 minutes over direct heat, turning two or three times. Baste with sauce. Cover and grill 30 to 35 minutes more, turning occasionally, until an instant-read meat thermometer registers 135°F. Transfer to cutting board and let stand 10 to 15 minutes. (Internal temperature will increase to 140°F. to 145°F. for medium-rare.) Discard any basting sauce. Reheat remaining bourbon sauce in saucepan. Slice beef and arrange on platter. Transfer sauce to a serving bowl and serve with beef. Serves 8.

Per serving: 575 calories, 40 g total fat, 17 g saturated fat, 120 mg cholesterol, 764 mg sodium, 27 g carbohydrates, 28 g protein, 58 mg calcium, 0 g fiber

pepper-steak kebabs with mango salsa

Green peppercorns are soft, underripe pepper berries, usually pickled in brine.

Prep time: 20 minutes plus marinating
Grilling time: 10 to 12 minutes

- 2 tablespoons green peppercorns in brine, drained
- 1 teaspoon coarsely ground black pepper
- ½ teaspoon salt
- 1½ pounds flank steak, pounded ½ inch thick

MANGO SALSA:

- 2 ripe mangoes, seeded, peeled and diced
- ⅓ cup finely chopped red onion
- 2 tablespoons minced green bell pepper
- 2 tablespoons minced red bell pepper
- 1 tablespoon sugar
- 2 tablespoons white wine vinegar
- ⅛ teaspoon salt

 ■

- 3 to 4 lemons, cut into wedges
  Metal skewers
- 2 tablespoons extra-virgin olive oil

1. Finely chop green peppercorns; transfer to a bowl. Stir in black pepper and salt. Rub mixture on both sides of steak. Cover and marinate in the refrigerator 1 hour.

2. Meanwhile, prepare grill according to manufacturer's instructions for direct grilling. Remove steak from refrigerator 20 minutes before grilling.

3. *Make mango salsa:* Combine all salsa ingredients in a medium bowl. Makes 2¼ cups.

4. Slice steak into 1¹⁄₂×2-inch pieces. Alternately thread 2 or 3 pieces *each* of steak and lemon wedges on each of 6 skewers. Brush steak with oil. Grill 5 to 6 minutes per side, until desired doneness. Serve with mango salsa. Makes 6 servings.

Per serving: 285 calories, 15.5 g total fat, 5 g saturated fat, 57 mg cholesterol, 412 mg sodium, 15 g carbohydrates, 23 g protein, 17 mg calcium, 1 g fiber

provençal beef stew

This stew is sophisticated enough to serve to company. It has the wonderful flavors of the south of France—red wine, orange peel, rosemary and olives.

Prep time: 25 minutes plus marinating
Baking time: 2 to 2¹⁄₂ hours

- 2 pounds bottom round steak, cut into ¾-inch pieces
- 1½ cups chopped onions
- 1½ cups chopped carrots
- 1½ cups red wine
- 1 cup chopped celery
- 3 large sprigs fresh rosemary, leaves removed, or 2 teaspoons dried rosemary
- 3 cloves garlic, crushed
- ¼ cup brandy
- 4 tablespoons plus 2 teaspoons extra-virgin olive oil, divided
- 3 strips orange peel
- 1 can (14½ oz.) chicken broth
- 2 tablespoons all-purpose flour
- ½ cup oil-cured olives
  Chopped fresh flat-leaf parsley, for garnish (optional)
  Polenta (optional)

1. Combine beef, onions, carrots, wine, celery, rosemary, garlic, brandy and 3 tablespoons of the oil in a large glass bowl. Stir well. Cover and marinate in the refrigerator for 2 hours.

2. Heat oven to 350°F. Remove beef with tongs from marinade (reserve marinade). Pat dry with paper towels. Heat 1 tablespoon of the oil in a medium Dutch oven over medium heat. Brown half the beef on all sides. Transfer to a large plate. Repeat with remaining beef and drippings.

3. Pour vegetables and marinade through a strainer set over a large bowl. Heat remaining 2 teaspoons oil over medium-high heat in same Dutch oven. Add vegetables; cook until onions begin to soften, 3 minutes. Add beef, reserved marinade, orange peel and broth. Bring to boil. Cover and bake 1 hour. Uncover and sprinkle flour over top. Cover and bake 30 minutes. Stir in olives; cover and bake 30 to 60 minutes more, until meat is tender. Divide stew among 6 shallow dishes. Sprinkle parsley over each bowl and serve with polenta, if desired. Makes 6 servings.

Per serving: 505 calories, 36 g total fat, 10 g saturated fat, 97 mg cholesterol, 801 mg sodium, 12 g carbohydrates, 33 g protein, 54 mg calcium, 2 g fiber

southwest brisket with corn cakes

The brisket can be made a day ahead and reheated, but the corn cakes should be prepared shortly before serving.

Prep time: 30 minutes
Baking time: 2 hours to 2 hours 15 minutes

- 1 boneless beef brisket, flat cut (1¾ to 2 lbs.)
- ¾ teaspoon salt
- 2 teaspoons olive oil, divided
- 1 large onion, chopped
- 1 tablespoon chili powder
- 1 jar (12 oz.) chili sauce
- 1 can (12 oz.) beer
- 1 teaspoon chopped chipotle chile in adobo*
  (see tip, page 95)

CORN CAKES:

- 1 can (8 oz.) cream-style corn
- 1¼ cups all-purpose flour
- ¾ cup milk
- 1 large egg
- 3 tablespoons sugar
- 1½ teaspoons baking powder
- ¾ teaspoon salt
- 1 can (8 oz.) whole-kernel corn, drained and patted dry
- 2 tablespoons chopped fresh cilantro
- 4 teaspoons olive oil
  ▪

  Avocado, red onion and red bell pepper, for garnish (optional)

1. ▪ Heat oven to 325°F. Sprinkle brisket with salt. Heat 1 teaspoon of the oil in a heavy Dutch oven over medium-high heat. Brown beef, 1 to 2 minutes per side. Transfer to a plate. Reduce heat to medium. Add remaining 1 teaspoon oil and the onion; cook 4 to 5 minutes, until softened. Add chili powder; cook, stirring, 1 minute. Stir in chili sauce, beer and chipotle. Add brisket and bring mixture to boil. Cover and bake 2 hours to 2 hours 15 minutes, until beef is fork-tender.

2. ▪ *Make corn cakes:* About 15 minutes before brisket is done, process cream-style corn, flour, milk, egg, sugar, baking powder and salt in a food processor, just until smooth. Transfer to a medium bowl; stir in whole-kernel corn and cilantro. Heat 1 teaspoon of the oil in a 12-inch nonstick skillet over medium heat. Spoon batter into skillet by scant ¼ cupfuls, 1 inch apart. Cook 1½ minutes, until bubbles appear evenly over top; turn and cook 1 minute more. Transfer to a plate. Cover and keep warm. Repeat process 3 more times with remaining batter, using 1 teaspoon oil per batch.

3. ▪ Transfer brisket to a cutting board. Cut across the grain into ¼-inch-thick slices. Transfer to a serving platter with Corn Cakes. Spoon some sauce over brisket. Serve with remaining sauce and, if desired, garnish with avocado, onion and bell pepper. Makes 8 servings.

Note: Can be found in ethnic section of supermarkets, or in Spanish or Latino specialty stores.

Per serving: 575 calories, 33 g total fat, 12.5 g saturated fat, 108 mg cholesterol, 1,323 mg sodium, 45 g carbohydrates, 24 g protein, 113 mg calcium, 2 g fiber

perfect easter ham

Perfect to look at, even better to eat, this ham will make a great centerpiece for a spring holiday feast. Heating time depends on the size of the ham (roughly 15 minutes per pound), but this can vary, so check the label for cooking instructions.

Prep time: 15 minutes plus standing
Baking time: 1 hour 50 minutes to 2 hours 35 minutes

- ¼ cup packed brown sugar
- 2 teaspoons grated orange peel
- 2 teaspoons grated lemon peel
- ¾ teaspoon ground ginger
- ½ teaspoon cinnamon
- 1 fully cooked (6 to 9 lbs.) bone-in smoked ham, shank portion
- 1 tablespoon whole cloves

1 cup port wine

⅔ cup fresh orange juice

¼ cup fresh lemon juice

GLAZE:

⅓ cup apricot preserves

2 tablespoons port wine

■

2 teaspoons chopped chives

Fresh fruit, for garnish (optional)

1. Heat oven to 300°F.

2. Combine brown sugar, orange and lemon peels, ginger and cinnamon in a bowl.

3. Score top and sides of ham with a knife in a crisscross pattern. Pat with spice mixture and stud with cloves.

4. Combine port and orange and lemon juices in a 13×9-inch roasting pan. Place ham, scored side up, in pan. Bake 30 minutes. Cover ham loosely with foil. Bake 1 hour 15 minutes to 2 hours more, basting every 30 minutes, until an instant-read thermometer inserted in center of ham registers 135°F.

5. *Make glaze:* Meanwhile, press preserves through a strainer into a cup to equal ¼ cup; stir in port. Uncover ham; brush with glaze. Bake 5 minutes. Let stand 15 minutes.

6. Skim fat from pan juices. Combine 1 cup of the juices and the chives in a bowl. (If there are more than 1 cup juices, return to roasting pan and bring to boil over medium-high heat. Gently boil until liquid is reduced to 1 cup.)

7. *To serve:* Cut a few slices from underside of ham to form a level cutting surface. Transfer ham, cut side down, to a large cutting board. Holding ham steady with a fork, cut along top of bone to cut off a boneless wedge of ham. Place ham wedge, cut side down, on carving board and slice. Transfer slices to a serving platter. Turn ham thin side up and repeat. Serve with sauce. Garnish with fresh fruit, if desired. Makes 12 servings.

Per 3-oz. serving: 155 calories, 5 g total fat, 1.5 g saturated fat, 46 mg cholesterol, 1,052 mg sodium, 8 g carbohydrates, 18 g protein, 12 mg calcium, 0 g fiber

herbed pork roast

Sardinia, an island off the coast of Southern Italy that's famous for roast pork, serves as the inspiration for this recipe. Thinly sliced and served at room temperature, it's a great dish for a crowd.

Prep time: 15 minutes plus standing
Baking time: 1 hour 45 minutes

1 4-pound boneless pork roast, tied

1 tablespoon slivered garlic

1 tablespoon olive oil

1 teaspoon salt

¼ teaspoon freshly ground pepper

1 small bunch fresh rosemary

1 small bunch fresh sage

Rosemary and sage sprigs, for garnish (optional)

1. Heat oven to 350°F. With a small, sharp knife, cut slits into all sides of pork and insert slivers of garlic into each. Brush all sides of pork with oil; sprinkle with salt and pepper. Place rosemary and sage under the string all around the roast. Transfer pork to a small roasting pan. Roast pork 1 hour 45 minutes, until a meat thermometer inserted in center of pork reaches 155°F.

2. Transfer pork to a cutting board. Let stand 30 minutes before slicing. Serve warm or at room temperature. (*Can be made ahead. After roasting, immediately wrap and refrigerate overnight. Before serving, let stand 30 minutes at room temperature.*) Garnish with herbs, if desired. Makes 8 servings.

Per serving: 425 calories, 26 g total fat, 9 g saturated fat, 134 mg cholesterol, 379 mg sodium, 1 g carbohydrates, 45 g protein, 39 mg calcium, 0 g fiber

grilled pork chops

Wood chips add great flavor to grilled foods, as this recipe demonstrates. Tip: Before grilling, be sure to soak wood chips in water, so they won't burn too quickly.

Prep time: 5 minutes plus soaking
Grilling time: 20 to 30 minutes

- **2 cups apple or hickory wood chips**
- **4 loin pork chops with bone, 1 inch thick (about 2½ lbs.)**
- **½ teaspoon salt**
- **¼ teaspoon freshly ground pepper**
- **2 teaspoons butter or margarine (optional)**
  Sliced zucchini and yellow squash, cooked (optional)

1. Combine wood chips and enough cold water to cover in a large bowl. Let stand 30 minutes.

2. Meanwhile, remove pork chops from refrigerator and prepare grill for indirect grilling. *For gas:* Remove cooking grate. Place disposable foil drip pan over one burner (if you have a three-burner gas grill, place pan over center burner).* Replace grate. Drain wood chips; place chips in a small foil pan on cooking grate, but not over drip pan. Add ½ cup water to pan. Light grill; close lid. Heat burners on High, 500°F. to 550°F., 10 to 15 minutes. Turn off burner under drip pan. Reduce heat to medium or medium-low on remaining burner(s). *For charcoal:* Open all vents. Build two equal piles of charcoal (30 to 60 total, depending on grill size) opposite each other on bottom grate near the grate's edge. Ignite charcoal; burn 25 to 30 minutes, until coals are covered with a light coating of gray ash (if one side seems hotter than the other, use long-handled tongs to rearrange coals). Place a disposable foil drip pan in center of bottom grate, between the piles of coals. Drain wood chips; add 1 cup to each pile of hot coals. Replace cooking grate.

3. Oil grill. Sprinkle both sides of pork chops with salt and pepper. Place chops directly over coals (or over lit burner, if using gas grill). Grill 1½ minutes per side, until browned. Transfer chops to area of grill directly over drip pan (or, if using gas grill, over unlit burner). Cover and smoke over medium heat (300°F. to 325°F.) 20 to 30 minutes, turning chops once, until instant-read meat thermometer inserted in center of each chop registers 160°F. If desired, top each chop with ½ teaspoon butter and serve with sliced zucchini and yellow squash. Serves 4.

*Note: If there is not enough room between heat source and cooking grate for drip pan, see tip, page 139.

Per serving: 215 calories, 12 g total fat, 4 g saturated fat, 82 mg cholesterol, 329 mg sodium, 0 g carbohydrates, 26 g protein, 7 mg calcium, 0 g fiber

shrimp tamales

Our tamales are wonderful party fare because they freeze so well. Dried corn husks are the traditional wrapping, but you also can wrap the tamales in foil.

Prep time: 1 hour • Cooking time: 40 to 45 minutes

- **28 dried corn husks (3 to 4 oz.) or fourteen 9-inch pieces of foil**
- **1 cup chicken broth**
- **⅔ cup canned cream-style corn**
- **⅓ cup milk**
- **2 cups masa harina* (see tip, page 25)**
- **3 medium poblano chiles* (see tip, page 95)**
- **1 large red bell pepper**
- **1 tablespoon olive oil**
- **1 cup finely chopped onions**
- **1 tablespoon finely chopped garlic**
- **½ pound peeled and deveined uncooked shrimp, chopped**
- **½ cup lard, butter or shortening**
- **1½ teaspoons baking powder**
- **½ teaspoon salt**
- **½ teaspoon sugar**
- **1 cup coarsely grated Chihuahua,* Muenster or Monterey Jack cheese**
- **½ cup coarsely grated Queso Fresco* or crumbled mild feta cheese**
  Guacamole (page 24) (optional)

1. Cover corn husks with hot tap water in a shallow baking dish. Soak, turning occasionally, until softened, about 30 minutes.

2. Bring chicken broth, creamed corn and milk just to boil in a small saucepan over medium heat. Gradually add broth mixture to masa harina in a medium bowl, stirring with a wooden spoon, until well blended; cool.

3. Heat broiler. Line a broiler pan with foil. Arrange poblanos and bell pepper on prepared pan and broil 4 inches from heat 10 to 15 minutes, turning peppers until skins are evenly charred. Wrap in foil and let stand 15 minutes. Peel, seed and dice peppers; transfer to a medium bowl.

4. Heat oil in a large skillet over medium-high heat. Add onions and cook 2 to 3 minutes. Add garlic, reduce heat to medium and cook 1 minute more. Cool, then combine with peppers and the uncooked shrimp in a bowl.

5. Beat lard, baking powder, salt and sugar in a large mixer bowl, until smooth. Gradually beat in masa harina mixture by spoonfuls, beating well after each addition. Continue to beat 5 to 8 minutes more, until mixture is light and fluffy. Stir in shrimp mixture and the cheeses (mixture will be stiff).

6. Drain and rinse corn husks; keep covered with a damp towel (or follow foil directions below). Flatten one husk on work surface (overlapping two husks if small). Spoon $1/4$ cup filling in center of husk. Spread into a 3-inch log. Roll up lengthwise. Secure each end by tying up with string or a strip of husk. Repeat with remaining husks and filling. *To prepare tamales with foil:* Cut each foil piece in half to make two 6×9-inch rectangles. Spread $1/4$ cup filling in center of each rectangle. Fold all sides in to form 2×3$1/2$-inch packets. *(Can be made ahead. Place tamales in resealable plastic storage bags and refrigerate up to 24 hours.)*

7. Place steamer rack in a Dutch oven over 1 inch of water. Arrange tamales in rack. Cover; bring to boil. Reduce heat to low and steam 30 minutes. Serve with guacamole, if desired. Makes 28 tamales.

Note: Available in most Hispanic markets.

Per tamale: 110 calories, 6.5 g total fat, 3 g saturated fat, 22 mg cholesterol, 173 mg sodium, 10 g carbohydrates, 4 g protein, 81 mg calcium, 1 g fiber

shrimp and bean stew EASY

This hearty Italian-influenced stew with sausage, white beans and garlic will become a quick-to-cook favorite. Be careful not to overcook the shrimp or it will become tough.

Prep time: 18 minutes · Cooking time: 10 to 11 minutes

- 1 **pound medium shelled and deveined shrimp**
- ¼ **teaspoon salt**
- ¼ **teaspoon freshly ground pepper**
- 1 **tablespoon olive oil**
- ¼ **pound Italian sausage with casings removed, crumbled (about 3 sausages)**
- 1 **tablespoon chopped garlic**
- 2 **cans (15 to 19 oz. each) cannellini or small white beans, drained and rinsed twice**
- 1 **can (14½ oz.) chicken broth**
- 1 **medium tomato, diced**
- 1 **tablespoon thinly sliced fresh basil**
  French bread (optional)

Sprinkle shrimp with salt and pepper. Heat oil in a 12-inch nonstick skillet over high heat. Add shrimp and cook 1 minute per side, until pink. Transfer to a bowl. Reduce heat to medium-high and add sausage; cook 3 to 4 minutes until browned. Add garlic; cook 30 seconds. Add beans and broth; bring to boil. Add tomato and cook 5 minutes more. Return shrimp to skillet and stir in basil. Serve with bread, if desired. Makes 4 servings.

Per serving: 440 calories, 16.5 g total fat, 4 g saturated fat, 194 mg cholesterol, 1,259 mg sodium, 31 g carbohydrates, 41 g protein, 126 mg calcium, 10 g fiber

orecchiette with shrimp

In the coastal region of Apulia at the heel of Italy, a small ear-shaped pasta called orecchiette (oh-rayk-kee-EHT-tay) is popular. It's perfect tossed with tomato, cauliflower and grilled shrimp. Tip: We grilled the shrimp in their shells to keep them moist, flavorful and tender, then peeled them before serving.

Prep time: 20 minutes · Cooking time: 22 to 30 minutes

- **1 pound unshelled medium shrimp**
- **4 tablespoons extra-virgin olive oil, divided**
- **4 tablespoons chopped fresh basil, divided**
- **2 tablespoons fresh lemon juice**
  Salt
- **¼ teaspoon freshly ground pepper**
- **1 small head cauliflower, cut into florets**
- **1 pound orecchiette pasta**
- **1 cup chopped onions**
- **1 tablespoon chopped garlic**
- **2 cups chopped fresh tomatoes**
- **¼ teaspoon red pepper flakes**
- **1 tablespoon chopped fresh flat-leaf parsley**
  Additional olive oil (optional)

1. With a small, sharp knife, cut along curved side of each shrimp to the tail; remove vein and leave shells on. Combine shrimp, 2 tablespoons *each* of the oil and basil, the lemon juice, ¼ teaspoon salt and the pepper in a medium bowl. Cover; refrigerate.

2. Heat and oil grill. Bring 6 quarts water to boil in a large saucepot or Dutch oven. Add 1 tablespoon salt and the cauliflower. Cook cauliflower until just tender, 5 to 8 minutes. Transfer with a slotted spoon to a large bowl. Reserve water.

3. Grill shrimp until shells are lightly charred and shrimp are just cooked through, 3 minutes per side. Cool slightly and remove shells.

4. Return reserved water to boil. Add pasta and cook according to package directions.

5. Heat remaining 2 tablespoons oil in a large skillet over medium-high heat. Add onions and garlic; cook 5 minutes. Reduce heat; stir in tomatoes, cauliflower, remaining 2 tablespoons basil, ¼ teaspoon salt and the red pepper flakes. Cook until tomatoes have softened, 8 to 10 minutes.

6. Drain pasta. Toss cauliflower sauce and shrimp with hot pasta in a large serving bowl. Divide among 6 shallow bowls. Sprinkle top with parsley and, if desired, drizzle additional oil over pasta. Makes 6 servings.

Per serving: 460 calories, 12 g total fat, 2 g saturated fat, 93 mg cholesterol, 591 mg sodium, 65 g carbohydrates, 24 g protein, 73 mg calcium, 4 g fiber

mussels provençal

We bring the taste of Provence to your table with steamed mussels, tomatoes, white wine, fennel, thyme, garlic and saffron. Serve with crusty bread to soak up the broth.

Prep time: 15 minutes · Cooking time: 23 minutes

- **2 bags (2½ lbs. each) mussels, scrubbed and debearded (see note, page 22)**
- **1 cup chopped fresh tomatoes**
- **1 cup white wine**
- **2 tablespoons olive oil**
- **3 cups chopped fennel (no substitutions)**
- **1 cup chopped onions**
- **2 tablespoons chopped garlic**
- **1 tablespoon fresh thyme leaves**
- **½ teaspoon saffron threads**
  Sliced French bread

1. Combine mussels, tomatoes and wine in a large Dutch oven. Cover and cook over medium heat until mussels open, about 8 minutes.

2. Remove mussels with a slotted spoon to a large bowl. (Discard any unopened mussels and empty shells.) Strain mussel liquid through a large strainer lined with cheesecloth and set over a bowl. Set mussels and broth aside.

3. Heat oil in same Dutch oven over medium heat. Add fennel, onions, garlic and thyme. Cook until fennel softens, about 10 minutes. Stir in saffron, reserved liquid and mussels. Simmer

5 minutes, until heated through. Divide mussels and liquid among 6 shallow bowls. Serve with bread. Makes 6 servings.

Per serving: 190 calories, 7.5 g total fat, 1 g saturated fat, 31 mg cholesterol, 374 mg sodium, 11 g carbohydrates, 15 g protein, 73 mg calcium, 1 g fiber

trout with pepper salad

Fish with grilled peppers, served over spinach, makes for a delicious—and colorful—meal. Pictured on page 124.

Prep time: 18 minutes • Grilling time: 12 minutes

4	trout (12 oz. each), with heads removed
1	teaspoon salt
¼	teaspoon freshly ground pepper

PEPPER SALAD:

3	assorted bell peppers (red, yellow, green), seeded and quartered
	Olive oil
1	tablespoon capers, drained
6	large fresh basil leaves, thinly sliced
1	teaspoon finely chopped garlic
½	teaspoon salt
⅛	teaspoon freshly ground pepper

1	large (12 to 14 oz.) bunch fresh spinach
1	tablespoon olive oil
1	tablespoon fresh lemon juice

1. Heat and oil grill. Sprinkle skin and cavity of each trout with salt and pepper.

2. *Make pepper salad:* Toss peppers with 1 tablespoon oil. Grill 6 minutes per side, until charred and tender. Wrap peppers in foil; let stand 5 minutes. Remove peel from peppers, cut into strips and toss in a bowl with 1 tablespoon oil and the remaining pepper salad ingredients.

3. Meanwhile, grill trout 6 minutes per side, until fish turns opaque. Remove skin from each trout and discard.

4. Toss spinach with oil and lemon juice in a bowl; divide among 4 serving plates. Arrange fish on spinach; top each trout with pepper salad. Makes 4 servings.

Per serving: 305 calories, 19 g total fat, 3 g saturated fat, 69 mg cholesterol, 1,103 mg sodium, 8 g carbohydrates, 28 g protein, 152 mg calcium, 3 g fiber

test kitchen tip

selecting whole fish

Here are some general guidelines to help you determine the quality of whole fish.

ODOR
Fresh fish shouldn't have an odor (sniff underneath the gill). It should simply smell like the ocean.

APPEARANCE
The eyes of a fish should be clear and protruding. Its tail should not be curled up or dried out. Red bruises indicate that the fish was hurt when it was caught. A fish's gills should appear cherry-red, with no white slime, and the scales should be tight, not loose. A fresh fish also should have good sheen.

FEEL
Fresh fish should hang stiffly, as opposed to limply. Its skin should be firm.

ONCE HOME
Rinse fresh fish as soon as you get it home before storing. Store fish in a colander half-filled with ice, then pour additional ice over the fish and set the colander over a large bowl. Store it in the refrigerator until preparing. It's best consumed the day of purchase, since you can't be sure whether it was caught yesterday or a week ago. If you're certain the fish is fresh, it can be frozen. Wrap it well in freezer wrap and freeze fish no longer than 3 months.

mediterranean menu

PANINI WITH GRILLED MUSHROOMS
page 19

TUNA ESPAÑOL
below

ROASTED ASPARAGUS
page 115

SWEET RICOTTA PUFFS WITH PEACHES
page 223

tuna español

Called escabèche (es-keh-BEHSH) in Spain, this dish has roots in the era when cooked fish and meat were preserved in spiced vinegar broths.

Prep time: 30 minutes • Cooking time: 21 to 26 minutes

- **4 tuna steaks, ½ inch thick (about 1½ lbs.)**
- **2 teaspoons kosher salt**
- **4 tablespoons extra-virgin olive oil, divided**
- **¼ cup peeled garlic cloves**
- **2 tablespoons chopped fresh flat-leaf parsley**
- **½ teaspoon cumin seeds**
- **⅛ teaspoon salt**
- **3 medium Hungarian wax or banana peppers, cut into ½-inch-wide strips (see tip, page 95)**
- **3 small onions, cut into very thin wedges**
- **2 teaspoons chopped fresh thyme leaves**
- **1 teaspoon chopped fresh oregano**
- **½ teaspoon sweet paprika**
- **1 bay leaf**
- **8 black peppercorns**
- **½ cup clam juice**
- **1 tablespoon white wine vinegar**

1. Sprinkle tuna steaks on both sides with kosher salt; let stand 10 minutes at room temperature.

2. Meanwhile, heat 1 tablespoon of the oil in a 12-inch skillet over medium-low heat. Add garlic and cook 4 to 5 minutes, turning occasionally, stirring until tender and lightly browned. Remove garlic with a slotted spoon to a cutting board; finely chop with parsley, cumin and salt. Set aside.

3. Increase heat to medium-high; heat the oil that's left in the skillet until very hot. Add tuna and sear 30 seconds per side; transfer to a clean plate.

4. Add 1 tablespoon of the oil to the skillet; reduce heat to medium. Add peppers and onions and cook 5 to 6 minutes, until just tender.

5. Reduce heat to medium-low; add garlic mixture, remaining 2 tablespoons oil, the thyme, oregano, paprika, bay leaf, peppercorns, clam juice and vinegar. Cover and simmer 10 to 12 minutes until peppers are tender. Add tuna to skillet; cover and simmer 2 to 3 minutes. Remove from heat and spoon sauce over steaks. Cover and let stand 2 minutes more for medium-rare, 3 minutes for medium. Discard bay leaf. Serve warm or at room temperature. Makes 4 servings.

Per serving: 380 calories, 21 g total fat, 4 g saturated fat, 54 mg cholesterol, 1,260 mg sodium, 12 g carbohydrates, 35 g protein, 77 mg calcium, 2 g fiber

pasta with grilled vegetables

Tomatoes and eggplant star in this subtle, smoky dish. The ridges (rigati) in the penne help the sauce cling to it.

Prep time: 15 minutes plus standing
Grilling time: 8 to 9 minutes

- **1 pound penne rigati or fusilli**
- **1 eggplant (about 1 lb.)**
- **2 pounds ripe tomatoes**
- **1 tablespoon chopped garlic**

Olive oil

1 cup packed fresh basil leaves, thinly sliced

½ teaspoon salt

¼ teaspoon freshly ground pepper

1. Heat grill. Cook penne or fusilli according to package directions.

2. Slice eggplant ³/₄ inch thick. Cut tomatoes in half. Wrap garlic, drizzled with 1 teaspoon oil, in foil. Set aside. Place 2 tablespoons oil in a cup. Brush one side of eggplant slices and cut side of tomatoes with oil. Place eggplant and tomatoes on grill, oiled side down. Grill tomatoes 3 minutes and eggplant 4 minutes, until vegetables are softened. Add garlic packet and grill 2 to 3 minutes. Turn vegetables; brush with remaining oil in the cup. Grill tomatoes 2 to 3 minutes more and eggplant 4 to 5 minutes more, until charred. Unwrap garlic and transfer with vegetables to a bowl. Cover and cool 5 minutes.

3. Skin tomatoes and chop. Return to bowl with any accumulated juices. Cut eggplant into ¹/₂-inch pieces. Stir in eggplant, basil, 2 tablespoons oil, salt and pepper. Drain pasta. Add vegetables to pasta and toss to coat. Makes 4 to 6 servings.

Per serving: 510 calories, 14.5 g total fat, 2 g saturated fat, 0 mg cholesterol, 258 mg sodium, 83 g carbohydrates, 15 g protein, 114 mg calcium, 7 g fiber

asian grilled eggplant

Eggplants are not all the same. They vary in color and size. And, although they all are mildly flavored, Italian and baby eggplants have a very delicate flesh. Asian varieties are the sweetest and have few seeds and a thin skin. When buying eggplant, look for those that are heavy for their size, firm and have taut, glossy skin that's free of cuts and bruises. Look for a bright green stem.

Prep time: 10 minutes • Grilling time: 10 to 12 minutes

1½ pounds Asian eggplants,* stems removed

2 tablespoons plus 2 teaspoons rice wine vinegar, divided

2 tablespoons plus 1½ teaspoons lite soy sauce, divided

1 tablespoon white miso paste**

1 teaspoon grated fresh ginger

1 tablespoon vegetable oil

1 large bunch watercress, trimmed

3 medium carrots, grated

1. Heat and oil grill or grill pan.

2. Meanwhile, slice eggplants in half lengthwise. With a small knife, score small shallow X's into the flesh of the eggplants. (Do not cut all the way through skin of eggplants.)

3. Whisk together 2 tablespoons *each* rice wine vinegar and soy sauce, the miso paste and ginger in a bowl. Set aside.

4. Combine oil and 1 teaspoon of the soy sauce in a cup. Brush mixture on both sides of eggplants. Grill eggplants until softened and lightly charred, 5 to 6 minutes per side.

5. Divide watercress among 4 serving plates. Toss carrots and remaining 2 teaspoons rice wine vinegar and ¹/₂ teaspoon soy sauce in a bowl.

6. Arrange eggplant slices on watercress; spoon miso mixture over top. Garnish with carrots. Makes 4 servings.

For Italian or baby eggplant, prepare recipe as directed *except* cut each eggplant lengthwise into ¹/₄-inch-thick slices. Brush both sides of slices with *2 tablespoons vegetable oil* and *2 teaspoons lite soy sauce* and grill 5 minutes per side, until softened and lightly charred. Divide slices among 4 plates.

**Note: Can be found in ethnic sections of supermarkets, or in Asian specialty stores.

Per serving: 120 calories, 4 g total fat, 0.5 g saturated fat, 0 mg cholesterol, 581 mg sodium, 19 g carbohydrates, 5 g protein, 149 mg calcium, 3 g fiber

grilled eggplant and peppers with yogurt

The aroma of eggplant and peppers on the grill is commonplace in Turkey. Grilled vegetables are often served with a garlicky yogurt. Here we've added poblano chiles to the mix to give the dish some heat.

Prep time: 15 minutes plus chilling and standing
Grilling time: 20 to 25 minutes

- **2 cups plain low-fat yogurt**
- **1 teaspoon finely chopped garlic**
- **¾ teaspoon salt, divided**
- **4 tablespoons olive oil, divided**
- **2 pounds Asian eggplants (about 8)**
- **3 large red bell peppers**
- **4 poblano or Anaheim chiles (see tip, page 95)**
- **1 tablespoon finely chopped fresh thyme**

1. Heat grill.

2. Place a large sieve over a bowl; line sieve with a triple layer of paper towels. Spoon yogurt into sieve; refrigerate 40 minutes. Discard drained liquid in bowl. Transfer drained yogurt to a small bowl; stir in garlic and ¼ teaspoon of the salt. Refrigerate.

3. Meanwhile, combine 3 tablespoons of the oil and the remaining ½ teaspoon salt in a bowl. Cut eggplants into long, ¾-inch-thick diagonal slices. Toss with oil mixture. Brush bell peppers with remaining 1 tablespoon oil.

4. Grill bell peppers over medium-high heat 20 to 25 minutes, turning as they blacken. After 10 minutes, add eggplant slices and poblanos to grill. Grill eggplant 10 to 12 minutes, turning occasionally, until tender; transfer to a large platter and cover with foil. Grill poblanos 8 to 10 minutes, turning as they blister and lightly blacken. Place all peppers and poblanos in a bowl. Cover tightly and let stand until cool.

5. Peel and seed bell peppers and poblanos; cut bell peppers in thick strips and poblanos into thin strips. Arrange on a platter, overlapping eggplant slices and bell pepper and poblano strips. Sprinkle thyme evenly over top. Spoon some yogurt sauce over vegetables and serve remaining sauce on the side. Makes 6 servings.

Per serving: 205 calories, 10.5 g total fat, 2 g saturated fat, 5 mg cholesterol, 355 mg sodium, 24 g carbohydrates, 7 g protein, 210 mg calcium, 4 g fiber

almond rice pilaf *EASY*

Here's the little black dress of side dishes—it goes with just about anything. And, there's no need to rush it to the table once it's finished. Covered, it can stand and stay hot for up to 20 minutes. For a crowd, simply double the ingredients.

Prep time: 10 minutes plus standing
Cooking time: 26 to 27 minutes

- **¼ cup sliced almonds**
- **1 tablespoon olive oil**
- **1 tablespoon butter (no substitutions)**
- **1 cup chopped onions**
- **1 tablespoon chopped garlic**
- **1½ cups long-grain rice**
- **1 can (14½ oz.) chicken broth plus enough water to equal 3 cups**
- **½ bay leaf**
- **1 tablespoon chopped fresh thyme or ½ teaspoon dried thyme**
- **2 tablespoons chopped fresh flat-leaf parsley**

1. Toast almonds over medium heat in a small skillet, stirring often, until golden brown, 2 to 3 minutes. Remove from heat and set aside.

2. Heat oil and butter in a Dutch oven over medium heat until butter melts. Add onions and cook, stirring, until golden, about 8 minutes. Stir in garlic and cook 1 minute more.

3. Stir in the rice until the grains are coated with oil and mixed with the onions. Add the broth, water and bay leaf and bring to boil; stir once. Reduce heat to low; cover pan tightly and cook rice 15 minutes. (Do not stir rice.)

4. Stir in thyme and parsley. Remove rice from heat and let stand, covered, 10 minutes. Discard bay leaf; spoon rice into a serving bowl and sprinkle with almonds. Makes 4 servings. (This recipe can be doubled.)

Per serving: 375 calories, 10.5 g total fat, 3 g saturated fat, 8 mg cholesterol, 474 mg sodium, 62 g carbohydrates, 7 g protein, 54 mg calcium, 2 g fiber

black-eyed pea salad EASY

Greens and black-eyed peas are often served hot, but our simple salad is a delicious twist. And thanks to the frozen black-eyed peas, it takes only minutes to prepare. Pictured on page 124.

Prep time: 15 minutes • Cooking time: 5 to 6 minutes

- 5 **tablespoons olive oil, divided**
- 1 **teaspoon finely chopped garlic**
- ½ **teaspoon cumin seeds**
- 1 **bunch (about 1 lb.) mustard greens or Swiss chard, trimmed and chopped**
- 3 **tablespoons red wine vinegar**
- 1 **teaspoon salt**
- ¼ **teaspoon freshly ground pepper**
- 1 **medium red bell pepper, diced**
- 1 **medium yellow bell pepper, diced**
- 2 **packages (10 oz. each) frozen black-eyed peas, cooked according to package directions and drained**

1. Heat 1 tablespoon of the oil in a large nonstick skillet over medium-high heat. Add garlic and cumin; cook 30 seconds. Add mustard greens and cook 1 minute, stirring, until wilted. Reduce heat and cook 3 to 4 minutes more (5 minutes for Swiss chard), until tender.

2. Combine remaining 4 tablespoons oil, the vinegar, salt, pepper and bell peppers in a bowl. Add black-eyed peas and mustard greens; toss.

(Can be made ahead. Cover and refrigerate up to 4 hours.) Makes 6 servings.

Per serving: 255 calories, 12 g total fat, 1.5 g saturated fat, 0 mg cholesterol, 413 mg sodium, 29 g carbohydrates, 11 g protein, 104 mg calcium, 6 g fiber

---

`test kitchen tip`

the best baked potato

Your favorite steak house may wrap potatoes in foil for baking, but, take it from us, cooking them that way is a major no-no. The covering traps moisture and steam, which continues to cook the potato; the result is soggy skin and boiled-potato-like texture. (Restaurants prepare potatoes this way because they cook them in advance and need them to stay hot.) Foil-wrapped potatoes also can be a health hazard. According to the Centers for Disease Control and Prevention, foil-wrapped potatoes provide the oxygen-free environment that toxins such as botulinum, which can live on the potato skin, need to grow. Here's the best way to bake a spud:

ARRANGE oven rack in center of oven. Heat oven to 425°F.

SCRUB four russet potatoes (8 oz. each), being careful not to break the skin. Pierce all sides with a fork.

ARRANGE potatoes 2 inches apart directly on oven rack. Bake 45 minutes, until a small knife easily pierces the center of each potato. Cut an "X" in the top of each potato and push ends to open. Sprinkle with salt and pepper and serve with butter, olive oil or sour cream, if desired.

asian-style green beans with cashews (EASY)

Tender-crisp beans tossed in a lemon-ginger vinaigrette make for the simplest of summer-fresh salads. Pictured on page 125.

Prep time: 15 minutes • Cooking time: 7 minutes

- **2 pounds green beans, trimmed**
- **3 tablespoons rice wine vinegar**
- **2 tablespoons vegetable oil**
- **1 teaspoon grated fresh ginger**
- **1 teaspoon salt**
- **¼ teaspoon sugar**
- **¼ teaspoon grated lemon peel**
- **⅔ cup sliced green onions**
- **½ cup chopped roasted cashews, divided**

1. Bring a large saucepan filled two-thirds with water to boil; add beans. Cook beans until just tender, about 7 minutes. Drain in a colander under cold running water.

2. Meanwhile, combine vinegar, oil, ginger, salt, sugar and lemon peel in a large bowl. Add beans, green onions and ¼ cup of the cashews; toss well and transfer to a serving bowl. Sprinkle top with remaining ¼ cup cashews. Serve immediately. Makes 6 cups.

Per ½ cup: 75 calories, 5 g total fat, 1 g saturated fat, 0 mg cholesterol, 233 mg sodium, 7 g carbohydrates, 2 g protein, 31 mg calcium, 2 g fiber

green beans with cilantro (EASY)

These lemony green beans make a great accompaniment to the Mediterranean-inspired dishes in this chapter, including Moroccan Chicken (page 138), Herbed Pork Roast (page 143) and Tuna Español (page 148).

Prep time: 20 minutes plus chilling
Cooking time: 7 to 8 minutes

- **2 pounds green beans, trimmed**
- **3 tablespoons extra-virgin olive oil, divided**
- **3 tablespoons chopped fresh cilantro**
- **1 teaspoon minced garlic**
- **¾ teaspoon salt**
- **1½ tablespoons white wine vinegar**
- **1 tablespoon fresh lemon juice**
  Sliced lemon, for garnish (optional)

1. Place a large steamer basket in a large saucepot; add water to fill to just under the basket. Bring water to boil. Add green beans to basket; cover and steam 7 to 8 minutes, until beans are tender.

2. Meanwhile, combine 2 tablespoons of the oil, the cilantro, garlic and salt in a large serving bowl. Add hot beans and toss. Cool, cover and refrigerate for 2 hours. *(Can be made ahead. Refrigerate up to 24 hours.)*

3. Combine remaining 1 tablespoon oil, the vinegar and lemon juice in a cup. Just before serving, add vinegar mixture to beans and toss to coat. Garnish with lemon slices, if desired. Serves 6.

Per serving: 105 calories, 7 g total fat, 1 g saturated fat, 0 mg cholesterol, 299 mg sodium, 10 g carbohydrates, 2.5 g protein, 51 mg calcium, 2 g fiber

corn and zucchini salad

Searing the corn and zucchini in a skillet over high heat gives them a great roasted taste. Pictured on page 125.

Prep time: 20 minutes • Cooking time: 23 to 29 minutes

- ¼ **pound fully cooked chorizo sausage, chopped**
- 1 **tablespoon olive oil**
- 6 **ears corn, kernels removed (4 cups)**
- 1 **tablespoon garlic, chopped**
- 1 **teaspoon chipotle chile in adobo,* finely chopped (see tip, page 95)**
- 2 **medium zucchini, cut in half crosswise**
- 1 **tablespoon fresh lime juice**
- ½ **teaspoon salt**

1. Heat a large nonstick skillet over medium-high heat, 2 minutes. Add chorizo and cook until edges begin to brown. Remove with a slotted spoon to a large serving bowl. Add oil and half the corn to the skillet. Cook, stirring often, until corn begins to brown on edges, 5 to 7 minutes. Transfer to bowl with chorizo. Repeat with remaining corn, garlic and the chipotle.

2. In the same skillet, cook zucchini until it begins to brown, 8 to 10 minutes. Transfer to a cutting board; cool, then dice. Stir into corn mixture with lime juice and salt. Makes 6 cups.

**Note:* Can be found in ethnic section of supermarkets, or in Spanish or Latino specialty stores.

Per ½ cup: 105 calories, 5 g total fat, 1.5 g saturated fat, 8 mg cholesterol, 226 mg sodium, 11 g carbohydrates, 4 g protein, 8 mg calcium, 2 g fiber

tabbouleh salad

Tabbouleh (tuh-BOO-luh) is a salad prepared with bulgur (parboiled and ground wheat) combined with tomatoes, green onions, parsley, mint, olive oil and lemon juice. Use peak-season red and yellow cherry tomatoes for delicious results.

Prep time: 30 minutes plus soaking and chilling

- 1½ **cups bulgur**
- 3 **cups boiling water**
- ¼ **cup olive oil**
- ¼ **cup fresh lemon juice**
- ¾ **teaspoon salt**
- ¼ **teaspoon ground red pepper**
  Pinch allspice
- 1 **cup red cherry tomatoes, halved**
- 1 **cup yellow cherry tomatoes, halved**
- ¾ **cup peeled, seeded and finely chopped cucumber**
- ¾ **cup fresh mint leaves, chopped**
- ½ **cup chopped green onions**
- ¼ **cup fresh parsley leaves, chopped**

1. Place bulgur in a large bowl and cover with the boiling water. Soak 30 minutes. Drain in a fine sieve lined with cheesecloth. Press out excess water with a spoon.

2. Whisk together oil, lemon juice, salt, red pepper and allspice in a large bowl. Add bulgur and remaining ingredients. Toss. Cover and refrigerate several hours. Makes 6 servings.

Per serving: 220 calories, 9.5 g total fat, 1.5 g saturated fat, 0 mg cholesterol, 307 mg sodium, 31 g carbohydrates, 5 g protein, 50 mg calcium, 8 g fiber

grilled red onions with watercress *EASY*

Wedges of onions are grilled until smoky and sweet, then chopped and tossed with watercress and a sherry vinaigrette.

Prep time: 15 minutes • Grilling time: 15 to 18 minutes

- **2 large red onions (1½ lbs.)**
- **1 tablespoon olive oil**
-    **Pinch cumin**

DRESSING:
- **2 tablespoons sherry vinegar**
- **¼ teaspoon cumin**
- **¼ teaspoon salt**
- **¼ cup olive oil**
  - ■
- **2 large bunches watercress, ends trimmed**

1. ■ Heat grill.

2. ■ Cut each onion into 1-inch-thick wedges, being sure to include part of the stem end in each wedge.

3. ■ Grill onions over medium coals 5 minutes per side. Press tops lightly with metal spatula to fan onions slightly; grill until outer wedges are charred and inner wedges are softened, 5 to 8 minutes. Cool 5 minutes. Remove tough outer layers. Coarsely chop onions and transfer to a bowl; toss with oil and the pinch of cumin.

4. ■ *Make dressing:* Whisk vinegar, the ¼ teaspoon cumin and the salt in a large bowl. Slowly whisk in oil until blended.

5. ■ Toss watercress with dressing; arrange on a large serving platter. Spoon onions on top. Serves 8.

Per serving: 115 calories, 8.5 g total fat, 1 g saturated fat, 0 mg cholesterol, 104 mg sodium, 9 g carbohydrates, 3 g protein, 93 mg calcium, 3 g fiber

the ultimate scalloped potatoes *EASY*

Have you given up on making scalloped potatoes because the dish always curdles? We've studied the problem, and found that the solution is in the ingredients. Use russet potatoes, which have a high starch content, to help the dish thicken properly. And call on heavy cream—not milk or half-and-half—to help prevent curdling. Another tip: Because potatoes can darken once sliced, prepare this dish right before you plan to bake it. And don't parboil or let the sliced potatoes stand in cold water before baking; doing so will make the dish watery. Pictured on page 127.

Prep time: 15 minutes • Baking time: 60 to 70 minutes

- **1 teaspoon butter or margarine, softened**
- **1 large clove garlic, peeled**
- **1 cup heavy or whipping cream**
- **⅓ cup milk**
- **1 teaspoon salt**
- **⅛ teaspoon freshly ground pepper**
- **2 pounds russet potatoes, peeled and sliced ⅛ inch thick**
- **1 cup coarsely shredded Gruyère cheese**
- **¼ cup finely shredded Parmesan cheese**

1. ■ Heat oven to 350°F. Butter a shallow 2-quart baking dish. Lightly crush garlic with the side of a knife. Heat cream, milk, garlic, salt and pepper in a small saucepan over medium-high heat, until small bubbles appear around edge of pan; remove from heat and let stand 10 minutes.

2. ■ Meanwhile, pat potato slices with paper towels. Arrange half the potatoes, overlapping slices, along bottom of the prepared dish. Pour half the cream mixture over the potatoes, then sprinkle with half the cheeses. Repeat with remaining potatoes, cream mixture and cheeses. Bake 60 to 70 minutes, until top is a deep brown and potatoes are tender when pierced with a knife. Makes 6 servings.

Per serving: 365 calories, 24 g total fat, 14.5 g saturated fat, 84 mg cholesterol, 573 mg sodium, 27 g carbohydrates, 11 g protein, 291 mg calcium, 2 g fiber

vanilla cheesecake

There's just something about a rich, creamy cheesecake that never fails to dazzle guests.

Prep time: 20 minutes plus standing and chilling
Baking time: 1 hour

CRUST:

- 1¼ cups graham-cracker crumbs
- ¼ cup sugar
- 3 tablespoons whole blanched almonds, toasted and finely ground
- 5 tablespoons butter or margarine, melted

FILLING:

- 1 vanilla bean, split, or 2 teaspoons vanilla extract
- 4 packages (8 oz. each) cream cheese, softened
- 1½ cups sugar
- 4 large eggs, at room temperature
- ⅓ cup sour cream
- Whole and sliced fresh strawberries, for garnish (optional)

1. Heat oven to 350°F.

2. *Make crust:* Combine graham-cracker crumbs, sugar, almonds and butter in a bowl until crumbs are evenly moistened. Press mixture into bottom of a 9-inch springform pan. Bake until golden brown, 10 minutes. Cool on a wire rack. Wrap bottom and side of pan with heavy-duty foil. Set aside.

3. *Make filling:* Reduce oven temperature to 325°F. Remove seeds from vanilla bean with tip of a small paring knife or spoon; set seeds aside. (Place bean in a canister with granulated or confectioners' sugar to make vanilla sugar, if desired.) Beat cream cheese in a mixer bowl on medium-high speed, 3 minutes. Scrape side of bowl with a rubber spatula. Beat in vanilla seeds. Gradually beat in sugar, scraping side of mixer bowl with a rubber spatula. Add eggs, one at a time, beating just until blended and mixture is completely smooth. Stir in sour cream and vanilla extract, if using. Pour filling into prepared pan. Place pan in a larger roasting pan and carefully add enough hot water to come halfway up side of springform pan.

4. Bake 1 hour. Turn oven off. Let cheesecake stand in oven 1 hour (do not open door). Remove from water bath and cool on wire rack 1 hour. Cover cheesecake and refrigerate 6 hours or overnight.

5. Remove ring from pan. Transfer cake to a flat serving plate. If desired, garnish top of cake with whole strawberries, and serve with sliced strawberries. Makes 12 servings.

Per serving: 525 calories, 36 g total fat, 21 g saturated fat, 170 mg cholesterol, 372 mg sodium, 41 g carbohydrates, 9 g protein, 84 mg calcium, 1 g fiber

---

test kitchen tip

no cracks about this cheesecake!

We've found the formula for a crack-free cheesecake:

USE A WATER BATH. This provides uniform heat, which is important, since temperature fluctuations are common inside and outside the oven. Thanks to the moist heat, this will result in a rich and creamy texture.

PRO TIP: Wrap the springform pan with double-thick, heavy-duty foil to make it watertight. Be careful not to spill any of the hot water into the batter when adding it to the roasting pan for the hot-water bath; use a teapot or a large liquid measure.

flan

Here's a luxuriously rich way to end a dinner party.

Prep time: 20 minutes plus chilling
Baking time: 60 to 65 minutes

- 1¼ **cups sugar, divided**
- 1½ **cups milk**
- ½ **cup heavy or whipping cream**
- 1 **Mexican cinnamon stick (canela) or**
  - 1 **cinnamon stick**
- 4 **large eggs**
- 1 **teaspoon vanilla extract**
  - **Pinch salt**

1. Heat oven to 325°F.

2. Melt ½ cup of the sugar in a small saucepan over medium heat, swirling pan occasionally, until sugar is amber in color, 10 minutes (do not stir). Pour caramel into the bottom of a 5-cup soufflé dish.

3. Bring milk, cream, remaining ¾ cup sugar and cinnamon stick to boil in a small saucepan over medium heat. Remove from heat, cover and let stand 10 minutes.

4. Meanwhile, whisk together eggs, vanilla and salt in a large bowl. Strain milk mixture through a sieve into eggs; whisk to combine. Discard cinnamon stick. Strain mixture again into prepared dish. Place dish in a roasting pan, making sure there is at least one inch of space between the edge of the dish and the pan. Add enough hot water to roasting pan to come halfway up side of the dish.

5. Bake until custard is just set, 60 to 65 minutes (mixture will jiggle slightly, but that's okay). Remove flan from oven. Let flan cool in hot-water bath 15 minutes. Remove dish from water bath and cool completely on a wire rack. Cover with plastic wrap and refrigerate overnight.

6. *To serve:* Run a knife around edge of soufflé dish. Place a serving plate slightly larger than soufflé dish on top. Invert flan onto plate. Makes 8 servings.

Per serving: 240 calories, 9.5 g total fat, 5 g saturated fat, 133 mg cholesterol, 77 mg sodium, 34 g carbohydrates, 5 g protein, 78 mg calcium, 0 g fiber

fruity scones

Slightly sweet like scones, but bursting with the intense flavor of dried fruit, our twist on this British Isles classic has tart dried cranberries and zesty orange peel. Tip: If the orange topping seems too moist to sprinkle, gently spread it with your fingertips.

Prep time: 12 minutes • Baking time: 16 to 18 minutes

- 1 **medium orange**
- ¼ **cup dried cranberries**
- 2 **cups self-rising all-purpose flour**
- ¼ **cup plus 2 teaspoons sugar, divided**
- 1 **teaspoon caraway seeds**
- ¼ **teaspoon salt**
- 1 **large egg**
- ¼ **cup plus 1 tablespoon milk, divided**
- 5 **tablespoons butter, cut up**

1. Heat oven to 400°F. Grease a large cookie sheet. Grate 1 teaspoon peel from orange. Cut orange in half and squeeze ¼ cup juice.

2. Combine orange juice and cranberries in a cup. Whisk together flour, the ¼ cup sugar, the caraway seeds and salt in a bowl. Beat egg and the ¼ cup milk in another cup. Cut butter into flour mixture until coarse crumbs form. Add orange juice and cranberry mixture and milk mixture, stirring just until dough forms a ball (do not overmix). Turn dough out onto a floured board. Lightly knead dough 5 or 6 times. Shape into a 6-inch circle on a prepared cookie sheet.

3. For topping, combine remaining 2 teaspoons sugar and the orange peel in a cup. Brush top of dough with remaining 1 tablespoon milk; sprinkle with orange topping. Cut into 8 wedges, but do not separate. Bake 16 to 18 minutes, until golden. Makes 8 scones.

Per scone: 235 calories, 8.5 g total fat, 5 g saturated fat, 47 mg cholesterol, 483 mg sodium, 35 g carbohydrates, 4 g protein, 124 mg calcium, 1 g fiber

rolled cinnamon-nut biscuits

Super tender and tangy-sweet, these buttermilk biscuits are wondrously easy to make.

Prep time: 15 minutes • Baking time: 11 to 13 minutes

FILLING:

- ½ cup walnuts, chopped
- 3 tablespoons cinnamon-sugar

- 2¼ cups buttermilk baking mix
- 3 tablespoons cinnamon-sugar
- ⅔ cup milk
- 3 tablespoons melted butter (no substitutions), divided
- ½ cup confectioners' sugar
- 1 tablespoon water

1. Arrange oven rack to upper third of oven. Heat oven to 425°F. Line a large cookie sheet with parchment paper.

2. *Make filling:* Combine nuts and the 3 tablespoons cinnamon-sugar in a bowl. Set aside 1 tablespoon for top of biscuits.

3. Whisk baking mix and the 3 tablespoons cinnamon-sugar in a bowl; stir in milk just until dough comes together. Turn dough out onto floured board. Flatten into a disk and fold in half. Repeat 6 times. Flatten dough into an 8×10-inch rectangle. Evenly brush dough with 2 tablespoons of the melted butter and sprinkle with filling. Starting from one long side, roll up; pinch seam. Slice roll crosswise into 8 equal pieces. Arrange 2 inches apart on cookie sheet. Brush tops with remaining 1 tablespoon butter and sprinkle with reserved filling.

4. Bake 11 to 13 minutes, until golden. Stir together confectioners' sugar and water in a bowl until smooth. Drizzle over hot biscuits. Serve warm. Makes 8 biscuits.

Per biscuit: 335 calories, 14.5 g total fat, 5 g saturated fat, 14 mg cholesterol, 468 mg sodium, 46 g carbohydrates, 5 g protein, 67 mg calcium, 1 g fiber

the perfect blueberry muffins

During blueberry season, you'll want to bake batch after batch of this recipe—for guests and family alike. Our version calls on a mix of crushed and whole blueberries for even more flavor, and a sprinkling of sugar on top to give them a subtle crunch with each bite.

Prep time: 10 minutes
Baking time: 30 minutes plus cooling

- 2 cups all-purpose flour
- 2 teaspoons baking powder
- ½ teaspoon salt
- ½ cup butter or margarine, softened
- 1 cup plus 1 tablespoon sugar, divided
- 2 large eggs
- ½ cup milk
- 1 teaspoon vanilla extract
- 2½ cups fresh blueberries

1. Heat oven to 375°F. Line twelve 3-inch or fourteen 2½-inch muffin-pan cups with paper liners.*

2. Combine flour, baking powder and salt in a bowl. Beat butter and 1 cup of the sugar in a large mixer bowl at medium speed until light and fluffy. Add eggs, one at a time, beating well after each addition. Add dry ingredients alternately with milk and vanilla, beginning and ending with dry ingredients, until batter is smooth.

3. Crush ½ cup of the berries and add to batter. Fold remaining 2 cups berries into batter with a rubber spatula. Spoon batter evenly into muffin-pan cups. Sprinkle with remaining 1 tablespoon sugar. Bake 30 minutes or until toothpick inserted in center comes out clean. Cool muffins in pan 5 minutes, then remove from pans onto a wire rack. Makes twelve 3-inch muffins.

*Note: Use paper liners to help retain the muffins' shape and to make them easy to remove from the pan.

Per 3-inch muffin: 250 calories, 9 g total fat, 5.5 g saturated fat, 58 mg cholesterol, 274 mg sodium, 39 g carbohydrates, 4 g protein, 69 mg calcium, 1 g fiber

the perfect eggs benedict

Eggs Benedict is the ultimate brunch dish; unfortunately, preparing it can be a little tricky. To help, our version calls on a foolproof technique and a make-ahead sauce. We also suggest adding vinegar to the cooking water when poaching the eggs, as this prevents the whites from spreading. For the hollandaise, whisk the melted butter and egg yolks in a double boiler over hot—not boiling—water, making sure the pan doesn't touch the water.

Prep time: 30 minutes • Cooking time: 10 minutes
Microwave used

HOLLANDAISE SAUCE:

- ¾ cup butter (no substitutions), cut up
- 3 large egg yolks
- 2 tablespoons fresh lemon juice
- ¼ teaspoon salt
- Pinch ground red pepper

- 2 tablespoons butter (no substitutions), divided
- 8 slices Canadian bacon
- 4 English muffins, split and toasted
- 1 tablespoon water

POACHED EGGS:

- 1 tablespoon distilled white vinegar
- 1 teaspoon salt
- 8 large eggs

Chopped fresh chives, for garnish (optional)

1. *Make hollandaise sauce:* Place butter in a 2-cup glass measure. Cover with plastic wrap, turning back one section to vent. Microwave on High 1 to 1½ minutes, until melted. In the top of a double boiler set above, not in, simmering water, whisk egg yolks and lemon juice until slightly thickened, 1 to 2 minutes. Remove top *only* of double boiler from water. Whisking constantly, slowly drizzle a few tablespoons melted butter into yolks in a thin, steady stream. Return top of double boiler to simmering water; continue to slowly add butter, whisking constantly, until sauce thickens. Whisk in salt and red pepper. Cover and remove pan from heat. *(Can be made ahead up to 1 hour. Let stand over hot water.)*

2. Heat oven to 200°F. Heat 1 tablespoon of the butter in a large skillet. Add bacon and cook 2 minutes per side, until lightly browned. Place on a cookie sheet and keep warm in oven.

3. Divide and spread toasted English muffin halves with remaining 1 tablespoon butter. Place halves on a cookie sheet and keep warm in oven.

4. Return double boiler to stovetop. Whisk 1 tablespoon water into hollandaise sauce. Cover and keep sauce warm over low heat while making eggs.

5. *Make poached eggs:* Fill a large, deep skillet with water. Add vinegar and salt. Cover and bring to a gentle boil over medium heat. Break one egg into a small cup. Carefully slip egg into gently boiling water. Repeat with remaining eggs, working in a clockwise direction. Reduce heat and simmer eggs 2 to 3 minutes, until whites are firm near the yolk. Remove with a slotted spoon in same order and place on a platter.

6. Arrange 2 muffin halves on each of 4 serving plates. Top each half with a slice of bacon. Remove eggs from platter with a slotted spoon, gently shaking off excess water. Place one egg over bacon. Divide and spoon hollandaise sauce over each serving. Sprinkle with chives, if desired. Makes 4 servings.

Per serving: 775 calories, 59 g total fat, 30.5 g saturated fat, 719 mg cholesterol, 2,045 mg sodium, 29 g carbohydrates, 31 g protein, 182 mg calcium, 1 g fiber

the perfect
omelet

If your omelets always turn out torn or misshapen, try this recipe. It's as easy as scrambling eggs!

Prep time: 10 to 15 minutes
Cooking time: 3 minutes per omelet

FOR EACH OMELET:

- 2 **large eggs**
- 2 **tablespoons water**
- ⅛ **teaspoon salt**
  Pinch freshly ground pepper
- 1 **tablespoon butter**
  Filling (below and right)

1. *For each omelet:* Whisk eggs, water, salt and pepper in a bowl until blended. Set aside.

2. Melt butter in a 10-inch nonstick skillet over medium heat, swirling to coat bottom and sides of skillet. Heat until bubbles begin to subside.

3. Pour in egg mixture. Cook 1 minute, until omelet starts to set. With spatula, gently push back edges of set egg and tilt pan to allow uncooked egg to flow onto exposed skillet. Cook 1 to 2 minutes, until top is set. With handle of skillet facing you, spoon ½ *cup desired filling* down one side of omelet.

4. Run knife around edge of egg. (Don't worry if edges tear; when omelet is folded over, you won't see it.) Gently roll one side of omelet over filling and slip onto plate, flipping to encase the filling. Serve omelet seam side down.

5. Repeat steps 1 through 4 three more times, for remaining omelets. Makes 4 omelets.

SPINACH AND FONTINA FILLING

Heat *1 tablespoon butter* in a skillet over medium heat. Add *½ cup chopped onion* and cook, stirring, until lightly browned. Chop *2 bags (10 oz. each) fresh spinach*. Add half the spinach to skillet with *½ teaspoon salt* and *¼ teaspoon freshly ground pepper*; cover and cook 2 minutes, until wilted. Stir in remaining spinach; cover and cook 2 minutes more. Drain spinach; transfer to a bowl and stir in *¼ pound diced fontina cheese*. Makes 2 cups (enough for 4 omelets).

Per omelet: 415 calories, 33.5 g total fat, 17.5 g saturated fat, 497 mg cholesterol, 1,160 mg sodium, 7 g carbohydrates, 23 g protein, 316 mg calcium, 4 g fiber

HAM AND CHEDDAR FILLING

Heat *1 tablespoon butter* in a skillet over medium-high heat. Add *2 tablespoons minced shallots* and cook, stirring, 1 minute. Stir in *½ pound chopped smoked ham*, *½ teaspoon chopped fresh thyme* or *pinch dried thyme* and *pinch freshly ground pepper*. Reduce heat to medium and cook until lightly browned. Transfer to a bowl; stir in *1 cup shredded sharp cheddar cheese*. Makes 2 cups (enough for 4 omelets).

Per omelet: 355 calories, 27 g total fat, 13 g saturated fat, 490 mg cholesterol, 1,373 mg sodium, 3 g carbohydrates, 24 g protein, 60 mg calcium, 0 g fiber

MUSHROOM AND GOAT CHEESE FILLING

Heat *1 tablespoon butter* in a skillet over medium-high heat. Add *1 pound sliced white mushrooms*, *2 tablespoons minced shallots*, *½ teaspoon salt* and *¼ teaspoon freshly ground pepper*. Cook, stirring, 6 to 7 minutes, until browned. Stir in *1 tablespoon chopped fresh tarragon* or *½ teaspoon dried tarragon*; cook 30 seconds. Transfer to a bowl. Add *2 ounces crumbled fresh goat cheese*. Makes 2 cups (enough for 4 omelets).

Per omelet: 345 calories, 28 g total fat, 14 g saturated fat, 470 mg cholesterol, 909 mg sodium, 8 g carbohydrates, 18 g protein, 84 mg calcium, 2 g fiber

---

m e n u
perfect brunch

**THE PERFECT OMELET WITH
SPINACH AND FONTINA FILLING**
left

THE PERFECT BLUEBERRY MUFFINS
page 157

SLICED IN-SEASON FRUIT

---

the perfect waffles (EASY)

What makes these waffles perfect? We used buttermilk for tangy flavor, then folded in beaten egg whites for the fluffiest, lightest waffles you've ever eaten. We doubt you'll have any waffles left over, but if you do, just wrap and place them in the freezer for a quick, toastable breakfast later in the week. Pictured on page 128.

Prep time: 20 minutes
Cooking time: 2 to 5 minutes per batch

- 2 **cups all-purpose flour**
- 3 **tablespoons sugar**
- 1 **tablespoon baking powder**
- ½ **teaspoon salt**
- ¼ **teaspoon baking soda**
- 3 **large eggs, separated**
- 2¼ **cups buttermilk**
- ¼ **cup butter or margarine, melted**
  Confectioners' sugar (optional)
  Pure maple syrup, sliced nectarines and fresh berries, for garnish (optional)

1. To keep waffles warm, heat oven to 200°F. Heat a waffle baker.

2. Combine flour, sugar, baking powder, salt and baking soda in a large bowl.

3. Whisk egg yolks in a medium bowl until lightly beaten. Whisk in buttermilk and melted butter until blended. Whisk buttermilk mixture into dry ingredients until smooth. Beat egg whites in a small mixer bowl until stiff but not dry. Fold egg whites into flour mixture with a rubber spatula just until blended. Makes about 6 cups batter.

4. Bake waffles in a waffle baker* according to manufacturer's directions, until crisp and golden brown, 2 to 5 minutes. Transfer each batch directly onto an oven rack to keep warm. Repeat. *(Can be made ahead. Cool waffles; freeze in resealable plastic storage bags up to 2 weeks. Reheat in toaster or 350°F. oven.)* Dust waffles with confectioners' sugar; serve with maple syrup and fruit, if desired. Makes five 8-inch-square waffles or 5 servings.

*Note: For best waffle removal, use a waffle baker with a nonstick grid.

Per serving: 385 calories, 13.5 g total fat, 7.5 g saturated fat, 157 mg cholesterol, 834 mg sodium, 52 g carbohydrates, 13 g protein, 315 mg calcium, 1 g fiber

bacon-maple corn muffins (EASY)

Treat overnight guests to these muffins that are made marvelous with hardwood-smoked bacon and maple syrup. Be sure to use self-rising flour; this convenient ingredient contains most of the leavening needed.

Prep time: 15 minutes • Baking time: 13 to 15 minutes

- 3 **slices hardwood-smoked bacon or regular bacon, chopped**
- ½ **cup finely chopped onion**
- 1 **cup self-rising all-purpose flour**
- 1 **cup yellow cornmeal**
- ½ **teaspoon baking soda**
- ½ **teaspoon salt**
- 1 **large egg**
- 1 **cup buttermilk**
- ⅓ **cup pure maple syrup (no substitutions)**

1. Heat oven to 425°F. Lightly coat twelve 2½-inch muffin-pan cups with vegetable cooking spray.

2. Heat a large skillet over medium-high heat. Add bacon and cook until crisp; transfer with a slotted spoon to a paper towel and drain. Cook onion in bacon drippings that remain in the skillet for 3 to 4 minutes, until tender. Set aside.

3. Whisk together flour, cornmeal, baking soda and salt in a medium bowl. Whisk egg, buttermilk and maple syrup in a small bowl. Stir buttermilk mixture, bacon, onion and all bacon drippings into dry ingredients, just until blended. Spoon batter evenly into prepared muffin cups. Bake 13 to 15 minutes, until golden. Makes 12 muffins.

Per muffin: 150 calories, 4.5 g total fat, 1.5 g saturated fat, 22 mg cholesterol, 348 mg sodium, 24 g carbohydrates, 4 g protein, 69 mg calcium, 1 g fiber

CREAM OF
GARDEN-FRESH
HERBS WITH
SHRIMP
pg. 170

COOKBOOK
AUTHOR
JULIA CHILD

chefs' favorites from your kitchen

With these recipes from renowned cookbook authors, chefs and restaurants around the country, you can treat family and friends to the most up-to-date tastes—in the comfort of your own home. So go ahead! Sneak a taste from the pan. Come as you are. And linger as long as you like!

JULIA CHILD'S DUCK
ROAST WITH POLENTA
pg. 182

no reservations required

ITALIAN
COLESLAW
pg. 177

WHITE GRAPE
GRANITA
pg.191

for the
best food
in town

CHOCOLATE
DECADENCE
pg.194

FRUIT SOUP
WITH SPICE
BROTH
pg.190

when guests ask
where you got these

world-class
recipes...

VEGETABLE TIAN
pg. 187
POACHED WHOLE
SALMON WITH
BASIL MAYONNAISE
pg. 186

GRILLED BANANA
SPLIT
pg. 190

just smile

GRILLED
FRESH
TOMATO
PIZZA WITH
THREE
CHEESES
pg. 177

OPEN-FACED
APRICOT PIE
pg. 200

easy-to-follow
recipes from our
guest chefs

BLUEBERRY SUGAR
SHORTCAKE WITH
WARM PEACH
COMPOTE
pg. 193

CHICKEN ADOBO
WITH SPICY BLACK
BEAN SALSA
pg. 178

help bring out the
culinary artist in you

NEW ENGLAND
SEPTEMBER SOUP
pg. 171
FROM COOKBOOK
AUTHOR
JASPER WHITE,
right

Chefs' Favorites from Your Kitchen **167**

what's for dinner?
ask a chef!

BEEF AND
RAVIOLI SOUP
pg. 170

CLASSIC
COUNTRY-STYLE
HEARTH LOAF
pg. 172

cream of carrot soup *EASY*

This sweet and creamy soup—from Janleone restaurant in Denver—will leave a lasting impression on those lucky enough to taste it. For garnish, use fresh dill sprigs and sautéed carrot shreds.

Prep time: 20 minutes
Cooking time: 25 minutes

- 2 pounds peeled and chopped carrots
- 3 cans (14½ oz. each) chicken broth
- ½ cup chopped fresh dill
- 2 tablespoons sugar
- ½ teaspoon salt
- ¼ teaspoon freshly ground pepper
- ¼ cup butter or margarine
- 1 medium onion, chopped
- ¼ cup all-purpose flour
- 1 cup heavy or whipping cream
- 1 cup milk

1. Bring carrots, broth, dill, sugar, salt and pepper to boil in a large Dutch oven. Reduce heat and simmer 20 minutes, until carrots are tender.

2. Meanwhile, melt butter in a large skillet over medium heat. Add onion and cook 4 to 5 minutes, until softened and just beginning to brown. Add flour and cook, stirring, 3 minutes. Stir into carrot mixture until combined.

3. Puree carrot mixture in blender in batches; transfer each batch to a large bowl, then return to Dutch oven. Stir in cream and milk. Cook over medium heat until heated through, 5 minutes (do not boil). Makes 8 cups.

Per 1 cup: 275 calories, 19 g total fat, 11.5 g saturated fat, 61 mg cholesterol, 927 mg sodium, 22 g carbohydrates, 4 g protein, 94 mg calcium, 4 g fiber

gazpacho

Castel Grisch Estate Winery and Restaurant in Watkins Glen, New York, shared this recipe with us. Completely do-ahead and made easy with prepared tomato juice, it's a great way to chill out on those too-hot-to-cook summer days. Remember this soup when you want to take advantage of the best of summer's freshest produce.

Total prep time: 30 minutes

- 2½ cups tomato or vegetable juice
- 1 cup peeled, seeded and finely chopped fresh tomatoes
- ½ cup finely chopped celery
- ½ cup finely chopped cucumber
- ½ cup finely chopped green bell pepper
- ½ cup finely chopped green onions
- 3 tablespoons white wine vinegar
- 2 tablespoons olive oil
- 1 large clove garlic, minced
- 2 teaspoons finely chopped fresh flat-leaf parsley
- 1½ teaspoons salt
- ½ teaspoon freshly ground pepper
- ½ teaspoon Worcestershire sauce

Combine tomato juice, tomatoes, celery, cucumber, bell pepper, green onions, vinegar, oil, garlic, parsley, salt, pepper and Worcestershire sauce in a large glass or stainless steel bowl. Cover and refrigerate overnight. Serve cold. Makes 5 cups.

Per 1 cup: 90 calories, 5.5 g total fat, 0.5 g saturated fat, 0 mg cholesterol, 1,160 mg sodium, 10 g carbohydrates, 2 g protein, 31 mg calcium, 2 g fiber

test kitchen tip

blender is best

For most recipes that call for pureeing, the food processor and blender work equally well. However, for cream soups we find that a blender gives the most velvety texture.

cream of garden-fresh herbs with shrimp

A Ladies' Home Journal reader tasted this creamy broth laden with shrimp at Heimann's Restaurant in St. Petersburg, Florida. She liked it so much she ordered a second bowl as her main course—then later asked us to obtain the recipe. We're glad she did! Pictured on page 161.

Prep time: 15 minutes · Cooking time: 20 minutes

- 2 **tablespoons butter**
- 2 **tablespoons all-purpose flour**
- 2 **cups beef broth**
- 1 **quart salted water**
- 3 **bay leaves**
- 20 **medium shrimp (about 9 oz.), shelled and deveined**
- 1½ **cups heavy cream**
- ¼ **teaspoon salt**
- ⅛ **teaspoon white pepper**
- ¼ **cup chopped fresh flat-leaf parsley**
- 2 **fresh sage leaves, chopped, or 1 tablespoon chopped fresh parsley and ¼ teaspoon dried sage**
- 1 **teaspoon chopped fresh thyme**
- 1 **teaspoon chopped fresh dill**
  Fresh sage leaves, for garnish (optional)

1. Melt butter in a medium saucepan. Whisk in flour until combined. Slowly whisk in beef broth. Simmer broth 15 minutes.

2. Meanwhile, bring water and bay leaves to boil in a medium saucepan. Add shrimp and cook 2 minutes, until opaque; drain. Discard bay leaves.

3. Stir cream into broth mixture and return to a simmer. Remove pan from heat. Stir in salt, white pepper, parsley, sage, thyme and dill. Divide soup among 4 serving bowls and arrange 5 shrimp on top of each serving. Garnish with sage leaves, if desired. Makes 4 servings.

Per serving: 440 calories, 40 g total fat, 24.5 g saturated fat, 216 mg cholesterol, 838 mg sodium, 7 g carbohydrates, 14 g protein, 100 mg calcium, 1 g fiber

beef and ravioli soup

When a reader claimed that this soup, from The Great Buffet in Sam's Town Hotel & Gambling Hall in Las Vegas, was the most delicious she had ever tasted, we couldn't wait to get the lowdown on how to make it. Pictured on page 168.

Prep time: 20 minutes · Cooking time: 35 minutes

- ½ **pound boneless beef top sirloin, cut into ¼-inch dice**
- 4 **tablespoons all-purpose flour, divided**
- 2 **tablespoons butter or margarine**
- 1 **celery rib, chopped**
- 1 **medium carrot, chopped**
- 1 **medium onion, chopped**
- 1 **tablespoon chopped garlic**
- ½ **teaspoon dried thyme**
- ½ **teaspoon white pepper**
- 2 **cans (14½ oz. each) beef broth**
- 1 **can (28 oz.) whole tomatoes in juice, chopped, juice reserved**
- 1 **cup water**
- ½ **teaspoon salt**
- 1 **package (9 oz.) refrigerated beef ravioli or one package (8 oz.) frozen beef tortellini**
- 1 **tablespoon cornstarch**
- 2 **tablespoons water**

1. Toss beef with 2 tablespoons of the flour in a bowl. Melt butter in a large Dutch oven over medium-high heat. Add beef and cook until beef is browned; transfer with a slotted spoon to a bowl and set aside.

2. Add celery, carrot, onion, garlic, thyme and white pepper to Dutch oven. Cook, stirring, 3 minutes, until vegetables are lightly browned. Add reserved browned beef, broth, tomatoes and their juice, 1 cup water and salt. Bring to boil; reduce heat to medium and cook 20 minutes, until vegetables are tender. Add beef ravioli and cook 10 minutes, stirring occasionally.

3. Meanwhile, combine remaining 2 tablespoons flour and the cornstarch with 2 tablespoons water in a cup until smooth. Stir into soup; bring to boil and boil 1 minute. Makes 4 servings.

Per serving: 490 calories, 24 g total fat, 7 g saturated fat, 104 mg cholesterol, 1,940 mg sodium, 44 g carbohydrates, 26 g protein, 126 mg calcium, 4 g fiber

new england september soup

From chef and cookbook author Jasper White comes this elegant soup that celebrates the great tastes of autumn and indulges in lobster—the ultimate catch of the day. Pictured on page 167.

Prep time: 1 hour • Cooking time: 2 hours

LOBSTER BROTH:
- 4 **small lobsters, cooked**
- 2 **cups chicken broth or water**
- 8 **cups water**
- 4 **ears yellow corn**
- 4 **sprigs fresh thyme or ½ teaspoon dried thyme**
- 1 **bay leaf**
- 1 **teaspoon whole black peppercorns**
  ■
- 1 **tablespoon butter (no substitutions)**
- 2 **cups thinly sliced onions**
- 1 **small sugar pumpkin or butternut squash (2 lbs.), peeled, seeded and cut into ½-inch-thick slices**
- ⅛ **teaspoon nutmeg**
- ½ **cup heavy or whipping cream or ¾ cup milk**
- ¾ **to 1 teaspoon kosher salt**
- ½ **teaspoon freshly ground pepper**
  Pinch ground red pepper
- 1 **tablespoon chopped fresh flat-leaf parsley**

1. *Make lobster broth:* Separate cooked tails and claws from lobsters. Crack tails and claws and remove meat with a fork. Cut lobster meat into

¾-inch dice; transfer to a small bowl, cover and refrigerate. You should have about 2½ cups. *(Can be made ahead. Refrigerate overnight.)* With a sharp knife, split lobster shells in half. Remove head sack (it can cause bitterness). Combine lobster shells, chicken broth and the 8 cups water in a large Dutch oven. Bring to boil over medium-high heat. Skim any foam from top.

2. Cut kernels from corncobs (you should have 2 cups corn kernels); set aside. *(Can be made ahead. Cover and refrigerate overnight.)* Break corncobs in half; add to lobster broth along with thyme, bay leaf and peppercorns. Reduce heat to medium and simmer broth, partially covered, 1 hour. Strain broth into a colander set over a bowl; discard shells, corncobs and herbs. *(Can be made ahead. Cool completely. Cover and refrigerate overnight.)* Makes about 5 cups.

3. Melt butter in a 4-quart Dutch oven or soup pot over medium heat. Add onions and cook, stirring, until softened and golden, 8 minutes. Stir in reserved lobster broth, corn kernels, pumpkin and nutmeg. Simmer mixture until pumpkin is very tender, 30 to 45 minutes.

4. Puree soup in batches in a blender or food processor. Strain mixture through a sieve into a medium saucepan and reheat over medium-low heat. Stir in cream, kosher salt, pepper and ground red pepper. Gently warm soup 5 minutes. Add reserved lobster meat and cook until lobster is just heated through, about 1 to 2 minutes. Divide soup among 8 shallow serving bowls and sprinkle with parsley. Makes 8 servings.

Per serving: 210 calories, 8 g fat, 4.5 g saturated fat, 57 mg cholesterol, 644 mg sodium, 24 g carbohydrates, 13 g protein, 97 mg calcium, 4 g fiber

goulash soup

This Hungarian tomato-and-beef soup, served at the Oak Chalet Restaurant in Bellmore, New York, is a hearty and satisfying meal in a bowl.

Prep time: 30 minutes • Cooking time: 1 hour

- 3 tablespoons butter
- 1 pound top round beef, cut into ½-inch cubes
- 1½ cups chopped onions
- 1 tablespoon minced garlic
- 2 tablespoons all-purpose flour
- 2 tablespoons paprika
- 3 tablespoons tomato paste
- 4 cans (14½ oz. each) chicken broth, plus enough water to equal 8 cups
- 1 can (14 oz.) whole tomatoes in juice, chopped, juice reserved
- 4 potatoes, peeled and grated
- 4 large carrots, diced
- 1 bay leaf
- ½ teaspoon dried marjoram
- ½ teaspoon caraway seeds, crushed
- ½ teaspoon freshly ground pepper
- ½ cup sour cream

1. Melt butter in a large Dutch oven over medium-high heat. Add beef and brown on all sides, 5 minutes. Transfer beef to a plate with a slotted spoon; set aside.

2. Add onions and garlic and cook 5 minutes. Add browned beef, flour and paprika; cook, stirring constantly, 3 minutes. Stir in tomato paste until smooth. Add chicken broth and water, tomatoes and their juice, potatoes, carrots, bay leaf, marjoram, caraway seeds and pepper. Bring to boil; reduce heat and simmer, stirring occasionally, until beef is just tender and vegetables are cooked through, 45 minutes. Remove bay leaf. Top each serving evenly with sour cream. Makes 14 cups.

Per 1 cup: 175 calories, 8 g total fat, 4 g saturated fat, 30 mg cholesterol, 633 mg sodium, 15 g carbohydrates, 10 g protein, 39 mg calcium, 2 g fiber

classic country-style hearth loaf

Daniel Leader, a highly regarded bread baker and chef, shared this recipe for his perfect rustic loaf. To give the bread a tangy-nutty flavor, he starts with a mixture called "poolish," which ferments overnight and is added to the dough the following day.

Prep time: 45 minutes plus chilling and rising
Baking time: 40 minutes

BRAN-WHEAT FLOUR:
- 3 pounds (9 cups) unbleached all-purpose flour, preferably organic
- 1 pound (3 cups) stone-ground whole wheat flour, preferably organic

POOLISH:
- ½ teaspoon active dry yeast
- ½ cup water, preferably spring water, at 75°F.

DOUGH:
- 2½ cups water, preferably spring water, at 75°F.
- ½ teaspoon active dry yeast
- 1 tablespoon fine sea salt
- 1 tablespoon shortening or butter, softened, or 2 teaspoons vegetable oil
  Butter (no substitutions) (optional)

1. *Make bran-wheat flour:* To measure, stir all-purpose and whole wheat flours in their packages or canisters to aerate, then gently dip a dry measuring cup into the flour, taking care not to pack the flour into the cup. Level off any excess with a metal spatula or flat knife. Combine the all-purpose and whole wheat flours in a large bowl. Cover.

2. *Make poolish:* Sprinkle yeast over $^1/_2$ cup water in another large bowl; let stand 1 minute. Stir with a wooden spoon, until yeast dissolves. Stir in $^3/_4$ cup of the bran-wheat flour. Vigorously stir mixture 100 strokes, until strands of gluten come off the spoon when you press back of spoon against the bowl and mixture is a pourable consistency. Scrape the sides of the bowl with a rubber spatula. Cover poolish with plastic wrap and refrigerate overnight.

3. *Make dough:* Remove poolish from refrigerator and let stand 2 hours, until mixture registers 75°F. when tested in center with an instant-read thermometer. The mixture should be bubbling slightly and have a wheaty aroma. Stir in the 2¹/₂ cups water and the ¹/₂ teaspoon yeast, until yeast is dissolved. Stir in 1 cup of the bran-wheat flour, until well combined. Add salt, then stir in 4 to 6 cups more bran-wheat flour, until mixture forms a thick mass that is difficult to stir. (The dough will be slightly sticky.)

4. Transfer dough to a lightly floured surface. Dip hands in flour to prevent sticking. Knead dough by pushing it down and forward with the heel of one hand, then pulling back from the top and folding the dough with the other hand. Knead dough vigorously 15 to 17 minutes, gradually adding enough bran-wheat flour (1¹/₂ to 2 cups) as necessary, until dough becomes smooth, elastic and strong. (Don't worry if you end up with a slightly tacky dough.) Press your finger into the dough and remove it. If the dough springs back, it's ready. Shape dough into a tight ball.

5. Grease a medium bowl with the 1 tablespoon shortening. Add dough, turning to grease top. Test temperature of the dough—it should reach 78°F. (If the temperature is too high, refrigerate dough for a few minutes. If the temperature is too low, place dough in a warm place for a few minutes.) Cover bowl with plastic wrap and let dough rise in a warm, draft-free place until doubled in bulk, 2 to 3 hours.

6. Punch dough down, pull up on sides and form into a ball. Cover and let rise in bowl 30 minutes.

7. Transfer dough to a floured surface. Punch down and knead briefly, 2 to 3 minutes. Divide dough in half. Flatten each piece with the heel of your hand, using firm direct strokes, then form each piece of dough into a ball.

8. Generously flour two 8×3-inch or 8¹/₂×3-inch bread baskets (or line two bowls of equal size with well-floured clean kitchen towels). Place loaves, smooth side down, in each prepared basket. Dust tops with flour. Cover with plastic wrap and let rise,

1¹/₂ to 2 hours, until increased in volume about 1¹/₂ times.

9. Meanwhile, arrange oven racks to center and upper third of oven. Place a 5×8-inch loaf pan on floor of oven. Heat oven to 450°F.

10. Lightly coat two large cookie sheets with vegetable cooking spray. Gently unmold loaves onto center of each prepared sheet. If desired, using a small, sharp knife or razor, score the loaves by making shallow cuts ¹/₄ to ¹/₂ inch deep along top of each loaf.

11. Place loaves in oven. Place 6 ice cubes in the loaf pan on floor of oven to create steam. Bake 20 minutes. Rotate cookie sheets and switch between racks. Reduce oven temperature to 400°F. Bake loaves 20 minutes more, until breads sound hollow when tapped and temperature registers 204°F. to 206°F. when stem end of an instant-read thermometer is inserted in center of each bread. (The loaves should have a rich caramel color and the crust should be firm.) Cool breads on wire rack at least 20 minutes. Slice breads and spread with butter, if desired. Makes 2 loaves; 8 to 10 slices per loaf.

Per slice: 500 calories, 4.5 g total fat, 0.5 g saturated fat, 0 mg cholesterol, 330 mg sodium, 115 g carbohydrates, 20 g protein, 65 mg calcium, 5 g fiber

test kitchen tip

follow the leader

Dan Leader shares his tips for making this recipe:

"You may not need to use all the flour called for in the recipe, depending on your flour's moisture content and whether it absorbs all the water," Leader says. "Just be careful not to use too much." He also advises not to skimp on the kneading time. "Fifteen to seventeen minutes is essential," he says. "Set a timer, if necessary, because if the dough is under-kneaded, the bread may collapse."

flatbread with chipotle steak and caramelized onions

At the California Grill at Disney's Contemporary Resort, Chef Clifford Pleau bakes this flatbread in a brick oven for the crispiest crust. We use a baking stone and a pan filled with ice cubes placed on an upper oven rack to achieve that same great texture. Cut into appetizer portions, the recipe makes a great starter. If you're serving steak as your entrée, you might prefer to serve the meatless mushroom-feta version, page 175.

Prep time: 40 minutes plus rising
Baking time: 10 minutes per batch

DOUGH:

1	cup warm water (110°F. to 115°F.)
1	teaspoon sugar
¼	teaspoon active dry yeast
1½	tablespoons extra-virgin olive oil
1¾	cups whole wheat flour
¾	to 1 cup all-purpose flour or bread flour
1	teaspoon salt
1	teaspoon freshly ground pepper

4	tablespoons extra-virgin olive oil, divided
2	tablespoons butter or margarine
4	large (3 lbs.) sweet onions, thinly sliced
1	tablespoon sugar
1	teaspoon salt, divided
3	medium chipotle chiles in adobo* (see tip, page 95)
1	(¾ to 1 lb.) boneless beef top loin steak, 1 to 1¼ inches thick
	Yellow cornmeal
	Sour cream

1. *Make dough:* Combine warm water and sugar in a small bowl; sprinkle yeast over top. Let stand 10 minutes until foamy; stir in 1½ tablespoons oil.

2. Combine whole wheat flour, ¾ cup of the all-purpose flour, the salt and pepper in a large bowl.

Stir in yeast mixture with a wooden spoon. Transfer dough to a lightly floured surface. Shape into a rough ball and knead 8 to 10 minutes, adding remaining ¼ cup all-purpose flour if necessary, until smooth and elastic. Transfer to a lightly oiled bowl. Cover bowl with a clean kitchen towel and let rise in a warm, draft-free place 1 hour.

3. Twenty minutes before baking, adjust oven rack to lowest position. Place a shallow baking pan on top rack of oven. Place baking stone** on lowest rack and heat oven to 500°F.

4. Meanwhile, heat 2 tablespoons of the oil and the butter in a 12-inch skillet over medium heat. Add onions, sugar and ½ teaspoon of the salt. Cook onions, stirring frequently, 30 to 40 minutes, until caramelized.

5. With flat side of a knife, mash chipotles to a paste. Stir 1 teaspoon of the paste into the caramelized onions; set remaining paste aside.

6. Transfer dough to a floured surface; knead 2 minutes. Return to bowl; cover and refrigerate 20 minutes.

7. Meanwhile, heat grill pan or cast-iron skillet 5 minutes over medium-high heat. Sprinkle both sides of steak with remaining ½ teaspoon salt. Oil pan and grill steak 5 minutes. Turn and brush top with remaining chipotle paste. Grill 8 to 10 minutes more for medium-rare (140°F.); transfer to a cutting board. Cover loosely with foil; keep warm.

8. Sprinkle a large cookie sheet generously with cornmeal. Divide dough into 4 equal pieces. On a lightly floured surface, shape 2 pieces of dough with a rolling pin into two 10×6-inch ovals. Transfer ovals to prepared sheet; brush tops with 1 tablespoon of the remaining oil. Divide and spread half the onion mixture over tops. Reserve remaining onion mixture.

9. Just before baking, carefully place 1 cup ice cubes in baking pan on top oven rack. Immediately slide 2 flatbreads, one at a time, onto baking stone. Bake 10 minutes, until crisp and lightly browned.

10. Transfer flatbreads to a large cutting board; cover loosely and keep warm. Repeat process, shaping and baking with remaining 2 pieces of dough, remaining 1 tablespoon oil and the reserved onion mixture.

11. Thinly slice steak across the grain. Divide steak over flatbreads. Cut into slices and serve with sour cream. Makes 16 slices.

*Note: Can be found in ethnic section of supermarkets or in Spanish or Latino specialty stores.

**Note: Can be found in specialty kitchenware shops.

Per slice: 225 calories, 8 g total fat, 3 g saturated fat, 17 mg cholesterol, 350 mg sodium, 26 g carbohydrates, 8 g protein, 35 mg calcium, 3 g fiber

MUSHROOM-FETA FLATBREAD

1. Prepare the dough as directed through step 3, page 174, except heat oven to 450°F.

2. Meanwhile, wrap *4 large cloves garlic* in foil. Bake 25 minutes, until softened. Cool; remove peel and mash to form a paste.

3. Heat grill. Combine *³⁄₄ teaspoon salt* and *¹⁄₂ teaspoon freshly ground pepper* in a cup. Cut *1 pound white mushrooms* in half. Slice *¹⁄₂ pound portobello mushroom caps* ¹⁄₂ inch thick. Arrange mushrooms in a grill basket. Brush both sides of mushrooms with *¹⁄₄ cup extra-virgin olive oil;* sprinkle with salt and pepper mixture. Grill mushrooms over medium heat 10 minutes, turning, until tender. Chop when cool.

4. Sprinkle a cookie sheet generously with *cornmeal.* Divide dough into 4 pieces. On a lightly floured surface, shape 2 pieces of dough with a rolling pin into two 10×6-inch ovals. Transfer ovals to prepared sheet. Combine *1 tablespoon* each *chopped fresh rosemary* and *thyme.* Spread half the garlic paste and 1¹⁄₂ teaspoons of the herbs on dough ovals; brush with *2 tablespoons oil.* Divide and sprinkle half the chopped mushrooms over herbs, pressing gently into the 2 dough ovals.

Proceed with step 9, page 174, and bake for 10 minutes, until lightly browned.

5. Transfer to cutting board; cover loosely and keep warm. Repeat with remaining dough, garlic paste, 1¹⁄₂ teaspoon of the herbs, *2 tablespoons oil* and the remaining chopped mushrooms.

6. Divide *6 ounces crumbled feta cheese* over tops of flatbreads; sprinkle with the remaining 1 tablespoon herbs. Makes 16 slices.

Per slice: 155 calories, 5.5 g total fat, 2.5 g saturated fat, 9 mg cholesterol, 376 mg sodium, 18 g carbohydrates, 5 g protein, 63 mg calcium, 2 g fiber

© Disney Enterprises, Inc.

---

test kitchen tip

mushroom matters

A shortlist of some popular mushroom varieties, along with how to handle them with care:

PORTOBELLO: Rich in flavor with a dense, meaty texture. An extremely mature form of cremini mushrooms. Large, with an open flat cap with dark gills. Available whole or packaged sliced or caps only. Remove stems before cooking.

SHIITAKE: Meaty and slightly smoky in flavor with a large, dark brown cap. Because the stems are usually tough, discard or use to flavor stocks or soups.

WHITE: Mild, earthy flavor, ranging in color from white to beige. ("Button" mushrooms are simply young white cultivated mushrooms.)

CLEANING AND STORING: Cool air is vital for keeping mushrooms fresh. Store in the refrigerator no longer than 3 days, arranged on a tray in a single layer, covered with a damp paper towel. Wipe with a damp paper towel to clean before using (do not to soak them in water, because they will absorb it and become soggy).

wild about wild rice

Sometimes referred to as "the caviar of grains," wild rice lends a nutty flavor and a pleasantly chewy texture to dishes. Here are a few tips on using and storing this opulent ingredient.

STORE uncooked wild rice indefinitely in a cool, dry place or in the refrigerator.

RINSE wild rice before using. Place the rice in a pan of warm water. Stir, then remove the particles that float to the top. Drain and repeat.

WILD RICE MATH: 1 cup uncooked wild rice makes about $2^2/_3$ cups of cooked wild rice.

MONEY-SAVING TIP: Though wild rice is expensive, you can make a little go a long way by combining a small amount with brown rice for a side dish. The cooking times for both are about the same.

walleye and wild rice cakes

This recipe, from the Manhattan Beach Lodge in Manhattan Beach, Minnesota, proves that crab cakes aren't the only cakes in town! Walleye (also known as walleyed pike) is a spiny-finned freshwater fish from the perch family, found in North America and Europe. If you can't get it, red snapper or orange roughy fillets work well in this recipe, too.

Prep time: 30 minutes plus chilling
Cooking time: 14 to 16 minutes

- **1 pound skinless walleye, red snapper or orange roughy fillets**
- **2 cups water**
- **½ cup cooked wild rice**
- **½ cup mayonnaise**
- **½ cup plain dry bread crumbs**
- **1½ teaspoons Old Bay seasoning**
- **1 large egg, lightly beaten**
- **½ teaspoon salt**
- **½ teaspoon freshly ground pepper**
- **½ teaspoon dry mustard**
- **2 tablespoons cornmeal, divided**
- **3 tablespoons butter or margarine, divided**
  Lemon wedges

1. Bring fillets and water to boil in a 12-inch nonstick skillet over medium-high heat. Reduce heat to low and simmer fillets 8 to 10 minutes until cooked through. (If fillets are thick, turn once halfway through cooking time.) Transfer fillets to a plate lined with paper towels; cool. Flake fish into small pieces with a fork. Set aside.

2. Combine rice, mayonnaise, bread crumbs, Old Bay seasoning, egg, salt, pepper and dry mustard in a large bowl. Add fish, stirring until well combined; cover and refrigerate 1 hour or overnight.

3. Line a jelly-roll pan with waxed paper; sprinkle with 1 tablespoon of the cornmeal. Shape fish mixture into eight ½-inch-thick patties. Transfer to waxed paper. Sprinkle tops with remaining 1 tablespoon cornmeal.

4. Melt 2 tablespoons of the butter in a 12-inch nonstick skillet over medium heat. Cook fish cakes 3 minutes. Add the remaining 1 tablespoon butter or margarine to skillet, turn cakes and cook 3 minutes more, until cakes are brown and heated through. Serve with lemon wedges. Makes 4 servings.

Per serving: 460 calories, 31 g total fat, 7.5 g saturated fat, 130 mg cholesterol, 634 mg sodium, 19 g carbohydrates, 27 g protein, 104 mg calcium, 1 g fiber

grilled fresh tomato pizza with three cheeses

Prep time: 20 minutes • Grilling time: 9 to 10 minutes

This quick entrée comes to us from cookbook author Michele Scicolone, a native of Brooklyn who travels to Italy at least twice a year, scouring the countryside for new culinary delights. Pictured on page 165.

- 2   plum tomatoes, chopped
- 1   tablespoon chopped fresh flat-leaf parsley
- 1   small clove garlic, minced
- 1   tablespoon olive oil
- ¼   teaspoon salt
- ¼   teaspoon freshly ground pepper
- ¼   cup crumbled Gorgonzola or blue cheese
- 2   ounces fresh mozzarella cheese, thinly sliced
- 2   tablespoons freshly grated Parmesan cheese
     Prepared pizza dough for one 12-inch pizza*
- 2   tablespoons fresh flat-leaf parsley or basil, cut into thin strips

1. Oil and heat grill. Combine tomatoes, parsley, garlic, oil, salt and pepper in a medium bowl. Toss the cheeses in another bowl. Flour a large cutting board. Pat or roll dough to a 12-inch circle. Slide dough off board onto heated grill; grill over low coals 2 to 3 minutes, until lightly browned.

2. Meanwhile, flour board again. Transfer pizza crust, cooked side up, onto board. Spread evenly with tomato mixture. Top with cheese mixture. Slide back onto grill. Cover and grill about 7 minutes more, moving pizza around to grill evenly, until crust is crisp and deep golden brown and cheese is just melted. Sprinkle with parsley or basil. Makes 4 to 6 servings.

*Note: Look for fresh or frozen pizza dough at a neighborhood bakery, pizza parlor or supermarket.

Per serving: 205 calories, 9.5 g total fat, 4 g saturated fat, 17 mg cholesterol, 728 mg sodium, 22 g carbohydrates, 9 g protein, 130 mg calcium, 1 g fiber

---

m e n u

michele scicolone's midsummer menu

MELON AND PROSCIUTTO

GRILLED FRESH TOMATO PIZZA WITH THREE CHEESES
left

ITALIAN COLESLAW
below

WHITE GRAPE GRANITA
page 191

CRISP BUTTER COOKIES

CHIANTI

---

italian coleslaw

Another gem from Michele Scicolone. Pictured on page 162.

Total prep time: 10 minutes plus chilling

- 1   medium fennel (about 1 lb.)
- 1   cup large green olives, pitted and sliced
- 3   cloves garlic, thinly sliced
- ¼   cup chopped fresh flat-leaf parsley
- ¼   cup olive oil
- 2   tablespoons red wine vinegar
     Pinch salt
     Pinch red pepper flakes

Trim brown spots from fennel; cut a thin slice off base of bulb. Discard green stems. Cut fennel in half lengthwise, then cut crosswise into thin slices. Combine fennel and remaining ingredients in a large bowl. Cover; refrigerate at least 1 hour. Makes 4 cups.

Per ½ cup: 180 calories, 18 g total fat, 2.5 g saturated fat, 0 mg cholesterol, 944 mg sodium, 4 g carbohydrates, 2 g protein, 74 mg calcium, 2 g fiber

chicken adobo with spicy black bean salsa ♥ LOW FAT

If the big, bold flavors of the tropics are your thing, you'll love this recipe from cookbook author Steven Raichlen. Raichlen calls for Scotch bonnet, one of the world's hottest chiles, to heat up the salsa, but you can use a milder chile if you like. The recipe is adapted from Miami Spice *(Workman Publishing, 1993). Pictured on page 167.*

Prep time: 10 minutes plus marinating
Grilling time: 10 to 12 minutes

ADOBO:

- ½ cup fresh lime juice
- 2 teaspoons minced garlic
- 1 teaspoon cumin
- ½ teaspoon dried oregano
- ½ teaspoon salt
- ¼ teaspoon freshly ground pepper
  ■
- 1½ pounds boneless, skinless chicken breasts

BLACK BEAN SALSA:

- 1½ cups cooked black beans or 1 can (19 oz.) black beans, rinsed and drained
- 1 ripe mango, peeled, seeded and diced
- ¼ cup chopped red onion
- ¼ cup chopped fresh cilantro or mint
- ½ Scotch bonnet chile, seeded and minced, or 1 teaspoon minced jalapeño chile (see tip, page 95)
- 3 tablespoons fresh lime juice
- 1 tablespoon extra-virgin olive oil (optional)
- 2 teaspoons brown sugar
  ■
  Cooked rice (optional)
  Sliced lime, for garnish (optional)

1. ■ *Make adobo:* Whisk all ingredients together in a glass bowl. Add chicken; cover and marinate in the refrigerator 1 to 2 hours, turning 2 or 3 times.

2. ■ Heat and oil grill.

3. ■ *Make black bean salsa:* Fifteen minutes before grilling chicken, combine all salsa ingredients in bowl.

4. ■ Remove chicken from marinade; pat dry with paper towels. Grill chicken 6 minutes; brush with marinade. (Discard remaining marinade.) Turn and grill 4 minutes more, or until cooked through.

5. ■ Transfer chicken to a cutting board and let rest 2 minutes; slice each breast ½ inch thick on the diagonal. Arrange breasts and salsa on 4 serving plates. Serve with rice and garnish with lime slices, if desired. Makes 4 servings.

Per serving: 325 calories, 5.5 g total fat, 1.5 g saturated fat, 89 mg cholesterol, 218 mg sodium, 30 g carbohydrates, 39 g protein, 55 mg calcium, 4 g fiber

stuffed chicken breasts with parsnip-potato puree

This flavorful and moist chicken recipe comes to us from husband-and-wife cooking team Mark Peel and Nancy Silverton, who oversee the Campanile Restaurant and La Brea Bakery in Los Angeles, California.

Prep time: 20 minutes • Roasting time: 30 to 35 minutes

GINGER-GARLIC BUTTER:

- 2 tablespoons butter or margarine, softened
- 2 tablespoons chopped fresh flat-leaf parsley
- 1 teaspoon grated fresh ginger
- 1 teaspoon minced garlic, mashed to a paste with side of knife
- 1 teaspoon grated lemon peel
- ¼ teaspoon salt
- ⅛ teaspoon freshly ground pepper
  ■
- 1 tablespoon olive oil
- 2 medium onions, sliced
- 4 chicken breast halves (2 to 2½ lbs.)

PARSNIP-POTATO PUREE:

- 1 pound parsnips, peeled
- 1 pound all-purpose potatoes, peeled
- 3 cloves garlic
- ¾ cup milk or heavy or whipping cream

3   tablespoons butter or margarine
¼   teaspoon salt
⅛   teaspoon white pepper
    Steamed green beans (optional)

1. Heat oven to 425°F. For ginger-garlic butter: Combine all ginger-garlic butter ingredients in a small bowl; refrigerate. Meanwhile, brush jelly-roll pan with the olive oil; add onions and toss. Gently separate skin from one end of each chicken breast. Spread one-quarter of the ginger-garlic butter under skin of each breast. Place chicken, skin side up, on top of onions. Roast 30 to 35 minutes, until chicken is cooked through and onions are softened.

2. *Make parsnip-potato puree:* Meanwhile, cut parsnips and potatoes into 1-inch chunks. Place vegetable steamer in a large Dutch oven; add 1 cup water. Arrange parsnips, potatoes and garlic in steamer. Cover Dutch oven and bring water to boil. Reduce heat to medium and steam until vegetables are tender, 20 minutes.

3. Heat milk just to boil in a small saucepan; remove from heat and stir in butter. In batches, transfer parsnip-and-potato mixture to a ricer or food mill and press vegetables into a large bowl. Stir in milk mixture, salt and pepper. Serve with chicken and onions and, if desired, green beans. Serves 4.

Per serving: 715 calories, 38.5 g total fat, 16 g saturated fat, 176 mg cholesterol, 586 mg sodium, 43 g carbohydrates, 48 g protein, 150 mg calcium, 9 g fiber

savannah jambalaya

Chef Elizabeth Terry, of Elizabeth on 37th in Savannah, Georgia, offers the following tip for her jambalaya: "For a great Southern slow-cooked flavor use a good-quality smoked ham."

Prep time: 20 minutes • Cooking time: 33 to 40 minutes

4   tablespoons olive oil, divided
1   to 1¼ pounds boneless, skinless
    chicken thighs
½   pound hot Italian sausage links
2   tablespoons butter or margarine
¼   pound country-smoked ham or prosciutto ham,
    cut into ¼-inch dice
1   cup finely chopped onions
1½ cups long-grain rice
1   can (28 oz.) whole tomatoes in juice, diced,
    juice reserved
1   cup chicken broth
1   pound medium shelled and deveined shrimp
½   cup finely chopped green bell pepper
1   teaspoon dried thyme
1   teaspoon dried oregano
½   teaspoon freshly ground pepper
¼   teaspoon salt
    Chopped fresh parsley, for garnish (optional)

1. Heat 1 tablespoon of the oil in a medium Dutch oven over medium-high heat. Add chicken and sausage; cook, stirring occasionally, 8 to 10 minutes until browned. Transfer to a cutting board with a slotted spoon; cool and cut into 1-inch pieces. Set aside.

2. Meanwhile, remove all but 1 tablespoon drippings from Dutch oven; add butter and melt over medium heat. Add ham and cook until browned, 3 to 5 minutes. Stir in onions and rice; cook 3 minutes. Add tomatoes and their juice, broth and reserved chicken and sausage. Bring to boil; cover and reduce heat to low. Cook until rice is tender and liquid is absorbed, about 25 minutes.

3. Meanwhile, combine remaining 3 tablespoons oil, the shrimp, bell pepper, thyme, oregano, pepper and salt in a medium bowl. Cover with plastic wrap and refrigerate.

4. When rice is almost tender, heat a large nonstick skillet over medium-high heat. Add shrimp mixture and cook, stirring occasionally, 3 to 5 minutes, until shrimp turn pink. Spoon shrimp over rice mixture. Garnish with parsley, if desired. Makes 6 servings.

Per serving: 640 calories, 28.5 g total fat, 8 g saturated fat, 228 mg cholesterol, 1,263 mg sodium, 47 g carbohydrates, 47 g protein, 120 mg calcium, 3 g fiber

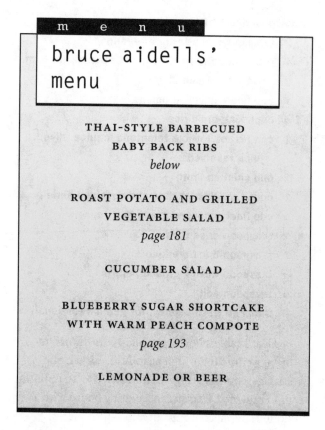

bruce aidells' menu

THAI-STYLE BARBECUED
BABY BACK RIBS
below

ROAST POTATO AND GRILLED
VEGETABLE SALAD
page 181

CUCUMBER SALAD

BLUEBERRY SUGAR SHORTCAKE
WITH WARM PEACH COMPOTE
page 193

LEMONADE OR BEER

thai-style barbecued baby back ribs

If your idea of heaven is a plate of spicy sausages or ribs, you're a kindred spirit of Bruce Aidells, founder of Aidells Sausage Company in San Francisco and author of The Complete Meat Cookbook *(Houghton Mifflin Company, 1998) and other cookbooks. To accompany these luscious ribs, Aidells suggests a salad of thinly sliced cucumbers tossed with white vinegar and sugar.*

Prep time: 15 minutes plus marinating and standing
Baking time: 45 to 60 minutes

THAI MARINADE:
¼ cup Asian fish sauce (nuoc mam or nam pla)
¼ cup chopped fresh cilantro
2 tablespoons peanut oil
2 tablespoons soy sauce
2 tablespoons fresh lime juice

2 tablespoons minced garlic
2 tablespoons sugar
2 stalks lemongrass,* bottom part only, outer leaves removed and tender center thinly sliced
1 tablespoon minced fresh ginger
2 teaspoons Asian sesame oil
■
4 to 4½ pounds pork loin back ribs (baby back ribs) or pork spareribs

THAI DIPPING SAUCE:
2 tablespoons fresh lime juice
2 tablespoons rice wine vinegar
1 tablespoon soy sauce
1 tablespoon hot Thai chili sauce or 1 teaspoon red pepper flakes
1 tablespoon sugar
1 teaspoon minced garlic
½ teaspoon Asian sesame oil

1. *Make Thai marinade:* Combine all marinade ingredients in a large shallow dish. Add ribs; cover, and marinate in the refrigerator overnight, turning occasionally.

2. Remove ribs from the refrigerator and let stand at room temperature 30 minutes. Meanwhile, arrange oven racks in the bottom and upper third of oven. Heat oven to 300°F.

3. Remove ribs from marinade, shaking off excess; reserve marinade for basting. Fill a roasting pan halfway with water; place on the bottom oven rack. Arrange ribs in one layer on two racks in a shallow roasting pan. Place pan on upper oven rack and bake 45 to 60 minutes, basting with marinade until the meat is very tender. (Do not baste the last 20 minutes of baking; discard any remaining marinade.) Temperature should reach 155°F. to 165°F. on an instant-read meat thermometer when inserted at the thickest part of the rib.

4. Transfer ribs to a cutting board; cover with foil and let stand 5 to 10 minutes. Cut into serving pieces and serve with Thai dipping sauce. Makes 6 servings.

5. *Thai dipping sauce:* Combine all Thai dipping sauce ingredients in a small bowl, stirring until sugar dissolves. Makes ¹⁄₃ cup.

Note: Can be found in produce aisle of supermarkets or in Asian specialty stores.

Per serving: 635 calories, 50 g total fat, 18 g saturated fat, 183 mg cholesterol, 745 mg sodium, 6 g carbohydrates, 39 g protein, 77 mg calcium, 0 g fiber

roast potato and grilled vegetable salad

This recipe from Bruce Aidells is a great way to load up on summer veggies! Roasted potatoes are tossed with grilled zucchini, yellow squash, eggplant, red onion, bell peppers and plenty of zesty garlic-mustard vinaigrette.

Prep time: 25 minutes
Baking time: 20 to 25 minutes

OVEN-ROASTED POTATOES:
- 1½ pounds small red or Yukon gold potatoes, cut into quarters
- 2 tablespoons olive oil
- ¼ teaspoon salt
- 1 teaspoon freshly ground pepper
- 2 tablespoons chopped fresh rosemary or
  - 2 tablespoons chopped fresh parsley and
  - 2 teaspoons dried rosemary, thyme or savory

GRILLED VEGETABLES:
- 2 bell peppers (red, yellow or green)
- 1 zucchini, thinly sliced lengthwise
- 1 yellow or pattypan squash, thinly sliced lengthwise
- 1 Asian eggplant, sliced lengthwise
- 1 red onion, quartered
- ¹⁄₃ cup olive oil

GARLIC-MUSTARD VINAIGRETTE:
- 1 clove garlic, minced
- 1½ teaspoons Dijon mustard
- ¾ teaspoon red wine vinegar
- ¼ teaspoon Worcestershire sauce
  Pinch salt
- ¼ teaspoon freshly ground pepper
- 2 tablespoons olive oil
- 1½ teaspoons chopped fresh herbs (such as basil, thyme, oregano or marjoram)
- ½ cup thinly sliced green onions
  Fresh thyme sprigs, for garnish (optional)

1. *Make oven-roasted potatoes:* Heat oven to 450°F. Combine potatoes with remaining roasted potato ingredients in a medium bowl. Spread potatoes on a large cookie sheet and roast, turning occasionally, until the potatoes are nicely browned on all sides, 20 to 25 minutes.

2. Meanwhile, heat grill.

3. *Make grilled vegetables:* Brush bell peppers and both sides of zucchini, yellow squash, eggplant and red onion with oil. Grill vegetables in batches 4 to 6 minutes per side, until softened and lightly charred. Transfer to a large plate and cool.

4. *Make garlic-mustard vinaigrette:* Combine garlic, mustard, vinegar, Worcestershire, salt and pepper in a small bowl. Gradually whisk in oil until mixture is thickened. Stir in herbs.

5. Coarsely chop eggplant, squash and onions. Peel and seed bell peppers and slice into thin strips.

6. Place the potatoes, grilled vegetables and green onions in a large bowl. Toss with half of the vinaigrette. Transfer salad to a shallow serving bowl or platter and pour on remaining vinaigrette. Garnish with fresh thyme, if desired. Makes 6 servings.

Per serving: 315 calories, 21.5 g total fat, 3 g saturated fat, 0 mg cholesterol, 167 mg sodium, 29 g carbohydrates, 4 g protein, 40 mg calcium, 4 g fiber

julia child's duck roast with polenta

"This is real food!" exclaims Julia Child about her trademark duck recipe. "Preparing a duck roast is a wonderful project for people who truly love cooking—the only people I write for." Julia recommends asking the butcher to prepare the duck for cooking for easier prep.

Prep time: 2 ½ hours plus marinating and chilling
Cooking time: 1 hour 25 to 1 hour 32 minutes

- **1** **whole duck (5½ to 5¾ lbs.), fresh or frozen, thawed;* neck and giblets reserved**
- **1** **teaspoon salt**
- **¼** **teaspoon dried thyme**
- **¼** **teaspoon allspice**
- **¼** **teaspoon paprika**
- **¼** **teaspoon freshly ground pepper**
- **¼** **teaspoon crumbled dried sage**

STOCK:

- **⅓** **cup diced onion**
- **⅓** **cup diced carrot**
- **⅓** **cup diced celery**
- **1** **can (14½ oz.) reduced-sodium chicken broth**
- **¼** **teaspoon dried thyme**
- **1** **bay leaf**
- **4** **fresh parsley sprigs**
- **1** **plum tomato, chopped**
- **2½** **cups water**
- **¼** **cup dry white vermouth**
- **¼** **teaspoon salt**
- **⅛** **teaspoon freshly ground pepper**
- ■
- **12** **pearl onions, peeled**
- **¼** **cup water**
- **¾** **pound assorted mushrooms (such as white, shiitake and brown), trimmed and halved**
- **1** **tube (16 oz.) refrigerated polenta, cut crosswise into 8 equal slices**
- **Steamed green beans (optional)**

1. ■ *Day before:* Remove leg-thigh portions from duck. Remove thigh bone by scraping along bone to separate from meat, keeping meat intact and attached to the drumstick. Cut at joint to remove thigh bone. Cut down each side of the breastbone and rib cage. Remove breast meat by scraping a sharp knife along rib cage. Leaving each breast covered with skin, trim off excess skin and fat; set aside. Trim excess fat and skin from legs and carcass; set aside. Chop the carcass into 2-inch pieces; transfer to bowl with neck and giblets and set aside. Prick the skin covering breast and leg-thighs with the tip of a small, sharp knife without piercing the meat.

2. ■ Combine salt, thyme, allspice, paprika, pepper and sage. Sprinkle spices on both sides of duck breasts and leg-thighs. Arrange on a plate. Cover and refrigerate overnight.

3. ■ Cut reserved fat and skin into thin strips. Cook very slowly in a small skillet over low heat, until melted (or rendered) to a clear, golden liquid, 25 to 30 minutes.

4. ■ *Make stock:* Heat 1 tablespoon melted duck fat in a large skillet over medium-high heat. (Transfer remaining fat to a cup; cover and refrigerate overnight.) Cook duck carcass, giblets and neck in 2 batches until well browned, turning occasionally, 5 to 10 minutes per batch. Transfer each batch with slotted spoon to a Dutch oven. Add diced onion, carrot and celery to the skillet. Cook until vegetables are lightly browned, 8 minutes; transfer to the Dutch oven with a slotted spoon. Discard fat from skillet. Add chicken broth to skillet and bring to boil, stirring to scrape up any browned bits. Transfer broth to the Dutch oven with thyme, bay leaf, parsley, tomato and the 2½ cups water. Bring to boil. Reduce heat; cover and simmer 1½ hours. Strain stock through a colander set over a large bowl, pressing on solids to extract as much liquid as possible. Discard solids; cool stock completely. Transfer to a large bowl; cover and refrigerate overnight.

5. ■ *Next day:* Discard fat from chilled stock. Bring stock to boil in a saucepan. Add vermouth and boil until liquid is reduced by half (1½ cups), 30 minutes; add salt and pepper. Set aside.

6. Melt 1 tablespoon reserved chilled duck fat in a small saucepan over medium heat. Add pearl onions and cook until browned on all sides, stirring occasionally, 5 to 8 minutes. Add the ¼ cup water and bring to boil. Cover and simmer onions 10 minutes, or until tender. Set aside, discarding liquid.

7. Melt 1 tablespoon more duck fat in a large skillet over medium-high heat. Add mushrooms and cook until softened. Transfer to a plate.

8. Melt another 1 tablespoon fat in same skillet over medium heat. Add the duck breasts and leg-thighs, skin side down. Cook leg-thighs 15 minutes, turning, until browned on both sides. Cook breasts 12 minutes, until well browned; turn and cook 3 minutes more for medium-rare. Transfer breasts to a plate. Cover skillet, reduce heat to low and cook leg-thighs, turning occasionally, 25 minutes more, until tender and cooked through.

9. Meanwhile, heat oven to 200°F. Melt 1 tablespoon fat in another large skillet. Add polenta slices and cook 5 minutes per side, until browned. Transfer slices to a cookie sheet and keep warm in oven.

10. Transfer leg-thighs to the plate with the duck breasts. Pour off fat from skillet and wipe clean. Return duck to skillet with onions, mushrooms and stock. Cover and simmer 4 to 5 minutes, turning duck occasionally, until duck is heated through. Remove skillet from heat. Remove duck to a cutting board; cut breast and leg-thighs into diagonal slices. Arrange 2 slices of polenta on each of 4 serving plates. Divide and arrange duck, onions and mushrooms on polenta. Reheat stock; spoon over duck. Serve with green beans, if desired. Makes 4 servings.

Note: To thaw, defrost in refrigerator up to 2 to 3 days. Once thawed, use within 2 days.

Per serving: 595 calories, 37.5 g total fat, 12.5 g saturated fat, 107 mg cholesterol, 1,481 mg sodium, 29 g carbohydrates, 31 g protein, 43 mg calcium, 5 g fiber

test kitchen tip
salts of the earth

Once upon a time, salt was rare and highly prized; in fact, Roman soldiers were paid, in part, with the commodity. Today, it is inexpensive and plentiful, and perhaps the most often-used seasoning in the world. While most recipes call for table salt, there are other varieties. Here are some common types available:

TABLE SALT contains additives to help keep it from clumping and to give it its pure whiteness. Iodine is added to many table salts, as it's an essential dietary nutrient. Uniodized salt is also available.

KOSHER SALT has no additives and is more coarsely ground than table salt. Some of the recipes in this book call for kosher salt for its enhanced texture; it also has a less salty flavor.

SEA SALT is derived from the evaporation of sea water. This process is more costly than mining the mineral from salt mines; however, some cooks prefer its flavor.

ROCK SALT is often called for in the freezing of homemade ice cream. Because it is unrefined, it has a grayish hue. Rock salt is inedible.

CANNING AND PICKLING SALT is additive-free so that it won't cloud brines. It is more finely ground than regular table salt.

SEASONED SALTS are blends of salt and other seasonings.

STORING SALT: With the exception of seasoned salts, all types of salts can be stored indefinitely at room temperature. Seasoned salts should be kept tightly capped at room temperature, and are best if used within one year.

balsamic marinated pork medallions

When asked for a quick weeknight supper one could easily prepare at home, chef Debra Ponzek, who's also the author of French Food, American Accent *(Clarkson Potter, 1996) offered this simple entrée. It calls on one of her favorite ingredients: dark, sweet balsamic vinegar.*

Total prep and cooking time: 28 minutes

- 1 tablespoon vegetable oil
- 4 (6 oz. each) boneless center cut pork chops, 1 to 1¼ inches thick
  Salt
  Freshly ground pepper
- ⅓ cup balsamic vinegar
- 1 tablespoon soy sauce
- 1 tablespoon butter or margarine
- 1 pound fresh spinach, stems removed

1. Heat oven to 400°F.

2. Heat oil in a large ovenproof skillet over medium-high heat 1 minute. Sprinkle pork with ¹/₂ teaspoon salt and ¹/₄ teaspoon pepper. Brown pork 3 minutes per side; add vinegar and soy sauce. Bake 8 to 12 minutes, until an instant-read meat thermometer inserted in center of one chop reaches 155°F. With a slotted spoon, transfer pork to a cutting board. Transfer sauce to a bowl; keep warm.

3. Add butter and spinach to skillet. Cook over medium-high heat 1 minute, until spinach wilts. Sprinkle with a pinch each salt and pepper. Slice pork and arrange on 4 serving plates. Serve with spinach and balsamic sauce. Makes 4 servings.

Per serving: 420 calories, 28 g total fat, 9.5 g saturated fat, 122 mg cholesterol, 728 mg sodium, 4 g carbohydrates, 37 g protein, 124 mg calcium, 3 g fiber

garlic-crusted whitefish

The Mity Nice Grill in Chicago serves this terrific dish. Part of what makes it so tasty is the cream cheese, which is spread over the bread-crumb-and-butter crust.

Total prep and cooking time: 1 hour 20 minutes

- 1¼ cups fresh bread crumbs
- 1 tablespoon olive oil
- 4 cloves garlic
- 1 package (8 oz.) cream cheese, softened
- 2 pounds russet potatoes, peeled and cut in half
  Salt
- 1½ cups milk
  Freshly ground pepper
- 6 tablespoons butter
- 1 tablespoon chopped fresh parsley
- 1 tablespoon butter, melted
- 4 (6 oz. each) whitefish fillets

1. Heat oven to 350°F. Spread bread crumbs in a pie plate. Bake 15 minutes, stirring twice; cool.

2. Heat oil in a small saucepan. Add garlic; cook over low heat 10 minutes. Transfer to a bowl and mash. Mix in cream cheese.

3. Boil potatoes, 2 teaspoons salt and water to cover in a large Dutch oven. Reduce heat and cook 30 minutes, until potatoes are fork-tender. Drain; transfer to a mixer bowl. Heat milk, ³/₄ teaspoon salt and ¹/₄ teaspoon pepper in saucepan until just warm. Beat hot milk and the 6 tablespoons butter into potatoes until smooth. Keep warm.

4. Increase temperature to 400°F. Toss bread crumbs, parsley and the 1 tablespoon melted butter in a bowl. Brush a jelly-roll pan with oil. Sprinkle fish with salt and pepper. Press one side of fish into crumbs; place crumb side down on pan. Spread cheese mixture over tops. Top with remaining crumbs. Bake 14 to 16 minutes until cooked through. Serve with potatoes. Makes 4 servings.

Per serving: 890 calories, 57 g total fat, 29 g saturated fat, 229 mg cholesterol, 819 mg sodium, 47 g carbohydrates, 47 g protein, 247 mg calcium, 5 g fiber

salsa-baked fish with jicama slaw

Bold and flavorful Mexican fare is the hallmark of Rick Bayless's two Chicago restaurants, the Frontera Grill and Topolobampo. We asked Bayless for a quick family-friendly recipe, and he gave us this dish. "It reminds me of the tastes of summer," Bayless says, "and it's great because it's just so simple."

Prep time: 30 minutes • Baking time: 20 minutes
Microwave used

- 4   **large cloves garlic, unpeeled**
- 2   **large (1 oz.) jalapeño chiles (see tip, page 95)**
- 1½ **pounds Yukon gold or baking potatoes, scrubbed and cut into ¼-inch-thick slices**
- 1   **tablespoon olive oil**
- 1½ **teaspoons salt, divided**
- ¼   **teaspoon freshly ground pepper**
- 1   **can (28 oz.) whole plum tomatoes, drained**
- ½   **cup finely chopped white onion**
- ⅓   **cup chopped fresh cilantro**
- 4   **(4 to 5 oz. each) boneless, skinless fish fillets (such as snapper, grouper, halibut, mahi-mahi or sea bass)**

JICAMA SLAW:
- 1   **small (1 lb.) jicama, peeled**
- 1   **small (8 oz.) seedless cucumber, unpeeled**
- 3   **tablespoons olive oil**
- 3   **tablespoons fresh lime juice**
- ½   **teaspoon salt**
- ¼   **cup chopped fresh cilantro**

1. Heat oven to 400°F. Arrange garlic and chiles in a small, heavy skillet. Cook 10 to 12 minutes over medium heat, turning occasionally, until softened and evenly charred. Cool.

2. Meanwhile, combine potatoes, oil, ½ teaspoon of the salt and the pepper in a shallow 3-quart glass baking dish. Cover with plastic wrap, turning back one corner to vent. Microwave on High until potatoes are fork-tender, 12 minutes.

3. Meanwhile, remove stems from chiles and peel garlic. Process chiles, garlic and ¾ teaspoon of the salt in a food processor, scraping sides of bowl, until finely chopped. Add tomatoes and pulse until coarsely chopped. Transfer to a bowl; stir in onion and cilantro.

4. Uncover potatoes and top with fish; sprinkle remaining ¼ teaspoon salt over fillets. Spoon tomato salsa over fish. Bake 20 minutes in oven until fish flakes easily when tested with a fork.

5. *Make jicama slaw:* Meanwhile, cut jicama into ¼-inch-thick slices, then cut slices crosswise into ¼-inch-thick strips. Repeat process with cucumber. Whisk together olive oil, lime juice and salt in a large bowl. Add jicama and cucumber strips and cilantro, tossing to coat.

6. Divide potatoes and fish among 4 serving plates. Serve with jicama slaw. Makes 4 servings.

Per serving: 495 calories, 16 g total fat, 2.5 g saturated fat, 47 mg cholesterol, 1,525 mg sodium, 55 g carbohydrates, 33 g protein, 139 mg calcium, 6 g fiber

---

test kitchen tip

what's whitefish?

Whitefish, a freshwater fish that's a cousin to trout and salmon, has a delicate flavor that sometimes borders on sweet. It's also a firm-textured fish, making it an excellent choice for the rich Garlic-Crusted Whitefish recipe on page 184.

If whitefish isn't available at your market, substitute haddock, lake trout or pike.

poached whole salmon with basil mayonnaise

Award-winning cookbook author James Peterson says, "When I want to pull out all the stops to impress my guests, a whole poached salmon with lemon and herbs is just the thing." To cook any large whole fish, Peterson recommends a fish poacher, which can be purchased at most gourmet food shops. Tip: Peel the skin off the salmon while it's still warm, and it will come off easily. Pictured on page 164.

Prep time: 30 minutes plus chilling
Cooking time: 1 hour to 1 hour 5 minutes

VEGETABLE BROTH:

- 8 fresh thyme sprigs or 1½ teaspoons dried thyme
- 1 large bunch fresh parsley
- 2 large bay leaves
- 1 large onion, sliced
- 2 carrots, sliced
- 2 celery ribs, sliced
- 8 cups water
- 1 tablespoon salt
- 3 cups white wine
- 14 whole black peppercorns, crushed (optional)

- 1 whole salmon (5 to 5½ lbs.), head removed

BASIL MAYONNAISE:

- ⅔ cup mayonnaise
- ⅔ cup sour cream
- ½ cup chopped fresh basil
- 1 tablespoon plus 1 teaspoon grated lemon peel
- 2 teaspoons fresh lemon juice
- 2 teaspoons chopped shallots
- 2 tablespoons milk
- ¼ teaspoon salt
- ¼ teaspoon freshly ground pepper

    Lemon wedges, fresh mint and thyme sprigs, for garnish (optional)

1. *Make vegetable broth:* Combine thyme, parsley and bay leaves in a piece of cheesecloth; tie ends of cheesecloth with kitchen string. Combine cheesecloth bundle, onion, carrots, celery, water and salt in a 4-quart pot. Cover and bring to boil over high heat. Reduce heat to medium-low and simmer gently, partially covered, 20 minutes. Add wine; simmer 10 minutes, then add peppercorns, if desired, and simmer 5 minutes more.

2. Strain broth into an 11-quart fish poacher on the stovetop over two burners. Arrange salmon in poacher, then add 15 cups cold water to cover the fish. Cover and bring liquid to boil over high heat (this will take 20 to 25 minutes). When the liquid begins to boil, uncover and reduce heat to medium-low to maintain a gentle simmer. Check the salmon for doneness after 10 to 15 minutes. Gently lift the poaching rack and insert an instant-read thermometer into the backbone, next to the center of the fish. (It's best to get someone to help with this, but if you must do it alone, set the rack with the salmon on a cutting board.) The temperature should register 132°F. (If you don't have a thermometer, insert a small paring knife along the backbone and peek in—the flesh should separate easily from the bone and should be pink instead of translucent red.)

3. *Make basil mayonnaise:* Combine all basil mayonnaise ingredients in a bowl. Cover and refrigerate. Makes 1²/₃ cups.

4. Remove salmon from poaching liquid, and carefully transfer to a large serving platter using 2 large spatulas. With a small knife, peel off the top skin, then gently turn the fish over and repeat. Cool and refrigerate. Garnish salmon with lemon wedges, mint and thyme sprigs, if desired. Serve with basil mayonnaise. Makes 8 servings.

Per serving: 370 calories, 30 g total fat, 7 g saturated fat, 81 mg cholesterol, 250 mg sodium, 2 g carbohydrates, 22 g protein, 53 mg calcium, 0 g fiber

vegetable tian

This recipe hails from France, the country where esteemed cookbook author James Peterson first discovered that cooking was his true passion. A tian was originally a Provençal earthenware dish, but the word is now used to mean any gratin that's Provençal in character. Provençal gratins typically include tomatoes and zucchini, but you can add any vegetable; only the tomatoes are essential. Pictured on page 164.

Prep time: 30 minutes
Baking time: 45 to 55 minutes

- 2   yellow or red bell peppers
- 6   tablespoons extra-virgin olive oil, divided
- 2   medium zucchini, cut diagonally into ¼-inch-thick slices, divided
- 2   teaspoons finely chopped fresh marjoram or thyme leaves, divided
- 2   teaspoons finely chopped garlic, divided
- ½   teaspoon salt, divided
- ¼   teaspoon freshly ground pepper, divided
- 40   large fresh basil leaves (2 cups loosely packed)
- 2   packages (9 oz. each) frozen artichoke hearts, thawed and patted dry
- 4   ripe tomatoes, cut into 4 wedges each, seeds removed
- ½   cup freshly grated Parmesan cheese

1. Heat broiler. Line a cookie sheet with foil. Place bell peppers on prepared sheet and broil 6 inches from heat source, turning occasionally, until evenly charred, 10 minutes. Cover peppers; let stand until cool enough to handle. Remove the charred skins. Cut peppers in half; seed and cut into ¼-inch strips.

2. Reduce oven temperature to 325°F. Heat 1 tablespoon of the oil in a 12-inch skillet over medium-high heat. Add half the zucchini in a single layer and cook, turning, until browned, 6 to 8 minutes. Sprinkle with 1 teaspoon of the marjoram, 1 teaspoon of the garlic, ¼ teaspoon of the salt and ⅛ teaspoon of the pepper. Cook 1 minute more, turning gently. Repeat with 1 tablespoon oil, remaining zucchini, 1 teaspoon marjoram, 1 teaspoon garlic, ¼ teaspoon salt and ⅛ teaspoon pepper.

3. Place basil leaves on a cutting board; drizzle with 4 teaspoons of the oil and chop coarsely. Spread evenly on bottom of a 3-quart shallow baking dish.

4. Toss artichokes in a bowl with 2 teaspoons of the oil; arrange in a single layer in the prepared dish. Top with zucchini. Arrange tomato wedges on top of zucchini, overlapping slightly. Arrange pepper strips in a crisscross pattern over tomatoes. Sprinkle evenly with Parmesan and drizzle with remaining 2 tablespoons oil. Bake 45 to 55 minutes or until most of the liquid evaporates from the tomatoes and vegetables are browned. Serve warm or at room temperature. Makes 8 servings.

Per serving: 195 calories, 15 g total fat, 4 g saturated fat, 10 mg cholesterol, 408 mg sodium, 11 g carbohydrates, 8 g protein, 199 mg calcium, 5 g fiber

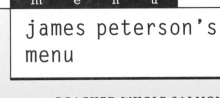

m e n u

james peterson's menu

POACHED WHOLE SALMON WITH BASIL MAYONNAISE
page 186

VEGETABLE TIAN
left

SUGAR SNAP PEAS

FRUIT SOUP WITH SPICE BROTH
page 190

CHARDONNAY

clams in green sauce

At Tony DaCaneca Tavern & Restaurant in Newark, New Jersey, flavorful fresh clams get spruced up with parsley, butter, onions, garlic and clam juice. Before serving, be sure to toss out clams that don't open after cooking.

Prep time: 15 minutes
Cooking time: 5 to 8 minutes

4 dozen fresh Littleneck clams, scrubbed
2 cups diced onions
4 tablespoons butter or margarine
2 tablespoons chopped fresh flat-leaf parsley
1 tablespoon chopped garlic
2 bottles (8 oz. each) clam juice
¼ teaspoon hot red pepper sauce
    Crusty bread (optional)

Combine clams, onions, butter, parsley and garlic in a medium Dutch oven. Add clam juice and hot pepper sauce. Cover with a tight-fitting lid. Bring to boil over medium-high heat. Cook until clams open, 5 to 8 minutes. Discard any unopened clams. Serve with crusty bread, if desired. Makes 4 servings.

Per serving: 305 calories, 14 g total fat, 7.5 g saturated fat, 107 mg cholesterol, 506 mg sodium, 14 g carbohydrates, 31 g protein, 147 mg calcium, 1 g fiber

creamed spinach

With this special side dish, Ruth's Chris Steak House in Metairie, Louisiana, offers the ultimate in comfort food. It's made rich and oh-so-yummy with butter and milk.

Prep time: 15 minutes • Cooking time: 18 to 22 minutes

½ cup butter or margarine
¼ cup all-purpose flour
2 tablespoons chopped onion
1 bay leaf
1 clove
1 teaspoon salt, divided
2 cups milk
3 pounds trimmed fresh spinach
2 tablespoons butter or margarine, softened
¼ teaspoon freshly ground pepper

1. Melt the ½ cup butter in a medium saucepan over medium heat. Add flour, stirring until light brown, 3 to 5 minutes. Stir in onion, bay leaf, clove and ½ teaspoon of the salt. Cook until onion begins to soften, 1 to 2 minutes. Whisk in milk, then stir until mixture reaches a boil and begins to thicken, 3 to 5 minutes. Reduce heat to low and cook 5 minutes more until mixture is thick and coats back of a spoon. Remove from heat; strain mixture through a fine sieve set over a medium saucepan. Set the saucepan aside.

2. Bring a large pot of water to boil. Add spinach and cook 1 minute. Immediately transfer spinach to a bowl of ice water. Drain spinach in a colander, then squeeze dry in a clean kitchen towel. Transfer spinach to a food processor and puree. Stir spinach into strained sauce. Cook over low heat until heated through, 5 minutes. Stir in the 2 tablespoons butter, the remaining ½ teaspoon salt and the pepper. Makes about 3 cups.

Per ½ cup: 266 calories, 21 g total fat, 13 g saturated fat, 57 mg cholesterol, 711 mg sodium, 14 g carbohydrates, 9 g protein, 347 mg calcium, 6 g fiber

potato croquettes

Cookbook author and teacher Joyce Goldstein shared this recipe with us. You can serve the croquettes as an appetizer, side dish or even a light main course.

Prep time: 30 minutes • Cooking time: 18 minutes

- **2 pounds boiling potatoes, such as russet or Yukon gold, peeled and quartered**
- **1¾ teaspoons salt, divided**
- **2 large egg yolks**
- **⅓ cup freshly grated Romano cheese**
- **¼ cup chopped green onions**
- **¼ cup pine nuts**
- **3 tablespoons chopped fresh parsley**
- **3 tablespoons chopped fresh mint**
- **¼ teaspoon freshly ground pepper**
- **1 bottle (48 oz.) vegetable oil**
- **3 large egg whites**
- **½ cup all-purpose flour**
- **1 cup plain dry bread crumbs**

1. Bring potatoes and enough cold water to cover by 2 inches to boil in a large saucepan. Add 1 teaspoon of the salt and cook until tender, 12 to 15 minutes. Drain and press potatoes into a large bowl with a potato ricer or food mill. Beat in yolks, cheese, green onions, pine nuts, parsley, mint, remaining ³/₄ teaspoon salt and the pepper.

2. Heat oven to 200°F. Line 2 jelly-roll pans with waxed paper. Shape potato mixture by rounded tablespoons into 2-inch-long ovals and place on prepared pans.

3. Heat oil to 375°F. in a deep 10-inch frying pan over medium heat. Beat egg whites in a bowl until frothy. Spread flour and bread crumbs on two separate plates. Dip ovals in flour, then egg whites, then coat in crumbs. Fry ovals, 5 to 6 at a time, until golden, 3 minutes. (Keep oil temperature between 325°F. and 350°F.) Transfer croquettes with a slotted spoon to a paper-towel-lined cookie sheet; keep warm in oven. Transfer to a serving dish. Serve immediately. Makes 30 croquettes.

Per croquette: 75 calories, 3.5 g total fat, 0.5 g saturated fat, 15 mg cholesterol, 153 mg sodium, 9 g carbohydrates, 2 g protein, 25 mg calcium, 1 g fiber

neiman marcus popovers *EASY*

These gems hail from the famous Dallas department store. Serve them hot from the oven for tea-time or breakfast.

Prep time: 20 minutes • Baking time: 1 hour

- **2 cups all-purpose flour**
- **¾ teaspoon salt**
- **½ teaspoon baking powder**
- **3 large eggs**
- **1¾ cups milk, at room temperature**
- **2 tablespoons butter or margarine, melted**

STRAWBERRY BUTTER (OPTIONAL):
- **½ cup unsalted butter (no substitutions), softened**
- **6 tablespoons strawberry preserves**

1. Heat oven to 450°F. Combine flour, salt and baking powder in a large mixer bowl; set aside. Whisk eggs in another bowl. Whisk in milk and melted butter. With mixer at low speed, stir milk mixture into dry ingredients. Increase speed to medium and beat batter 2 minutes.

2. Meanwhile, grease popover cups of a six-cup (5 oz. each) popover pan. Heat in oven 5 minutes. Divide and pour batter into prepared cups. Bake 10 minutes. Reduce oven temperature to 350°F. Bake popovers 40 minutes.

3. With a small, sharp knife cut a small slit in the top of each popover. Bake 10 minutes more, until popovers are a deep golden brown. Unmold popovers and serve immediately with strawberry butter. Makes 6 popovers.

4. *Strawberry butter:* Beat butter in a small mixer bowl until light and fluffy. Beat in preserves. Makes 1¹/₄ cups.

Per popover (without strawberry butter): 246 calories, 8 g total fat, 4 g saturated fat, 122 mg cholesterol, 403 mg sodium, 33 g carbohydrates, 10 g protein, 136 mg calcium, 1 g fiber

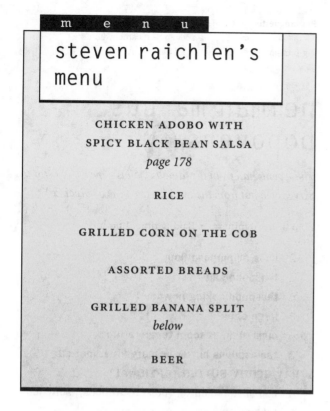

m e n u

steven raichlen's menu

CHICKEN ADOBO WITH
SPICY BLACK BEAN SALSA
page 178

RICE

GRILLED CORN ON THE COB

ASSORTED BREADS

GRILLED BANANA SPLIT
below

BEER

grilled banana split

This recipe is adapted from The Barbecue Bible *(Workman Publishing, 1998) by Steven Raichlen. Here, the award-winning cookbook author gives this traditional sundae a tropical twist with rum, coconut ice cream and macadamia nuts. Choose bananas that are still slightly firm, not overripe, to hold up best on the grill. Pictured on page 165.*

Prep time: 15 minutes plus marinating
Grilling time: 6 to 8 minutes

MAPLE SAUCE:
- 1 cup pure maple syrup (no substitutions)
- ½ cup dark rum
- ¼ cup sugar
- ½ teaspoon cinnamon
- ¼ teaspoon freshly grated nutmeg

  ▪

- 4 slightly green bananas, peeled
- 2 pints coconut or vanilla ice cream

- 1 cup heavy or whipping cream, beaten until stiff
- ¼ cup toasted coconut shavings or shredded coconut
- 2 tablespoons toasted chopped macadamia nuts

1. ▪ Clean grill rack. Heat and oil grill.

2. ▪ *Make maple sauce:* Whisk together maple syrup, rum, sugar, cinnamon and nutmeg in a large bowl until sugar dissolves.

3. ▪ Place bananas on clean grill and cook, turning frequently, until lightly browned on all sides and almost tender, 6 to 8 minutes. Transfer to a cutting board and slice diagonally into ½-inch-thick slices. Stir hot bananas into maple sauce and marinate in refrigerator 3 hours.

4. ▪ Place 2 scoops of ice cream in the center of 4 shallow bowls; divide and spoon banana mixture over each scoop. Divide and top each with whipped cream, toasted coconut and macadamia nuts. Makes 4 servings.

Per serving with ½ cup ice cream: 325 calories, 36 g total fat, 21 g saturated fat, 107 mg cholesterol, 63 mg sodium, 115 g carbohydrates, 5 g protein, 106 mg calcium, 1 g fiber

fruit soup with spice broth

"This soup is delicate and intriguing because the fruits are served in a light syrup scented with exotic spices," says James Peterson, author of Splendid Soups *(Bantam, 1993) and other cookbooks. "Sometimes I like to make this soup with unusual tropical fruits to keep the conversation going with people guessing what's what," he adds, "but use whatever fruits you have available." Pictured on page 163.*

Total prep time: 30 minutes plus standing and chilling

- 1 vanilla bean, cut lengthwise in half
- 1 ¼-inch-thick slice fresh ginger
- 1 star anise, crushed

1 2-inch cinnamon stick or ½ teaspoon
    cinnamon
½ cup sugar
4 cups water
    Juice of 1 orange (about ½ cup)
1 mango or papaya (1 lb.), peeled, seeded and
    cut into ¼-inch dice
2 kiwis (8 oz.), peeled and cut into
    ¼-inch dice
1 cup red berries (such as raspberries, red
    currants or halved wild strawberries or
    small strawberries)
½ medium pineapple, peeled, cored and cut into
    ½-inch dice
    Fresh mint, for garnish (optional)

1. Combine vanilla bean, ginger, star anise, cinnamon stick (or cinnamon, if using), sugar, water and orange juice in a 4-quart pot with a tight-fitting lid. Bring mixture to a slow simmer over medium-low heat. Cover pot and simmer mixture 5 minutes. Remove from heat and let stand 1 hour.

2. Remove and reserve vanilla bean. Strain syrup through a fine sieve into a large bowl; discard ginger, star anise and cinnamon stick. Scrape the seeds from each half of the vanilla bean and stir into the strained syrup. (If desired, use vanilla bean to make vanilla sugar by placing the dry bean in sugar.)

3. Stir mango, kiwis, berries and pineapple into syrup and refrigerate 2 hours. *(Can be made ahead. Cover and refrigerate up to 4 hours.)* Divide soup among 6 chilled serving bowls. Garnish with mint, if desired. Makes 6 servings.

Per serving: 180 calories, 1 g total fat, 0 g saturated fat, 0 mg cholesterol, 4 mg sodium, 46 g carbohydrates, 1 g protein, 29 mg calcium, 4 g fiber

white grape granita EASY LOW FAT

Michele Scicolone's recipe makes for a light, refreshing finish to her menu (page 177) or any summer evening dinner. White grape juice is always available on the supermarket shelf, and seedless green grapes are available year-round. But you can use red grapes as well, which will give the ice a beautiful blush. Pictured on page 163.

Total prep time: 15 minutes plus chilling and freezing

1   cup water
½   cup sugar
3   cups green or red seedless grapes (1 lb.),
     stems removed
1½ cups chilled white grape juice
     Green seedless grapes and fresh mint sprigs,
     for garnish (optional)

1. Combine water and sugar in a small saucepan. Bring to a simmer over medium-low heat. Cook, stirring occasionally, until sugar is dissolved, 5 minutes. Transfer to a small bowl and cool completely. Refrigerate until cold, 30 minutes.

2. Meanwhile, place a metal 13×9-inch baking pan and a metal spoon in the freezer.

3. Puree grapes in a food processor or blender. Strain puree through a fine-mesh sieve set over a large bowl, pressing solids with a rubber spatula to extract juice; discard peel. Stir in grape juice and chilled sugar syrup. Pour mixture into frozen pan.

4. Freeze grape mixture until ice crystals form around edges of pan, about 30 minutes. With the frozen metal spoon, scrap the ice crystals from edges of pan and stir into the mixture. Freeze mixture 2 to 2½ hours more, stirring every 30 minutes, until all of the liquid is frozen.

5. Scoop granita into 6 small serving bowls and garnish with grapes and mint sprigs, if desired. Makes 6 servings.

Per serving: 155 calories, 0 g total fat, 0 g saturated fat, 0 mg cholesterol, 7 mg sodium, 40 g carbohydrates, 0 g protein, 8 mg calcium, 0 g fiber

warm blueberry phyllo stack with almonds

Emily Luchetti, cookbook author and executive pastry chef at San Francisco's Farallon restaurant, shared with us this showstopping summertime dessert, which she created with Darcy Tizio, pastry chef at Farallon. As with all of Luchetti's signature desserts, this stunning "stack" of crisp almond-phyllo pastry, vanilla ice cream and warm blueberry sauce is a contrast of textures and temperatures—luscious but not too filling.

Prep time: 45 minutes
Baking time: 12 to 14 minutes per batch

BLUEBERRY COMPOTE:
- **2 pints fresh blueberries**
- **¼ cup sugar**
- **2 tablespoons fresh lemon juice**
- **3 tablespoons unsalted butter (no substitutions)**

ALMOND SUGAR:
- **1 cup whole natural almonds (see tip, page 193)**
- **⅔ cup sugar**

  ■

- **8 sheets (12×17 inches) phyllo dough**
- **6 tablespoons unsalted butter (no substitutions), melted**
- **1 quart premium vanilla ice cream**

1. ■ Heat oven to 350°F.

2. ■ *Make blueberry compote:* Bring all blueberry compote ingredients except butter to boil over high heat in a medium saucepan. Add butter and cook 3 to 5 minutes, until some berries have popped and juice is slightly thickened. *(Can be made ahead. Cool. Transfer to an airtight container and refrigerate up to 2 days.)*

3. ■ *Make almond sugar:* Bake nuts on a jelly-roll pan until toasted, 8 to 9 minutes, stirring once. Cool completely. Process cooled almonds and sugar in a food processor until finely ground. *(Can be made ahead. Transfer to an airtight container and store at room temperature up to 2 days.)*

4. ■ On a flat surface, cover phyllo sheets with a lightly dampened clean kitchen towel. Remove 1 phyllo sheet and place it lengthwise in front of you; brush with melted butter. Sprinkle with 3 tablespoons almond sugar. Repeat process with 3 more sheets phyllo, arranging each sheet directly on top of first sheet, buttering and sprinkling each layer with 3 tablespoons almond sugar.

5. ■ Line a large cookie sheet with parchment paper. Cut phyllo stack into fifteen 3-inch squares; discard trimmings. Transfer squares with spatula to prepared cookie sheet. Carefully place another empty cookie sheet directly on top of squares so the stacks bake flat. Bake 12 to 14 minutes, until lightly browned. (Check squares at 12 minutes by lifting top cookie sheet with a potholder.) Transfer squares to a wire rack; cool completely.

6. ■ Meanwhile, prepare another phyllo stack with remaining 4 sheets phyllo, butter and almond sugar. Repeat cutting stack into squares. Bake and cool squares completely.

7. ■ Place a jelly-roll pan in freezer until cold, about 15 minutes. Using a 1½- to 2¼-inch ice-cream scoop, place 20 scoops of ice cream on cold pan. Cover with plastic wrap and return to freezer until ready to use. *(Can be made ahead; freeze up to 24 hours.)*

8. ■ *To serve:* Arrange 1 phyllo square on each of 10 serving plates. Top each with a scoop of ice cream, then 1 heaping tablespoon of blueberry compote. Repeat with another phyllo square, ice cream and 1 heaping tablespoon compote. Cover each with remaining phyllo squares. Serve immediately. Makes 10 servings.

Per serving: 460 calories, 28 g total fat, 13 g saturated fat, 64 mg cholesterol, 113 mg sodium, 51 g carbohydrates, 6 g protein, 112 mg calcium, 3 g fiber

blueberry sugar shortcake with warm peach compote

For a sweet finish to his inspired menu (page 180), Bruce Aidells didn't have to travel far: This luscious shortcake is from his wife, Nancy Oakes, the executive chef and co-owner of one of San Francisco's top-rated restaurants, Boulevard. Self-rising flour takes the guesswork out of assembling the shortcake, and the peach filling can be made ahead and gently reheated. "If the peaches are really ripe and flavorful, I don't bother to cook them," Aidells says. "I just toss them with sugar and fresh lemon juice to taste." Pictured on page 166.

Prep time: 25 minutes • Baking time: 35 to 40 minutes

SHORTCAKE:

- 2¼ **cups self-rising cake flour**
- ⅓ **cup plus 2 tablespoons granulated sugar, divided**
- 1 **cup fresh blueberries**
- 1 **cup heavy or whipping cream**
- 2 **tablespoons unsalted butter, melted (no substitutions)**

PEACH COMPOTE:

- 3 **tablespoons butter (no substitutions)**
- ⅓ **cup firmly packed brown sugar**
- 8 **ripe peaches (2 to 2½ lbs.), peeled and sliced into eighths**

  Fresh mint sprigs, for garnish (optional)
  Whipped cream (optional)

1. *Make shortcake:* Heat oven to 375°F. Grease a large cookie sheet. Whisk together flour and ⅓ cup of the granulated sugar in a large bowl. Gently stir in blueberries. Add cream and mix gently with rubber spatula, just until mixture comes together. (Dough will be crumbly.) Turn dough out onto prepared cookie sheet; press into a round and let rest 5 minutes. Pat dough to a 6-inch circle about 1½ inches thick. Brush top and side with melted butter; sprinkle top with remaining 2 tablespoons granulated sugar. Bake 35 to 40 minutes, until golden brown and toothpick inserted in center comes out clean. Cool on cookie sheet 5 minutes. Transfer to a wire rack and cool completely.

2. *Make peach compote:* Meanwhile, melt butter in a large nonstick skillet over medium-high heat. Stir in brown sugar and cook 2 minutes, until sugar begins to melt. Add peaches and cook until peaches are heated through, 3 to 4 minutes.

3. Set aside ½ cup peach compote for garnish. Split shortcake in half horizontally; transfer bottom half to a serving platter. Spoon peach compote on bottom half. Arrange top half of shortcake over fruit. Garnish top half of shortcake with reserved peach compote and, if desired, mint sprigs. Serve with whipped cream, if desired. Makes 8 servings.

Per serving: 410 calories, 19 g total fat, 11.5 g saturated fat, 60 mg cholesterol, 410 mg sodium, 58 g carbohydrates, 4 g protein, 39 mg calcium, 2 g fiber

---

test kitchen tip

storing and toasting nuts

Nuts are highly perishable due to the high percentage of natural oils they contain. When making any recipe with nuts, always taste them before using—especially during the summer months, when heat can cause nuts to turn rancid even more quickly. But properly stored, nuts will stay fresh for some time. Purchase them in sealed packages or vacuum-packed cans. Once opened, store nuts in an airtight container in the freezer (they'll keep up to one year).

It's also a good idea to toast frozen nuts before using them in desserts to bring out their full flavor. To toast, spread nuts on a jelly-roll pan or cookie sheet and bake at 350°F. for 8 to 10 minutes, until golden and fragrant. Be sure to cool the nuts completely before grinding—if they're too hot, they'll form a paste.

chocolate decadence

With almost 2½ pounds of bittersweet chocolate, Jacques Torres' luscious creation is the definition of decadent. It's exactly the sort of dessert patrons expect from Torres, executive pastry chef of Le Cirque 2000 restaurant in New York City, cookbook author and host of the national public TV series Dessert Circus. *The recipe comes from Torres' book,* Dessert Circus at Home *(William Morrow, 1999). Pictured on page 163.*

Prep time: 40 minutes plus standing and chilling
Baking time: 30 to 35 minutes
Microwave used

CAKE:

- **2** packages (8 oz. each) plus 2 ounces bittersweet or semisweet chocolate squares, finely chopped
- **10** large eggs, separated
- **10** tablespoons unsalted butter, softened (no substitutions)
- **¾** cup almond flour or toasted almond flour,* or ½ cup whole blanched almonds
- **2** tablespoons light corn syrup
- **¼** cup dark rum (optional)
- **12** tablespoons sugar

TRUFFLE GANACHE (FILLING/FROSTING):

- **2** cups heavy or whipping cream
- **2** packages (8 oz. each) plus 5 ounces bittersweet or semisweet chocolate squares, finely chopped
- **¼** cup Grand Marnier or orange-flavored liqueur, or grated peel of 1 orange

  ■

  Fresh raspberries and mint sprigs, for garnish (optional)

1. ■ Heat oven to 325°F. Grease a 15½×10½×1-inch jelly-roll pan with vegetable shortening or butter. Line bottom of pan with parchment paper. Set aside.

2. ■ *Make cake:* Place chocolate in a medium microwaveproof bowl. Cover with plastic wrap, turning back one edge to vent. Microwave on High

1½ minutes; stir and microwave 30 to 45 seconds more, until chocolate is melted and completely smooth. Keep chocolate covered so it remains warm.

3. ■ Beat egg yolks, butter, almond flour (if using whole blanched almonds, process nuts with 2 tablespoons of the sugar in food processor until finely ground) and corn syrup in a large mixer bowl on medium-high speed, until light and fluffy. Beat in rum, if desired.

4. ■ Beat egg whites in a clean mixer bowl with clean beaters on medium speed, until foamy. Beat in sugar (or remaining 10 tablespoons sugar, if using whole blanched almonds) 1 tablespoon at a time. Increase speed to medium-high and beat to stiff peaks. Gently fold whites into almond mixture with a rubber spatula, until almost combined. Gently fold in the warm chocolate, until well combined. Spread batter into prepared pan. Bake cake 30 to 35 minutes, until top springs back when lightly touched and a toothpick inserted in center comes out clean. Cool cake completely on a wire rack.

5. ■ *Make truffle ganache:* Line the bottom of another 15½×10½×1-inch jelly-roll pan with parchment paper. Set aside. Heat heavy cream in a medium saucepan over medium heat, until bubbles begin to form around edge of pan. Place chocolate in a medium bowl and pour half of the hot cream over chocolate. Whisk chocolate slowly until smooth. Gradually add remaining hot cream, whisking until chocolate is completely smooth. Stir in orange-flavored liqueur. Pour ganache into prepared pan. Let stand at room temperature until ganache is cool and spreadable (the consistency of icing), about 45 to 60 minutes. Makes about 3¾ cups.

6. ■ Carefully invert cake onto a cutting board lined with parchment or waxed paper. Peel off parchment from bottom of cake. Trim ¼ inch from edges of cake. Cut cake crosswise into three 10×5-inch pieces. With a long, flat spatula, lift one piece onto a flat serving platter. Spread ¾ cup of the ganache over top. Repeat layering two more times. Frost sides with ½ cup of the ganache, keeping sides and top as smooth as possible. Refrigerate cake until ganache becomes firm, 15 to 20 minutes. Fill a large pastry bag fitted with a #2 round tip with the remaining 1 cup ganache. Decoratively pipe ganache along top and bottom edge of cake (or use the tines of a fork to draw lines along the cake). *(Can be made ahead. Cover and refrigerate cake up to 3 days. Let stand at room temperature 2 hours before serving.)* Garnish cake with fresh raspberries and mint sprigs, if desired. Makes twenty 1/2-inch-thick slices.

Note: Almond flour and toasted almond flour can be found in specialty baking supply shops or through baking mail order sources.

Per slice: 510 calories, 39 g total fat, 20 g saturated fat, 154 mg cholesterol, 44 mg sodium, 42 g carbohydrates, 7 g protein, 69 mg calcium, 2 g fiber

sweet potato cheesecake

Here's a terrific twist on traditional cheesecake from the Calico Restaurant in Rhinebeck, New York. Baked sweet potatoes are mashed, and added with spices and cream cheese. Try it in place of sweet potato pie for a melt-in-your-mouth autumn dessert.

Prep time: 1 hour plus chilling
Baking time: 1 hour 40 to 1 hour 43 minutes

- **1 pound sweet potatoes, scrubbed**

PASTRY:
- **1½ cups all-purpose flour**
- **⅓ cup granulated sugar**
- **½ cup butter, cut up (no substitutions)**
- **1 large egg**
- **1 large egg yolk**

- **1 tablespoon all-purpose flour**
- **2 teaspoons cinnamon**
- **½ teaspoon ginger**
- **¼ teaspoon nutmeg**
- **1 cup whole milk ricotta**
- **12 ounces cream cheese, softened**
- **½ cup granulated sugar**
- **¼ cup firmly packed brown sugar**

- **2 large eggs**
- **2 large egg yolks**

1. Heat oven to 400°F. Line a baking pan with foil. Prick sweet potatoes with a fork; arrange on prepared pan. Bake 60 to 70 minutes, until very soft. Cool; cut in half and scoop out flesh. Mash and set aside. (You should have 1¼ cups.)

2. *Make pastry:* Meanwhile, combine the 1½ cups flour and the sugar in a large bowl. With pastry blender or 2 knives, cut in butter until mixture resembles fine crumbs. Beat 1 egg and 1 egg yolk together in a cup; add to flour mixture, tossing with a fork until mixture begins to hold together. On a lightly floured surface, shape pastry into a ball, then flatten into a disk. Wrap and refrigerate 1 hour.

3. On a lightly floured surface with a floured rolling pin, roll pastry to an 11-inch circle, ¼ inch thick. Using the bottom of a 9-inch springform pan as a guide, cut pastry into a 9-inch circle. Lightly butter bottom of pan, then transfer pastry to pan. Press edge of pastry against side of pan. Bake pastry until golden, 20 to 23 minutes. Cool on a wire rack.

4. Reduce oven temperature to 250°F. Combine the 1 tablespoon flour, cinnamon, ginger and nutmeg in a cup.

5. Process ricotta in a food processor until very smooth, 1 minute. Transfer to a large mixing bowl. Add cream cheese, granulated and brown sugars and beat at medium speed, scraping down sides of bowl with a rubber spatula, until smooth and fluffy. Beat in sweet potatoes. At low speed, beat in 2 eggs and 2 egg yolks, one at a time. Add flour-spice mixture and beat just until smooth.

6. Pour filling into prepared crust. Bake cheesecake until firm, 1 hour 20 minutes. Cool on a wire rack. Cover and refrigerate overnight. To serve, run a small knife around side of pan; detach ring. Makes 12 servings.

Per serving: 410 calories, 23 g total fat, 13.5 g saturated fat, 169 mg cholesterol, 130 mg sodium, 42 g carbohydrates, 9 g protein, 98 mg calcium, 1 g fiber

orange vacherin jeanette

TV cooking star, chef and author Jacques Pépin gave us easy-to-follow, step-by-step directions for this perfect do-ahead dessert. The melt-in-your-mouth frozen layer cake with orange cream is from his book, The Art of Cooking *(Knopf, 1988).*

Prep time: 45 minutes plus freezing
Baking time: 3 to 3½ hours

1 **tablespoon butter, softened**
MERINGUE:
  5 **large egg whites**
1¼ **cups sugar**
ORANGE CREAM:
  4 **cups heavy cream**
  ¼ **cup sugar**
  2 **tablespoons Grand Marnier liqueur**
1½ **tablespoons grated orange peel**

  ½ **pint fresh raspberries**
RASPBERRY SAUCE:
  2 **packages (10 oz.) frozen raspberries in syrup, thawed**
  ⅛ **teaspoon lemon juice**

1. ■ Heat oven to 200°F. Trace two 12×4-inch rectangles 2 inches apart on a sheet of parchment paper large enough to fit a large cookie sheet. Grease paper with the butter; place, buttered side down, on cookie sheet. Lift the paper and turn it over, then place the paper back on the cookie sheet.

2. ■ *Make meringue:* Beat egg whites in a mixer bowl on medium-high speed to stiff peaks, 3 to 5 minutes. Quickly pour in the sugar (this should take no more than 10 seconds, or 20 seconds if using a hand mixer). Increase speed to high and beat 15 seconds. (The sugar will not dissolve; it will still be grainy when rubbed between your fingers. Don't worry: This produces a brittle, dry and tender meringue.)

3. ■ Fit a large pastry bag with a ¾-inch plain tip. Spoon half of the meringue into pastry bag.

(Tip: To make filling the bag easy, place bag in a tall glass or blender container). Starting at one corner of the parchment, pipe meringue, following outline, and fill in one rectangle. Smooth top of rectangle with a large metal spatula. Repeat with remaining meringue for second rectangle. Pipe any remaining meringue into oval shapes on parchment.

4. ■ Bake 3 to 3½ hours. (The meringues should feel completely dry. If they turn pale golden, that's okay.) Transfer the meringues on parchment paper to a wire rack and cool completely.

5. ■ *Make orange cream:* Meanwhile, beat all orange cream ingredients in a large mixer bowl to firm peaks. Cover and refrigerate.

6. ■ Cut a 14×6-inch piece of cardboard; wrap with foil. Peel one meringue rectangle from parchment and place, bottom side down, on cardboard. (Don't worry if meringue breaks; it will be covered completely with cream. Just gently shape to reassemble.) Spread top with 4 cups of orange cream. Peel ovals from parchment and crumble; sprinkle evenly over orange cream. Peel remaining rectangle from parchment and place, bottom side up, over crumbs.

7. ■ Transfer cake to a cookie sheet. Spread 2 cups of the orange cream over top and sides of cake. Fill a large pastry bag, fitted with a ¾-inch star tip, with remaining orange cream. Pipe remaining cream on the top, the sides and a border along the base. Gently press fresh raspberries onto cake. Freeze, uncovered, 6 hours, until completely firm. *(For longer freezing time, cover loosely with plastic wrap, then with foil, and freeze up to 2 days. Refrigerate 1 hour before serving.)*

8. ■ *To serve:* Slice Vacherin and serve with raspberry sauce. Makes 12 servings.

9. ■ *Raspberry sauce:* Puree thawed raspberries in syrup in a blender. Strain through a sieve into a bowl; discard solids. Stir lemon juice into puree. Makes 2 cups.

Per serving with 1 tablespoon sauce: 415 calories, 30.5 g total fat, 19 g saturated fat, 111 mg cholesterol, 63 mg sodium, 34 g carbohydrates, 3 g protein, 59 mg calcium, 2 g fiber

key lime pie

This version of the classic dessert is hard to beat. A reader spotted it at the Rock Festival Cafe in New York City (formerly the American Festival Cafe). Though the dessert is no longer featured on the regular menu, you might just spot it as a special there from time to time.

Prep time: 10 minutes plus chilling
Baking time: 20 minutes

- 1¼ cups graham-cracker crumbs
- 2 tablespoons granulated sugar
- 6 tablespoons butter or margarine, melted
- 3 large egg yolks
- 1 can (14 oz.) sweetened condensed milk
- 1 teaspoon grated lime peel
- ½ cup fresh lime juice
- 1 cup heavy or whipping cream
- 2 tablespoons confectioners' sugar

1. Heat oven to 350°F. Combine graham-cracker crumbs, granulated sugar and butter in a medium bowl. Press crumbs into a 9-inch pie plate. Bake 5 minutes, until the crust is golden. Cool on a wire rack.

2. Meanwhile, whisk together egg yolks and condensed milk in a medium bowl until smooth. Gradually whisk in lime peel and juice until blended. Pour filling into prepared crust. Bake 15 minutes. Cool on a wire rack 20 minutes. Chill 2 hours. *(Can be made ahead. Cover loosely and refrigerate overnight.)*

3. Beat cream in a mixer bowl to soft peaks. Gradually beat in confectioners' sugar and beat to stiff peaks. Spread whipped cream over top of pie. Makes 8 servings.

Per serving: 460 calories, 27 g total fat, 15.5 g saturated fat, 161 mg cholesterol, 278 mg sodium, 48 g carbohydrates, 7 g protein, 173 mg calcium, 1 g fiber

---

test kitchen tip

key points about key lime pie

Originally a specialty of Florida, the Key Lime Pie can now be found across the country in a variety of versions. Here are some commonly asked questions about this ever-popular dessert:

Q. WHAT ARE KEY LIMES? Key limes grow only in Florida and the Caribbean; they have a thin, yellow-green skin, and a highly aromatic pulp. They're smaller than the Persian lime (the bright-green lime more commonly found at the supermarket), and contain a moderate amount of seeds.

Q. DO I NEED REAL KEY LIMES TO MAKE A KEY LIME PIE? Purists might claim that the recipe should call for key limes to be truly authentic. However, we feel that the more widely available Persian lime works well to bring out the fresh, tingly and tart flavors of the pie.

Q. I HAVE AN OLD RECIPE FOR KEY LIME PIE THAT DOES NOT CALL FOR BAKING THE CUSTARD. WILL THE CUSTARD THICKEN WITHOUT BAKING? Once upon a time, some key lime pie recipes did not call for baking the custard. The raw egg yolks were simply stirred into the lime juice and sweetened condensed milk, then chilled. The custard indeed set up without baking. Today, however, thorough cooking is needed to kill harmful bacteria that may be present in raw eggs. Though our custard calls for a baking step, it still retains the much-loved cool and creamy qualities of the classic.

lemon icebox cake

We developed this recipe after a reader told us about an ice-box cake she tried at a well-known New York City restaurant. The version she enjoyed was served in individual cakes, but ours is assembled in one pan.

Prep time: 1 hour plus chilling and freezing
Baking time: 10 minutes • Microwave used

CARAMEL SAUCE:

1½   **cups sugar**
½   **cup water**
½   **vanilla bean, split lengthwise**
⅔   **cup heavy or whipping cream**

COMPOTE:

2   **cups fresh or frozen huckleberries, blackberries or blueberries**
⅓   **cup sugar**
1   **tablespoon fresh lemon juice**

CRUST:

1¼   **cups graham-cracker crumbs**
⅓   **cup unsalted butter, melted (no substitutions)**
■
1   **cup heavy or whipping cream**
2   **jars (11 oz. each) prepared lemon curd**
1   **package (8 oz.) cream cheese, softened**
¾   **cup heavy or whipping cream**

MERINGUE:

6   **large egg whites, at room temperature**
1   **cup sugar**

1. ■ Day One: *Make caramel sauce:* Bring sugar, water and vanilla bean to boil in a 2-quart heavy saucepan over medium-high heat. Cook 5 minutes (do not stir). Cover and cook 5 minutes, until sugar dissolves. Uncover and cook 5 minutes more, swirling pan until syrup is amber. Remove from heat; with a long-handled spoon, slowly stir in cream (mixture will bubble). Carefully discard vanilla bean. Return to heat; reduce heat to low and simmer, stirring, until caramel is smooth. Transfer to a bowl; refrigerate 1½ hours until cool. *(Can be made ahead. Cover and refrigerate up to 24 hours. Microwave on High 1 minute; stir. Microwave 15 to 30 seconds more, until room temperature and pourable.)*

2. ■ *Make compote:* Combine berries and sugar in a small saucepan. Cook over medium heat, until berries soften and mixture becomes juicy, 5 minutes. Strain berry mixture through a fine sieve into a small bowl. Transfer berries to another bowl. Return juice to saucepan and bring to boil; cook over medium-low heat until syrupy, 10 minutes. Pour syrup over berries; stir in lemon juice. Cool. *(Can be made ahead. Cover and refrigerate up to 24 hours.)*

3. ■ *Make crust:* Heat oven to 350°F. Combine crumbs and butter in a bowl. Reserve 2 tablespoons of the crumb mixture in a cup. Press remaining crumbs into the bottom of a 9-inch springform pan. Bake 10 minutes, until crust is golden brown. Cool completely on a wire rack. *(Can be made ahead. Cover crust and reserved crumb mixture and let stand at room temperature up to 24 hours.)*

4. ■ Day Two: Beat 1 cup cream in mixer bowl to firm peaks. Fold in 1 cup lemon curd. Cover and refrigerate.

5. ■ Measure ³⁄₄ cup cooled caramel sauce and pour into a large mixer bowl (reserve remaining sauce). Add cream cheese and beat at medium speed just until smooth. Add the ³⁄₄ cup cream and beat just until mixture thickens (will be the consistency of whipped cream). Cover and refrigerate.

6. ■ *To assemble:* Spread another ¹⁄₂ cup lemon curd evenly over crust. (Reserve remaining curd for another use.) Gently spread caramel-cream mixture evenly over curd. Sprinkle top with reserved 2 tablespoons crumb mixture. Gently spread lemon curd-cream mixture evenly over crumbs. Drizzle reserved caramel sauce with spoon in a zigzag pattern completely over lemon cream. Place in freezer.

7. ■ *Make meringue:* Combine egg whites and sugar in a large stainless-steel mixer bowl. Place bowl over medium saucepan half filled with gently simmering water. Heat mixture, whisking constantly, until sugar is completely dissolved and temperature reaches 160°F. on an instant-read thermometer, about 5 minutes. Remove bowl from water; beat egg-sugar mixture to just-stiff, shiny peaks. Spoon meringue into a pastry bag fitted with a

½-inch round tip; pipe decoratively over cake. Freeze overnight.

8. Day Three: Thirty minutes before serving, transfer cake to a cookie sheet and let stand at room temperature. Just before serving, position oven rack 8 inches from heat source. Heat broiler. Place cake on rack and broil cake just until meringue is golden, 1 to 2 minutes. Remove side from pan. Cut into wedges. Serve immediately with compote. Makes 16 servings.

Per serving: 495 calories, 30.5 g total fat, 18 g saturated fat, 170 mg cholesterol, 147 mg sodium, 52 g carbohydrates, 6 g protein, 54 mg calcium, 4 g fiber

white-chocolate and berry terrine with raspberry sauce

A reader enjoyed this exquisite dessert at a bridal shower given at Clifton–The Country Inn, in Charlottesville, Virginia, and asked us to get the recipe. We found it a stunning dessert indeed, and it's perfect for any special occasion, as it's not too rich or sweet. Make-ahead tip: You can unmold the terrine and refrigerate it up to 2 hours before serving.

Total prep and cooking time: 40 minutes plus chilling
Microwave used

WHITE-CHOCOLATE MOUSSE:

- 1 envelope unflavored gelatin
- ¼ cup cold water
- 7 ounces domestic or imported white-chocolate squares
- ½ cup sugar
- 2 large eggs
- 1 large egg yolk
- 1 tablespoon Chambord or raspberry liqueur
- 2 cups heavy or whipping cream
- 1 pint fresh strawberries, sliced
- 1 pint fresh blackberries
- 1 pint fresh raspberries

RASPBERRY SAUCE:

- 1 package (10 oz.) frozen raspberries in syrup, thawed

    ■

    Fresh mint sprigs, for garnish (optional)

1. *Make white-chocolate mousse:* Line a 9×5-inch loaf pan with plastic wrap. Sprinkle gelatin over cold water in a 1 cup glass measure; let stand 2 minutes to soften. Microwave on High 40 seconds; stir 2 minutes, until gelatin completely dissolves. Cool slightly.

2. Bring a medium saucepan half full with water to a simmer. Meanwhile, place chocolate in a medium microwaveproof bowl. Microwave on High 1 to 2 minutes; stir until smooth. Set aside.

3. Combine sugar, eggs, egg yolk and liqueur in a medium stainless-steel bowl. Place bowl over simmering water, and beat with handheld mixer until mixture doubles in volume and temperature registers 160°F. on an instant-read thermometer, about 5 minutes. Beat in dissolved gelatin. Remove from heat; fold in melted chocolate. Cool to room temperature. Beat cream in a mixer bowl to soft peaks; gently fold into white-chocolate mixture.

4. Arrange half of the strawberries in one layer in bottom of prepared pan; spread top with one-third of mousse. Arrange a layer of blackberries on top, then spread with another third of mousse. Top with raspberries, then remaining mousse and strawberries. Cover and refrigerate overnight.

5. *To serve:* Uncover mousse. Place a serving plate over top of pan. Holding bottom of pan and plate, invert and remove pan. Peel off wrap. Serve with raspberry sauce. Garnish with mint sprigs, if desired. Make 12 servings.

6. *Raspberry sauce:* Bring thawed raspberries in syrup to boil in a small saucepan; reduce heat and simmer 5 minutes. Transfer to a food processor and puree. Strain through a fine sieve into a bowl. *(Can be made ahead. Cover and refrigerate overnight.)* Makes ³/₄ cup.

Per serving: 335 calories, 21.5 g total fat, 12.5 g saturated fat, 107 mg cholesterol, 43 mg sodium, 34 g carbohydrates, 4 g protein, 86 mg calcium, 4 g fiber

open-faced apricot pie

As the author of comprehensive cookbooks on cakes, pies and pastries, Rose Levy Beranbaum knows her desserts, and apricot pie is one of her seasonal favorites. We think she really struck gold with this to-die-for version. Her tip for piecrust success? "I partially bake the pie shell before adding the fruit, which keeps the bottom crust flaky and crisp." Pictured on page 166.

Prep time: 25 minutes plus chilling
Baking time: 1 hour 15 minutes to 1 hour 30 minutes

FLAKY PIECRUST:

- **8**   **tablespoons cold unsalted butter, divided**
- **1⅓**   **cups all-purpose flour (measure according to instructions in step 2)**
- **¼**   **teaspoon salt**
- **⅛**   **teaspoon baking powder**
- **2½**   **to 3½ tablespoons ice water**
- **1½**   **teaspoons cider vinegar**

  ■

- **1**   **tablespoon beaten egg white**
- **6**   **tablespoons sugar**
- **2**   **tablespoons cornstarch**
- **2**   **pounds fresh apricots, halved and pitted**
- **½**   **cup fresh raspberries**
- **⅓**   **cup apricot preserves, melted**

1. *Make flaky piecrust:* Cut 5 tablespoons of the butter into ³/₄-inch cubes. Refrigerate 30 minutes. Cut remaining 3 tablespoons butter into ³/₄-inch cubes. Place in freezer 30 minutes.

2. To measure the flour, stir in its package to aerate, then gently dip a dry measuring cup into the flour, without packing the flour into the cup. Level off any excess with a spatula. Place the flour, salt and baking powder into a large plastic storage bag; seal and place in freezer 30 minutes.

3. Process the chilled dry ingredients in a food processor to combine. Add the refrigerated butter cubes and pulse 20 to 30 seconds, until the mixture resembles coarse meal. Add frozen butter cubes and pulse 10 times, until the frozen butter is the size of small peas.

4. Add 2¹/₂ tablespoons of the ice water and the vinegar and pulse 6 times. If mixture does not hold together, add half the remaining 1 tablespoon water and pulse; repeat one more time, if necessary. The mixture should be in particles and should not hold together without being pinched. With floured hands, gently gather dough into a ball. Wrap, flatten into a disk and refrigerate 2 hours or overnight.

5. Cover a rolling pin with a cloth stockinette; on a floured pastry cloth (or between 2 sheets of lightly floured plastic wrap), roll dough into a 14-inch circle. Fit into a 9-inch pie pan. Trim edge, leaving a ¹/₂-inch border; turn under and flute. Cover and refrigerate 1 hour or overnight.

6. Arrange oven rack at lowest position; place cookie sheet on rack. Heat oven to 425°F. Line pastry with parchment or foil; fill with dried beans or uncooked rice and bake 20 minutes. Carefully remove parchment and beans or rice. Prick bottom and sides of shell with a fork and bake 5 to 10 minutes more (check after 3 minutes and prick again if upper layer of pastry bubbles up), until crust is pale golden. Cool crust on a wire rack 3 minutes; brush bottom and sides with egg white.

7. Meanwhile, combine sugar and cornstarch in a bowl. Add apricots and toss to coat. Let stand 15 minutes.

8. Decoratively arrange apricots, cut sides up, in crust. Cover edge of crust loosely with foil and bake 50 to 60 minutes, until filling is bubbly and apricots are tender. (If apricots begin to darken, cover loosely with another sheet of foil.) Cool pie on a wire rack.

9. Arrange raspberries over apricots. Strain preserves through a sieve and brush over fruit. Makes 6 servings.

Per serving: 405 calories, 16 g total fat, 9.5 g saturated fat, 41 mg cholesterol, 121 mg sodium, 62 g carbohydrates, 5 g protein, 36 mg calcium, 3 g fiber

sweets
for all
seasons

From spring's berries to winter's juicy pears, every time of year brings its own cherished flavors. This chapter showcases seasonal tastes swirled into sorbets, nestled between layers of tender cakes, bubbling in cobblers and cradled in the buttery crusts of tarts, pies and pastries.

STRAWBERRY
SHORTBREAD
TARTS
pg. 210

THE PERFECT
SOUR CHERRY PIE
pg. 218

SWEET RICOTTA
PUFFS WITH PEACHES
pg. 223

PECAN-NECTARINE
LAYER CAKE
pg. 216

savor the **parade** of summer's **fresh fruits**

STRAWBERRY-
CARAMEL-SAUCED
SUNDAES
pg. 209

the last bite
of an inspired
dessert

TARTE TATIN
pg.226

CHERRY
CLAFOUTI
pg. 219

APPLE PIE, RIGHT
pg. 228
PLUM CROSTATA,
LEFT
pg. 224

is the sweetest
memory guests take home

SKILLET SOUFFLÉ
pg. 209

APPLE AND PEAR SAUCE
pg. 225

dessert on a

LEMON MOUSSE
pg. 240

weeknight?
you bet!

PEAR TARTLETS
pg. 234

PEANUT BUTTER
CHIP BARS
pg. 231

(it's what we call
sweet and simple)

with each season comes

HALLOWEEN
CUPCAKES
pg. 230

sweet inspirations

CARROT AND
FRUIT BUNDT
CAKE
pg. 225

skillet soufflé

A soufflé baked in a skillet might not be traditional, but it sure is easy—and every bit as elegant as the classic. Pictured on page 205.

Prep time: 15 minutes • Baking time: 15 minutes

- **2 pints fresh strawberries, hulled, divided**
- **⅓ cup strawberry preserves**
- **1 tablespoon framboise (raspberry-flavored liqueur)**
- **2 tablespoons unsalted butter (no substitutions)**
- **8 large egg whites**
- **¼ teaspoon cream of tartar**
- **¼ teaspoon salt**
- **¼ cup plus 2 tablespoons sugar, divided**

1. Heat oven to 375°F.

2. Mash 1 cup of the strawberries and the strawberry preserves with a potato masher in a bowl; stir in framboise liqueur.

3. Start to melt butter in a deep ovenproof 10-inch or 11-inch skillet over low heat.

4. Meanwhile, beat egg whites, cream of tartar and salt to soft peaks in a large mixer bowl. Gradually beat in ¼ cup of the sugar. Beat to stiff peaks. Fold strawberry mixture into whites, one-third at a time, just until blended.

5. Increase heat to medium-low. Pour mixture into the skillet, gently spreading it to the sides and mounding in the center. Cook 2 minutes. Transfer skillet to oven and bake soufflé 15 minutes, until set. Slice remaining 3 cups strawberries and transfer to a bowl. Toss with remaining 2 tablespoons sugar. Serve soufflé immediately with berries. Makes 8 servings.

Per serving: 135 calories, 3 g total fat, 2 g saturated fat, 8 mg cholesterol, 133 mg sodium, 23 g carbohydrates, 4 g protein, 17 mg calcium, 2 g fiber

strawberry-caramel-sauced sundaes

Remember this recipe when strawberry season comes around. Swirl strawberries into the still-warm homemade caramel sauce, then spoon it over ice cream and sorbet for a to-die-for summer sundae. Pictured on page 203.

Prep time: 10 minutes • Cooking time: 13 to 18 minutes

STRAWBERRY-CARAMEL SAUCE:
- **½ cup sugar**
- **¼ cup water**
- **2 tablespoons orange juice**
- **1 cup heavy or whipping cream**
   Pinch salt
- **½ teaspoon vanilla extract**
- **1 pint fresh strawberries, hulled and quartered**

- **2 pints vanilla ice cream**
- **1 pint strawberry sorbet**
   Fresh strawberries, for garnish (optional)

1. Bring sugar and water to boil in a medium saucepan over medium-high heat. Reduce heat to medium and cook, swirling pan occasionally, until mixture is caramel-colored, 5 to 10 minutes. Remove from heat. Carefully stir in orange juice with a long-handed wooden spoon (mixture will bubble). Stir vigorously until blended.

2. Return pan to heat; stir in heavy cream and salt. Bring to boil; reduce heat and simmer sauce until thickened and reduced to 1 cup, about 8 minutes. Stir in vanilla. Pour sauce into a medium bowl and stir in strawberries.

3. Scoop ice cream and sorbet into 8 serving dishes. Divide and spoon Strawberry-Caramel Sauce over top. Garnish with strawberries, if desired. Makes 8 servings.

Per serving: 355 calories, 18.5 g total fat, 11.5 g saturated fat, 70 mg cholesterol, 88 mg sodium, 46 g carbohydrates, 3 g protein, 114 mg calcium, 1 g fiber

strawberry shortbread tarts

Shortbread topped with a tart layer of lemon curd and fresh strawberries make this dessert as delicious as it is simple. Pictured on page 202.

Prep time: 20 minutes • Baking time: 10 minutes

- 1 cup all-purpose flour
- ⅓ cup cold butter, cut up (no substitutions)
- 2 tablespoons sugar
- 1 large egg yolk
- 1 tablespoon cold water
- ¾ cup prepared lemon curd, stirred until smooth
- ½ cup mascarpone cheese or sour cream
- 1½ pints fresh strawberries, hulled and sliced
  Grated lemon peel and fresh mint sprigs, for garnish (optional)

1. Heat oven to 400°F. For shortbread, grease a large cookie sheet. Process flour, butter and sugar in a food processor until mixture resembles fine meal. Beat egg yolk and cold water. Drizzle over flour; pulse just until dough starts to cling together.

2. Gather dough into a ball; divide and shape into 8 equal balls. Place balls 3 inches apart on cookie sheet; press balls with floured fingers into 3¹/₂-inch circles.

3. Bake circles 10 minutes, until golden brown in the center. Let stand on the cookie sheet 2 minutes; cool on a wire rack.

4. Meanwhile, for lemon filling, gently fold lemon curd and mascarpone in a bowl just until combined. Place shortbreads on 8 serving plates. Divide and spread lemon filling on shortbreads. Divide and arrange berries on filling. Garnish with lemon peel and mint sprigs, if desired. Makes 8 servings.

Per serving: 310 calories, 17 g total fat, 9.5 g saturated fat, 60 mg cholesterol, 109 mg sodium, 38 g carbohydrates, 5 g protein, 46 mg calcium, 2 g fiber

strawberry-almond tart

You won't need to spend hours preparing this berry beauty—but your guests will think you did!

Prep time: 20 minutes plus cooling
Baking time: 20 to 25 minutes
Microwave used

- ½ cup sugar
- ½ cup almond paste, crumbled
- 10 tablespoons butter, softened
- 3 large eggs
- ½ teaspoon vanilla extract
- ⅓ cup all-purpose flour
- 1 tablespoon cornstarch
- ⅓ cup apricot preserves
- 2 teaspoons white rum
- 2 pints fresh strawberries, hulled and sliced
  ¼ inch thick

1. Heat oven to 375°F. Lightly coat bottom and sides of a 10-inch tart pan with removable bottom with vegetable cooking spray. Line the outside of the pan with foil.

2. Combine sugar and almond paste in a mixer bowl. Beat at medium speed 2 to 3 minutes to break up paste. Beat in butter, scraping with a rubber spatula, until smooth. Beat in eggs, one at a time, until blended; add vanilla.

3. Sift flour and cornstarch in a bowl. Stir into almond mixture. Spread in pan. Bake 20 to 25 minutes, until top springs back when gently pressed with a finger. Cool in pan on a wire rack.

4. Remove sides of pan. Microwave preserves in a microwaveproof cup on High 40 seconds. Strain through a sieve into a small bowl; discard solids. Stir in rum. Brush a thin layer over tart. Arrange overlapping slices of berries on top of tart. Brush top with remaining preserves. Makes 8 servings.

Per serving: 345 calories, 20.5 g total fat, 10 g saturated fat, 118 mg cholesterol, 178 mg sodium, 37 g carbohydrates, 5 g protein, 59 mg calcium, 2 g fiber

strawberries-and-cream cake

Filled with fresh strawberries and frosted with whipped cream, this glorious dessert serves 24, making it a great party cake for graduations and other springtime celebrations.

Prep time: 1¹/₂ hours plus cooling
Baking time: 20 minutes per cake

- **2** recipes White Cake Batter (see recipe, right)
  Buttercream Filling (see recipe, below right)
- **1** cup finely chopped fresh strawberries
- **¹/₃** cup strawberry jelly, melted
- **2** cups heavy or whipping cream
- **¹/₄** cup confectioners' sugar
  Sliced strawberries, blueberries and mint sprigs, for garnish (optional)

1. Heat oven to 350°F. Line a 15¹/₂×10¹/₂-inch jelly-roll pan with foil; lightly coat foil with vegetable cooking spray.

2. Make one recipe of white cake batter. Spread batter evenly in prepared pan. Bake 20 minutes, until toothpick inserted in center comes out clean.

3. Cool cake in the pan on a large wire rack 10 minutes; invert cake onto rack. Remove pan and foil; cool completely. Meanwhile, repeat process with another recipe of white cake batter. *(Can be made ahead. Cover and freeze cakes up to 1 month. Thaw at room temperature 30 minutes.)*

4. Make the buttercream filling; stir in the chopped strawberries.

5. Place 1 cake layer on a large platter; tuck 4 strips of waxed paper under cake. Brush top of cake with melted jelly. Spread buttercream over jelly; top with second cake layer.

6. Beat cream and confectioners' sugar in a mixer bowl at medium-high speed to stiff peaks. Spread over top and sides of cake. Remove waxed-paper strips. Garnish cake with sliced strawberries, blueberries and mint sprigs, if desired. Refrigerate up to 2 hours before serving. Makes 24 servings.

WHITE CAKE BATTER:
Combine *2 cups sifted all-purpose flour, 2 teaspoons baking powder* and *¹/₂ teaspoon salt* in a bowl; set aside. Beat *²/₃ cup butter or margarine, softened,* in a large mixer bowl at medium-high speed until smooth. Gradually beat in *1¹/₄ cups sugar,* scraping bowl occasionally with rubber spatula, until light and fluffy, about 5 minutes. Add *4 large egg whites;* beat 1 minute more. Beat in *1 teaspoon vanilla extract.* With mixer at low speed, add flour mixture alternately with *³/₄ cup milk,* beginning and ending with flour mixture, until blended. Proceed as directed in recipe.

BUTTERCREAM FILLING:
Beat *6 tablespoons butter, softened (no substitutions),* in a large mixer bowl until smooth. Add *2 cups confectioners' sugar, 3 tablespoons heavy or whipping cream* and *¹/₂ teaspoon vanilla;* beat until light and fluffy. Makes 1¹/₃ cups.

Per serving: 415 calories, 22 g total fat, 13.5 g saturated fat, 67 mg cholesterol, 343 mg sodium, 52 g carbohydrates, 4 g protein, 99 mg calcium, 1 g fiber

---

test kitchen tip

strawberry smarts

Here's how to select the best strawberries—and keep them that way:

BUY berries with a natural healthy sheen, and look for caps that are pert and green (not wilted or brown).

STORE in the refrigerator in a container (layer and separate with paper towels). Fresh berries will keep three to five days.

WASH and then hull only when ready to use.

SERVE at room temperature for best flavor.

2. Heat oven to 350°F. Butter two large cookie sheets. On a lightly floured surface with a floured rolling pin, roll one piece of dough ⅛ inch thick. Cut with a 2- or 3-inch flower or scalloped cookie cutter. With a ¾-inch round cutter, cut out circles in the center of half of the 3-inch cutouts. (For 2-inch cutouts, use a ½-inch-wide star tip.) Place 1 inch apart on sheets. Bake 8 minutes, or until edges are golden. Cool on wire racks. Repeat with remaining dough, re-rolling scraps.

3. Spread plain cookies with mango butter. Top with cookies that have cutouts. Makes 2 dozen 3-inch cookies, or 5 dozen 2-inch cookies. *(Can be made ahead. Store in freezer in airtight containers up to 1 month.)*

Per 3-inch cookie: 175 calories, 8.5 g total fat, 5 g saturated fat, 38 mg cholesterol, 96 mg sodium, 23 g carbohydrates, 2 g protein, 7 mg calcium, 0 g fiber

fruit sandwich cookies

Why save the prettiest cookies for Christmas? Welcome guests (or treat yourself!) any time of year with these buttery, shaped beauties. Look for mango butter in the jams and jellies aisle of the supermarket. Or, substitute lemon curd, if you wish. Pictured on page 201.

Prep time: 35 minutes plus chilling
Baking time: 8 minutes per batch

- 1 cup butter, softened (no substitutions)
- 2 cups confectioners' sugar
- 1 tablespoon grated lime peel
- 2 large eggs
- 3 cups all-purpose flour
- ⅛ teaspoon salt
- ¼ cup to ½ cup prepared mango butter or lemon curd

1. Beat butter, sugar and lime peel in a mixer bowl until fluffy. Beat in eggs, one at a time, until blended. Gradually beat in flour and salt. Divide dough into 4 pieces and shape into disks; wrap in plastic wrap and refrigerate 2 hours or overnight.

tuiles

These classic wafer-thin cookies get their name from the French word for "tile." Their curved shapes resemble the rounded tiles of rooftops. Try serving them as a crunchy counterpoint to the luscious Strawberry-Caramel-Sauced Sundaes, page 209. The cookies are pictured on page 201.

Prep time: 20 minutes
Baking time: 5 to 6 minutes per batch

- 2 large egg whites
- ½ cup sugar
- ¼ cup all-purpose flour
- 3 tablespoons butter, melted and cooled (no substitutions)
- 1 teaspoon grated orange peel
- 6 ounces white chocolate squares, melted and cooled

1. Heat oven to 350°F. Generously coat a large cookie sheet with vegetable cooking spray. Whisk egg whites and sugar in a bowl. Add flour; whisk until smooth. Add melted butter and orange peel; whisk until well blended.

2. Drop batter by level measuring teaspoonfuls 6 inches apart on sheet, making only 4 cookies per sheet. Bake 5 to 6 minutes, until golden.

3. Let cookies cool on cookie sheet 30 seconds to 1 minute. Working quickly, loosen each cookie with a thin metal spatula and immediately drape over a rolling pin to cool, pressing cookies lightly to mold onto rolling pin. (If cookies harden to cookie sheet, return to oven for 1 minute to soften, then drape over rolling pin.) Cool on wire racks. Repeat with remaining batter.

4. Spoon melted chocolate into a heavy-duty plastic storage bag; snip off one corner of the bag. Pipe tops of cookies with chocolate; let stand until chocolate is firm. Makes about 4 dozen cookies.

Per cookie: 35 calories, 2 g total fat, 1 g saturated fat, 2 mg cholesterol, 13 mg sodium, 5 g carbohydrates, 0 g protein, 8 mg calcium, 0 g fiber

lemon-pistachio checkerboards

No special equipment is needed to make these treats—just use an empty waxed paper box to help keep the logs in shape as they chill. Pictured on page 201.

Prep time: 15 minutes plus chilling
Baking time: 11 to 13 minutes per batch

- 2¼ **cups all-purpose flour**
- ½ **teaspoon baking powder**
- ¾ **cup butter, softened (no substitutions)**
- ¾ **cup sugar**
- 1 **large egg**
- 2 **teaspoons grated lemon peel**
- 2 **drops yellow food coloring**
- ¼ **cup shelled unsalted pistachios, finely chopped**
- ⅛ **teaspoon almond extract**
- 3 **drops green food coloring**

1. Combine flour and baking powder in a bowl. Beat butter and sugar in a large mixer bowl. Beat in egg. Stir in flour mixture just until blended. (If

necessary, mix with hands until the dough comes together.)

2. Divide dough in half. Knead lemon peel and yellow coloring into half of the dough. Knead pistachios, almond extract and green coloring into the other half. Use your hands to blend the colors evenly. Divide each kind of dough into two pieces. Roll each into a 12-inch rope.

3. Line an empty, smaller waxed paper or plastic wrap box (12¼×2×2 inches) with waxed paper, letting paper extend at sides. Place a pistachio rope and a lemon rope in box, side by side. Press to flatten. Repeat with remaining dough, placing opposite kinds on top of each other. Press to flatten; cover and refrigerate overnight.

4. Heat oven to 350°F. Use butter to grease two cookie sheets. Unwrap log; cut into scant ¼-inch-thick slices. Place 1 inch apart on sheets. Bake 11 to 13 minutes, until just golden. Cool on wire racks. Makes about 4 dozen cookies.

Per cookie: 65 calories, 3.5 g total fat, 2 g saturated fat, 13 mg cholesterol, 37 mg sodium, 8 g carbohydrates, 1 g protein, 6 mg calcium, 0 g fiber

---

test kitchen tip

softening butter

Did you know softened butter is not the same as butter at room temperature? Read on:

Softened butter should actually be fairly stiff. Don't be tempted to use the microwave, because butter melts easily, making it too soft for baking. For best results, remove a stick of butter from the refrigerator. Keep wrapped and place on a cutting board. With a rolling pin, give each side of the butter a few whacks to make it just pliable.

---

berry-rhubarb tiramisu

A glorious summertime take on the ever-popular dessert.

Prep time: 35 minutes plus standing and chilling
Cook time: 23 to 25 minutes

- **4** cups sliced fresh rhubarb
- **¾** cup plus ⅓ cup sugar, divided
- **1** vanilla bean, split lengthwise in half
- **1** pint strawberries, hulled and sliced
- **3** large egg yolks
- **¼** cup water
- **8** ounces (1 cup) mascarpone cheese
- **1½** cups heavy or whipping cream, beaten until stiff
- **1½** packages (3 oz. each) ladyfingers
- **6** whole strawberries, for garnish (optional)

1. Bring rhubarb, ³⁄₄ cup sugar and half of the split vanilla bean to boil, stirring, in saucepan. Reduce heat to medium and cook, stirring occasionally, 15 minutes, until rhubarb softens. Transfer to bowl. Remove vanilla bean. With small knife, scrape out seeds. Discard pod. Stir seeds and strawberries into rhubarb mixture. Refrigerate, stirring occasionally, until cold.

2. Meanwhile, combine yolks, remaining ¹⁄₃ cup sugar, remaining half of vanilla bean and ¹⁄₄ cup water in a large stainless-steel bowl. Place bowl over a large saucepan with 1 inch of gently simmering water. Cook mixture, stirring constantly, 8 to 10 minutes, until mixture is thickened and temperature registers 160°F. on an instant-read thermometer. Remove bowl from water and whisk until cool. Remove vanilla bean; scrape out seeds into egg yolk mixture and whisk in mascarpone. Discard pod. Gently fold in whipped cream. Arrange half of the ladyfingers in bottom of a 1¹⁄₂- to 2-quart serving dish. Spread with half the fruit mixture. Cover with half the cream mixture. Repeat layering, ending with cream mixture. *(Can be made ahead. Cover; refrigerate overnight.)* Garnish with whole strawberries, if desired. Serves 8 to 10.

Per serving: 550 calories, 29 g total fat, 17.5 g saturated fat, 198 mg cholesterol, 54 mg sodium, 70 g carbohydrates, 6 g protein, 143 mg calcium, 1 g fiber

berry crumble

Here's a simple three-step dessert that's a breeze to put together, allowing you to spend more time with the lucky recipients. When selecting, look for blackberries that are deep-colored and plump, and blueberries that are firm, consistent in size and blue with a silverish frost.

Prep time: 15 minutes • Baking time: 40 to 45 minutes

- **3** cups fresh blueberries
- **3** cups fresh blackberries
- **1** tablespoon fresh lemon juice
- **8** tablespoons granulated sugar, divided
- **¾** cup plus 4 tablespoons all-purpose flour, divided
- **½** cup firmly packed brown sugar
- **½** teaspoon cinnamon
- **6** tablespoons butter or margarine, cut into small pieces
- **½** cup chopped walnuts
  Vanilla ice cream (optional)

1. Heat oven to 375°F. Combine blueberries, blackberries, lemon juice, 6 tablespoons of the granulated sugar and 2 tablespoons of the flour in a large bowl. Transfer to a 2-quart shallow baking dish.

2. Combine remaining flour and granulated sugar, brown sugar and cinnamon in a medium bowl. With a pastry blender or 2 knives, cut in butter until mixture resembles coarse crumbs. Stir in walnuts. Sprinkle evenly over fruit.

3. Bake 40 to 45 minutes, until top is brown and fruit is bubbly. Cool on a wire rack. Serve warm or at room temperature with vanilla ice cream, if desired. Makes 8 servings.

Per serving: 340 calories, 14 g total fat, 6 g saturated fat, 23 mg cholesterol, 11 mg sodium, 54 g carbohydrates, 4 g protein, 46 mg calcium, 5 g fiber

raspberry crème brûlée tartlets

Sweet raspberries are hidden under a satiny custard and sealed with a thin layer of caramelized sugar. You'll need to broil the brown sugar only until it melts; it will become crisp after chilling.

Prep time: 1 hour plus chilling
Baking time: 25 to 28 minutes

PASTRY:
- 1½ cups all-purpose flour
- 1½ teaspoons granulated sugar
- ½ teaspoon salt
- ½ cup cold unsalted butter, cut up (no substitutions)
- 6 to 8 tablespoons ice water

CUSTARD FILLING:
- 2 cups heavy or whipping cream
- 6 large egg yolks
- ⅓ cup granulated sugar
- 2 teaspoons cornstarch
- Pinch salt
- ½ vanilla bean, split lengthwise in half
- 1 cup fresh raspberries
- 12 teaspoons brown sugar

1. *Make pastry:* Combine flour, sugar and salt in a large bowl. With a pastry blender or 2 knives, cut in butter until mixture resembles coarse crumbs. Add ice water, 1 tablespoon at a time, tossing vigorously with a fork after each addition, until pastry holds together. Divide pastry into 6 equal pieces and flatten each piece into a disk. Cover disks with plastic wrap and refrigerate overnight.

2. *Make custard filling:* Heat cream in a medium saucepan over medium heat until tiny bubbles form around the edge. Whisk yolks, sugar, cornstarch and salt in a medium bowl until well blended. Gradually stir in hot cream in a thin, steady stream. Return mixture to saucepan; add vanilla bean. Cook, stirring constantly, over medium-low heat, 5 to 10 minutes, until temperature reaches 170°F. on an instant-read thermometer and mixture coats the back of a spoon.

3. Strain custard through a fine sieve into a medium bowl. Scrape seeds from vanilla bean with a small knife; add to custard. Discard pod. Cover surface of custard with plastic wrap and refrigerate overnight.

4. On a lightly floured surface with a floured rolling pin, roll each pastry disk into a 6-inch circle. Fit rounds into six 4½-inch individual tart pans with removable bottoms. Fold overhang in, pressing against sides of tart pans so that pastry extends ¼ inch above rim. Prick bottoms of tart shells with a fork. Place in freezer 20 minutes.

5. Heat oven to 425°F. Line each tart shell with foil and fill with dried beans or pie weights. Place tart pans on a cookie sheet and bake 15 minutes. Remove foil and beans from shells. Bake 10 to 13 minutes more, until golden brown. Cool on a wire rack. Remove tart crusts from pans.

6. Divide raspberries among tart crusts. Spoon custard evenly over fruit. Refrigerate until custard is set, 20 minutes or up to 2 hours.

7. Heat broiler. Arrange tartlets on a cookie sheet. Sift 2 teaspoons brown sugar over each tartlet. Broil 4 inches from heat, about 1 minute or until sugar is melted and caramelized. Refrigerate tartlets 30 minutes or up to 3 hours before serving. Makes 6 servings.

Per serving: 685 calories, 50 g total fat, 29.5 g saturated fat, 263 mg cholesterol, 248 mg sodium, 52 g carbohydrates, 8 g protein, 94 mg calcium, 2 g fiber

summer pudding

In this classic pudding, slices of white bread line a charlotte pan, and gently simmered blackberries, blueberries and raspberries are piled into the mold. The dessert is then refrigerated, while the berries seep into the bread, coloring it a beautiful red. Served with whipped cream, it's a great do-ahead summer dessert.

Prep time: 20 minutes plus chilling
Cooking time: 15 minutes plus standing

- **2 cups fresh blueberries**
- **2 cups fresh blackberries**
- **⅔ cup sugar**
- **⅓ cup water**
- **1 strip (2 inches) lemon peel**
- **1 vanilla bean, split lengthwise in half**
- **1 cup fresh raspberries**
- **10 to 12 slices thin white bread, crusts removed**
  Whipped cream (optional)

1. Combine blueberries, blackberries, sugar, water, lemon peel and vanilla bean in a medium stainless-steel saucepan. Bring to boil over medium heat. Reduce heat and simmer 5 minutes. Stir in raspberries; cook 5 minutes more. Remove from heat; cover and let stand 15 minutes. Remove vanilla bean and lemon peel with a slotted spoon. Discard lemon peel. Scrape seeds from vanilla bean with a small spoon or tip of knife and stir into fruit. Discard pod. Let fruit cool to room temperature, about 15 to 20 minutes.

2. Meanwhile, butter a 6-cup charlotte pan, soufflé dish or glass bowl. Trim and cut 2 to 3 slices of bread to fit bottom of the pan. Cut and trim enough slices to fit tightly along the sides (plug in any small gaps with extra pieces of bread). Spoon fruit into prepared pan. Cover top of fruit with remaining bread, filling in any open spaces with smaller pieces of bread. Trim edge of bread along sides of dish. Arrange a piece of plastic wrap directly over the top, leaving a 1-inch overhang. Place a plate directly on top of pudding. Weigh the plate down with a large, heavy can. Refrigerate overnight.

3. Remove can, plate and plastic wrap. Run a thin knife along the sides of the pudding. Place a large serving plate on top of pan and invert pudding onto plate. Serve with whipped cream, if desired. Makes 6 servings.

Per serving: 265 calories, 2.5 g total fat, 1 g saturated fat, 2 mg cholesterol, 235 mg sodium, 58 g carbohydrates, 4 g protein, 68 mg calcium, 5 g fiber

pecan-nectarine layer cake

This tall beauty gets a little kick with a spirited dash of bourbon—both in the cake and the filling. Feature it at your next midsummer night's feast. To give the layers the lightest, most tender texture, we call for cake flour, not all-purpose flour. Pictured on page 203.

Prep time: 45 minutes plus chilling
Baking time: 20 to 25 minutes

CAKE:
- **1 cup pecan halves, toasted**
- **2 cups cake flour (not self-rising)**
- **1½ teaspoons baking soda**
- **½ teaspoon nutmeg**
- **½ teaspoon cinnamon**
- **½ teaspoon salt**
- **1 cup buttermilk, at room temperature**
- **¼ cup bourbon**
- **¾ cup butter, softened (no substitutions)**
- **1 cup firmly packed brown sugar**
- **1 cup granulated sugar**
- **3 large eggs at room temperature, separated**

- **10 medium nectarines**
- **2 tablespoons granulated sugar**

WHIPPED CREAM:

1½ **cups heavy or whipping cream**

¼ **cup confectioners' sugar**

2 **tablespoons bourbon**

■

Mint leaves, for garnish (optional)

1. *Make cake:* Heat oven to 350°F. Lightly grease bottoms of three 9-inch round cake pans. Line with waxed paper. Grease and flour paper and sides of pans. Process nuts in a food processor or blender until finely ground.

2. Combine pecans, flour, baking soda, nutmeg, cinnamon and salt in a large bowl. Combine buttermilk and ¼ cup bourbon in a cup. Beat butter 30 seconds in a large mixer bowl on medium-high speed. Add brown sugar and the 1 cup granulated sugar and beat until light and fluffy, about 4 minutes. Add egg yolks, one at a time, beating well after each addition. Reduce speed to medium-low. Add flour mixture, alternating with buttermilk mixture, beginning and ending with flour mixture.

3. In another clean mixer bowl with clean beaters, beat egg whites on medium-high speed just to stiff peaks. Gently fold into batter with a rubber spatula. Divide batter and spread evenly into the prepared pans. Bake 20 to 25 minutes, until tops are golden and a toothpick inserted in center of layers comes out clean. Cool layers in pans on wire racks, 15 minutes. Remove from cake pans; peel off waxed paper and cool completely. Refrigerate 1 hour, until firm.

4. Meanwhile, peel, pit and cut nectarines into ¼-inch-thick slices. Transfer to a medium bowl and toss with the 2 tablespoons granulated sugar.

5. *Make whipped cream:* Beat cream in a mixer bowl until thickened. Gradually add confectioners' sugar and bourbon and continue to beat just to stiff peaks.

6. *To assemble:* Remove 10 nectarine slices for garnish; set aside. Place one cake layer on a serving plate; cover with half of the remaining nectarines in a single layer. Spread top with one-third of the whipped cream, covering evenly to edge. Top with second cake layer, half of remaining whipped cream and remaining nectarines. Top with third cake layer, then remaining whipped cream. Garnish top with reserved nectarines. *(Can be made ahead. Refrigerate up to 3 hours.)* Garnish with mint leaves, if desired. Makes 12 servings.

Per serving: 585 calories, 33 g total fat, 15 g saturated fat, 126 mg cholesterol, 427 mg sodium, 69 g carbohydrates, 6 g protein, 82 mg calcium, 3 g fiber

test kitchen tip

nectarine know-how

Nectarines—similar in flavor and texture to peaches (without the fuzz)—are one of the treats of summer. They're usually at their peak between June and September. Here's how to enjoy them at their best:

CHOOSE nectarines that have a healthy golden yellow skin with no tinges of green. The pretty blush color on the skin of the fruit has to do with the variety of nectarine, not ripeness. Nectarines should be firm and unblemished in the store. Complete ripening them at home in a loosely closed paper bag for several days at room temperature.

USE the ripened fruit as soon as possible. Refrigerate ripe nectarines for up to 5 days.

SERVE nectarines at room temperature for best flavor. As with peaches, it's a personal choice as to whether or not you peel them.

seven secrets to perfect pie crusts

Some say the perfect, flaky, all-American pie crust of our grandmothers' days are becoming a lost art. Nonsense! Follow these tips, and you'll be an expert pie-baker for years to come:

1. **CHILL EVERYTHING.** Place flour in a bowl in the freezer 15 minutes, or, if you have space, keep a package of flour in the refrigerator just for pies.

2. **TO MEASURE FLOUR AND FAT:** Use nested measuring cups. Stir flour in canister or package to aerate; spoon into a measuring cup. Level off excess with a metal spatula.

3. **USE PIE PLATES** made of standard glass or dull metal. Do not use shiny metal plates, which can result in a soggy bottom crust.

4. **IF PASTRY CRACKS** while rolling it out, too little water was added. Start over from the beginning.

5. **IF BOTTOM OF PASTRY** splits before it's filled, patch it by dampening a scrap of pastry and pressing gently over hole.

6. **IF CRUST SHRINKS,** you've stretched it too much in the pie plate. Always drape sides of the plate generously with pastry, and don't pull up on the pastry to flute edges.

7. **IF A CRUST FAILS TO BROWN,** you've either used too little fat or too much liquid. Or, when you rolled it out, too much flour was used.

the perfect sour cherry pie

What makes this pie perfect? The crust, for starters—we used a combination of shortening (for flakiness) and butter (for flavor). For proper consistency, we thickened the filling with tapioca. The hardest part might be buying the cherries! If you're lucky, you'll spot them at your local farmers' market; otherwise, look for frozen sour (tart) cherries in selected supermarkets. Pictured on page 202.

Prep time: 30 minutes plus chilling and standing
Baking time: 60 to 70 minutes

PASTRY:
- 2¼ cups all-purpose flour
- 3 tablespoons sugar
- ½ teaspoon salt
- ½ teaspoon grated lemon peel
- 9 tablespoons butter, cut up (no substitutions)
- ⅓ cup vegetable shortening, chilled
- 5 to 6 tablespoons ice water

CHERRY FILLING:
- 5 cups fresh sour (tart) cherries or 1½ pounds frozen sour (tart) cherries
- ¾ cup sugar
- 3 tablespoons instant tapioca
- ¼ teaspoon almond extract

- 1 large egg, separated
- 2 teaspoons sugar

1. *Make pastry:* Combine flour, sugar, salt and lemon peel in a bowl. With a pastry blender or 2 knives, cut in butter and shortening until mixture resembles coarse crumbs. Add ice water, tossing with a fork, until pastry holds together. (For food processor: Pulse flour, sugar, salt and lemon peel to combine. Add butter and shortening and pulse until mixture resembles coarse crumbs. Sprinkle 3 tablespoons water onto flour mixture. Pulse 3 times. Add 2 tablespoons water and pulse until pastry just comes together, adding more water if necessary.) Shape pastry into 2 balls, one slightly larger than the other. Flatten into disks and wrap in plastic wrap; refrigerate up to 1 hour.

2. *Make filling:* Pit cherries. Stir together cherries, sugar, tapioca and almond extract in a large bowl. Let stand 15 minutes (45 minutes for frozen cherries), stirring occasionally.

3. Adjust oven rack to lowest position. Heat oven to 425°F. On a lightly floured surface, roll larger pastry disk into a 12-inch circle. Fit pastry into a 9-inch pie plate, leaving a 1-inch overhang. Cover with plastic wrap and refrigerate. Roll remaining pastry into a 10-inch square. Using a pastry wheel or sharp knife, trim edges of pastry and cut pastry into ten 1-inch-wide strips.

4. Lightly beat egg white until foamy, and brush bottom of pie pastry. Spoon in filling. Beat egg yolk with 1 tablespoon water and brush edge of pastry. Weave strips over filling for lattice crust. Trim ends and flute edge. Brush strips and edge with yolk mixture. Sprinkle with 2 teaspoons sugar. Place on a cookie sheet. Bake 10 minutes. Cover edge of pastry with foil. Bake 50 minutes more or until juices in center bubble (60 minutes for frozen cherries). If lattice darkens, cover loosely with foil. Cool on a wire rack. Makes 8 servings.

Per serving: 475 calories, 23 g total fat, 10.5 g saturated fat, 61 mg cholesterol, 321 mg sodium, 64 g carbohydrates, 5 g protein, 23 mg calcium, 1 g fiber

cherry clafouti

Though cherries are the traditional choice for this classic country dessert from southern France, any fruit—plums, peaches or berries—can be used. Serve warm. Pictured on page 204.

Prep time: 20 minutes • Baking time: 35 to 40 minutes

- 1½ **pounds fresh red or white sweet cherries, pitted**
- ½ **pint fresh blackberries or raspberries**
- ½ **cup plus 2 tablespoons granulated sugar, divided**
- 2 **tablespoons Kirsch (cherry-flavored liqueur)**
- 3 **large eggs**
- ½ **cup crème fraîche (see tip, right)**
- ½ **cup milk**
- ½ **cup all-purpose flour**
  Confectioners' sugar

1. Heat oven to 425°F. Combine cherries, blackberries, 2 tablespoons of the granulated sugar and the Kirsch in a large bowl. Transfer to a shallow 6-cup baking dish. Bake until fruit is hot and steamy, 8 to 10 minutes. Strain fruit in a large strainer set over a bowl; reserve 2 tablespoons juice. Return fruit to baking dish. Reduce oven temperature to 350°F.

2. Meanwhile, beat eggs in a large mixer bowl on medium-high speed, until foamy, 2 minutes. Beat in remaining ½ cup granulated sugar, the crème fraîche, milk, flour and the 2 tablespoons of reserved fruit juice, until well blended. Pour batter over fruit. Bake until filling is set and top is golden brown, 35 to 40 minutes. Cool on a wire rack until warm. Dust top with confectioners' sugar. Makes 8 servings.

Per serving: 260 calories, 8.5 g total fat, 4.5 g saturated fat, 94 mg cholesterol, 41 mg sodium, 40 g carbohydrates, 5 g protein, 76 mg calcium, 2 g fiber

---

test kitchen tip

oh-so *fraîche!*

Often used in French cooking, crème fraîche is a dairy product that's similar to sour cream, but has a softer flavor and milder taste. If you can't find the product in your area, try this substitute:

HEAT 1 cup heavy or whipping cream in a small saucepan over low heat until warm (90°F. to 100°F.). Transfer cream to a small bowl. Stir in 2 tablespoons buttermilk.

LET the mixture stand, covered, at room temperature for 24 to 30 hours until thickened. Do not stir mixture.

STORE, covered, in the refrigerator for up to a week. Stir before using. Makes 1 cup.

cherishing cherries

Fresh cherry season is short—sweet cherries appear May through July, while tart cherries are generally available in June and July. Here's how to make the most of these short months!

SELECT firm, plump, shiny, blemish-free cherries. Avoid fruit that's bruised or very soft.

USE fresh cherries as soon after purchasing as possible. Refrigerate the cherries, covered, for up to 4 days.

TO FREEZE, rinse and dry the fruit, pitting if desired. Place in freezer bags and freeze 6 to 12 months.

old-fashioned cherry-peach cobbler

Everybody loves the all-time favorite cobbler—and this one is most definitely worth adding to your repertoire.

Prep time: 45 minutes • Baking time: 30 to 35 minutes

- ¾ **cup sugar**
- 2 **tablespoons cornstarch**
- ¼ **teaspoon cinnamon**
- 5 **cups Bing cherries, pitted and halved**
- 4 **large ripe peaches (1½ lbs.), cut into ½-inch-thick slices**
- 1 **tablespoon fresh lemon juice**
- 1 **teaspoon vanilla extract**

BISCUITS:
- 2 **cups all-purpose flour**
- ¼ **cup sugar**
- 2 **teaspoons baking powder**
- ¼ **teaspoon salt**
- ½ **cup cold butter or margarine, cut into small pieces**
- 1 **cup heavy or whipping cream**

1. Heat oven to 400°F. Combine sugar, cornstarch and cinnamon in a 6-quart Dutch oven. Whisk until blended. Stir in cherries, peaches and lemon juice until juicy. Bring to boil over medium-high heat, stirring frequently. Reduce heat to medium and simmer 2 minutes. Stir in vanilla. Pour into a 3-quart glass baking dish.

2. *Make biscuits:* Pulse flour, sugar, baking powder and salt in a food processor to combine. Add butter and process until mixture resembles coarse meal. Transfer flour mixture into a large bowl; pour cream over top, then stir with a fork until mixture comes together (dough will be soft).

3. Turn out onto a lightly-floured surface and gently knead 3 times until smooth. Roll to a 10½-inch square. Cut into 16 squares. Arrange squares over filling, slightly overlapping in an oval, leaving center open. Bake 30 to 35 minutes, until fruit is bubbly in center and biscuits are browned. (If biscuits become too brown, cover loosely with foil during the last 5 minutes of baking.) Cool on a wire rack. Serve warm or at room temperature. Makes 12 servings.

Per serving: 350 calories, 16 g total fat, 9.5 g saturated fat, 48 mg cholesterol, 215 mg sodium, 50 g carbohydrates, 4 g protein, 76 mg calcium, 2 g fiber

cherry-pecan upside-down cake

Here's a no-fuss cake that's perfect for in-season cherries.

Prep time: 35 minutes • Baking time: 35 to 40 minutes

- 3 **cups fresh sour (tart) cherries**
- ¾ **cup unsalted butter or margarine, softened, divided**
- ½ **cup firmly packed light brown sugar**
- ⅓ **cup pecans, chopped**

1½ cups all-purpose flour

1½ teaspoons baking powder

¼ teaspoon salt

3 large eggs, at room temperature, separated

¾ cup granulated sugar, divided

1½ teaspoons vanilla extract

½ cup milk

1. Pit cherries into a colander; drain and set aside. Heat oven to 350°F.

2. Combine ¼ cup of the butter, the brown sugar and pecans in a 10-inch cast iron or heavy oven-proof skillet. Cook over medium heat, stirring until butter melts and mixture is blended. Bring to a simmer and cook 1 minute, stirring constantly. Remove skillet from heat. Arrange cherries in a single layer over brown sugar mixture.

3. Combine flour, baking powder and salt in a small bowl, stirring until blended; set aside. Beat egg whites in a small mixer bowl on low speed until foamy. Increase speed to medium and gradually beat in ¼ cup of the granulated sugar; beat to soft peaks. Set aside. Beat remaining ½ cup butter in a large mixer bowl, until creamy. Gradually beat in remaining ½ cup granulated sugar; beat 2 minutes until light and fluffy. Beat in egg yolks and vanilla until blended. On low speed, beat in flour mixture in thirds, alternately with milk, just until blended. Gently fold in whites, one-third at a time, until no white streaks remain. Pour batter into skillet and spread gently to cover cherries.

4. Bake cake 35 to 40 minutes, until a toothpick inserted in center comes out clean. Cool 3 minutes in pan. Run knife around edge of cake; using pot holders, carefully invert onto a serving plate. Spoon any glaze remaining in pan over cake. Cool completely. Makes 12 servings.

Per serving: 300 calories, 15.5 g total fat, 8 g saturated fat, 86 mg cholesterol, 136 mg sodium, 38 g carbohydrates, 4 g protein, 71 mg calcium, 1 g fiber

peaches-and-cream frozen tart

An easy graham-cracker crust overflows with a wonderful combination of vanilla ice cream and peach sorbet. Ripe peaches complete the dessert, making every bite a summer-fresh delight.

Total prep time: 20 minutes plus freezing

1¼ cups graham-cracker crumbs

½ cup toasted sliced almonds, divided

⅓ cup butter or margarine, melted

1 pint vanilla ice cream

1 pint peach sorbet

3 ripe peaches, peeled, pitted and cut into eighths

1. Heat oven to 350°F. Wrap bottom of a 10-inch tart pan with removable bottom with foil. Process graham-cracker crumbs and ¼ cup of the almonds in a food processor, pulsing until finely ground. Add melted butter and pulse to combine. Press crumbs evenly on bottom and up sides of prepared pan; place on a jelly-roll pan. Bake crust 6 to 7 minutes, until golden. Cool completely on a wire rack. Freeze 2 hours.

2. Refrigerate ice cream 10 to 15 minutes to soften. Transfer to a medium bowl and quickly stir just until smooth. Immediately spread ice cream on top of crust. Cover with plastic wrap and freeze 2 hours, until firm.

3. Refrigerate sorbet 10 to 15 minutes, until softened. Transfer to a medium bowl; stir just until smooth. Uncover tart and spread sorbet over ice-cream layer. Cover and freeze 2 hours or until firm. *(Can be made ahead. Cover and freeze up to 2 days.)*

4. Remove sides of pan and transfer tart to a serving plate. Arrange peach slices on top and sprinkle with remaining ¼ cup almonds. Refrigerate tart 10 to 15 minutes before serving. Makes 8 to 10 servings.

Per serving: 315 calories, 17.5 g total fat, 7.5 g saturated fat, 33 mg cholesterol, 169 mg sodium, 37 g carbohydrates, 6 g protein, 115 mg calcium, 2 g fiber

handfuls of heaven

At first glance, a white peach may look like any other fresh peach—but once you take a bite, you'll discover the delicious difference. Like their name implies, rather than orange-yellow flesh, they have a much lighter pink or whitish interior. A white peach may be the sweetest, juiciest, most delicate fruit you'll ever taste.

Before the 1930s, white peaches were more common than their yellow counterparts. But they soon proved too fragile for shipping, so mostly yellow peaches were harvested commercially. Then in the 1980s, a hardier variety of white peach was developed. They're better travelers and even sweeter than the heirloom varieties.

White peaches are in season in late summer. Look for creamy white skin with flashes of vibrant pink and no green. If placed in a paper bag, white peaches ripen twice as fast as yellow ones—usually in about a day.

white peach ice cream

This homemade ice cream is just the way to show off white peaches' seductive, subtle floral flavor.

Prep time: 30 minutes plus chilling and freezing

- 2 **pounds white peaches**
- 1 **cup sugar, divided**
- 2 **teaspoons fresh lemon juice**
  Pinch salt
- 1 **pint heavy or whipping cream**
- ¾ **cup milk**
- 4 **large egg yolks**
- ¼ **cup light corn syrup**
  Sliced white peaches and fresh mint sprigs, for garnish (optional)

1. Bring a large saucepan of water to boil. Add peaches and let stand in hot water 1 minute. Remove peaches with a slotted spoon to a bowl. When cool, peel skin, cut in half and remove pits. Finely chop enough peach halves to equal 1 cup; set aside.

2. Puree remaining peaches in a food processor with ½ cup of the sugar, the lemon juice and salt. Cover and refrigerate.

3. For custard, heat cream and milk in a saucepan over medium-high heat, until small bubbles form around edge of pan.

4. Meanwhile, whisk yolks, remaining ½ cup sugar and the corn syrup in a bowl. Gradually whisk in half the hot cream mixture; return to saucepan. Cook over medium heat, stirring, until slightly thickened, about 2 minutes (160°F. on a candy thermometer). Stir in chopped peaches. Transfer to a large bowl and refrigerate until cold, 2 hours or overnight.

5. Stir chilled peach puree into cold custard. Transfer to a 2-quart ice-cream maker and freeze according to manufacturer's directions. Place in freezer for at least 3 hours, until firm. Serve with sliced peaches and mint, if desired. Makes about 7 cups.

Per ½ cup: 330 calories, 20 g total fat, 12 g saturated fat, 153 mg cholesterol, 54 mg sodium, 36 g carbohydrates, 3 g protein, 66 mg calcium, 1 g fiber

sweet ricotta puffs with peaches

We add elegance to these Sicilian fritters by serving them with peaches in vin santo, a sweet Italian white wine. Pictured on page 203.

Prep time: 35 minutes plus chilling
Cooking time: 80 seconds to 2 minutes per batch

PEACHES:

- 6 large ripe peaches
- ½ cup vin santo wine or sweet sherry
- 2 to 4 teaspoons granulated sugar

SWEET RICOTTA PUFFS:

- 1 container (15 oz.) whole-milk ricotta
- 2 large eggs
- 3 tablespoons granulated sugar
- ½ teaspoon grated orange peel
- ¾ cup all-purpose flour
- 1¾ teaspoons baking powder
- Pinch salt
-
- 1½ cups olive oil
- Confectioners' sugar
- Fresh mint sprigs, for garnish (optional)

1. *Make peaches:* Peel and pit peaches. Cut into ½-inch-thick wedges. Combine in a large bowl with wine and sugar. Cover and refrigerate 2 hours.

2. *Make sweet ricotta puffs:* Whisk all sweet ricotta puffs ingredients in a medium bowl until smooth. Line a large cookie sheet with a double thickness of paper towels. Heat oven to warm or lowest setting.

3. Heat oil in a large skillet over medium-high heat, about 9 minutes. (Drop a small bit of dough into oil; if it starts to bubble immediately, the oil is ready for frying. Discard bit of dough.) Drop 6 pieces of dough by level tablespoons, scraping with a small spatula or another spoon, into hot oil. Fry 40 to 60 seconds per side, until golden and puffed. Transfer fritters with a slotted spoon to prepared cookie sheet. Turn oven off. Place fritters in oven and repeat process with remaining dough.

4. Sprinkle fritters with confectioners' sugar. Arrange 4 fritters on each of 10 shallow dessert plates. Spoon peach and wine mixture among dessert plates, arranging peaches alongside fritters. Garnish with mint, if desired, and serve immediately. Makes 10 servings.

Per serving: 300 calories, 17.5 g total fat, 5.5 g saturated fat, 64 mg cholesterol, 149 mg sodium, 28 g carbohydrates, 8 g protein, 148 mg calcium, 2 g fiber

---

test kitchen tip

it's a peach

There is perhaps no more luscious taste than a perfectly ripe peach. Peaches are at their best between June and September—so get them while you can. Here's how to pick the cream of the crop:

SELECT peaches that are firm but yield slightly to pressure when pressed. The fruit should be well-shaped and without blemishes or soft spots. Skin color varies from variety to variety, and is not a good indication of ripeness. However, the peaches should have no tinges of green.

STORE peaches at room temperature until slightly soft (placing them in a paper bag expedites the ripening process), then in the refrigerator for up to 5 days.

PEEL the fuzzy skin off of a peach by inserting a fork in one end of the fruit. Dip the peach in boiling water for 20 seconds, then peel the skin from the peach with a paring knife, starting from the stem end. It should slip off easily.

plum crostata

A crostata, a rustic open-faced Italian fruit tart, is a perfect way to show off ruby-red plums. For the most delicious results, choose ripe plums that give slightly when gently squeezed. Pictured on page 205.

Prep time: 20 minutes plus chilling
Baking time: 25 to 30 minutes

PASTRY:

- 1¼ **cups all-purpose flour**
- 2 **tablespoons sugar**
- ¼ **teaspoon salt**
- ½ **cup cold butter, cut into small pieces (no substitutions)**
- 4 **tablespoons ice water**

FILLING:

- 6 **tablespoons sugar**
- 1 **tablespoon cornstarch**
- 1 **pound plums, pitted and cut into eighths (about 3 cups)**
- ½ **teaspoon grated orange peel**
- ¼ **teaspoon cinnamon**
- 1 **large egg yolk**
- 1 **tablespoon water**

1. *Make pastry:* Pulse flour, sugar and salt in a food processor to combine. Add butter and pulse until mixture resembles coarse crumbs. Add ice water and pulse just until mixture begins to hold together. Transfer to a board; shape into a ball, then flatten into a disk. Wrap in plastic wrap and refrigerate 30 minutes.

2. *Make filling:* Heat oven to 425°F. Combine sugar and cornstarch in a cup. On a lightly floured surface, roll pastry to a 12-inch circle. Transfer circle onto a large cookie sheet lined with foil. Toss plums with sugar and cornstarch mixture, orange peel and cinnamon. Arrange plum slices in center of pastry, leaving a 1½-inch border. (Spoon any remaining sugar and cornstarch mixture over fruit, if necessary.)

3. Beat egg yolk and water with a fork in another cup. Fold edge of pastry over plums, leaving some of the plums showing in the center of the pastry. Lightly brush pastry edge with egg-water mixture.

4. Bake crostata 25 to 30 minutes, until pastry is golden and fruit is bubbly. Cool on cookie sheet on a wire rack 5 minutes. Carefully loosen crostata from foil with a large spatula. Remove foil and transfer crostata to a wire rack to cool. Serve warm or at room temperature. Makes 6 servings.

Per serving: 345 calories, 16 g total fat, 9.5 g saturated fat, 50 mg cholesterol, 253 mg sodium, 48 g carbohydrates, 4 g protein, 14 mg calcium, 2 g fiber

pineapple sorbet EASY

If you like piña colada, you'll love this refreshing dessert featuring the flavors of that tropical drink. The recipe is foolproof, too. All you have to do is puree the mixture with the rum, and voilà—it's ready to serve! Tip: Don't confuse cream of coconut with coconut milk—they're two different products. Cream of coconut is often located where cocktail mixes are found.

Total prep time: 5 minutes plus 4 to 5 hours chilling

- 1 **can (20 oz.) pineapple chunks in juice**
- ⅔ **cup cream of coconut, chilled**
- **Pinch salt**
- 2 **tablespoons light rum**

1. Combine pineapple chunks and juice, cream of coconut and salt in a shallow stainless-steel bowl. Cover and freeze until firm, 4 to 5 hours.

2. Puree pineapple mixture and rum in a blender until smooth. Serve immediately. Makes 4 servings.

Per serving: 375 calories, 26 g total fat, 6 g saturated fat, 0 mg cholesterol, 48 mg sodium, 33 g carbohydrates, 1 g protein, 22 mg calcium, 1 g fiber

carrot and fruit bundt cake LOW FAT

Instead of a whopping cup of vegetable oil—the usual amount in a carrot cake—we used apple sauce and just ¹/₄ cup of canola oil, a heart-healthier fat. Bake a day ahead to allow flavors to mellow. Pictured on page 208.

Prep time: 30 minutes • Baking time: 1 hour 15 to 20 minutes

3	cups all-purpose flour
2	teaspoons baking powder
1½	teaspoons baking soda
1½	teaspoons cinnamon
½	teaspoon salt
½	cup dried apricots, finely diced, divided
½	cup dried currants, divided
¼	cup crystallized ginger, finely chopped
1	cup granulated sugar
1	cup firmly packed brown sugar
2	large eggs
2	large egg whites
1	cup applesauce
¼	cup canola oil
1¼	pounds carrots, shredded (4 cups)
1	tablespoon vanilla extract

GLAZE:

1	can (6 oz.) pineapple juice
½	cup fresh orange juice
2	tablespoons honey
2	tablespoons toasted pecans, chopped

1. Heat oven to 350°F. Grease and flour a 12-cup fluted kugelhopf mold or bundt pan. Combine flour, baking powder, baking soda, cinnamon and salt in a large bowl. Set aside 2 tablespoons of the apricots and 1 tablespoon of the currants in a bowl for glaze. Stir remaining apricots and currants and the crystallized ginger into flour mixture.

2. Stir together granulated sugar and next seven ingredients in another large bowl until well blended, breaking up any lumps of brown sugar with a spoon. Stir into flour mixture. Pour batter into prepared pan.

3. Bake 1 hour 15 to 20 minutes, until a toothpick inserted into center of cake comes out clean. Let cake cool in pan on a wire rack 10 minutes. Unmold cake onto rack and cool completely.

4. *Make glaze:* Meanwhile, combine all glaze ingredients in a medium saucepan. Bring to boil. Reduce heat and boil gently 12 to 15 minutes, until glaze thickens and is reduced to ¹/₃ cup. Pour into a small bowl and let cool 15 minutes. Stir reserved 2 tablespoons apricots and 1 tablespoon currants into glaze. Spoon glaze over top of cooled cake, pressing fruit to stick to cake. Sprinkle top with pecans, pressing to stick. Makes 12 servings.

Per serving: 435 calories, 7.5 g total fat, 1 g saturated fat, 35 mg cholesterol, 386 mg sodium, 88 g carbohydrates, 6 g protein, 103 mg calcium, 4 g fiber

apple and pear sauce EASY

This sauté is simply sublime served over vanilla ice cream. Pictured on page 206.

Prep time: 20 minutes • Cooking time: 13 minutes

2	tablespoons butter or margarine
2	tablespoons sugar
2	Golden Delicious apples, peeled, cored and cut into ½-inch chunks
2	Bosc or Bartlett pears, peeled, cored and cut into ½-inch chunks
1	tablespoon brandy
1	pint vanilla ice cream

Melt butter in a nonstick skillet over medium heat. Add sugar; cook until sugar just begins to melt, 2 minutes. Stir in apples and pears. Increase heat to medium-high. Cover; cook fruit 10 minutes, stirring frequently, until fruit is golden and tender. Add brandy; cook, uncovered, 1 minute more. Divide ice cream into 4 serving bowls; top with sauce. Serves 4.

Per serving: 302 calories, 14 g fat, 8 g saturated fat, 45 mg cholesterol, 111 mg sodium, 44 g carbohydrates, 3 g protein, 98 mg calcium, 3 g fiber

tarte tatin

Golden Delicious apples work well in this classic, because they hold their shape after baking. Pictured on page 204.

Prep time: 45 minutes plus chilling
Baking time: 35 minutes

PASTRY:

1¼	cups all-purpose flour
1	tablespoon sugar
¼	teaspoon salt
6	tablespoons unsalted butter, cut up (no substitutions)
1	large egg yolk
2	to 3 tablespoons ice water

CARAMEL:

¼	cup water
½	cup sugar

APPLES:

4	tablespoons unsalted butter (no substitutions)
⅓	cup sugar
3	pounds Golden Delicious apples (5 to 6), peeled, cored and quartered

1. *Make pastry:* Pulse flour, sugar and salt in food processor to combine. Add butter and pulse 4 to 5 times, until mixture resembles coarse crumbs. Add egg yolk; pulse to blend. Add ice water; pulse until mixture just begins to come together. Shape pastry into a ball and flatten into a disk. Wrap in plastic wrap and refrigerate 30 minutes or overnight.

2. *Make caramel:* Bring water and sugar to boil in a small saucepan over medium-high heat. Cook, swirling pan, until syrup turns dark amber, 10 minutes. Quickly pour caramel into a 9½-inch deep-dish glass pie plate, tilting the plate so the bottom is evenly coated. Set aside.

3. *Make apples:* Melt butter in a 12-inch nonstick skillet. Add sugar and cook 2 minutes. Add apples and cook, gently stirring, until almost tender and lightly caramelized, 25 to 30 minutes.

4. Heat oven to 375°F. Let apples cool slightly in pan. With a spoon, arrange apples, cored side up, in two layers on top of caramel in pie plate.

5. On a lightly floured surface, roll pastry into an 11-inch circle; place on top of apples. Fold up overhanging pastry along rim of pie plate. Bake until pastry is golden brown and filling is bubbly, 35 minutes.

6. Cool tart on a rack 10 minutes. Invert a plate (larger than the pie plate) on top of pie plate. Carefully invert tart onto plate. (If any apples stick to pie plate, remove with a small knife and replace on pastry.) Serve warm or at room temperature. Makes 8 servings.

Per serving: 380 calories, 15.5 g fat, 9 g saturated fat, 65 mg cholesterol, 133 mg sodium, 59 g carbohydrates, 3 g protein, 16 mg calcium, 3 g fiber

sour cream-apple pie

This heavenly crumb pie is filled with Golden Delicious apples, apple brandy and vanilla bean custard.

Prep time: 30 minutes plus chilling
Baking time: 50 to 55 minutes
Microwaved used

PASTRY:

1½	cups all-purpose flour
1	tablespoon granulated sugar
¼	teaspoon salt
5	tablespoons butter or margarine, cut up
2	tablespoons vegetable shortening
4	to 5 tablespoons ice water

CRUMB TOPPING:

½	cup all-purpose flour
¼	cup firmly packed brown sugar
⅛	teaspoon nutmeg
⅛	teaspoon ginger
3	tablespoons butter or margarine

FILLING:

2	tablespoons apple brandy
1	vanilla bean, split lengthwise in half, or 1 teaspoon vanilla extract
½	cup sour cream
½	cup plus 2 tablespoons granulated sugar

2   tablespoons all-purpose flour
4   large Golden Delicious apples (2 lbs.),
     peeled, cored and cut into ½-inch wedges
     (6 cups)

1. *Make pastry* Pulse flour, granulated sugar and salt in a food processor to combine. Add butter and shortening. Pulse until mixture resembles coarse crumbs. Gradually add ice water through feed tube, 1 tablespoon at a time, until mixture starts to hold together. Shape pastry into a ball and flatten into a thick disk. Wrap in plastic wrap and refrigerate 30 minutes. On a lightly floured surface, roll pastry into a 12-inch circle. Fit into a 9-inch pie plate, trim edges and flute. Place pastry shell in freezer 10 minutes.

2. Meanwhile, arrange oven rack in lower third of oven. Heat oven to 425°F.

3. *Make crumb topping:* Combine flour, brown sugar, nutmeg and ginger in a medium bowl. With pastry blender or 2 knives, cut in butter until mixture resembles coarse crumbs.

4. *Make filling:* Microwave the brandy in a microwaveproof cup on High 40 seconds, until hot. If using vanilla bean, add and let stand 10 minutes. Combine sour cream, granulated sugar and flour (and vanilla extract, if using) in a large bowl. Remove vanilla bean, reserving brandy; scrape seeds from bean and stir into sour cream mixture. Discard pod (or reserve for another use, such as flavoring granulated sugar). Add apples and reserved brandy, tossing to coat. Spoon filling into frozen pastry shell. Sprinkle topping evenly over filling. Bake 15 minutes. Cover edges of crust loosely with foil. Reduce heat to 375°F. and bake 35 to 40 minutes more, until filling is bubbly and topping is golden. Cool on a wire rack 1 hour. (*Can be made ahead. Cool completely. Wrap well and freeze up to 2 weeks. Thaw at room temperature 4 hours. Reheat in a 350°F. oven 15 minutes.*) Serve warm or at room temperature. Makes 8 servings.

Per serving: 435 calories, 18.5 g total fat, 10 g saturated fat, 37 mg cholesterol, 196 mg sodium, 65 g carbohydrates, 4 g protein, 35 mg calcium, 4 g fiber

---

test kitchen tip

the apple of your pie

There are some 2,500 varieties of apples grown in this country—and some are better than others for baking, cooking and eating. Here's a sampling of apples and their suggested uses.

CORTLAND: A slightly tart red apple with green highlights. Good for eating and baking.

CRISPIN: A sweet, yellow-green apple. All-purpose.

CRITERION: A sweet, yellow apple with a red blush. All-purpose.

FUJI: A sweet, greenish yellow apple with a red blush. All-purpose.

GOLDEN DELICIOUS: A solidly yellow apple that ranges from tangy to sweet. All-purpose.

GRANNY SMITH: A green apple with very tart flesh. All-purpose.

JONAGOLD: A yellow apple with orange to red blush, it ranges from tangy to sweet. All-purpose.

JONATHAN: A red apple with yellow undertones that's full-flavored and mildly tart. All-purpose.

NORTHERN SPY: A moderately tart, red, striped or blushed apple. Good for eating and baking.

ROME BEAUTY: A red, striped apple with green tinges that's slightly tart. Good for baking and cooking.

WINESAP: A deep purplish red apple that has a tangy, winelike taste. All-purpose.

YORK IMPERIAL: A deep red apple with green stripes, it is slightly tart. Good for baking and cooking.

apple appeal

A few tips for enjoying the ultimate fall fruit:

SELECT apples that are firm and have smooth, unblemished skins. The rough patches on the skin, called russeting, generally do not affect the flavor of the apple.

STORE apples in the refrigerator crisper in the plastic bag in which they were purchased. Apples purchased in bulk can be stored in a cool, moist place. Apples kept at room temperature will lose their crispness and flavor 10 times faster than if stored in the refrigerator.

apple pie

Our all-American pie gets an extra dose of flavor from Calvados, an apple brandy that hails from Normandy, France. Applejack is an easy-to-find stateside substitute, as is regular brandy. Pictured on page 205.

Prep time: 30 minutes plus chilling
Baking time: 63 to 67 minutes

PASTRY:

- 2¼ cups all-purpose flour
- 2 tablespoons confectioners' sugar
- ½ teaspoon salt
- ½ cup cold unsalted butter, cut into ½-inch cubes (no substitutions)
- ¼ cup vegetable shortening, chilled
- ⅓ cup orange juice
- 1½ to 2 tablespoons ice water

FILLING:

- 2½ pounds Gala and Golden Delicious apples, peeled, cored and cut into ½-inch-thick wedges
- ½ cup firmly packed brown sugar
- 3 tablespoons cornstarch
- 2 tablespoons Calvados, applejack or brandy
- 1 teaspoon cinnamon
- 1 tablespoon unsalted butter (no substitutions)
- 1 tablespoon heavy or whipping cream
- 1 tablespoon granulated sugar

1. *Make pastry:* Whisk together flour, confectioners' sugar and salt in a large bowl. With a pastry blender or 2 knives, cut in butter and shortening until mixture resembles coarse crumbs. With a fork, gradually stir in orange juice and 1½ tablespoons ice water. When dough begins to come together (adding remaining ½ tablespoon water, if necessary), turn dough out onto surface and gently press into a disk. Cut in half and shape into 2 disks. Wrap each disk in plastic wrap and refrigerate 1 hour. *(Can be made ahead. Refrigerate up to 3 days.)*

2. *Make filling:* Toss all filling ingredients except butter together in a large bowl.

3. Arrange oven rack in lower third of oven. Line a cookie sheet with foil and place on oven rack.

4. Heat oven to 425°F. On a lightly floured surface, with a floured rolling pin roll one pastry disk out to an 11½-inch circle; fit into a 9-inch pie plate. Trim overhang to ½ inch. Place in freezer 5 minutes. Arrange one layer of tightly packed apple wedges, spoke-fashion, in prepared pie shell. (This will prevent empty space between apples and top crust.) Repeat with remaining apples, stacking layers until pastry is full. Pour any juices left in bowl over the fruit; dot with butter. Roll remaining pastry into a 10-inch circle. If desired, cut out three flowers with a 1½-inch flower-shape cookie cutter. Arrange pastry over apples. Gently press flower cutouts on top of pie; trim and flute edge. Brush top with cream. Sprinkle top evenly with granulated sugar.

5. Place pie plate on a hot cookie sheet; bake 25 minutes, until edge of crust is golden. Reduce oven temperature to 400°F. Cut a vent in center of a piece of foil; cover pie. Bake pie 38 to 42 minutes more, until top is golden and filling is bubbly. Uncover; cool completely on a wire rack. Serves 8.

Per serving: 455 calories, 20.5 g total fat, 10 g saturated fat, 37 mg cholesterol, 154 mg sodium, 66 g carbohydrates, 4 g protein, 31 mg calcium, 3 g fiber

cranberry-nut tart

This lovely tart can be made ahead and frozen up to two weeks. If you plan on using fresh cranberries for the filling, October through December is peak season. Otherwise, frozen cranberries work fine.

Prep time: 20 minutes plus chilling
Baking time: 56 to 63 minutes

PASTRY:

- 1½   cups all-purpose flour
- ¼   teaspoon salt
- ½   cup butter, softened (no substitutions)
- ½   cup granulated sugar
- 1   large egg yolk
- 1   tablespoon ice water

FILLING:

- ⅓   cup toasted shelled pistachios
- ¼   cup whole blanched almonds
- 1   cup granulated sugar, divided
- ½   cup butter, softened (no substitutions)
- 2   large eggs
- 3   tablespoons all-purpose flour
- ⅛   teaspoon almond extract
- 1½   cups fresh or frozen cranberries

  ▪

Confectioners' sugar, for garnish (optional)

1. *Make pastry:* Combine flour and salt in a medium bowl; set aside. Beat butter and granulated sugar in a large mixer bowl at medium-high speed until creamy. Beat in egg yolk and water. With mixer at low speed, beat in flour mixture just until mixture holds together. Flatten into a thick disk. Wrap well in plastic wrap and refrigerate 1 hour or overnight.

2. Heat oven to 350°F. On a lightly floured surface, roll pastry into a 13-inch circle, ¼ inch thick. Fit into a 10-inch fluted tart pan with removable bottom. Fold in sides, trim edge of pastry and prick bottom with tines of a fork. Place in freezer 10 minutes. Line pastry shell with foil; fill with dried beans or pie weights. Bake 8 minutes.

Remove foil and beans. Bake 8 to 10 minutes more, until golden. Cool on a wire rack.

3. *Make filling:* Process pistachios, almonds and ¼ cup of the granulated sugar in a food processor until nuts are finely ground, about 1 minute. Add butter and ½ cup of the granulated sugar and process until combined, scraping sides of bowl once. Add eggs, flour and almond extract; pulse until blended.

4. Combine cranberries and remaining ¼ cup granulated sugar in a small bowl. Place tart pan on a jelly-roll pan. Pour nut mixture into crust and smooth top with a spatula. Sprinkle cranberry-sugar mixture over top. Bake 40 to 45 minutes, until filling is set and golden. Cool on a wire rack. Remove sides of pan. *(Can be made ahead. Cool completely. Wrap and freeze up to 2 weeks. Thaw at room temperature 4 hours. Reheat in 350°F. oven 15 minutes.)* Sift confectioners' sugar over top of tart, if desired. Makes 12 servings.

Per serving: 360 calories, 20 g total fat, 10.5 g saturated fat, 95 mg cholesterol, 213 mg sodium, 42 g carbohydrates, 5 g protein, 27 mg calcium, 2 g fiber

test kitchen tip
pastry traditions

Ever wonder why some tart and pie pastry recipes call for eggs, and others don't? The difference may be in the pastry tradition from which the recipe hails. A pastry that contains egg is likely patterned after one of the two classic French pastries called pâte brisée and pâte sucrée (the latter contains sugar). These pastries are crisp, rich and buttery. They're also quite different from the eggless pastries of the traditional American pie-crust recipe, which often calls for shortening to help attain its renowned light and flaky texture.

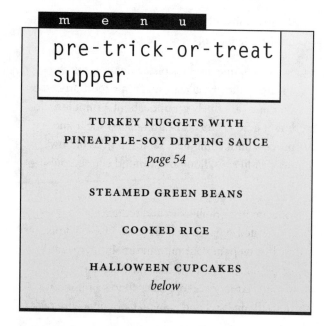

menu

pre-trick-or-treat supper

TURKEY NUGGETS WITH
PINEAPPLE-SOY DIPPING SAUCE
page 54

STEAMED GREEN BEANS

COOKED RICE

HALLOWEEN CUPCAKES
below

halloween cupcakes

Use your imagination! Design spooky and silly shapes out of melted and cooled chocolate to top these fun party cakes. Tip: To make piping the shapes easier, sketch them onto paper. Place paper under a sheet of waxed paper, and trace with the melted and cooled chocolate. Pictured on page 208.

Prep time: 20 minutes plus decorating and chilling
Baking time: 20 to 22 minutes

2½ cups all-purpose flour
2 teaspoons baking powder
½ teaspoon salt
½ cup fresh orange juice
½ teaspoon grated orange peel
¼ cup vegetable oil
2 teaspoons vanilla extract
3 large eggs, separated
1 cup butter or margarine, softened
1¼ cups granulated sugar

FROSTING:
1 box (16 oz.) confectioners' sugar
½ cup plus 6 tablespoons butter or margarine, softened
¼ cup heavy or whipping cream
1 teaspoon vanilla extract

Orange paste food coloring
¾ cup semisweet chocolate chips, melted and cooled

■

1 package (12 oz.) white chocolate chips, melted and cooled
1 package (12 oz.) semisweet chocolate chips, melted and cooled

DECORATIONS:
14 sliced natural almonds, 14 heart-shaped sprinkles, 7 semisweet chocolate mega chips, 14 blue nonpareils, and bat and pumpkin sprinkles

1. ■ *Make cupcakes:* Heat oven to 350°F. Line twenty-two 2½-inch muffin-pan cups with paper liners.

2. ■ Combine flour, baking powder and salt in a medium bowl. Whisk together orange juice and peel, oil and vanilla in a glass measure. Set both aside.

3. ■ Beat egg whites in a small mixer bowl to soft peaks; set aside. Beat butter and granulated sugar in a large mixer bowl until light and fluffy, 3 minutes. Add egg yolks, one at a time, beating well after each addition. Beat in flour mixture, alternating with orange juice mixture, beginning and ending with flour mixture, until just combined. Fold egg whites into batter with a rubber spatula.

4. ■ Divide batter into prepared muffin-pan cups. Bake 20 to 22 minutes, until golden, and a toothpick inserted in center of a cupcake comes out clean. Transfer to wire racks; cool in pans 5 minutes. Remove cupcakes from pans and cool completely. *(Can be made ahead. Wrap well and freeze up to 2 weeks.)*

5. ■ *Make frosting:* Beat confectioners' sugar, butter, cream and vanilla in a large mixer bowl until light and fluffy. (Makes 2¾ cups.) Divide frosting evenly among 3 bowls. Reserve one bowl as white frosting. Put a small amount of orange food coloring on a toothpick and stir into one bowl of frosting until well blended. (Color will darken as frosting stands.) Stir the ¾ cup semisweet chocolate, melted, into remaining frosting. Spread 1 tablespoon white frosting on each of seven cupcakes. Ice the remaining cupcakes with orange and chocolate frostings. Spoon remaining frosting of each color into three disposable pastry bags fitted with a #2 round or star tip. Set everything aside.

6. Fit two additional large disposable pastry bags with #2 round tips; fill one with the melted white chocolate and the other with the melted semisweet chocolate.

7. For decorations, line cookie sheets with waxed paper and pipe as directed in the following steps.

8. *For stand-up skeletons and white spiderwebs:* Pipe white chocolate into spiderweb and skeleton shapes onto cookie sheet lined with waxed paper. Refrigerate until firm, 30 minutes. Pipe dots of semisweet chocolate onto white spiderwebs for flies, and attach sliced almonds for wings. Pipe semisweet chocolate for skeleton eyes and mouths; attach red hearts. Refrigerate until firm.

9. *For stand-up cats and tombstones:* Pipe semisweet chocolate into cat and tombstone shapes onto cookie sheet lined with waxed paper. Refrigerate until firm, 30 minutes. Pipe white chocolate for cats' eyes and whiskers; attach red hearts for noses. Attach blue nonpareils for pupils. Pipe "RIP" with white chocolate on tombstones. Refrigerate until firm.

10. Carefully peel off paper from skeletons, white spiderwebs, cats and tombstones (they're fragile). Gently press on tops of cupcakes.

11. *For black spiderwebs:* Pipe semisweet chocolate into spiderweb shapes directly on tops of cupcakes. Attach mega chips for spider bodies; dot white chocolate and attach blue nonpareils for eyes. Pipe semisweet chocolate for spider legs.

12. Pipe edges of cupcakes decoratively with reserved frostings and attach bat and pumpkin sprinkles. Makes 22 cupcakes.

Per cupcake: 390 calories, 22 g total fat, 12 g saturated fat, 75 mg cholesterol, 267 mg sodium, 47 g carbohydrates, 3 g protein, 40 mg calcium, 0 g fiber

peanut butter chip bars

Busy week ahead? Make up a batch of these on the weekend, then freeze extra bars for a treasure trove of ready-made desserts all week. Pictured on page 207.

Prep time: 10 minutes • Baking time: 25 to 30 minutes

1¼	cups all-purpose flour
1	teaspoon baking powder
¼	teaspoon salt
½	cup butter or margarine
1	cup sugar
½	cup peanut butter
2	large eggs
1	teaspoon vanilla extract
1	cup semisweet chocolate chips

1. Heat oven to 350°F. Line a 9-inch square baking pan with foil, leaving one inch of foil over sides of pan. Grease bottom and sides of foil with vegetable shortening. Whisk together flour, baking powder and salt in a medium bowl; set aside.

2. Melt butter in a medium saucepan over medium heat. Stir in sugar and cook until well combined, 2 to 3 minutes. Stir in peanut butter and cook until mixture is smooth, 3 minutes. Remove pan from heat. Beat in eggs and vanilla with a spoon. Stir in flour mixture, until smooth. Pour batter into prepared pan. Sprinkle top with chips.

3. Bake until edges are golden and toothpick inserted in center comes out clean, 25 to 30 minutes. Cool completely on a wire rack. Remove from pan; peel off foil and cut into twelve 2×2³/₄-inch bars. *(Can be made ahead. Store at room temperature in an airtight container up to 2 days, or wrap well and freeze up to 2 weeks.)* Makes 12 bars.

Per bar: 325 calories, 18 g fat, 8 g saturated fat, 56 mg cholesterol, 228 mg sodium, 38 g carbohydrates, 6 g protein, 39 mg calcium, 1 g fiber

pumpkin crème caramel

Here's a velvety custard with just the right touch of pumpkin and fresh ginger, made complete with soothing caramel syrup. It's just the right ending to an autumn dinner party.

Prep time: 35 minutes • Baking time: 1 hour

- 1 cup granulated sugar, divided
- ⅓ cup water
- 1 cup milk
- 1 cup heavy or whipping cream
- ¼ teaspoon salt
- 1 2-ounce piece (⅓ cup) ginger, peeled and cut into ¼-inch slices
- 5 large eggs
- 1 large egg yolk
- 1 teaspoon vanilla extract
- 1 cup solid pack pumpkin

1. Dissolve ²/₃ cup of the sugar and the water in a medium saucepan over medium-high heat. Bring to boil. Boil, stirring occasionally, until syrup is golden brown, about 8 to 10 minutes. Meanwhile, warm a 1½-quart soufflé dish in hot tap water. Remove dish from water and immediately pour in caramel syrup, tilting dish to coat bottom evenly. Set aside and keep warm.

2. Heat oven to 350°F. Combine milk, cream, remaining ⅓ cup sugar, the salt and ginger in a medium saucepan. Bring to boil; remove from heat. Meanwhile, whisk together eggs, egg yolk and vanilla in a large bowl. Beating constantly, gradually add hot milk mixture to egg mixture, then strain through a fine sieve into another large bowl; discard ginger. Whisk pumpkin into custard until smooth. Pour into prepared soufflé dish.

3. Place dish in a large roasting pan. Carefully pour enough boiling water into roasting pan to reach halfway up sides of dish. Place in oven and immediately reduce temperature to 325°F. Bake 1 hour or until a knife inserted in center comes out clean. Remove from water bath and transfer to a wire rack. Cool completely. Cover and refrigerate 4 hours or overnight. To serve, run a knife around edge of custard and invert onto a large serving plate. Makes 10 servings.

Per serving: 210 calories, 12 g total fat, 6 g saturated fat, 149 mg cholesterol, 99 mg sodium, 23 g carbohydrates, 5 g protein, 68 mg calcium, 1 g fiber

apricot frangipane bars

Here, the humble cookie bar soars to the level of a lovely dessert! The layer of mashed apricots lends a tart contrast to the sweet almond topping.

Prep time: 30 minutes plus cooling
Baking time: 30 to 35 minutes

- 2½ cups water
- 2 cups (12 oz.) dried apricots
- 1 cup granulated sugar, divided
- 2¼ cups all-purpose flour
- ⅛ teaspoon salt
- ½ cup cold butter, cut up (no substitutions)
- ¼ cup vegetable shortening
- 3 to 5 tablespoons ice water

ALMOND TOPPING:

- 1 cup granulated sugar
- 1 tub (7 oz.) or 1 can (8 oz.) almond paste
- ¾ cup butter, softened (no substitutions)
- 4 large eggs
- ½ cup all-purpose flour
- 1 teaspoon vanilla extract
- ½ teaspoon almond extract
- ⅛ teaspoon salt
- Confectioners' sugar

1. For the apricot filling, bring the water, apricots and $^3/_4$ cup of the granulated sugar to boil in a small saucepan. Reduce heat and simmer until the apricots are tender, about 20 minutes. Remove from heat and mash with a fork until smooth. Cool completely.

2. Heat oven to 400°F. Meanwhile, for the crust, combine flour, remaining $^1/_4$ cup granulated sugar and the salt in a medium bowl. With a pastry blender or 2 knives, cut in butter and shortening until mixture resembles coarse crumbs. Add the ice water, 1 tablespoon at a time, tossing with a fork until mixture is moist enough to hold together. Pat pastry into a $15^1/_2 \times 10^1/_2$-inch jelly-roll pan. Smooth top of pastry with rolling pin. Bake 15 to 17 minutes, until golden brown. Cool the crust completely in the pan on a wire rack.

3. *Make almond topping:* Beat the granulated sugar, almond paste and butter in a large mixing bowl at medium speed until light and fluffy. Add eggs, one at a time, beating well after each addition. Beat in flour, vanilla, almond extract and salt at low speed, until smooth.

4. Reduce oven temperature to 350°F. Spread apricot filling evenly over the baked crust. Top evenly with almond topping. Bake 30 to 35 minutes, until a toothpick inserted in center comes out clean. Cool completely in the pan on a wire rack. Cut into 3×1-inch bars. Sprinkle with confectioners' sugar. Makes 50.

Per bar: 150 calories, 7 g total fat, 3 g saturated fat, 29 mg cholesterol, 64 mg sodium, 20 g carbohydrates, 2 g protein, 16 mg calcium, 1 g fiber

poached pears with star anise LOW FAT EASY

In this recipe, star anise brings the poached pears to life.

Prep time: 10 minutes • Cooking time: 50 to 55 minutes

- 1 **bottle (750 ml) white wine**
- 4 **cups water**
- 1 **cup sugar**
- 1 **star anise**
- 4 **Bosc pears, peeled and cored, stem intact**

Combine wine, water, sugar and star anise in a medium non-reactive Dutch oven. Bring to boil. Add pears; reduce heat and simmer pears until tender, about 30 to 40 minutes. Remove pears with a slotted spoon. Bring liquid to boil and cook poaching liquid until it has reduced by a third and has slightly thickened. Pour liquid over pears. Makes 4 servings.

Per serving: 405 calories, 0.5 g total fat, 0 g saturated fat, 0 mg cholesterol, 18 mg sodium, 73 g carbohydrates, 1 g protein, 38 mg calcium, 4 g fiber

test kitchen tip
peerless pears

Most pears are great for snacking out of hand. But some are better for baking, while others work well in salads. Here's a pear primer:

COOKING CHOICES: Bartlett pears, both the yellow and red versions, hold their shape when cooked in any way. Also, the golden brown, full-flavored Bosc pear makes a good choice for baking, poaching or broiling.

SALADS: Try the Comice pear—the sweetest and juiciest of them all—or the mellow-flavored Anjou. Or, to add dramatic color to a salad, try a Red Bartlett pear.

pear tartlets

In these individual fruit pastries, there's no crust to fuss with—just a mixture of flour, ground almonds, chopped pears and pear brandy that's spread on the bottom of each pan. Bartletts or Red Bartletts work beautifully in this recipe, or substitute Anjous. Pictured on page 207.

Prep time: 20 minutes • **Baking time:** 35 to 37 minutes

- **4** ripe Bartlett pears (about 1¾ lbs.), peeled and cored, divided
- **½** pound whole blanched almonds, toasted and cooled
- **1** cup sugar
- **½** cup all-purpose flour
- **2** large eggs
- **¼** cup butter, melted (no substitutions)
- **2** teaspoons Poire William (pear brandy) or brandy
  Whipped cream, for garnish (optional)

1. Heat oven to 375°F. Coat six 4½-inch tartlet pans with removable bottoms with vegetable cooking spray. Transfer tartlet pans to a large jelly-roll pan or cookie sheet.

2. Slice 3 of the pears ¼ inch thick. Chop remaining pear. Set both aside.

3. Process almonds in a food processor until fine. Add sugar and flour; pulse to combine. Add eggs, melted butter and pear brandy. Process until smooth, scraping sides of bowl with a rubber spatula. Add chopped pear and process until smooth.

4. Divide batter among the prepared tartlet pans and spread mixture in bottoms and halfway up the sides of pans. Divide and arrange reserved pear slices in a single row, overlapping slightly, on top of batter in pans.

5. Bake 35 to 37 minutes, until filling is set and edges are lightly browned. Cool tartlets on a wire rack. Remove sides and bottoms of pans and transfer pear tartlets to 6 serving plates. Serve with whipped cream, if desired. Makes 6 servings.

Per serving: 555 calories, 29.5 g total fat, 7 g saturated fat, 92 mg cholesterol, 104 mg sodium, 68 g carbohydrates, 11 g protein, 126 mg calcium, 7 g fiber

banana cream napoleons

Ooh-la-la! This dazzling dish nestles fruit, caramel and whipped cream between layers of phyllo for a mouthwatering study of texture and taste. When you prepare the phyllo layers, toasted nuts and caramel sauce ahead, the dessert is easy to assemble at the last minute. Pictured on page 201.

Prep time: 1 hour • **Baking time:** 19 to 22 minutes

PASTRY:
- **6** tablespoons granulated sugar
- **¼** teaspoon cinnamon
- **6** sheets phyllo dough, divided
- **6** tablespoons unsalted butter, melted (no substitutions)
- **¼** cup pecans, toasted, cooled and finely chopped

CARAMEL SAUCE:
- **3** tablespoons unsalted butter (no substitutions)
- **½** cup packed dark brown sugar
- **¼** cup heavy or whipping cream
- **3** tablespoons granulated sugar
- **2** tablespoons orange juice
- **1** teaspoon vanilla extract

FILLING:
- **¾** cup heavy or whipping cream
- **¼** cup sour cream

2 tablespoons granulated sugar, divided
1 tablespoon dark rum
5 firm, ripe bananas, peeled
1 tablespoon unsalted butter, melted
   (no substitutions)
½ teaspoon grated orange peel
   ■
¼ cup pecans, toasted and chopped
   Fresh mint sprigs, for garnish (optional)

1. ■ *Make pastry:* Heat oven to 350°F. Combine granulated sugar and cinnamon in a small bowl.

2. ■ Place one sheet of the phyllo on work surface (keep remaining phyllo covered with plastic wrap and a clean kitchen towel). Brush sheet lightly with butter. Sprinkle top with 1 tablespoon cinnamon-sugar and 1 tablespoon of the pecans. Repeat process 3 times. Top stack with 1 more sheet of phyllo, brush with butter and sprinkle with 1 tablespoon cinnamon-sugar. With long side facing you and using a long sharp knife, cut phyllo stack into 5 parallel strips lengthwise, then cut stack into 4 even strips crosswise, making 20 rectangles.

3. ■ Grease a large cookie sheet. Arrange 18 of the rectangles ¼ inch apart on prepared cookie sheet. Bake rectangles 6 to 8 minutes, until lightly browned. Carefully transfer each rectangle with a spatula to wire racks; cool rectangles and cookie sheet completely.

4. ■ Brush remaining phyllo sheet lightly with butter, then sprinkle sheet with remaining 1 tablespoon cinnamon-sugar. Cut into 4 rectangles. Stack rectangles. Roll up jelly-roll style from a long side. Slice roll crosswise into ¼-inch-wide strips. Toss strips gently to separate and spread out onto the same greased cookie sheet.

5. ■ Cut remaining 2 rectangles crosswise into ⅛-inch-wide strips and add to cookie sheet. Bake strips 5 to 6 minutes, or until golden. Cool strips on pan on wire rack. (*Can be made ahead. Arrange baked rectangles and strips between sheets of waxed paper in airtight containers and let stand at room temperature up to 3 days.*)

6. ■ *Make caramel sauce:* Meanwhile, melt butter in a medium skillet over medium heat. Add brown sugar, cream and granulated sugar. Bring to boil, stirring frequently. Reduce heat and simmer 5 minutes, stirring occasionally with a long-handled wooden spoon, until sugar dissolves. Stir in orange juice and vanilla. (Mixture may bubble up, but that's okay.) Remove skillet from heat and set aside.

7. ■ *Make filling:* Increase oven temperature to 425°F. Beat cream, sour cream, 1 tablespoon of the granulated sugar and the rum in a small mixer bowl on high speed until stiff. Cover; refrigerate.

8. ■ Grease another large cookie sheet. Cut bananas crosswise into 1-inch-thick slices, discarding ends. Toss bananas with remaining 1 tablespoon granulated sugar, melted butter and orange peel in a medium bowl. Arrange slices, cut side down, on prepared cookie sheet in a single layer. Bake 8 minutes, until tender. Set aside.

9. ■ *To assemble:* Just before serving, reheat caramel sauce over low heat. Meanwhile, fill a large pastry bag fitted with a ½-inch-wide star tip with whipped-cream mixture. Arrange 1 phyllo rectangle on each of 6 large dessert plates. Pipe about one-third of whipped cream on top of rectangles, then divide and top each serving with half of the bananas, cut side down. Drizzle each serving with about 1 teaspoon caramel sauce. Top each with another rectangle. Pipe another third of the whipped cream on rectangles and top with remaining bananas. Top each serving with remaining rectangles. Drizzle each serving with 1 teaspoon caramel sauce. Pipe remaining whipped cream on top of each and arrange strips of phyllo in cream. Drizzle a little caramel sauce over and around Napoleons; sprinkle with toasted pecans. Serve immediately with remaining caramel sauce and garnish with mint sprigs, if desired. Makes 6 servings.

Per serving: 705 calories, 44 g total fat, 23.5 g saturated fat, 110 mg cholesterol, 123 mg sodium, 77 g carbohydrates, 4 g protein, 71 mg calcium, 2 g fiber

brown sugar angel cake with ginger whipped cream

In a league of its own—this cake sets itself apart from the rest not just for the wonderful flavor of the cake, but also thanks to the luscious ginger-infused whipped cream. Confectioners' sugar adds a lovely finish.

Prep time: 20 minutes • Baking time: 40 to 45 minutes

ANGEL FOOD CAKE:

- 1   cup cake flour (not self-rising)
- ½   teaspoon nutmeg
- ¼   teaspoon baking soda
- 1½   cups firmly packed brown sugar
- 1½   teaspoons cream of tartar
- ¼   teaspoon salt
- 12   large egg whites, at room temperature
- 2   teaspoons confectioners' sugar

GINGER WHIPPED CREAM:

- 1   cup heavy or whipping cream
- 3   tablespoons confectioners' sugar
- ½   teaspoon ginger

1. ▪ Heat oven to 350°F.

2. ▪ *Make angel food cake:* Sift flour, nutmeg and baking soda into a medium bowl. Repeat process. Press brown sugar through a sieve into another bowl. Set both aside.

3. ▪ Combine cream of tartar and salt in a cup. Beat egg whites in a large mixer bowl on medium-low speed until foamy, about 3 minutes. Add cream of tartar and salt mixture and beat 1 minute. Increase speed to medium and beat to soft peaks, about 8 minutes. Add brown sugar, 1 tablespoon at a time, until sugar is blended and soft peaks form. Sift half of the flour mixture over egg whites. Gently stir in flour mixture with a large wire whisk. Sift remaining flour mixture over batter; whisk gently just until combined. Pour batter into an ungreased 10-inch tube pan. Run a knife through batter to remove any air pockets. Bake 40 to 45 minutes or until top of cake springs back when lightly touched

with fingertip. Immediately invert pan onto a funnel or bottle and cool 1 hour. Run knife around sides of pan and tube to unmold cake. Transfer to a serving plate. Dust top with confectioners' sugar.

4. ▪ *Make ginger whipped cream:* Beat cream in a large mixer bowl at medium-high speed to soft peaks. Beat in confectioners' sugar and ginger to stiff peaks. Serve cake with ginger whipped cream. Makes 12 servings.

Per serving: 230 calories, 7.5 g total fat, 4.5 g saturated fat, 27 mg cholesterol, 144 mg sodium, 37 g carbohydrates, 5 g protein, 40 mg calcium, 0 g fiber

black-raspberry linzer tartlets

We made this classic Austrian dessert into individual tartlets and packed every buttery bite with a thick layer of sweet berry preserves. To make arranging the lattice easier, place the pastry strips in the freezer until firm.

Prep time: 1 hour 20 minutes plus chilling
Baking time: 40 minutes

PASTRY:

- 3   cups (12 oz.) hazelnuts
- 1   cup granulated sugar
- ¼   teaspoon salt
- 1   cup cold unsalted butter, cut up (no substitutions)
- 2   large egg yolks, lightly beaten
- 2   teaspoons grated lemon peel
- 1   teaspoon vanilla extract
- 2   cups all-purpose flour
- ½   teaspoon cinnamon
- ¼   teaspoon nutmeg
       Pinch cloves
       ▪

- 2   jars (10 or 12 oz. each) premium-quality black-raspberry or black-currant preserves
- 1   large egg white
- 1   teaspoon water
       Confectioners' sugar

1. *Make pastry:* Heat oven to 350°F. Spread hazelnuts on a baking sheet. Bake 12 to 15 minutes, until lightly browned and skins are crackly. Wrap nuts in a clean kitchen towel and let stand 5 minutes. Rub nuts in towel to remove skins; cool completely. Transfer to a food processor and pulse until finely ground.

2. Combine granulated sugar and salt in a large bowl. With a pastry blender or 2 knives, cut in butter until mixture resembles coarse crumbs. Stir in yolks, lemon peel and vanilla. Combine ground hazelnuts, flour, cinnamon, nutmeg and cloves in another bowl. With a pastry blender, cut nut-flour mixture, 1 cup at a time, into butter-sugar mixture until just blended and crumbly.

3. Measure 1⅓ cups crumbs and flatten into a thin disk; cover with plastic wrap. Divide remaining crumb mixture into 8 equal pieces. Press pieces into bottoms and up sides of eight 4½-inch individual tart pans with removable bottoms; cover with plastic wrap. Refrigerate pastry disk and tart shells 2 hours or overnight.

4. Heat oven to 400°F. Spread preserves over bottoms of tart shells. Refrigerate. For lattice top, roll pastry disk between 2 sheets of lightly floured waxed paper into a 9×8-inch rectangle. Place in freezer about 15 minutes, until firm. Cut rectangle lengthwise into sixteen ½-inch-wide strips, then cut strips in half. Carefully arrange 4 strips over each tart in a lattice pattern; trim edges. Lightly beat egg white and water in a cup and brush over lattice.

5. Place tartlets on a cookie sheet and bake 15 minutes. Reduce oven temperature to 350°F. Bake 25 minutes more, until pastry is browned and filling is bubbly. (If pastry browns too quickly, cover loosely with foil.) Cool tartlets completely on wire racks. Remove sides of pans. Sift confectioners' sugar over tarts. Makes 8 servings.

Per serving: 895 calories, 51.5 g total fat, 16.5 g saturated fat, 115 mg cholesterol, 113 mg sodium, 107 g carbohydrates, 11 g protein, 121 mg calcium, 7 g fiber

winter fruit compote with dried tart cherries

Some heavy winter meals call for a light dessert—and this one, featuring the flavors of the season, fits the bill.

Prep time: 30 minutes · Cooking time: 5 to 8 minutes

- 4 **navel oranges, rinsed**
- 2 **tablespoons sour cream**
- ½ **cup port wine**
- ⅓ **cup plus 1 tablespoon granulated sugar, divided**
- 1 **ripe Bosc pear, peeled, cored and cut into eight slices**
- 1 **Golden Delicious apple, peeled, cored and cut into eight slices**
- ¼ **cup dried sour (tart) cherries**
- 2 **cups thinly sliced fresh pineapple**
- ½ **cup heavy or whipping cream**

1. Grate ¼ teaspoon orange peel and combine with sour cream in a small bowl; set aside.

2. With a sharp paring knife, cut peel and white pith from oranges. Remove segments and squeeze juice from membranes. Strain juice into a small saucepan and reserve orange segments in a serving dish. Add port and ⅓ cup of the sugar to saucepan; cook, stirring, over medium heat, until sugar is dissolved. Add pear, apple, and cherries. Simmer until tender, 5 to 8 minutes. Gently stir into oranges. Stir in pineapple slices.

3. Beat cream with remaining 1 tablespoon sugar in a large mixing bowl to stiff peaks. Fold in sour cream mixture. Serve compote with whipped cream mixture. Makes 6 servings.

Per serving: 270 calories, 9 g total fat, 5 g saturated fat, 29 mg cholesterol, 14 mg sodium, 45 g carbohydrates, 2 g protein, 49 mg calcium, 3 g fiber

praline-banana cream pie

The brown sugar filling and toasted pecan crust give this decadently rich and creamy pie its great praline taste. When preparing the filling, stir it constantly, but gently. Stirring too vigorously can cause the custard to break down and prevent it from thickening properly.

Prep time: 30 minutes plus chilling
Baking time: 25 to 27 minutes

PASTRY:

- ⅓ **cup pecan halves, lightly toasted**
- 3 **tablespoons granulated sugar**
- 1 **cup plus 2 tablespoons all-purpose flour**
- ¼ **teaspoon salt**
  Pinch cinnamon
- 5 **tablespoons cold butter, cut up (no substitutions)**
- 1 **tablespoon vegetable shortening**
- 4 **to 5 tablespoons ice water, divided**
- 1 **large egg**

FILLING:

- ½ **cup firmly packed brown sugar**
- ⅓ **cup cornstarch**
  Pinch salt
- 2⅔ **cups half-and-half cream**
- 4 **large egg yolks**
- 2 **teaspoons vanilla extract**
- 2 **tablespoons butter or margarine**
- 2 **ripe bananas, peeled and thinly sliced**

SPICED WHIPPED CREAM:

- 1 **cup heavy or whipping cream**
- 2 **tablespoons granulated sugar**
- 1 **tablespoon amber rum**
- ⅛ **teaspoon cinnamon**

1. *Make pastry:* Process pecans and granulated sugar in a food processor until finely ground. Combine nut mixture with flour, salt and cinnamon in a bowl. With a pastry blender or 2 knives, cut in butter and shortening until mixture resembles coarse crumbs. Add 3 to 4 tablespoons of the ice water, 1 tablespoon at a time, tossing vigorously with a fork after each addition, until pastry holds together. Shape pastry into a ball, then flatten into a disk. Cover with plastic wrap and refrigerate 1 hour or overnight.

2. On a floured surface, with a floured rolling pin roll pastry into a 13-inch circle; fit into a 9-inch pie plate. Trim overhang to 1 inch. Fold overhang under and flute. Prick bottom with a fork. Place in freezer 20 minutes.

3. Heat oven to 400°F. Line pastry shell with foil and fill with dried beans or pie weights. Bake 15 minutes. Remove foil and beans. Meanwhile, beat egg and remaining 1 tablespoon ice water in a cup. Brush pastry with egg glaze and bake 10 to 12 minutes more until golden brown. Cool on a wire rack.

4. *Make filling:* Combine brown sugar, cornstarch and salt in a saucepan. Whisk in cream. Bring to boil over medium heat, stirring; boil 1 minute. Remove from heat. Beat egg yolks in a small bowl. Gradually whisk in 1 cup of the hot mixture. Return mixture to saucepan. Cook, whisking constantly, until mixture boils; boil 1 minute. Remove from heat. Whisk in vanilla and butter until smooth. Cool 10 minutes. Arrange banana slices evenly in baked crust; pour filling on top. Cover surface with plastic wrap. Chill 3 hours or until filling is firm.

5. *Make spiced whipped cream:* Beat cream in a large mixer bowl to soft peaks. Beat in sugar, rum and cinnamon to stiff peaks. Spoon into a pastry bag fitted with a large star tip; pipe decoratively over top of pie. Makes 10 servings.

Per serving: 465 calories, 30.5 g total fat, 16.5 g saturated fat, 184 mg cholesterol, 199 mg sodium, 42 g carbohydrates, 6 g protein, 113 mg calcium, 1 g fiber

citrus tartlets

These individual tartlets, bursting with sweet orange-, lemon- and lime-flavored curd, are the quintessential winter dessert. When preparing the curd, heat gently but do not let it boil, which can cause the eggs to scramble. The lime-sugared orange slices make for an extra-elegant finish. Pictured on page 201.

Prep time: 1 hour plus chilling
Baking time: 12 to 15 minutes
Microwave used

CITRUS CURD:
- 6 tablespoons fresh orange juice
- 5 teaspoons fresh lemon juice
- 5 teaspoons fresh lime juice
- 6 large egg yolks, at room temperature
- ¾ cup sugar
- 6 tablespoons unsalted butter, melted (no substitutions)
- Pinch salt

TART CRUSTS:
- 1⅔ cups all-purpose flour
- ¼ cup sugar
- ⅛ teaspoon salt
- ½ cup unsalted butter (no substitutions), divided
- 3 tablespoons shortening
- 1 tablespoon fresh orange juice

ORANGE SLICES:
- 9 thin slices navel orange (about 2 oranges)
- ¾ cup sugar
- ⅓ cup brandy
-
- 1 tablespoon sugar
- 1 teaspoon grated lime peel

1. *Make citrus curd:* Combine all citrus curd ingredients in a food processor and puree until smooth. Transfer to a small, heavy saucepan. Cook, stirring, over medium-low heat, 4 to 5 minutes, until mixture thickens and registers 180°F. on an instant-read thermometer. Pour mixture through a fine sieve into a medium bowl. Place bowl into a larger bowl. Add enough ice water to large bowl to reach halfway up bowl with curd. Stir curd occasionally, until cold and thick, 30 minutes.

Remove curd from ice water. Cover top of curd with plastic wrap and refrigerate 2 hours. *(Can be made ahead. Refrigerate up to 24 hours.)*

2. *Make tart crusts:* Pulse flour, sugar and salt in a food processor. Add ¼ cup of the butter, cut up, and shortening and pulse until coarse crumbs form. Microwave remaining ¼ cup butter in a 1-cup glass measure covered with plastic wrap, 30 seconds or just until melted. Cool slightly. Stir in orange juice. Add melted butter mixture to flour mixture and pulse again, until moist and crumbly. Gather dough into a ball and divide into 6 equal pieces. Press into six 4½-inch tartlet pans with removable bottoms. Arrange tart pans on a large jelly-roll pan. Place in freezer 10 minutes.

3. Heat oven to 400°F. Bake tart shells 12 to 15 minutes, until golden brown, rotating the jelly-roll pan after 11 minutes. Transfer to a wire rack; cool in pans.

4. *Make orange slices:* Cut each orange slice in half. Lightly coat a 20-inch sheet of waxed paper with vegetable cooking spray. Combine sugar and brandy in a 12-inch skillet. Add orange slices and bring to boil; reduce heat and cook 10 to 12 minutes, until sauce is syrupy and oranges are tender. Lightly coat a metal spatula with vegetable cooking spray and transfer orange slices to prepared waxed paper; cool.

5. *To assemble:* Divide and spread citrus curd into crusts. *(Can be made ahead. Cover loosely and refrigerate up to 24 hours.)* Top each tart with 3 overlapping orange slices.

6. Just before serving, combine 1 tablespoon sugar and lime peel in a cup. Divide and sprinkle oranges with lime-sugar mixture. Makes 6 tartlets.

Per tartlet: 765 calories, 39 g total fat, 20 g saturated fat, 285 mg cholesterol, 85 mg sodium, 92 g carbohydrates, 7 g protein, 46 mg calcium, 1 g fiber

weeknight desserts

Who says there's no time for a homemade dessert on weeknights? Flag the two recipes on this page, keep the following items in stock and you'll always have a sweet treat for your family:

- Butter and sugar
- Peach halves in heavy syrup
- Heavy or whipping cream
- Vanilla extract
- Natural almonds
- Prepared lemon curd
- Crystallized ginger

Another super-quick-fix recipe, the Apple and Pear Sauce, appears on page 225.

lemon mousse

Take whipped cream, fold in a jar of lemon curd and top with crystallized ginger, and you've got an instant dessert. Pictured on page 206.

Total prep time: 10 minutes

- **½ pint heavy or whipping cream**
- **⅔ cup prepared lemon curd**
- **2 teaspoons crystallized ginger, finely chopped
  Fresh mint sprigs, for garnish (optional)**

Beat heavy cream in a large mixer bowl to stiff peaks. Fold in lemon curd with a rubber spatula just until combined. *(Can be made ahead. Cover and refrigerate up to 2 hours.)* Divide mousse among 4 dessert bowls. Sprinkle the top of each serving with ½ teaspoon ginger. Garnish with mint sprigs, if desired. Makes 4 servings.

Per serving: 348 calories, 25 g fat, 14 g saturated fat, 81 mg cholesterol, 65 mg sodium, 36 g carbohydrates, 4 g protein, 40 mg calcium, 1 g fiber

baked peaches with cream

Asked to come up with a sophisticated dessert using canned peaches, we developed this treat. Baked with cream and sugar until lightly caramelized, then sprinkled with toasted almonds, the dessert makes a sweet and simple finish if there ever was one.

Prep time: 15 minutes
Baking time: 12 to 15 minutes

- **2 teaspoons butter or margarine**
- **2 cans (15½ oz. each) peach halves in heavy syrup, well drained**
- **1 tablespoon sugar**
- **½ cup heavy or whipping cream**
- **½ teaspoon vanilla extract**
- **2 tablespoons sliced natural almonds, toasted**

1. Heat broiler. Coat the bottom of a broilerproof 8×8 baking pan with butter.

2. Pat peach halves dry with paper towels; arrange, cut side down, in prepared dish, then sprinkle tops with sugar. Broil peaches 5 inches from heat source 8 to 10 minutes, until edges of fruit are browned.

3. Meanwhile, combine cream and vanilla in a 1-cup glass measure.

4. Remove peaches from broiler; pour cream mixture into dish. Reduce oven temperature to 425°F. Bake peaches 12 to 15 minutes, until sauce is bubbly. Sprinkle with toasted almonds. Serve warm. Makes 4 servings.

Per serving: 275 calories, 14.5 g total fat, 8 g saturated fat, 46 mg cholesterol, 41 mg sodium, 39 g carbohydrates, 2 g protein, 33 mg calcium, 0 g fiber

CHOCOLATE
BABY CAKES
pg. 270

the year in chocolate

BITTERSWEET
CHOCOLATE TART
pg. 266

Oh, chocolate, how do we love thee? Let us count the ways: In cookies and cakes, tortes and tarts, puddings and mousses, sorbets and sauces. . . Come along and indulge in our chapter-long love song to America's favorite flavor.

there's just

THE PERFECT
CHOCOLATE CAKE
pg. 258

EASY
CHOCOLATE
SOUFFLÉS
pg. 271

no end to
our affection for our
favorite confection

CHOCOLATE-
CHERRY
PUDDING CAKE

EASY FUDGE
pg. 280

CHOCOLATE
SHEET CAKE
pg. 256

what we've
done

ZEBRA
BROWNIES
pg. 254

CARAMEL-
CHEESE
BROWNIES
pg. 254

BROWNIE WAFFLES
À LA MODE
pg. 274

with the
humble brownie
will come as a
sweet surprise

whoever said *heaven* can wait

CHOCOLATE-
PEAR CAKE
pg. 264

CHOCOLATE
ESPRESSO CAKE
pg. 261

DOUBLE-
CHOCOLATE
VANILLA
CUPCAKES
pg. 256

hadn't tried our *heavenly* chocolate cakes

CHOCOLATE ANGEL
FOOD CAKE
pg. 257

CHOCOLATE-
COCONUT BARS
pg. 252

Our idea of a
chocolate
bar...

KILLER
BROWNIES
pg. 253

peanut butter-chocolate chip cookies

Get ready for the best of both worlds! Peanut butter cookies—crisscrossed tops and all—get a sprinkling of chocolate chips borrowed from that other cookie classic, the chocolate chip cookie.

Prep time: 12 minutes
Baking time: 8 minutes per batch

- 1¼ **cups all-purpose flour**
- ¾ **teaspoon baking soda**
- ½ **teaspoon baking powder**
- ¼ **teaspoon salt**
- ½ **cup butter or margarine, softened**
- ½ **cup smooth or chunky peanut butter**
- 1 **cup sugar**
- 1 **large egg**
- 1 **teaspoon vanilla extract**
- 1 **cup semisweet chocolate chips**

1. Heat oven to 375°F. Combine flour, baking soda, baking powder and salt in a medium bowl; set aside. Beat butter in a large mixer bowl until creamy. Beat in peanut butter and sugar until smooth. Beat in egg and vanilla. Stir in flour mixture until blended. Stir in chocolate chips.

2. Roll dough into 1-inch balls and arrange 2 inches apart on an ungreased cookie sheet. Flatten with a fork, making a crisscross design. Bake 8 minutes, until edges are golden. Let cookies stand on sheet 1 minute. Transfer cookies to wire racks to cool completely. Repeat with remaining dough. Makes 3½ dozen.

Per cookie: 90 calories, 5 g total fat, 2 g saturated fat, 11 mg cholesterol, 80 mg sodium, 11 g carbohydrates, 2 g protein, 8 mg calcium, 0 g fiber

the perfect chocolate chip cookies

How did we create the most buttery-crisp, chewy, chocolate-studded cookie ever? After testing the recipe dozens of times, we found the secret: Just the right amount of oats and an exact proportion of granulated to brown sugar so that the cookies are chewy, rather than cakey. Feel free to omit the walnuts if you're not a nut lover.

Prep time: 20 minutes plus standing
Baking time: 13 to 14 minutes per batch

- 2¼ **cups all-purpose flour**
- ¼ **cup quick-cooking oats**
- 1 **teaspoon baking soda**
- ½ **teaspoon salt**
- 1 **cup butter, softened (no substitutions)**
- 1 **cup firmly packed brown sugar**
- ¾ **cup granulated sugar**
- 2 **large eggs**
- 2 **teaspoons vanilla extract**
- 1 **package (12 oz.) semisweet chocolate chips (2 cups)**
- 2 **cups chopped walnuts**

1. Heat oven to 375°F. Combine flour, oats, baking soda and salt in a medium bowl; set aside.

2. Beat butter and sugars in a large mixer bowl at medium speed until creamy, 2 minutes. Add eggs, one at a time, beating well after each addition. Beat in vanilla. At low speed, gradually beat in flour mixture until blended. Stir in chips and nuts.

3. Drop dough by heaping tablespoonfuls 2 inches apart on 2 large ungreased cookie sheets. Bake 13 to 14 minutes, until golden brown. Let cookies stand on sheets 2 minutes. Transfer cookies to wire racks to cool completely. Repeat with remaining dough. Makes about 45 cookies.

Per cookie: 165 calories, 9.5 g total fat, 4 g saturated fat, 21 mg cholesterol, 101 mg sodium, 19 g carbohydrates, 2 g protein, 15 mg calcium, 0 g fiber

chocolate madeleines

For this recipe, you'll need to use madeleine molds. These are special tins that give these spongy cookies their classic scallop-shell lines. Look for the mold in specialty shops or from mail-order catalogs that specialize in kitchenware.

Prep time: 15 minutes plus standing
Baking time: 10 minutes per batch

- 2 tablespoons unsweetened cocoa
- 1¼ cups unsalted butter (no substitutions)
- 1¼ cups granulated sugar
- 1 cup all-purpose flour
- ¼ teaspoon salt
- 6 large egg whites, at room temperature
- 4 ounces semisweet chocolate squares, melted (see tip, page 265) and cooled
- 2 ounces unsweetened chocolate squares, melted (see tip, page 265) and cooled
- 1 teaspoon vanilla extract
  Confectioners' sugar, for garnish (optional)

1. Heat oven to 350°F. Generously butter 2 madeleine molds. Sprinkle pans with cocoa; tap out the excess.

2. Melt butter in a small saucepan over medium heat until golden brown, skimming any foam on the surface. Strain the clear butter liquid through a fine sieve into a small bowl; discard the browned or milky solids. Cool to room temperature.

3. Combine granulated sugar, flour and salt in a medium bowl; set aside. Beat egg whites in a large mixer bowl on medium speed until frothy, 2 to 3 minutes. Reduce speed to low; beat in flour mixture just until combined. Beat in butter, cooled chocolates and vanilla. Let batter stand 5 minutes until thickened.

4. Spoon batter into a heavy-duty plastic storage bag. Snip off one corner. Pipe a strip of batter down center of each mold, filling each ⅔ full. (Batter will spread during baking.) Bake cookies until firm to the touch in center, 10 minutes. Immediately invert onto a sheet of waxed paper; cool completely. Repeat process with remaining batter, cooling madeleine molds and buttering and dusting them with cocoa between each batch. *(Can be made ahead. Store cookies in an airtight container at room temperature up to 1 week.)* Sift confectioners' sugar over madeleines, if desired. Makes 41 cookies.

Per cookie: 110 calories, 7.5 g total fat, 4.5 g saturated fat, 16 mg cholesterol, 25 mg sodium, 11 g carbohydrates, 1 g protein, 5 mg calcium, 0 g fiber

chocolate buttons

This recipe makes 9 dozen cookies, so you'll have plenty to freeze for future munching. The cookies are chock-full of hazelnuts—toasted to bring out maximum flavor.

Prep time: 40 minutes
Baking time: 5 to 8 minutes per batch

- 1 cup toasted hazelnuts, minced
- 6 tablespoons all-purpose flour
- 6 tablespoons unsweetened cocoa
- ⅛ teaspoon ground cloves (optional)
  Pinch salt
- ½ cup butter, softened (no substitutions)
- ½ cup plus 2 tablespoons sugar
- ½ teaspoon vanilla extract
- 2 large egg whites

1. Heat oven to 350°F. Grease 2 cookie sheets. Combine nuts, flour, cocoa, cloves (if using) and salt in a small bowl; set aside. Beat butter and sugar in a large mixer bowl until light. Add vanilla and egg whites, one at a time, beating well after addition, until blended. Gradually add nut mixture; beat at medium speed 1 minute.

2. Spoon batter into a pastry bag fitted with a ½-inch plain tip. Pipe ¾-inch rounds 2 inches apart on prepared cookie sheets. Bake 5 to 8 minutes. Transfer cookies to wire racks to cool completely. Repeat with remaining batter. Makes 9 dozen cookies.

Per cookie: 25 calories, 2 g total fat, 1 g saturated fat, 2 mg cholesterol, 12 mg sodium, 2 g carbohydrates, 0 g protein, 6 mg calcium, 0 g fiber

chocolate-hazelnut biscotti

Think big! We doubled the size of these twice-baked coffeehouse favorites—now there's more cookie to dip!

Prep time: 30 minutes plus standing
Baking time: 1 hour 14 minutes to 1 hour 20 minutes

- 2 **cups all-purpose flour**
- ¾ **cup unsweetened cocoa**
- 2 **teaspoons instant espresso powder**
- 1½ **teaspoons baking powder**
- ½ **teaspoon salt**
- 2 **large eggs**
- 2 **large egg whites**
- 1½ **cups sugar**
- ¼ **cup butter or margarine, melted**
- ¼ **cup vegetable oil**
- 1 **ounce unsweetened chocolate square, melted (see tip, page 265)**
- 2 **teaspoons vanilla extract**
- ¾ **cup toasted and skinned hazelnuts, chopped**

1. Position rack in center of oven. Heat oven to 325°F. Grease a large cookie sheet. Combine flour, cocoa, espresso powder, baking powder and salt in a medium bowl; set aside.

2. Whisk together eggs, egg whites, sugar, melted butter, oil, melted chocolate and vanilla in a large bowl. Stir in flour mixture until smooth, then stir in nuts. Form dough into a 15×4½-inch log on prepared cookie sheet. Bake 50 minutes, until toothpick inserted in center comes out clean. Cool 15 minutes. (Keep oven on.)

3. With serrated knife, cut log on an angle into ½-inch-thick slices. Lay slices flat on prepared cookie sheet. Bake 12 to 15 minutes, until cookies feel firm in center; turn over and bake 12 to 15 minutes more. Transfer to wire racks to cool completely. *(Can be made ahead. Store in an airtight container and freeze up to 1 month.)* Makes 18 biscotti.

Per cookie: 225 calories, 11 g total fat, 3 g saturated fat, 30 mg cholesterol, 142 mg sodium, 31 g carbohydrates, 4 g protein, 84 mg calcium, 1 g fiber

---

test kitchen tip

send something sweet

Go ahead—make someone's day! Send them a care package of cookies. For safe arrival, follow these tips:

CHOOSE GOOD TRAVELERS: Some cookies will take the voyage through the postal system better than others. Slice-and-bake cookies, most drop cookies, cutouts and uncut bars travel well; frosted and filled cookies do not.

SEND THEM FRESH: Pack the cookies just after baking and cooling. Avoid sending them near the end of the week, as they could get delayed over the weekend.

WRAP 'EM: Using plastic wrap, wrap the cookies either singly or back-to-back in pairs.

PACK 'EM: Pack cookies in heavy boxes lined with plastic or foil.

STACK 'EM: Fill the box starting with the sturdiest and heaviest cookies on the bottom. Follow with a layer of filler (such as bubble wrap; foam packing pieces; or crumpled tissue paper, paper towels or waxed paper). Continue layering, ending with a generous layer of filler to help prevent shifting.

Be sure to include a card inside the box with the recipient's address. Use strapping tape to seal the box shut securely, and mark the box "perishable."

chocolate checkerboards

These charming cookies are a classic favorite—and irresistibly yummy to boot. Best of all, they call for just a handful of ingredients, which you may already have on hand.

Prep time: 1 hour plus freezing
Baking time: 7 to 9 minutes per batch

2⅔	cups all-purpose flour
½	teaspoon baking powder
¾	cup butter or margarine, softened
¾	cup sugar
1	large egg
1½	teaspoons vanilla extract
2	ounces unsweetened chocolate squares, melted (see tip, page 265)

1. Combine flour and baking powder in a bowl; remove 1 tablespoon of the flour mixture to a cup and set aside.

2. Beat butter and sugar in a mixer bowl until light and fluffy. Beat in egg and vanilla. At low speed, gradually beat in flour mixture until blended; gather into a ball. For chocolate dough, remove 1¼ cups dough and transfer to a bowl. Stir in melted chocolate and reserved flour mixture until blended.

3. Divide each portion of chocolate and vanilla doughs into thirds. Press each third into a 6×2-inch rectangle. Transfer rectangles to a large cookie sheet; place in freezer 10 minutes until firm. Working with one rectangle at a time, cut in half crosswise, then cut each half in thirds lengthwise to make six 3×½-inch strips. Repeat cutting remaining rectangles to make a total of 36 strips.

4. Place a sheet of plastic wrap on a smooth surface. Working on surface, attach three strips side by side using one vanilla strip and two chocolate strips, alternating flavors and pressing gently to adhere. Top with another layer of three strips, alternating flavors from the bottom layer (two vanilla strips and one chocolate strip). Repeat

process for final layer with three more strips. Gently press top and sides, smoothing surface to form a 3×1¾-inch checkerboard log about 1¾ inches high. Repeat for another log. Then, make two more logs with remaining strips, starting with two vanilla strips and one chocolate strip on the bottom and topping with alternating-flavored layers; wrap tightly and freeze 3 hours until firm enough to slice.

5. Heat oven to 375°F. Grease 2 large cookie sheets. Cut twelve ¼-inch-thick slices from each log; arrange 1 inch apart on prepared sheets. Bake cookies, one sheet at a time, 7 to 9 minutes, until edges are just golden. Transfer cookies to wire racks to cool completely. Makes 4 dozen cookies.

Per cookie: 70 calories, 6 g total fat, 2 g saturated fat, 12 mg cholesterol, 36 mg sodium, 8 g carbohydrates, 1 g protein, 6 mg calcium, 0 g fiber

chocolate-coconut bars (EASY)

Oh what a joy! Our bar cookies with chocolate and coconut topping will remind you of a favorite coconut-almond candy bar. They're a great, informal treat to tote to summer cookouts, family reunions and picnics. Pictured on page 248.

Prep time: 15 minutes · Baking time: 45 to 50 minutes
Microwave used

CHOCOLATE LAYER:

4	ounces unsweetened chocolate squares
⅔	cup butter or margarine
¾	cup granulated sugar
½	cup firmly packed brown sugar
2	large eggs
½	teaspoon vanilla extract
1	cup all-purpose flour
	Pinch salt
1	cup whole natural almonds, toasted and chopped

COCONUT TOPPING:

½	cup granulated sugar
1	large egg

1 tablespoon all-purpose flour
½ teaspoon baking powder
½ teaspoon vanilla extract
1 bag (7 oz.) shredded coconut

1. Heat oven to 325°F. Line a 13×9-inch baking pan with foil. Grease foil and sprinkle with flour.

2. *Make chocolate layer:* Combine chocolate and butter in a large microwaveproof bowl. Cover bowl with plastic wrap, turning back one section to vent. Microwave on High 1½ minutes, until almost melted; stir until smooth. Beat in sugars, eggs and vanilla with a wooden spoon until smooth. Beat in flour and salt. Spread evenly in prepared pan. Sprinkle top with almonds.

3. *Make coconut topping:* Whisk together granulated sugar, egg, flour, baking powder and vanilla in a bowl, 30 seconds. Stir in coconut. Pour topping evenly over chocolate layer. Bake 45 to 50 minutes, until golden and just set in middle. Cool completely in pan on a wire rack.

4. To cut bars, lift cookies out of pan with foil. Peel off foil. Cut lengthwise into 1½-inch-wide strips, then cut crosswise at 1¾-inch intervals to form rectangles. *(Can be made ahead. Cover and freeze up to 1 week. Thaw at room temperature.)* Makes 42 bars.

Per bar: 130 calories, 8 g total fat, 4.5 g saturated fat, 23 mg cholesterol, 57 mg sodium, 15 g carbohydrates, 2 g protein, 19 mg calcium, 1 g fiber

killer
brownies

If you bake these double-chocolate, extra-fudgy brownies ahead, wrap well in plastic wrap and don't cut them until ready to serve. Pictured on page 248.

Prep time: 15 minutes • Baking time: 28 to 30 minutes
Microwave used

8 ounces unsweetened chocolate squares
½ cup plus 3 tablespoons butter or margarine,
    cut up

2 cups sugar
4 large eggs
1 teaspoon vanilla extract
1 cup all-purpose flour
¼ teaspoon salt
1 package (12 oz.) semisweet chocolate chips
    (2 cups)
1½ cups walnuts, chopped and toasted

1. Heat oven to 350°F. Line a 13×9-inch baking pan with foil. Grease foil. Combine chocolate and butter in a large microwaveproof bowl. Cover bowl with plastic wrap, turning back one section to vent. Microwave on High 3 minutes; stir until smooth. Whisk in sugar, then eggs and vanilla. Stir in flour and salt. Fold in chocolate chips and walnuts. Pour into prepared pan.

2. Bake 28 to 30 minutes, until center is just set. Cool completely in pan on a wire rack. To cut bars, lift brownies out of pan with foil. Peel off foil. Cut into 2-inch squares. Makes 2 dozen brownies.

Per brownie: 310 calories, 20 g total fat, 9.5 g saturated fat, 50 mg cholesterol, 89 mg sodium, 34 g carbohydrates, 4 g protein, 25 mg calcium, 1 g fiber

test kitchen tip
lining the pan

Many of our bar cookie recipes specify lining the baking pan with foil. That's because it makes it easier to get the bars out of the pan after baking. It also makes cleanup easier (just throw away the foil lining). To adapt this technique to your favorite bar cookie or brownie recipes, simply line the pan with foil, letting the foil slightly extend over the edge of pan. Grease the foil if the recipe calls for a greased pan. Spread cookie dough evenly in the pan, then bake and cool bars in pan as directed. Lift the bars out, using the extra overhanging foil. Cut bars into desired shapes (for great shape ideas, see tip, page 137).

1. Heat oven to 325°F. Grease and flour an 8-inch square baking pan.

2. Heat butter and unsweetened chocolate in a large saucepan over medium-low heat, until melted and smooth, stirring frequently. Remove from heat. Whisk in sugar, eggs and vanilla. Sift flour, baking powder and salt onto butter-chocolate mixture; stir in just until blended.

3. Place melted and cooled white chocolate in a heavy-duty plastic storage bag. Snip one corner from bag.

4. Spread half of the batter in prepared pan; gently squeeze half of the white chocolate in stripes over batter. Repeat with remaining batter and white chocolate. Bake 25 to 28 minutes, until a toothpick inserted in center comes out clean. Cool completely in pan on a wire rack. Cut into squares. Makes 16 brownies.

Per brownie: 190 calories, 10 g total fat, 6 g saturated fat, 42 mg cholesterol, 103 mg sodium, 23 g carbohydrates, 2 g protein, 25 mg calcium, 1 g fiber

zebra brownies

Kids love these fun brownies striped with two kinds of chocolate. Tuck them into lunch boxes for a treat they'll look forward to all morning. Or, tote a batch to the office—your colleagues will appreciate them just as much, if not more! Pictured on page 244.

Prep time: 15 minutes • Baking time: 25 to 28 minutes

½	**cup butter or margarine**
3	**ounces unsweetened chocolate squares**
1	**cup sugar**
2	**large eggs**
1	**teaspoon vanilla extract**
1	**cup all-purpose flour**
½	**teaspoon baking powder**
⅛	**teaspoon salt**
2	**ounces white chocolate squares, melted (see tip, page 265) and cooled**

caramel-cheese brownies

Here's a tasty twist on traditional brownies. Gooey caramel and rich cream cheese are marbleized, then sandwiched between brownie batter in the pan before baking, making every bite melt-in-your-mouth yummy. Pictured on page 244.

Prep time: 40 minutes • Baking time: 40 minutes
Microwave used

1	**package (8 oz.) cream cheese, softened**
1	**large egg**
20	**caramels, unwrapped**
1	**tablespoon water**

BROWNIES:

1	**cup butter or margarine**
1	**cup unsweetened cocoa**
1½	**cups granulated sugar**
½	**cup firmly packed brown sugar**

4 large eggs
1¼ cups all-purpose flour
1 teaspoon vanilla extract
¼ teaspoon salt

1. Heat oven to 350°F. Line a 13×9-inch baking pan with foil, letting foil extend at ends. Grease foil.

2. Whisk cream cheese and egg in a medium bowl until smooth; set aside. Combine caramels with water in a small microwaveproof bowl. Cover with plastic wrap, turning back one section to vent. Microwave on Medium (50% power) 1 minute; stir. Microwave 1 minute more. Stir mixture until caramels are melted. Set aside and cool slightly while making brownies.

3. *Make brownies:* Place butter in a large microwaveproof bowl. Cover bowl with plastic wrap, turning back one section to vent. Microwave on Medium (50% power) 1 to 1½ minutes, until melted. Whisk in cocoa until smooth; let stand 5 minutes to cool slightly. Whisk both sugars into cocoa mixture until combined. Add eggs, one at a time, whisking after each addition, until blended. Stir in flour, vanilla and salt.

4. Spread 1¾ cups brownie batter in prepared pan. Gently stir melted caramels into cream-cheese mixture just until marbleized, then slowly pour over brownie layer, spreading evenly to cover. Spread remaining brownie batter evenly over cream cheese-caramel layer (there may be a few spots where it won't cover completely).

5. Bake 40 minutes, until a toothpick inserted in center has crumbs clinging to it. Cool completely in pan on a wire rack.

6. To cut bars, lift brownies out of pan with foil. *(Can be made ahead. Wrap well and freeze up to 1 month. Thaw at room temperature 2 hours.)* Peel off foil. Cut into twelve 3×3-inch squares, then cut each square in half diagonally into triangles. Makes 24 brownies.

Per brownie triangle: 245 calories, 13 g total fat, 8 g saturated fat, 76 mg cholesterol, 162 mg sodium, 31 g carbohydrates, 4 g protein, 34 mg calcium, 0 g fiber

one-pan chocolate cake with coconut icing

Here's a grandmotherly cake that's quick and comforting.

Prep time: 10 minutes · Baking time: 25 to 30 minutes

Unsweetened cocoa
½ cup butter or margarine
4 ounces unsweetened chocolate squares
1½ cups sugar
2 teaspoons vanilla extract, divided
1¾ cups buttermilk
3 large eggs
1¾ cups all-purpose flour
1 teaspoon baking soda
1 teaspoon salt
½ teaspoon baking powder
1 can (15 oz.) sweetened condensed milk
1¾ cups shredded coconut

1. Heat oven to 350°F. Grease a 13×9-inch baking pan and sprinkle with cocoa, tapping out excess. Heat butter and chocolate in a large saucepan over medium heat, until melted and smooth, stirring frequently; remove from heat. Stir in sugar and 1 teaspoon of the vanilla until smooth. Gradually whisk in buttermilk, then eggs.

2. Add flour, baking soda, salt and baking powder, whisking until smooth. Pour batter evenly into prepared pan. Bake 25 to 30 minutes, until a toothpick inserted in center comes out clean. Cool 5 minutes in pan on a wire rack. Heat broiler.

3. Stir remaining 1 teaspoon vanilla into sweetened condensed milk until blended; spread over top of warm cake. Sprinkle evenly with coconut. Place cake under broiler at closest position to heat source; broil 2 to 3 minutes until coconut is golden. Cool cake completely in pan on wire rack. Makes 24 servings.

Per serving: 240 calories, 11 g total fat, 7 g saturated fat, 43 mg cholesterol, 262 mg sodium, 34 g carbohydrates, 4 g protein, 91 mg calcium, 1 g fiber

double-chocolate vanilla cupcakes

These cute cupcakes with satiny chocolate frosting are old-fashioned, from-the-heart, bake-sale classics! Pictured on page 247.

Prep time: 40 minutes • Baking time: 21 to 23 minutes
Microwave used

CUPCAKES:

1	bar (4 oz.) German sweet baking chocolate, chopped
3	tablespoons heavy or whipping cream
2½	cups all-purpose flour
1	tablespoon baking powder
¾	teaspoon salt
¾	cup butter or margarine, softened
1	cup granulated sugar
1	tablespoon vanilla extract
3	large eggs
3	large egg yolks
¾	cup milk

FROSTING:

2	ounces unsweetened chocolate squares
¼	cup butter or margarine, cut up
1½	cups confectioners' sugar
⅓	cup sour cream
½	teaspoon vanilla extract

1. *Make cupcakes:* Heat oven to 350°F. Line eighteen 2¾-inch muffin-pan cups with cupcake/muffin liners. Microwave chocolate and cream in a small microwaveproof bowl on High 1 minute. Whisk until smooth and chocolate is melted. Set aside.

2. Combine flour, baking powder and salt in a bowl; set aside. Beat butter, granulated sugar and vanilla in a mixer bowl at medium-high speed, until fluffy. Beat in eggs, one at a time, beating well after each addition. Beat in yolks. With mixer at low speed, add flour mixture alternately with milk, beginning and ending with flour mixture, until blended.

3. Remove 1⅓ cups batter to a bowl; set aside. Spoon remaining batter into muffin-pan cups. By teaspoonfuls, spoon chocolate mixture into center of each cup. With another teaspoon, spoon reserved 1⅓ cups batter over chocolate (batter does not have to cover chocolate completely). Bake 21 to 23 minutes, until a toothpick inserted in center of cupcakes comes out clean. Remove from pans and cool completely on wire racks.

4. *Make frosting:* Combine chocolate and butter in a small microwaveproof bowl. Cover bowl with plastic wrap, turning back one section to vent. Microwave on High 1½ minutes. Stir until chocolate is melted. Transfer to mixer bowl and beat in remaining ingredients until smooth. Frost cupcakes. *(Can be made ahead. Wrap and freeze up to 1 month. Thaw at room temperature 2 hours.)* Makes 18 cupcakes.

Per cupcake: 335 calories, 18 g total fat, 10.5 g saturated fat, 105 mg cholesterol, 304 mg sodium, 40 g carbohydrates, 4 g protein, 81 mg calcium, 1 g fiber

chocolate sheet cake ⓔⓐⓢⓨ

A rich, fudgy one-layer cake from deep in the heart of Texas. For a twist, the frosting features Mexican Ibarra chocolate, which is flavored with almonds and cinnamon. Pictured on page 244.

Prep time: 20 minutes • Baking time: 40 minutes
Microwave used

CAKE:

2	cups all-purpose flour
2	cups sugar
1	teaspoon baking soda
½	teaspoon baking powder
½	teaspoon salt
¾	cup unsweetened cocoa
1	cup boiling water
2	large eggs
1	cup buttermilk

1 teaspoon vanilla extract

1 cup butter or margarine, melted and cooled

FROSTING:

1½ disks (4½ oz.) Ibarra chocolate (Mexican chocolate),* finely chopped; or 4½ ounces semisweet chocolate squares, finely chopped, and ¼ teaspoon cinnamon

½ cup butter or margarine, cut up

½ cup heavy or whipping cream
■
¾ cup pecans, toasted and chopped

1. Heat oven to 350°F. Grease a 13×9-inch baking pan. Line bottom with waxed paper; grease and flour paper.

2. *Make cake:* Whisk together flour, sugar, baking soda, baking powder and salt in a large bowl; set aside. Whisk cocoa and boiling water in a medium bowl until smooth. Stir cocoa mixture into flour mixture with a rubber spatula. (Mixture will be dry.) Whisk eggs, buttermilk, vanilla and butter in a medium bowl. Whisk buttermilk mixture into cocoa mixture, until smooth. Pour batter into prepared pan. Bake 40 minutes, until a toothpick inserted in center of cake comes out clean.

3. *Make frosting:* Meanwhile, place Ibarra chocolate (or semisweet chocolate and cinnamon) and butter in a medium microwaveproof bowl. Cover bowl with plastic wrap, turning back one section to vent. Microwave on High 1½ minutes, until chocolate is melted; stir until smooth. Add cream. Cover and microwave 1½ minutes more, just until cream is hot. Stir until frosting is completely smooth and shiny.

4. Cool cake in pan on a wire rack 5 minutes. Pour frosting evenly over hot cake. Sprinkle pecans over top. Cool cake completely. Makes 12 servings.

*Available in most Hispanic supermarkets.

Per serving: 575 calories, 35 g total fat, 18 g saturated fat, 112 mg cholesterol, 494 mg sodium, 64 g carbohydrates, 6 g protein, 65 mg calcium, 3 g fiber

chocolate angel food cake LOW FAT

Chocolate lovers rejoice! Here's an almost no-fat cake you can enjoy without guilt. Best of all, you can freeze it to satisfy future chocolate cravings without overindulging. Pictured on page 247.

Prep time: 25 minutes plus cooling
Baking time: 40 to 45 minutes

⅔ cup sifted cake flour (not self-rising)

⅓ cup unsweetened cocoa

1½ cups granulated sugar, divided

12 large egg whites, at room temperature

1½ teaspoons vanilla extract

1½ teaspoons cream of tartar

½ teaspoon salt

Confectioners' sugar (optional)

1. Heat oven to 375°F. Sift flour, cocoa and ¾ cup of the granulated sugar together 3 times; set aside.

2. Beat egg whites in a large mixer bowl at low speed until foamy, about 5 minutes. Add vanilla, cream of tartar and salt. Gradually increase speed to medium while beating in remaining ¾ cup granulated sugar, 1 tablespoon at a time, 5 minutes. When sugar is incorporated, continue beating to stiff peaks, 2 minutes more.

3. Sift one-third of the flour mixture over whites; gently fold in with rubber spatula. Repeat process 2 more times.

4. Pour batter into an ungreased 10-inch tube pan. Run a knife through batter to remove any air pockets. Bake 40 to 45 minutes, until top of cake springs back when lightly touched with fingertip. Invert and hang pan on neck of a bottle to cool.

5. Run a thin knife around sides of pan and tube to unmold cake. Invert pan. Turn cake upright onto serving plate. Sift confectioners' sugar over cake, if desired. Makes 14 servings.

Per serving: 120 calories, 0.5 g total fat, 0 g saturated fat, 0 mg cholesterol, 126 mg sodium, 27 g carbohydrates, 4 g protein, 26 mg calcium, 0 g fiber

the perfect chocolate cake

Looking for chocolate paradise? This is it! Our secret to perfection is using cocoa powder instead of melted chocolate for the most intense flavor. (Nearly a pound of chocolate in the frosting doesn't hurt matters, either.) Our shiny chocolate ganache topping and lots of light, airy chocolate curls add a gorgeous finish. Pictured on page 242.

Prep time: 1 hour plus standing and decorating
Baking time: 25 minutes

CAKE:

1	cup unsweetened cocoa, sifted
1½	cups boiling water
3	cups all-purpose flour
1	teaspoon baking soda
½	teaspoon salt
1½	cups unsalted butter, softened (no substitutions)
2¼	cups sugar
4	large eggs, at room temperature
2	teaspoons vanilla extract

FROSTING:

1¼	cups sugar
½	cup water
6	large egg yolks, at room temperature
2	cups unsalted butter, softened (no substitutions)
8	ounces unsweetened chocolate squares, melted (see tip, page 265) and slightly cooled
6	ounces semisweet chocolate squares, melted (see tip, page 265) and slightly cooled
2	teaspoons vanilla extract
	Pinch salt

GANACHE TOPPING:

3	ounces semisweet chocolate squares, finely chopped
⅓	cup heavy or whipping cream

CHOCOLATE SHAVINGS:

1	(4 oz.) piece semisweet chocolate or 4 ounces semisweet chocolate squares

1. Arrange oven racks in middle and bottom third of oven. Heat oven to 350°F. Grease three 9-inch round cake pans. Line bottoms with waxed paper; grease paper. Sprinkle paper lightly with flour, shaking out excess.

2. *Make cake:* Whisk together cocoa and boiling water in a bowl until smooth. Let stand until cooled.

3. Combine flour, baking soda and salt in a bowl; set aside.

4. Beat butter in a large mixer bowl at medium-high speed, until creamy. Add sugar and beat until light and fluffy, 3 to 5 minutes. Add eggs, one at a time, beating well after each addition. Add vanilla. Scrape side of bowl with rubber spatula. Beat in flour mixture at low speed. Scrape side and bottom of mixer bowl with rubber spatula. Slowly beat in cocoa mixture. Increase speed to medium and beat until completely smooth, 1 to 2 minutes.

5. Pour batter into prepared pans. Arrange 2 pans on middle rack and 1 pan in center of bottom rack. Bake 15 minutes. Switch one pan from middle rack with the pan from the bottom rack. Bake 10 minutes more, until a toothpick inserted in centers comes out clean. Cool in pans on wire racks 15 minutes. Invert and remove pans; peel off paper. Invert cakes again, right side up, on racks and cool completely.

6. *Make frosting:* Combine sugar and water in a small saucepan. Bring to boiling over medium heat. Boil, without stirring, until syrup reaches 238°F. on a candy thermometer, 5 to 8 minutes. Meanwhile, beat egg yolks in a small mixing bowl just until combined. Gradually stir about half of the sugar mixture into the egg yolks. Return all of the egg yolk mixture to saucepan. Cook and stir for 2 minutes more. Cool to room temperature.

7. Beat butter in another large mixer bowl until creamy and very smooth. With mixer at high speed, gradually add cooled sugar mixture, beating until combined. Reduce speed to medium-high; slowly beat in melted chocolates. Beat in vanilla and salt. Scrape sides and bottom of mixer bowl with rubber spatula and beat until chocolate is well incorporated. (The frosting should be smooth and creamy.)

8. Place 1 cake layer on a flat serving plate. Spread 1 cup of the frosting over top of layer with a metal spatula. Repeat with remaining cake layers and 2 cups of frosting. Frost sides with 1½ cups frosting, keeping sides and top as smooth as possible. Fill a large pastry bag fitted with a ½-inch star tip with remaining ½ cup frosting. Pipe a decorative border around top of cake.

9. *Make ganache topping:* Place chocolate in a small bowl. Bring cream to boil in a small saucepan over medium-high heat; immediately pour over chocolate. Let stand 3 minutes; stir until mixture is smooth. Let stand 8 to 10 minutes more, just until ganache begins to thicken. Carefully pour ganache over center of top of cake, and quickly smooth over top with a small metal spatula just to the decorative border. Let stand 15 minutes, until set.

10. *Make chocolate shavings:* Meanwhile, rub a 4-ounce piece of chocolate with palm of hands to warm slightly. (This will make it easier to make shavings.) Using a swivel-blade vegetable peeler, peel chocolate toward you to form shavings. (If using semisweet chocolate squares, grate on the large holes of a standing grater set over a piece of waxed paper.) Transfer shavings to a large plate. Continue making shavings until there are enough to cover side of cake. Very gently press shavings onto side of cake. Store cake in refrigerator. Makes 20 servings.

Per serving: 675 calories, 47.5 g total fat, 28 g saturated fat, 199 mg cholesterol, 153 mg sodium, 64 g carbohydrates, 7 g protein, 45 mg calcium, 4 g fiber

test kitchen tip

great ways with grated chocolate

Some chocolate lovers feel you can never have too much chocolate. For that camp, we suggest sneaking grated semisweet chocolate into recipes whenever you can. Just a few ideas:

A DUSTING WILL DO
Sprinkle on top of a frosted cake. Use grated semisweet chocolate on white frosting and grated white chocolate on dark frosting.

RICE MADE NICER
Grate 1 ounce semisweet chocolate square; divide evenly over tops of four ½-cup servings of rice pudding.

PERFECT PARFAITS
Sprinkle semisweet grated chocolate between layers of ice cream and raspberry sauce in parfait glasses.

A BETTER BANANA CAKE
Grate 2 ounces semisweet chocolate squares into your favorite two-layer banana cake or spice cake recipe after batter is prepared. Bake as directed.

CHOCOLATE FOR BREAKFAST
Sprinkle grated semisweet chocolate over confectioners' sugar-dusted pancakes.

FUSS-FREE FROSTING
Brush top of cake with melted semisweet chocolate. Let stand until slightly tacky and sprinkle with grated white chocolate. Let stand until set.

chocolate-caramel layer cake

Talk about a showpiece! This chocolaty beauty gets extra opulence from a creamy caramel filling and beautiful brittle-glazed pecans arranged on the top. No wonder we chose it to grace the cover of our first-ever recipe annual—it's a great choice when you've got something wonderful to celebrate. Pictured on the cover.

Prep time: 1 hour 15 minutes plus standing and chilling
Baking time: 30 to 33 minutes

- ¾ **cup unsweetened cocoa**
- 1 **cup boiling water**
- 2 **cups cake flour (not self-rising)**
- 1 **teaspoon baking soda**
- ½ **teaspoon baking powder**
- ¼ **teaspoon salt**
- 1 **cup butter (no substitutions)**
- ½ **cup plain low-fat yogurt**
- 2½ **teaspoons vanilla extract**
- 1½ **cups sugar**
- 3 **large eggs, at room temperature**

CARAMEL FILLING:

- ½ **cup sugar**
- 2 **tablespoons water**
- ¼ **cup heavy or whipping cream**
- ¾ **cup unsalted butter (no substitutions)**
  Dash salt

CHOCOLATE ICING:

- 6 **ounces bittersweet or semisweet chocolate squares, finely chopped**
- ½ **cup heavy or whipping cream**
- 2 **tablespoons light corn syrup**

CARAMELIZED PECANS:

- 1 **cup sugar**
- ⅓ **cup water**
- 1 **cup pecan halves, lightly toasted**

1. Whisk together cocoa and boiling water in a small bowl until smooth. Cool to room temperature. Meanwhile, heat oven to 350°F. Grease two 9-inch round cake pans. Line bottoms with waxed paper; grease paper. Sprinkle paper lightly with flour, shaking out excess.

2. Stir together flour, baking soda, baking powder and salt in a large bowl; set aside. Remove butter from refrigerator and place one unwrapped stick between two sheets of waxed paper. With a rolling pin, give each side of the butter a few whacks to make it pliable but not too soft. (Softened butter should have the consistency of raw cookie dough.) Transfer to a large mixer bowl. Repeat with other stick of butter.

3. Whisk yogurt and vanilla into cocoa mixture. Beat butter and sugar on medium-high speed, until blended, 2 minutes. Add eggs, one at a time, beating well after each addition until light and fluffy. At low speed, alternately beat in flour mixture and cocoa mixture, beginning and ending with the flour. (Mixture may look curdled but that's OK.) Divide batter evenly between prepared pans.

4. Bake 30 to 33 minutes, until a toothpick inserted in center comes out clean. Cool cakes in pans on wire racks 10 minutes. Invert and remove pans; peel off paper. Invert cakes again, right side up on racks, and cool completely.

5. *Make caramel filling:* Bring sugar and water to boil in a small 1½-quart saucepan over medium heat, stirring. Increase heat to medium-high and cook, without stirring, until syrup turns light amber in color, 5 to 6 minutes. Remove from heat and gradually stir in cream. (Mixture will bubble vigorously.) Stir until smooth. Pour caramel into a large mixer bowl; let stand until cool, 40 minutes. Add butter and salt; beat at medium speed until smooth. Cover with plastic wrap and refrigerate 1 hour until firm.

6. *Make chocolate icing:* Place chocolate in a small bowl. Bring cream and corn syrup to boil in a small saucepan over medium-high heat; immediately pour over chocolate. Let stand 3 minutes; stir until mixture is smooth. Let stand at room temperature until icing thickens, about 1 hour.

7. *Make caramelized pecans:* Lightly butter a jelly-roll pan. Bring sugar and water to boil in a small saucepan over medium heat, stirring. Increase heat to medium-high and cook, without stirring, until mixture turns light amber in color, 9 to 10 minutes. Remove from heat and stir in pecans. Immediately spread on prepared pan in a single layer. Let stand until cool. Break into pieces. *(Can be made ahead. Cover and let stand at room temperature overnight.)*

8. Beat caramel filling again, 30 to 60 seconds, until fluffy. Measure $^3/_4$ cup caramelized pecans, then finely chop and stir into caramel filling. (Reserve remaining caramelized pecans for top of cake.)

9. Place 1 cake layer on a flat serving plate. Spread caramel filling over top with a metal spatula. Top with second layer. Refrigerate cake 10 minutes, until filling is set.

10. Spread chocolate icing with a small metal spatula over top and sides of cake. *(Can be made ahead. Refrigerate cake until icing is firm. Then cover loosely and refrigerate up to 24 hours. Let stand at room temperature 4 hours before serving.)* Arrange remaining caramelized pecans over top of cake. Makes 16 servings.

Per serving: 550 calories, 34 g total fat, 18 g saturated fat, 110 mg cholesterol, 274 mg sodium, 61 g carbohydrates, 5 g protein, 97 mg calcium, 1 g fiber

chocolate espresso cake

Another tall beauty. Pictured on page 246.

Prep time: 45 minutes • Baking time: 22 to 25 minutes
Microwave used

- **1 tablespoon instant espresso powder**
- **1¼ cups hot water**
- **2 ounces unsweetened chocolate squares, chopped**
- **2 cups all-purpose flour**
- **½ cup unsweetened cocoa**
- **1½ teaspoons baking soda**
- **¼ teaspoon baking powder**
- **¼ teaspoon salt**
- **¾ cup butter or margarine, softened**
- **1 cup granulated sugar**
- **¾ cup firmly packed brown sugar**
- **3 large eggs, at room temperature**
- **½ teaspoon vanilla extract**

FROSTING:
- **8 ounces semisweet chocolate squares, chopped**
- **1½ cups unsalted butter, softened**
- **1 teaspoon instant espresso powder dissolved in 1 teaspoon hot water**
- **2 cups confectioners' sugar**

1. Heat oven to 350°F. Grease three 9-inch round cake pans. Line bottoms with waxed paper; grease paper. Sprinkle paper lightly with flour, shaking out excess. Dissolve espresso powder in the 1$^1/_4$ cups hot water; stir in chocolate until melted. Cool.

2. Combine flour, cocoa, baking soda, baking powder and salt in a bowl; set aside. Beat butter and sugars in a mixer bowl until light and fluffy. Add eggs, one at a time, beating well after each addition. Add vanilla. With mixer at low speed, add flour mixture alternately with chocolate mixture, beginning and ending with flour mixture, until blended.

3. Spread batter in prepared pans. Bake 22 to 25 minutes, until a toothpick inserted in center of cakes comes out clean. Cool in pans on wire racks 20 minutes. Invert and remove pans; peel off paper. Invert cakes again, right side up, on racks and cool completely.

4. *Make frosting:* Meanwhile, microwave chocolate in a microwaveproof bowl on High 1 to 2 minutes; cool just to room temperature. Beat butter on medium-high speed in a large mixer bowl until light and fluffy. Add espresso-water mixture. Beat in confectioners' sugar until light and fluffy. Beat in cooled chocolate.

5. Place 1 cake layer on a flat serving plate. Spread with scant 1 cup frosting. Top with second layer and another scant 1 cup frosting. Top with third layer and spread top and sides with remaining frosting. Makes 12 servings.

Per serving: 735 calories, 45.5 g total fat, 27 g saturated fat, 146 mg cholesterol, 358 mg sodium, 83 g carbohydrates, 6 g protein, 91 mg calcium, 3 g fiber

ice cream chocolate roll

A good old-fashioned ice cream roll never goes out of style! We paired the chocolate cake with pistachio ice cream, but feel free to use your favorite flavor.

Prep time: 30 minutes plus chilling and freezing
Baking time: 11 to 12 minutes

- ½ cup plus 3 tablespoons unsweetened cocoa, divided
- ⅓ cup all-purpose flour
- ¼ teaspoon baking soda
- ¼ teaspoon salt
- 4 large eggs, at room temperature, separated
- ⅓ cup plus ½ cup sugar, divided
- ½ ounce semisweet chocolate square, grated
- 2 pints premium ice cream

1. Heat oven to 375°F. Line a 15½×10½×1-inch jelly-roll pan with waxed paper; grease paper. Sprinkle paper lightly with flour, shaking out the excess.

2. Sift ½ cup of the cocoa, the flour, baking soda and salt into a bowl; set aside.

3. Beat egg yolks and ⅓ cup of the sugar in a mixer bowl at medium-high speed 5 minutes, until thick and pale golden. Set aside.

4. Beat egg whites in another mixer bowl at medium-high speed until foamy. Gradually add remaining ½ cup sugar and beat just to stiff peaks. With a rubber spatula, fold one-third of whites into yolk mixture to lighten. Fold in remaining whites in two additions, just until blended. Sift one-third of cocoa-flour mixture over yolk mixture; gently fold in until almost blended. Repeat folding in remaining cocoa-flour mixture in two additions, just until blended. Gently fold in grated chocolate. Spread batter evenly in prepared pan. Bake 11 to 12 minutes, until center springs back when lightly pressed with a fingertip.

5. Meanwhile, sift remaining 3 tablespoons cocoa over a clean kitchen towel to cover surface. When cake is done, immediately invert onto towel; carefully remove pan and peel off waxed paper. Lifting from the long side, roll hot cake up with towel, jelly-roll fashion. Completely cool cake in towel.

6. Refrigerate ice cream 20 to 25 minutes to soften.

7. Unroll cooled cake. Gently spread softened ice cream over top, then reroll cake (don't worry if it cracks slightly). Transfer cake, seam side down, to a serving plate. Cover with plastic wrap and freeze 4 hours. *(Can be made ahead. Wrap well and freeze up to 1 week.)* Makes 10 to 12 servings.

Per serving: 240 calories, 11.5 g total fat, 6.5 g saturated fat, 110 mg cholesterol, 135 mg sodium, 33 g carbohydrates, 6 g protein, 79 mg calcium, 2 g fiber

chocolate hazelnut roll

Prep time: 30 minutes plus standing
Baking time: 18 minutes • Microwave used

CAKE:
- 8 ounces bittersweet or semisweet chocolate squares, chopped
- 1½ teaspoons vanilla extract
- 2 teaspoons instant espresso powder
- 8 large eggs, at room temperature
- ¾ cup granulated sugar
- 3 tablespoons unsweetened cocoa, divided

FILLING:
- ⅔ cup chocolate-hazelnut spread (Nutella)
- 1 teaspoon vegetable oil
- 2 tablespoons unsweetened cocoa
- 2 tablespoons warm water
- 1 cup heavy or whipping cream, chilled
- ¼ cup granulated sugar
- Confectioners' sugar and unsweetened cocoa

1. *Make cake:* Heat oven to 350°F. Line a 15½×10½×1-inch jelly-roll pan with foil. Grease foil. Microwave chocolate in a large microwaveproof bowl on High 1 to1½ minutes. Let stand 5 minutes; stir until melted and smooth. Combine vanilla and espresso powder in a cup. Set both aside.

2. Beat eggs and sugar in a large mixer bowl on high speed until thick and pale yellow, 5 minutes. With a rubber spatula, fold one-third of egg mixture into chocolate until blended (be sure to scrape bottom of bowl to incorporate all chocolate). Sift 2 tablespoons of the cocoa over chocolate mixture; then fold in vanilla-espresso mixture and remaining egg mixture until just blended.

3. Pour batter into prepared pan. Bake 18 minutes, until a few moist crumbs cling to a toothpick when inserted in center of cake. Sift remaining 1 tablespoon cocoa over top of cake, and cover with a clean damp kitchen towel. Let cool completely in pan, about 40 minutes.

4. *Make filling:* Stir together hazelnut spread and oil in a small bowl until smooth; set aside. Stir cocoa and water in a large mixer bowl until smooth. Add cream and sugar. On high speed, beat mixture until very stiff, 6 minutes.

5. Run a knife around edge of cake to loosen from pan; sift confectioners' sugar over top. Cover cake with a piece of waxed paper, then arrange a cookie sheet on top of paper. Invert cake so that one long side faces you. Remove pan and peel off foil. (If cake doesn't come out of pan, pull at one edge of foil.) Drop spoonfuls of hazelnut spread over cake, then spread, leaving a 1-inch border along the other long side opposite you. Place a serving platter or board along this side. Holding waxed paper, slide cake onto platter. Spread whipped cream filling to cover hazelnut layer. Using waxed paper as a guide and starting with long side that is covered with filling, roll up cake onto platter. *(Can be made ahead. Cover and refrigerate up to 1 hour.)*

6. To serve, sift top of cake lightly with confectioners' sugar and cocoa. Cut crosswise with a serrated knife into fourteen 1-inch-thick slices. Makes 14 servings.

Per serving: 270 calories, 16 g total fat, 7 g saturated fat, 127 mg cholesterol, 48 mg sodium, 29 g carbohydrates, 6 g protein, 47 mg calcium, 1 g fiber

---

magical treats with melted chocolate

Transform melted semisweet chocolate into these quick-fix treats and garnishes. See tip, page 265, to find out how to melt chocolate.

SWEET STIRRINGS
Dip only the bowls of 8 teaspoons into 2 ounces melted semisweet chocolate squares; refrigerate 5 minutes or just until set. Serve with coffee.

CHOCOLATE PRETZELS
Dip 15 pretzel twists halfway into 2 ounces melted semisweet chocolate squares. Refrigerate on waxed-paper-lined cookie sheet 5 minutes, until set.

CHOCOLATE BANANA ROCKETS
Cut 2 bananas in half crosswise; insert popsicle sticks into each half. Freeze until firm. Peel bananas. Dip bananas completely into 2 ounces melted semisweet chocolate squares. Freeze until chocolate is firm, 15 minutes.

CHOCOLATE RIMS
Melt 1 ounce semisweet chocolate square on a small microwaveproof plate on High 1 minute. Place a wineglass upside down in chocolate on plate and rotate clockwise to coat $1/8$ inch around rim (coats 8 glasses). Turn upright; let set before filling. Use for serving puddings, ice cream, cream cordials and other drinks.

CHOCOLATE LEAVES
Brush the underside of clean, pesticide- and toxin-free stiff leaves (rose or lemon) with melted semisweet chocolate. Cool and carefully peel off leaves. Use to decorate pies, cakes and other desserts.

chocolate-banana torte

Dressed up with chocolate chips and bananas, this cake is really a simple, one-bowl cake in delicious disguise.

Prep time: 15 minutes • Baking time: 20 to 25 minutes

- **6** large ripe bananas, divided
- **2** large eggs
- **1** cup granulated sugar
- **½** cup vegetable oil
- **2** teaspoons vanilla extract, divided
- **1¼** cups all-purpose flour
- **1** teaspoon baking soda
- **¼** teaspoon salt
- **1¼** cups miniature semisweet chocolate chips
- **1** cup heavy or whipping cream
- **3** tablespoons confectioners' sugar, plus more for garnish

1. Heat oven to 350°F. Grease three 8-inch round cake pans. Line bottoms with waxed paper; grease paper. Sprinkle paper lightly with flour, shaking out excess.

2. Mash 3 of the bananas in a bowl. Stir in eggs, granulated sugar, oil and 1 teaspoon of the vanilla. Stir in flour, baking soda and salt until blended. Stir in chocolate chips; pour evenly into prepared pans. Bake 20 to 25 minutes, until a toothpick inserted in center of cakes comes out clean. Cool in pans on wire racks 5 minutes. Invert and remove pans; peel off paper. Invert cakes again, right side up, on racks and cool completely.

3. Beat cream, 3 tablespoons confectioners' sugar and remaining 1 teaspoon vanilla to stiff peaks. Reserve ⅓ cup whipped cream for top of cake. Chop 3 bananas; fold into remaining whipped cream. Place one cake layer on platter. Spread with half of banana cream. Repeat layering cake, cream and a final layer of cake. Sprinkle with confectioners' sugar. Top with reserved cream. Makes 12 servings.

Per serving: 470 calories, 25 g total fat, 10 g saturated fat, 63 mg cholesterol, 180 mg sodium, 61 g carbohydrates, 4 g protein, 28 mg calcium, 1 g fiber

chocolate-pear cake

Chocolate and pears pair well, as this luscious one-pan cake demonstrates. It's studded with chunks of semisweet chocolate, but if you prefer, you can use ⅓ cup semisweet chocolate chips instead. Pictured on page 246.

Prep time: 25 minutes • Baking time: 30 to 35 minutes

- **1** cup cake flour (not self-rising)
- **3** tablespoons unsweetened cocoa
- **½** teaspoon baking powder
- **3** ripe Bartlett pears (1½ lbs.), peeled and cored
- **⅔** cup granulated sugar
- **½** cup butter or margarine, softened
- **2** large eggs
- **2** ounces semisweet chocolate squares, cut into ¼-inch chunks
  Confectioners' sugar, for garnish (optional)

1. Heat oven to 350°F. Grease and flour a 9-inch springform pan. Combine flour, cocoa and baking powder in a small bowl; set aside.

2. Cut each pear lengthwise into quarters, then cut each quarter lengthwise in half. Place granulated sugar in a large mixer bowl; remove 1 tablespoon to a small cup and set aside. Beat remaining sugar and butter on medium speed 2 minutes, until light and fluffy. Beat in eggs, one at a time, until blended. On low speed, beat in flour mixture just until blended. Stir in chocolate chunks.

3. Spread 1½ cups batter in prepared pan. Arrange all the pear slices with tapered ends toward center, overlapping around edge of pan (do not cover center with fruit). Sprinkle reserved 1 tablespoon granulated sugar over pears, then spread top with a light coating of remaining batter (it will not cover fruit completely). Bake 30 to 35 minutes, until a toothpick inserted in center of cake comes out clean. Cool cake in pan on a wire rack. Remove side of pan and sift confectioners' sugar over top, if desired. Serve warm or at room temperature. Makes 10 servings.

chocolate-raspberry torte

What? No butter? You won't miss it in this sinfully delicious soufflé-style chocolate cake. The stiffly beaten egg whites give the dessert its ultra-light texture, while chocolate gives it richness.

Prep time: 35 minutes • Baking time: 40 minutes

- ½ **cup plus 2 teaspoons unsweetened cocoa, divided**
- 1 **cup all-purpose flour**
- ½ **teaspoon baking powder**
- ½ **teaspoon baking soda**
- ¼ **teaspoon salt**
- 1¼ **cups granulated sugar, divided**
- 1 **cup 1% low-fat milk**
- 1 **ounce unsweetened chocolate, melted (see tip, right)**
- 1½ **teaspoons vanilla extract**
- 4 **large egg whites, at room temperature**
- ¼ **cup seedless raspberry jam**
- 1 **pint fresh raspberries and fresh mint leaves, for garnish (optional)**
- 1 **tablespoon confectioners' sugar**

1. Heat oven to 350°F. Lightly coat a 9-inch round cake pan with vegetable cooking spray. Coat bottom and sides with 2 teaspoons of the cocoa. Sift flour, baking powder, baking soda and salt into a large bowl. Whisk in 1 cup of the granulated sugar; set both aside.

2. Combine milk and remaining ½ cup cocoa in a small saucepan. Whisk over medium heat 5 minutes, until mixture thickens. Remove from heat and whisk in melted chocolate and vanilla until smooth. Whisk cocoa mixture into flour mixture until blended.

3. Beat whites in a large mixer bowl on medium speed until foamy. Gradually beat in remaining

¼ cup granulated sugar. Gradually increase speed to medium-high and beat to stiff peaks. Gently fold one-third of whites into chocolate mixture with rubber spatula, then fold in remaining whites until smooth. Pour batter into prepared pan. Bake 40 minutes, until a toothpick inserted in center of cake comes out clean. Cool in pan on a wire rack 15 minutes. Invert and remove pan. Invert again, right side up, on rack and cool completely.

4. Split cake into two layers. Remove top layer; place bottom layer onto a serving plate. Spread jam over bottom layer; place top layer over jam, cut side down. Garnish with raspberries and mint leaves, if desired. Sift confectioners' sugar over top. Makes 12 servings.

test kitchen tip

make it melt

Hints for melting chocolate:

IN THE MICROWAVE: Coarsely chop chocolate and place in a microwaveproof bowl or cup. Microwave on High 1 minute; stir. Repeat in 30-second increments until melted. Keep in mind chocolate pieces won't appear melted until stirred.

ON THE STOVETOP: Coarsely chop chocolate. Make sure all utensils are dry (the smallest amount of water can cause the chocolate to stiffen and become grainy). Melt chocolate in a heavy saucepan over low heat. (Or, place chocolate in top of a double boiler over hot, not boiling, water.) Stir chocolate frequently until completely melted.

bittersweet chocolate tart

Here, a rich custard full of the sophisticated taste of bittersweet chocolate is encased in a shortbread crust. Pictured on page 241.

Prep time: 30 minutes plus freezing
Baking time: 39 to 43 minutes

CRUST:

- 1 **cup all-purpose flour**
- ½ **cup confectioners' sugar**
- ¼ **teaspoon salt**
- 6 **tablespoons cold unsalted butter, cut up (no substitutions)**
- 1 **large egg yolk**
- 1 **teaspoon vanilla extract**

FILLING:

- 1 **cup heavy or whipping cream**
- 8 **ounces bittersweet chocolate squares, cut up**
- 1 **large egg, lightly beaten**

 ▪

 Whipped cream (optional)
 Chocolate shavings and fresh mint sprigs, for garnish (optional)

1. ▪ *Make crust:* Heat oven to 350°F. Process flour, confectioners' sugar and salt in a food processor to blend. Add butter and pulse until mixture is the texture of fine meal. Beat egg yolk and vanilla with a fork in a cup. Drizzle over flour mixture. Pulse just until dough begins to hold together. With floured fingers, press dough evenly in bottom and up the side of a 9½-inch tart pan with removable bottom. Prick bottom of tart shell with a fork; place in freezer 15 minutes. Bake 22 to 23 minutes, until golden brown. Cool on a wire rack while making filling. (Leave oven on.)

2. ▪ *Make filling:* Heat cream over medium heat in a small saucepan until hot. Meanwhile, pulse chocolate in clean bowl of food processor, until chopped. With motor on, pour hot cream through feed tube and process until chocolate melts. Add egg and process until blended.

3. ▪ Pour filling into crust. Bake 17 to 20 minutes, until filling is set but still jiggly in center (it will continue to set as it cools). Cool tart in pan on wire rack. Remove side of pan. Top with a dollop of whipped cream and garnish with chocolate shavings and mint sprigs, if desired. Serve warm or at room temperature. Makes 12 servings.

Per serving: 310 calories, 22.5 g total fat, 13 g saturated fat, 85 mg cholesterol, 68 mg sodium, 27 g carbohydrates, 4 g protein, 32 mg calcium, 2 g fiber

rich chocolate tart with cappuccino sauce

This will remind you of the most scrumptious brownie you've ever had—and then some! The filling, featuring two kinds of chocolate, is baked in a pastry crust and served with a robust cappuccino sauce.

Prep time: 35 minutes plus chilling
Baking time: 35 minutes

PASTRY:

- 1 **cup all-purpose flour**
- 3 **tablespoons sugar**
- ¼ **teaspoon salt**
- ½ **cup unsalted butter, cut up (no substitutions)**

FILLING:

- ½ **cup unsalted butter (no substitutions)**
- 4 **ounces semisweet chocolate squares**
- 2 **ounces unsweetened chocolate squares**
- ½ **cup sugar**
- ½ **cup heavy or whipping cream**
- 1 **teaspoon vanilla extract**
- 3 **large eggs, lightly beaten**

CAPPUCCINO SAUCE:

- 2 **cups milk**
- 1 **to 2 tablespoons coarsely ground espresso coffee beans (do not use instant powder)**
- 1 **cinnamon stick**
- 4 **large egg yolks**
- ⅓ **cup sugar**

CHOCOLATE DECORATIONS:

2 ounces semisweet chocolate squares, melted
   (see tip, page 265) and cooled

2 ounces white chocolate squares, melted
   (see tip, page 265) and cooled

■

Whipped cream (optional)

1. *Make pastry:* Combine flour, sugar and salt in a food processor; pulse. Add butter and process until pastry begins to hold together. Shape into a ball. Roll into a 10-inch circle between 2 sheets of lightly floured waxed paper. Refrigerate 5 minutes. Remove bottom sheet of waxed paper and fit pastry into a 9-inch tart pan with removable bottom. Place in freezer 1 hour.

2. Heat oven to 400°F. Remove top sheet of waxed paper and place pastry-lined pan on a cookie sheet. Bake 15 minutes or until golden. Cool on a wire rack. Reduce oven temperature to 350°F.

3. *Make filling:* Meanwhile, melt butter with chocolates in a double boiler over simmering water. Remove from heat and stir in sugar, cream and vanilla, then eggs. Pour into tart shell and place on cookie sheet. Bake 20 minutes or until just set. Remove sides of pan and cool completely on wire rack. Serve with cappuccino sauce, chocolate decorations and, if desired, whipped cream. Makes 8 servings.

4. *Make cappuccino sauce:* Meanwhile, bring milk to boil in a medium saucepan. Remove from heat; stir in ground coffee and cinnamon. Let stand 20 to 30 minutes. Strain coffee mixture through a sieve lined with cheesecloth into a clean saucepan and reheat over medium heat. Meanwhile, whisk egg yolks with sugar in a small bowl. Gradually whisk in hot milk; add to saucepan and cook over medium-low heat, stirring constantly, just until mixture is thickened and coats back of a spoon. (Do not boil.) Strain through a sieve into a clean bowl. Cover surface with plastic wrap and refrigerate at least 2 hours. *(Can be made ahead. Refrigerate up to 4 hours.)* Makes 1½ cups.

5. *Make chocolate decorations:* Place cooled chocolates separately into two small heavy-duty plastic storage bags. Line cookie sheet with waxed paper or parchment paper. Snip 1 corner of each bag and squeeze chocolates into desired designs on prepared cookie sheet. Refrigerate until firm. *(Can be made ahead. Cover and refrigerate on parchment in an airtight container up to 2 days.)* Peel away paper.

Per serving with 2 tablespoons sauce: 643 calories, 46 g total fat, 26.5 g saturated fat, 240 mg cholesterol, 131 mg sodium, 56 mg carbohydrates, 9 g protein, 109 mg calcium, 3 g fiber

test kitchen tip

a love that's true

We are truly a chocolate-loving nation. In fact, each year Americans eat about 12 pounds of chocolate per capita. Here are some other tidbits to know about our faithful friend:

THE BITTER TRUTH
The best-loved chocolate in America is milk chocolate. However, 22 percent of the U.S. population prefers dark (bittersweet) chocolate.

WHOM DO YOU LOVE?
The top-selling chocolate items for home baking are cocoa and semisweet baking chips. And what do we bake the most? Chocolate chip cookies, of course!

YOUR CHEATING HEART
If your recipe calls for unsweetened or semisweet chocolate squares, cocoa powder may be substituted (except in candy, pie fillings, puddings or coatings). Just follow package directions for proper amounts. Use real cocoa, though—not sweetened cocoa or hot chocolate mixes. Want to use Dutch process cocoa? That's okay, too, except in angel food cake, because it won't yield the same light and airy texture.

chocolate syrup for grown-ups

Chocolate meets more than a glass of milk in these very adult stir-ins.

THE QUINTESSENTIAL ADULT MILK SHAKE

Combine 3 tablespoons Kahlua or coffee-flavored liqueur, 2 tablespoons chocolate syrup and ³⁄₄ cup milk or half-and-half cream in a tall glass. Cover top, shake well and add ice.

COCOA RUM

Combine 2 tablespoons rum, 2 tablespoons chocolate syrup, 1 tablespoon crème de cacao and ³⁄₄ cup milk in a tall glass. Add ice.

CHOCOLATE MARTINI

Combine 1¹⁄₂ ounces vodka (3 tablespoons), 1 teaspoon white crème de cacao and ¹⁄₂ teaspoon white crème de menthe in a shaker or covered glass with 3 ice cubes. Shake and pour into a chilled martini glass.

MOCHACCINO

Stir ³⁄₄ cup cold brewed coffee, ¹⁄₃ cup milk and 3 tablespoons chocolate syrup in a tall glass. Add ice.

MOCHA SODA

Pour 3 tablespoons chocolate syrup into bottom of a tall glass. Gradually add ¹⁄₂ cup cold brewed coffee to fill glass halfway; stir until smooth. Add ¹⁄₂ cup seltzer and ice to taste.

brownie-almond tart

Heavy cream and corn syrup are added to brownie batter to create a satiny filling for this decadent treat. Serve in small slivers, garnished with berries.

Prep time: 20 minutes plus chilling and standing
Baking time: 55 to 60 minutes • Microwave used

ALMOND CRUST:

5	tablespoons butter or margarine
¹⁄₃	cup confectioners' sugar
²⁄₃	cup all-purpose flour
¹⁄₄	cup ground, toasted almonds

CHOCOLATE FILLING:

2	ounces unsweetened chocolate squares
¹⁄₂	cup butter or margarine, cut up
¹⁄₂	cup granulated sugar
3	large eggs
¹⁄₃	cup heavy or whipping cream
¹⁄₃	cup light corn syrup
1	tablespoon all-purpose flour
1	teaspoon vanilla extract
¹⁄₄	teaspoon salt
1	tablespoon confectioners' sugar

CHOCOLATE DRIZZLE:

1	ounce semisweet chocolate square, chopped
1	teaspoon butter or margarine

■

Fresh raspberries, for garnish (optional)

1. *Make almond crust:* Heat oven to 350°F. Beat butter in a large mixer bowl on medium speed until creamy; beat in confectioners' sugar. With mixer at low speed, beat in remaining crust ingredients until coarse crumbs form. Press into bottom of an 8-inch springform pan. Bake 20 minutes until lightly browned. Cool 10 minutes on a wire rack.

2. *Make chocolate filling:* Meanwhile, combine chocolate and butter in a medium microwaveproof bowl. Cover bowl with plastic wrap, turning back one section to vent. Microwave on High 1 to 1¹⁄₂ minutes; stir until smooth. Whisk in remaining chocolate-filling ingredients.

3. Pour filling over almond crust. Bake 35 to 40 minutes, until a toothpick inserted in center comes out barely clean. Cool in pan on a wire rack. (*Can be made ahead. Cover and freeze up to 1 month.*) Run knife around edge; remove side of pan. Sprinkle top of brownie with confectioners' sugar.

4. *Make chocolate drizzle:* Place chocolate and butter in a small microwaveproof bowl. Cover bowl with plastic wrap, turning back one section to vent. Microwave on High 1 to 1½ minutes until melted. Stir until smooth. Cool slightly. Transfer to a heavy-duty plastic storage bag. Snip a small hole in corner of bag and drizzle over top of tart. Let stand until chocolate is set, about 30 minutes. Cut into 12 wedges. Garnish with raspberries, if desired. Makes 12 brownies.

Per brownie: 305 calories, 21 g total fat, 12 g saturated fat, 97 mg cholesterol, 206 mg sodium, 29 g carbohydrates, 4 g protein, 32 mg calcium, 1 g fiber

chocolate cheesecake

No chocolate chapter would be complete without a big, all-American, luscious chocolate cheesecake.

Prep time: 15 minutes plus chilling
Baking time: 55 minutes

6	ounces semisweet chocolate squares
2	ounces unsweetened chocolate squares
¼	cup brewed coffee or water
1	cup (20 cookies) chocolate-wafer crumbs
¼	cup butter or margarine, melted
3	packages (8 oz. each) cream cheese
1	cup sugar
2	large eggs
1	cup sour cream
1	teaspoon vanilla extract
	Boiling water
	Confectioners' sugar and chocolate curls for garnish (optional)

1. Melt chocolates with coffee in a double boiler over gently simmering water. Cool.

2. Heat oven to 350°F. Wrap outside of an 8- or 9-inch springform pan with heavy-duty foil. Combine wafer crumbs and butter in a bowl. Press crumbs into bottom of pan.

3. Beat cream cheese in a large mixer bowl until smooth. Beat in sugar until light and fluffy. Add eggs, one at time. At low speed, beat in chocolate mixture. Add sour cream and vanilla, beating just until blended. Pour batter into prepared pan. Place in a large roasting pan in oven and pour boiling water in roasting pan to come halfway up sides of springform pan.

4. Bake 55 minutes or until sides of cheesecake are puffed and center is just set. Remove from water bath and cool completely on a wire rack. (*Can be made ahead. Cover and refrigerate up to 2 days.*) Remove sides of pan. Garnish top with confectioners' sugar and chocolate curls, if desired. Makes 16 servings.

Per serving: 365 calories, 27 g total fat, 16 g saturated fat, 88 mg cholesterol, 213 mg sodium, 27 g carbohydrates, 6 g protein, 65 mg calcium, 1 g fiber

test kitchen tip
blooming chocolate

Ever unwrap a square of chocolate only to find a grayish layer on the surface? Don't throw it out! Though the gray color (called "bloom") may not look appetizing, it will disappear when heated, and it does not hurt the quality of the chocolate. The bloom is caused by storing the chocolate in conditions that are too humid or too warm.

m e n u

dazzle your valentine

CREAM OF GARDEN-FRESH HERBS
WITH SHRIMP
page 170

BALSAMIC MARINATED PORK
MEDALLIONS
page 184

ALMOND-RICE PILAF
page 150

STEAMED SUGAR-SNAP PEAS

EASY CHOCOLATE SOUFFLÉS
page 271

chocolate baby cakes

When these cuties started appearing on restaurant menus all over, we just had to develop our own recipe. They're opulent, yet surprisingly easy. One bite and you'll agree—these are the sweetest little baby cakes! Pictured on page 241.

Prep time: 15 minutes • Baking time: 10 to 12 minutes
Microwave used

> **Granulated sugar**
> ¾ **cup unsalted butter or margarine, cut into pieces**
> 5 **ounces semisweet chocolate squares, chopped**
> 1 **ounce unsweetened chocolate square, chopped**
> 3 **large eggs, at room temperature**
> 3 **large egg yolks, at room temperature**

> ⅓ **cup confectioners' sugar**
> 1 **teaspoon vanilla extract**
> ⅛ **teaspoon salt**
> ⅓ **cup all-purpose flour**
> **Whipped cream (optional)**
> 6 **fresh strawberries, halved, and 1 ounce semisweet chocolate square, melted, for garnish (see tip, page 265) (optional)**

1. Heat oven to 400°F. Lightly coat six 4-ounce ramekins with vegetable cooking spray; coat bottom and sides with granulated sugar. Combine butter with semisweet and unsweetened chocolates in a medium microwaveproof bowl. Cover bowl with plastic wrap, turning back one section to vent. Microwave on High 1 minute; stir until chocolate melts. Place in freezer about 5 minutes, stirring occasionally, until cool.

2. Meanwhile, beat eggs, egg yolks, confectioners' sugar, vanilla and salt in a large mixer bowl on high speed 2 to 3 minutes, until pale yellow and thick. Beat in cooled chocolate mixture. Beat in flour, scraping sides of bowl, just until blended.

3. Divide batter evenly among prepared ramekins; place 2 inches apart on a large cookie sheet. Bake 10 to 12 minutes, until cakes are slightly puffed and feel firm at edges and soft in the center when pressed with a fingertip. Cool cakes in dishes 5 minutes, then invert onto 6 serving plates. Serve warm. If desired, serve with whipped cream and garnish each plate with a strawberry drizzled with melted chocolate. Makes 6 servings.

Per serving: 500 calories, 39.5 g total fat, 22.5 g saturated fat, 275 mg cholesterol, 91 mg sodium, 35 g carbohydrates, 7 g protein, 45 mg calcium, 2 g fiber

easy chocolate soufflés

A soufflé that can be made ahead? Hard to believe, but heavenly news! Prepare the soufflés up to six hours before your party, refrigerate and bake just before serving. They're delicious and float-off-the-plate light. Pictured on page 243.

Prep time: 20 minutes • Baking time: 18 to 20 minutes
Microwave used

- ¼ cup butter or margarine
- 5 ounces semisweet chocolate squares, chopped
- 3 large eggs, at room temperature, separated
- ½ cup sugar
- ¼ cup all-purpose flour
- 2 tablespoons unsweetened cocoa
- ½ teaspoon vanilla extract
- ½ cup heavy or whipping cream, beaten until stiff

1. Heat oven to 375°F.

2. Combine butter and chocolate in a large microwaveproof bowl. Cover bowl with plastic wrap, turning back one section to vent. Microwave on High 1 to 1½ minutes. Stir until smooth; set aside.

3. Beat egg whites in a small mixer bowl on medium speed until foamy. Gradually beat in sugar. Continue beating until stiff peaks form.

4. Stir egg yolks, flour, cocoa and vanilla into chocolate mixture. With a rubber spatula, gently fold in one-third of whites to lighten, then fold in remaining whites. Spoon batter evenly into four 6-ounce individual baking dishes; place on a jelly-roll pan. *(Can be made ahead. Cover with plastic wrap and refrigerate up to 6 hours.)* Bake 18 to 20 minutes, until tops are puffed and barely set in center. Serve immediately with whipped cream. Makes 4 servings.

Per serving: 560 calories, 37 g total fat, 21.5 g saturated fat, 231 mg cholesterol, 180 mg sodium, 56 g carbohydrates, 8 g protein, 86 mg calcium, 3 g fiber

toffee ice-cream layer cake

A perfect dinner-party choice, this creamy and cool dessert serves twelve and can be made ahead.

Prep time: 15 minutes plus chilling and freezing
Baking time: 10 minutes

CRUST:
- 1 cup (20 cookies) chocolate-wafer crumbs
- ½ teaspoon cinnamon
- 2 tablespoons butter or margarine, melted
  ▪
- 1 quart premium coffee ice cream
- 3 bars (1.4 oz.) chocolate-covered toffee candy, crushed, or 1 bag (6 oz.) chocolate-covered toffee candy bits, divided
- 1 quart premium chocolate ice cream
- 12 chocolate-wafer cookies, broken up
- 1 quart premium vanilla ice cream
  Heavenly Hot Fudge Sauce (see recipe, page 278)

1. *Make crust:* Heat oven to 350°F. Combine crumbs and cinnamon in a bowl. Stir in butter until crumbs are moistened. Press into bottom of a 9-inch springform pan. Bake 10 minutes. Cool.

2. Refrigerate coffee ice cream to soften slightly, 30 minutes. Quickly spread onto cooled crust and sprinkle with ⅔ cup of the toffee candy. Freeze until firm, 1 hour. Refrigerate chocolate ice cream to soften slightly, 30 minutes. Quickly spread onto coffee layer and sprinkle top with broken chocolate wafers. Freeze 1 hour. Repeat, softening vanilla ice cream; spread on top of chocolate layer and sprinkle with remaining toffee candy. Cover and freeze overnight. *(Can be made ahead. Wrap and freeze up to 1 week.)*

3. To serve, unwrap cake and refrigerate 20 minutes. Run a small, sharp knife around edge of pan. Loosen side of pan and transfer cake to platter. Serve with Heavenly Hot Fudge Sauce. Serves 12.

Per serving: 505 calories, 34 g total fat, 16 g saturated fat, 93 mg cholesterol, 262 mg sodium, 47 g carbohydrates, 5 g protein, 150 mg calcium, 0 g fiber

the verdict on chocolate

Chocolate has taken the rap for causing all sorts of problems, from acne to tooth decay! Well, the jury's back in—and finds our beloved ingredient "not guilty!"

MYTH: Chocolate causes acne.
FACT: Scientists can find no link between eating chocolate—even large amounts of it—and blemishes.

MYTH: Chocolate raises blood cholesterol.
FACT: Foods derived from plants contain no cholesterol, and chocolate, produced from the cocoa tree, is no exception. The cocoa butter in chocolate, though a saturated fat, is largely composed of stearic acid—a fatty acid that does not elevate blood cholesterol levels.

MYTH: Chocolate is loaded with caffeine.
FACT: Chocolate does contain caffeine, but not very much. An ounce of milk chocolate has just 5 mg, compared to 100 to 150 mg in a cup of coffee, about 20 mg in a cup of regular tea and 30 to 50 mg in a 12-ounce can of cola.

MYTH: Chocolate causes tooth decay.
FACT: Research indicates that chocolate is probably less harmful to teeth than other sweets with the same sugar content, and does not necessarily cause the growth of bacteria that promote plaque formation and cavities. The worst culprits are sticky foods that cling to the teeth—including, of course, sticky candies covered with chocolate. Plain chocolate, on the other hand, is quickly "rinsed" from the teeth by saliva.

chocolate-peanut butter ice-cream pie

Here's the best way to soften the ice cream for this dreamy treat: Remove the ice cream from the freezer and refrigerate 30 minutes before spooning into the crust. To serve, allow the frozen pie to soften in the refrigerator 20 minutes before cutting into wedges.

Prep time: 30 minutes plus freezing
Baking time: 10 minutes

CRUST:
- 15 chocolate cream sandwich cookies
- ½ cup dry-roasted peanuts
- ¼ cup butter or margarine, melted

FILLING:
- 3 pints premium chocolate ice cream, softened
- 8 packages (1.6 oz. each) milk chocolate-covered peanut-butter cups, coarsely chopped
- 1 cup heavy or whipping cream
- 2 tablespoons confectioners' sugar

CHOCOLATE SAUCE:
- 1 cup prepared hot fudge topping
- ¼ cup strong-brewed coffee
- 2 tablespoons coffee-flavored liqueur

1. *Make crust:* Heat oven to 375°F. Process cookies and peanuts in a food processor to fine crumbs. Reserve 1 tablespoon crumbs for garnish. Combine remaining crumbs with the melted butter in a medium bowl. Press crumbs into bottom and up sides of a 9-inch pie plate. Bake 10 minutes or until set. If necessary, press crumbs into place with a wooden spoon. Cool on a wire rack.

2. *Make filling:* Combine ice cream with chopped peanut-butter cups in a large bowl. Spoon into cooled crust. Cover surface with plastic wrap; freeze 6 hours or overnight.

3. Beat cream and sugar in a small mixer bowl to stiff peaks. Spoon whipped cream over pie; sprinkle with reserved crumbs.

4. *Make Chocolate Sauce:* Heat fudge topping in a small saucepan; stir in the coffee and liqueur. Serve sauce warm with pie. Makes 16 servings.

Per serving: 470 calories, 29.5 g total fat, 16.5 g saturated fat, 65 mg cholesterol, 223 mg sodium, 49 g carbohydrates, 7 g protein, 86 mg calcium, 2 g fiber

chocolate-cherry pudding cake

A scrumptious cake with dried cherries, chocolate chips and pecans comes with a soothing dose of warm fudge pudding in every bite. Pictured on page 243.

Prep time: 20 minutes • Baking time: 35 minutes

- 1 **cup all-purpose flour**
- 12 **tablespoons unsweetened cocoa, divided**
- ¾ **cup granulated sugar**
- 2 **teaspoons baking powder**
- ¼ **teaspoon salt**
- ¾ **cup milk**
- 3 **tablespoons butter or margarine, melted**
- 1 **teaspoon vanilla extract**
- ½ **cup dried tart cherries**
- ½ **cup semisweet chocolate chips**
- ½ **cup chopped pecans**
- ¾ **cup firmly packed brown sugar**
- 1½ **cups water**
  Vanilla ice cream (optional)

1. Heat oven to 350°F. Grease a 9-inch square baking dish. Combine flour and 6 tablespoons of the cocoa in a large bowl. Stir in granulated sugar, baking powder and salt until blended. Add milk, butter, vanilla, cherries and chocolate chips until blended. Spread evenly in prepared baking dish; sprinkle top with pecans.

2. Whisk remaining 6 tablespoons cocoa and the brown sugar in a medium saucepan until blended.

Whisk in the water. Bring to boil, whisking occasionally. Pour mixture over batter in pan, tilting pan to cover evenly. Bake 35 minutes, until a toothpick inserted in center of bottom cake layer comes out clean. Cool 15 minutes. Serve warm with ice cream, if desired. Makes 12 servings.

Per serving: 265 calories, 9.5 g total fat, 4 g saturated fat, 10 mg cholesterol, 173 mg sodium, 47 g carbohydrates, 3 g protein, 88 mg calcium, 1 g fiber

---

test kitchen tip

unsweetened chocolate ideas

It's surprising what rich flavor a little unsweetened chocolate can bring to both sweet and savory recipes. See the tip on page 265 for the best ways to melt chocolate.

ALWAYS ROOM FOR MORE CHOCOLATE
For chocolate-chocolate chip cookies, stir 1 ounce melted unsweetened or semisweet chocolate square into your favorite chocolate chip cookie dough. Reduce baking time 1 to 2 minutes.

MARBLE A CAKE
For a marble cake, stir 1 ounce melted unsweetened chocolate square into ½ cup prepared white or yellow cake batter in a bowl. Pour remaining white batter into baking pans; spoon chocolate batter over top and swirl batters with a knife to marbleize. Bake as directed.

GOOD GRAVY
To enrich gravy, stir in 1 teaspoon shaved unsweetened chocolate to 1 cup of dark gravy for beef, lamb and pork.

SOUTH-OF-THE-BORDER TIP
Add ½ ounce of unsweetened chocolate to 3 to 4 cups of your favorite chili recipe or beef or pork stew.

brownie waffles
à la mode

We call for our dessert waffles to be baked in a heart-shaped waffle iron for a pretty presentation, then we top them with cinnamon ice cream and a hot fudge sauce. The result is the sweetest way to say "I love you" for a special birthday, Valentine's Day or anniversary. Pictured on page 245.

Prep time: 25 minutes plus standing and freezing
Cooking time: 1 to 2 minutes per batch
Microwave used

CINNAMON ICE CREAM:
- 1   pint premium vanilla ice cream, softened
- ½   teaspoon cinnamon

HOT FUDGE SAUCE:
- 6   ounces bittersweet or semisweet chocolate squares, chopped
- ½   cup milk
- ¼   cup light corn syrup
- 2   tablespoons butter or margarine
- 1   tablespoon sugar
- 1   teaspoon instant espresso powder

WAFFLES:
- ¼   cup butter or margarine, cut up
- 1   ounce unsweetened chocolate square, chopped
- ½   cup all-purpose flour
- 3   tablespoons unsweetened cocoa
- ¼   teaspoon baking powder
- ¼   teaspoon baking soda
- ¼   teaspoon salt
- 2   large eggs
- ½   cup sugar
- 1½ teaspoons vanilla extract
- 3   tablespoons cold brewed coffee
- ½   cup chopped walnuts

   Chopped walnuts, for garnish (optional)

1. *Make cinnamon ice cream:* Combine ice cream and cinnamon in a small bowl, stirring quickly until blended. Cover and freeze until firm.

2. *Make hot fudge sauce:* Meanwhile, combine chocolate, milk, corn syrup, butter and sugar in a medium saucepan. Cook over medium-low heat, stirring frequently, until chocolate melts; whisk until smooth. Reduce heat to low and simmer 2 minutes, stirring occasionally, until slightly thickened. Stir in espresso powder. Remove from heat and keep warm.

3. *Make waffles:* Combine butter and chocolate in a small microwaveproof bowl. Cover with plastic wrap, turning back one corner to vent. Microwave on High 1 minute; stir until smooth. Place in freezer 5 minutes until cool.

4. Heat oven to 200°F. Lightly coat a nonstick 7½-inch heart-shaped waffle baker* with nonstick cooking spray. Heat on medium-low heat.

5. Sift flour, cocoa, baking powder, baking soda and salt in a bowl. Whisk eggs, sugar and vanilla in another bowl until blended, then whisk in cooled melted chocolate. Sift flour mixture again over chocolate mixture; add coffee and walnuts and stir just until blended. Pour ½ cup batter into waffle baker. Cook according to manufacturer's directions, just until cooked through, about 1 to 2 minutes. (Waffles will not be crisp. Do not overcook—batter burns easily.) Transfer to a cookie sheet; keep warm in oven. Repeat process with remaining batter (spreading batter in baker, if batter becomes too thick).

6. Separate and arrange 3 waffle hearts on each of 6 serving plates; top each serving with one scoop of ice cream and drizzle with hot fudge sauce. Garnish with additional walnuts, if desired. Makes 6 servings.

*Note: If you don't have a nonstick waffle baker, use the regular kind, but be sure to grease the grids well and follow the manufacturer's directions for the amount of batter to use.

Per serving with sauce: 645 calories, 41 g total fat, 20.5 g saturated fat, 135 mg cholesterol, 362 mg sodium, 70 g carbohydrates, 10 g protein, 139 mg calcium, 3 g fiber

chocolate shortcake with cherries

A triple-chocolate shortcake made with bittersweet chocolate and cocoa is filled with Bing cherries and mounds of white chocolate whipped cream for a dessert that's straight out of a die-hard chocolate fan's dreams.

Prep time: 40 minutes plus standing
Baking time: 23 to 25 minutes
Microwave used

SHORTCAKE:

2	**cups all-purpose flour**
½	**cup granulated sugar**
⅓	**cup Dutch process cocoa**
2½	**teaspoons baking powder**
½	**teaspoon salt**
½	**cup cold unsalted butter, cut up (no substitutions)**
3	**ounces bittersweet or semisweet chocolate squares, finely chopped**
½	**cup milk**
1	**large egg**

GLAZE:

2	**teaspoons heavy or whipping cream**
2	**teaspoons granulated sugar**

FILLING:

5	**cups fresh Bing cherries, pitted and halved**
½	**cup granulated sugar**
1	**tablespoon fresh lemon juice**

WHITE CHOCOLATE WHIPPED CREAM:

3	**ounces white chocolate squares, finely chopped**
1½	**cups heavy or whipping cream, divided**
1	**teaspoon vanilla extract**
	Fresh mint leaves, for garnish (optional)

1. Heat oven to 400°F. Lightly coat a 9-inch round cake pan with vegetable cooking spray. Set aside.

2. *Make shortcake:* Combine flour, sugar, cocoa, baking powder and salt in a large bowl. With a pastry blender or 2 knives, cut in butter until mixture resembles fine crumbs. Stir in chocolate. Beat milk and egg in a glass measure. Gradually add milk mixture to flour mixture, tossing with a fork, until flour mixture is just moistened and dough begins to hold together. On a lightly floured surface, gather dough into a ball; knead gently 3 to 4 times, just until smooth. Gently press into prepared pan.

3. *Make glaze:* Brush top of dough with cream, then sprinkle evenly with sugar.

4. Bake 23 to 25 minutes, until top of shortcake is golden and a toothpick inserted in center comes out clean. Cool in pan on a wire rack 10 minutes. Run a small knife around edge of pan and invert onto rack. Remove pan and invert cake again, right side up, on rack and cool completely.

5. *Make filling:* Meanwhile, gently combine cherries with sugar and lemon juice. Let stand 30 minutes, stirring occasionally. Set aside.

6. *Make white chocolate whipped cream:* Combine chocolate and ¼ cup of the cream in a small microwaveproof bowl. Microwave on High 30 to 60 seconds, stirring every 10 seconds, until mixture is smooth. Let stand until cool, about 15 minutes. Beat remaining 1¼ cups cream and the vanilla in a large mixer bowl until thickened. Add white chocolate mixture and beat just to soft peaks.

7. *To assemble:* Split shortcake in half horizontally. Transfer bottom half to a large dessert plate. Spoon half the filling over bottom, then top with half the whipped cream. Cover cream with remaining half of shortcake; spoon on remaining cream and cherries. Garnish with mint leaves, if desired. Cut into 8 wedges. Makes 8 servings.

Per serving: 660 calories, 38.5 g total fat, 22.5 g saturated fat, 123 mg cholesterol, 360 mg sodium, 77 g carbohydrates, 9 g protein, 190 mg calcium, 3 g fiber

ultra-rich chocolate pudding EASY

The richness of this family favorite comes through in every spoonful. It's best served chilled. To prevent the formation of a skin, before refrigerating, place plastic wrap directly on the surface.

Prep time: 10 minutes plus chilling
Cooking time: 10 minutes

- 2 **cups milk**
- ⅔ **cup sugar, divided**
- 2 **tablespoons cornstarch**
- 2 **large egg yolks**
- ½ **teaspoon vanilla extract**
- 2 **ounces unsweetened chocolate squares, finely chopped**
- 1 **tablespoon butter or margarine**

1. Heat milk and ⅓ cup of the sugar in a medium saucepan until bubbles appear at edge.

2. Meanwhile, whisk remaining ⅓ cup sugar, the cornstarch, yolks and vanilla in a bowl. Gradually whisk hot milk into yolk mixture. Return yolk mixture to saucepan. Cook over medium heat, stirring constantly, until mixture thickens and comes to a boil; boil 1 minute.

3. Remove from heat; immediately sprinkle chocolate over top and let stand 2 minutes. Whisk in chocolate and butter until smooth. Pour into 4 dessert bowls. Cover tops directly with plastic wrap. Refrigerate until cold, 3 hours. Makes 4 servings.

Per serving: 350 calories, 17.5 g total fat, 10 g saturated fat, 131 mg cholesterol, 95 mg sodium, 49 g carbohydrates, 7 g protein, 173 mg calcium, 1 g fiber

test kitchen tip
is it love— or the chocolate?

Is there really such thing as an addiction to chocolate? Chocoholics may sometimes feel they can't get enough of it, but it's not the same as the powerful physical addiction to nicotine. However, there is some evidence that chocolate can be a mood booster. The reason: It contains phenylethylamine (PEA), a substance that causes the brain to produce chemicals that duplicate the walking-on-air feeling of being in love.

warm chocolate mousse

Psssst—here's a secret: Chocolate's flavor is more intense when it's warm. Knowing that, doesn't a warm chocolate mousse make perfect sense?

Prep time: 25 minutes plus chilling
Baking time: 33 to 35 minutes

- 4 **ounces unsweetened chocolate squares**
- 6 **tablespoons butter (no substitutions)**
- ⅔ **cup water**
- ¾ **cup sugar, plus extra for coating pan, divided**
- 6 **large eggs, separated**
  Pinch salt
  Boiling water
- ¾ **cup heavy or whipping cream, beaten until stiff**

1. Heat chocolate, butter and the ⅔ cup water in a saucepan over medium-low heat, stirring, until chocolate is melted; whisk until smooth. Pour into a bowl and refrigerate 30 minutes, whisking occasionally, until cool.

2. Meanwhile, heat oven to 350°F. Grease a 2½-quart 2-inch deep baking dish; coat with some of the sugar.

3. Beat yolks and ½ cup of the sugar in a mixer bowl until pale yellow and thick. Beat egg whites and salt in a clean mixer bowl with clean beaters to soft peaks. Gradually beat in remaining $\frac{1}{4}$ cup sugar; beat until stiff. Whisk yolk mixture into cooled chocolate. Gently fold in beaten whites, one-third at a time, with whisk, just until blended. Pour into prepared baking dish.

4. Place baking dish in a shallow roasting pan on center oven rack. Pour boiling water into roasting pan to come halfway up sides of baking dish. Bake 33 to 35 minutes, until top springs back when lightly pressed in center. Remove baking dish from water bath; cool on a wire rack 10 minutes. Serve with whipped cream. Makes 12 servings.

Per serving: 235 calories, 18.5 g total fat, 9.5 g saturated fat, 142 mg cholesterol, 107 mg sodium, 16 g carbohydrates, 4 g protein, 32 mg calcium, 1 g fiber

super-chocolate sorbet

We did it! We combined the rich chocolate taste of a premium ice cream and the low-fat profile of a sorbet. And it's easy, too.

Total prep time: 10 minutes plus freezing

- ½ **cup water**
- 2 **ounces semisweet chocolate squares**
- ⅓ **cup light corn syrup**
- 2 **tablespoons coffee-flavored liqueur**
- 1 **cup low-fat (1%) milk, at room temperature**

1. Heat water, chocolate, corn syrup and liqueur in a medium saucepan over low heat until chocolate is melted. Stir in milk.

2. Immediately transfer to an ice-cream maker and freeze according to manufacturer's directions. Makes 2 cups.

Per ½ cup: 190 calories, 5 g total fat, 3 g saturated fat, 2 mg cholesterol, 65 mg sodium, 35 g carbohydrates, 3 g protein, 94 mg calcium, 1 g fiber

test kitchen tip

ways to love chocolate chips

Sure, semisweet morsels are at their traditional best in the chocolate chip cookie, but true chocolate fans are always on the lookout for ways to sprinkle them into something good. Here are a few of our favorite ideas:

INSTANT FROSTING
Sprinkle ½ cup chocolate chips over hot cake or brownies. Let stand 5 minutes, until melted, then spread.

CHOCOLATE CHIP-PECAN PIE
Add ½ cup chocolate chips and no more than ½ cup sugar to your favorite pecan pie filling before baking.

DESSERT SCONES
Add no more than ⅓ cup sugar to your favorite scone recipe. Stir in ⅓ cup miniature chocolate chips. Bake as directed.

DARK BARK
Melt 1⅓ cups chocolate chips. Add ½ cup each raisins and peanuts. Pour into a foil-lined 8-inch square pan; refrigerate 30 minutes. Cut into 1¾-inch squares. Makes 16.

CHOCOLATE PIZZA
Place one 9-inch unbaked prepared refrigerated pie crust on a cookie sheet. Sprinkle top with ¼ cup each miniature chocolate chips and chopped nuts; cut into 8 wedges and bake at 450°F. 9 to 12 minutes.

choosing chocolate

When it comes to baking, chocolate can be called for in many forms. Here are the most common:

UNSWEETENED COCOA
Sometimes called unsweetened cocoa powder, this product is used almost exclusively for baking. It is pure chocolate, with most of the cocoa butter removed.

DUTCH PROCESS OR EUROPEAN-STYLE COCOA
These cocoa powders are similar to unsweetened cocoa powder, but the acids have been neutralized, giving them a gentler flavor and a dark, reddish hue.

UNSWEETENED CHOCOLATE
This product, used mostly in baking and cooking, is made from pure chocolate and cocoa butter, with no sugar added. It's sometimes called baking or bitter chocolate.

SEMISWEET AND BITTERSWEET CHOCOLATE
Though there are some differences between these two chocolates, they can be used interchangeably in recipes. Semisweet chocolate is pure chocolate with added cocoa butter and sugar; bittersweet chocolate is usually darker and less sweet than semisweet.

MILK CHOCOLATE
The favorite chocolate of Americans, this chocolate has milk or cream added to the cocoa butter, sugar and pure chocolate. The result is a creamy texture, lighter color and a milder flavor than bittersweet or semisweet chocolates.

heavenly hot fudge sauce

Watch out! Once you've tasted this easy homemade version, there's no going back to the stuff in the jar. It's a great all-purpose sauce over ice cream, pound cake or lavish desserts such as the Toffee Ice-Cream Layer Cake, page 271.

Total prep time: 10 minutes
Microwave used

- **8 ounces unsweetened chocolate squares, coarsely chopped**
- **1⅓ cups heavy or whipping cream**
- **1⅓ cups sugar**
- **¼ cup butter (no substitutions)**
- **2 teaspoons vanilla extract**

1. Combine chocolate and heavy or whipping cream in a medium microwaveproof bowl. Microwave on High 1 1/2 minutes. Stir until chocolate is completely melted.

2. Stir in sugar. Microwave 1 minute more. Stir to dissolve sugar, then stir in butter and vanilla until smooth. Serve warm. *(Can be made ahead. Cool. Cover and refrigerate up to 1 week. Microwave on High 1 1/2 to 2 minutes, stirring after 1 minute, until warm and smooth.)* Makes 3 cups.

Per tablespoon: 70 calories, 5 g total fat, 3 g saturated fat, 11 mg cholesterol, 12 mg sodium, 7 g carbohydrates, 1 g protein, 8 mg calcium, 0 g fiber

almond chocolate sauce

Here's another quick-fix sauce. This one's made elegant with a little liqueur in the mix.

Total prep time: 5 minutes
Microwave used

- **2 ounces semisweet chocolate squares, chopped**
- **¼ cup heavy or whipping cream**
- **2 tablespoons almond-flavored or hazelnut-flavored liqueur**

Combine chocolate and cream in a small microwaveproof bowl. Microwave on High 45 seconds; whisk until smooth. Whisk in liqueur. Makes ½ cup.

Per tablespoon: 70 calories, 5 g total fat, 3 g saturated fat, 10 mg cholesterol, 4 mg sodium, 6 g carbohydrates, 0 g protein, 8 mg calcium, 0 g fiber

mint chocolate sauce

Ice cream topped with this refreshing sauce and served with a sampling of dainty cookies will end the evening on a sweet and simple note.

Total prep time: 5 minutes
Microwave used

- **2 ounces semisweet chocolate squares, chopped**
- **⅓ cup heavy or whipping cream**
- **½ teaspoon peppermint extract**

Combine chocolate and cream in a small microwaveproof bowl. Microwave on High 45 seconds; whisk until smooth. Whisk in peppermint extract. Makes ½ cup.

Per tablespoon: 70 calories, 6 g total fat, 3.5 g saturated fat, 13 mg cholesterol, 5 mg sodium, 5 g carbohydrates, 0 g protein, 9 mg calcium, 0 g fiber

peanut butter-chocolate sauce

Some people just can't resist the combination of peanut butter and chocolate. If you're in that camp, you're in for a treat.

Total prep time: 5 minutes
Microwave used

- **2 ounces semisweet chocolate squares, chopped**
- **⅓ cup heavy or whipping cream**
- **3 tablespoons smooth peanut butter**
- **1 tablespoon light corn syrup**

Combine chocolate and cream in a small microwaveproof bowl. Microwave on High 45 seconds; whisk until smooth. Whisk in peanut butter and corn syrup. Makes ⅔ cup.

Per tablespoon: 90 calories, 7 g total fat, 3 g saturated fat, 11 mg cholesterol, 29 mg sodium, 6 g carbohydrates, 2 g protein, 9 mg calcium, 1 g fiber

test kitchen tip
storing chocolate

To keep chocolate baking squares and chips at their luscious best, follow these storage tips:

Store chocolate, tightly covered, in a cool, dry place (between 60°F. and 78°F.).

It's a good idea to refrigerate chocolate during warmer months. To do so, wrap tightly in foil and seal in a plastic bag to prevent the odors of other foods from penetrating the chocolate. Be sure to leave the chocolate wrapped when bringing it back to room temperature. Otherwise, moisture could condense on the surface, causing it to become grainy and clumpy when heated.

chocolate hazelnut bonbons

All you need for these delectable bonbons are three ingredients and foil truffle cups. They also make lovely holiday gifts, and can be made up to three weeks ahead of time.

Total prep time: 40 minutes plus chilling

- **4** **ounces semisweet chocolate squares, melted (see tip, page 265) and cooled**
- **24** **one-inch foil truffle cups**
- **½** **cup chocolate-hazelnut spread (Nutella)**
- **2** **ounces semisweet chocolate squares, melted (see tip, page 265) and cooled**
- **¼** **cup chopped hazelnuts**

1. Line a jelly-roll pan with foil. Place the 4 ounces cooled chocolate squares in a large, heavy-duty plastic storage bag. Cut a ¼-inch hole in one corner of bag. Pipe a ¼-inch deep layer of chocolate into bottoms of 6 of the foil truffle cups. Spread onto sides of cup with a plastic drink stirrer (or toothpick); invert cups onto prepared jelly-roll pan. Repeat process with remaining chocolate and cups. Refrigerate cups 10 minutes, until hardened.

2. Turn cups right-side up. Fill a heavy-duty plastic storage bag with hazelnut spread and cut a ½-inch hole in one corner of bag. Pipe hazelnut spread up to ¼ inch from top of cups. Refrigerate cups 10 minutes.

3. Smooth tops of hazelnut filling. Place the 2 ounces cooled chocolate squares in a heavy-duty plastic storage bag. Cut a ¼-inch hole in one corner of bag. Pipe chocolate over hazelnut filling and tap cups lightly to spread chocolate. Sprinkle tops with chopped hazelnuts. Refrigerate 10 minutes, until chocolate is firm. *(Can be made ahead. Cover and let stand at room temperature up to 3 weeks.)* Makes 24 bonbons.

Per bonbon: 60 calories, 3.5 g total fat, 1.5 g saturated fat, 0 mg cholesterol, 6 mg sodium, 8 g carbohydrates, 1 g protein, 5 mg calcium, 1 g fiber

easy fudge

No prior candymaking experience required—in fact, you don't even need a candy thermometer! Five ingredients and a microwave are all it takes to make this fiendishly delicious fudge. Pictured on page 243.

Prep time: 15 minutes plus standing
Microwave used

- **8** **ounces semisweet chocolate squares, coarsely chopped**
- **2** **cups milk chocolate chips**
- **1** **can (14 oz.) fat-free sweetened condensed milk**
- **2** **tablespoons light corn syrup**
- **½** **cup white chocolate chips**

1. Line an 8-inch square baking pan with plastic wrap, extending over the sides.

2. Combine semisweet and milk chocolates, condensed milk and corn syrup in a 2-quart microwaveproof bowl. Microwave on High 2 to 2½ minutes, until chocolate *begins* to melt (do not overheat); stir until smooth.

3. Immediately, spread half of the fudge mixture into pan; sprinkle with white chocolate chips. Spread remaining fudge mixture on top. Let stand at room temperature 5 hours, until firm. Holding plastic wrap, lift out fudge and cut into 1-inch squares. Makes 64 squares.

Per square: 75 calories, 3 g total fat, 2 g saturated fat, 0 mg cholesterol, 11 mg sodium, 11 g carbohydrates, 1 g protein, 35 mg calcium, 0 g fiber

GOLDEN ONION
AND BACON
TARTLETS
pg. 290

OYSTERS IN
GRUYÈRE SAUCE
pg. 291

holiday
happenings

PÂTÉ IN
SAVORY PUFFS
pg. 291

Here's everything you need to make your holiday season a festive one: Quick and elegant bites for a party of nibbles and cheer; perfect menus for turkey (or prime rib!) and all the trimmings, and, of course, our annual lineup of splendid cookies, desserts and gifts.

start your
holiday

WATERCRESS
SALAD WITH
BELGIAN
ENDIVE
pg. 293

FROM LEFT:
MIMOSA,
CHAMPAGNE
COCKTAIL,
KIR ROYALE
pg. 289

SALMON AND
CAVIAR CREPES
pg. 292

feast right,

TURNIP AND
TURNIP GREENS
SOUP
pg. 293

SHRIMP WITH
PEPPER-
CILANTRO DIP
pg. 290

with a **soup**, salad
or something
festive to **sip**

the bird
may take

BLUE
CHEESE-
WALNUT DIP
pg. 289

LHJ'S CLASSIC
THANKSGIVING
TURKEY
pg. 294
CORN BREAD
STUFFING
pg. 298

WINTER SQUASH
WITH SAGE BUTTER
pg. 299
PEAS PARISIENNE
pg. 301

center stage, but side dishes make the meal

see menu, pg. 295

MIXED NUT STRUDEL
pg. 304

FROM TOP: GERMAN
SANDWICH COOKIES
pg. 317
RUGELACH
pg. 316
CHOCOLATE CHIP
DROPS
pg. 314

nothing

says

THE PERFECT
PUMPKIN PIE
pg. 304

CHOCOLATE-WALNUT
MERINGUE BARS
pg. 315
VANILLA WREATHS
pg. 312

happy holidays

more succinctly

than homemade sweets

CLOCKWISE FROM TOP:
CARROT CAKE
pg. 306
KENTUCKY POUND
CAKE
pg. 306
CORNMEAL
CAT'S TONGUES
pg. 307

a gift from
the hands is a gift
from the **heart**

WHITE
CHOCOLATE
CANDIES
pg. 320

SHORTBREAD
COOKIES
pg. 314
ALMOND
PEARS
pg. 310

champagne cocktail

There's nothing like a traditional champagne cocktail to add exuberance to the festivities. Pictured on page 282.

Total prep time: 5 minutes

- **1 sugar cube**
- **1 teaspoon brandy**
- **2 to 3 dashes (⅛ teaspoon) bitters**
- **⅔ cup chilled champagne**
- **1 maraschino cherry**

Place sugar cube in bottom of a fluted champagne glass. Add brandy and bitters. Slowly add champagne. When bubbles settle, add cherry. Serve immediately. Makes 1 drink.

Per serving: 135 calories, 0 g total fat, 0 g saturated fat, 0 mg cholesterol, 8 mg sodium, 5 g carbohydrates, 0 g protein, 15 mg calcium, 0 g fiber

kir royale

Champagne adds effervescent appeal to the kir—that classic white wine and crème de cassis aperitif from France. Pictured on page 282.

Total prep time: 5 minutes

- **1 2-inch strip lemon peel**
- **1 teaspoon crème de cassis (black currant-flavored liqueur)**
- **⅔ cup chilled champagne**

Twist lemon strip around the handle of a small wooden spoon. Pour crème de cassis into a fluted champagne glass. Slowly add champagne. When bubbles settle, add lemon twist. Serve immediately. Makes 1 drink.

Per serving: 120 calories, 0 g total fat, 0 g saturated fat, 0 mg cholesterol, 8 mg sodium, 3 g carbohydrates, 0 g protein, 15 mg calcium, 0 g fiber

mimosa

The ultimate brunch bubbly! Pictured on page 282.

Total prep time: 5 minutes

- **⅓ cup fresh orange juice, chilled**
- **¼ teaspoon Cointreau or Triple Sec (orange-flavored liqueur)**
- **⅓ cup chilled champagne**
  Orange wedge, for garnish (optional)

Combine orange juice and Cointreau in a fluted champagne glass. Slowly add champagne. Garnish with orange wedge, if desired. Serve immediately. Makes 1 drink.

Per serving: 95 calories, 0 g total fat, 0 g saturated fat, 0 mg cholesterol, 5 mg sodium, 9 g carbohydrates, 1 g protein, 16 mg calcium, 0 g fiber

blue cheese-walnut dip

Serve with fall fruits, such as sliced apples and pears, and French bread slices. Pictured on page 284.

Total prep time: 15 minutes

- **½ pound Maytag or Danish blue cheese**
- **½ cup unsalted butter, softened (no substitutions)**
- **½ cup plus 2 teaspoons finely chopped toasted walnuts, divided**

Combine cheese and butter in a food processor. Process mixture, scraping down sides of bowl with a rubber spatula, until smooth. Stir in ½ cup walnuts. *(Can be made ahead. Transfer to airtight container. Cover and refrigerate up to 24 hours. Let stand at room temperature for 3 hours to soften.)* Transfer dip to a small platter or serving bowl; sprinkle top with remaining 2 teaspoons walnuts. Makes 1¾ cups.

Per tablespoon: 73 calories, 7 g total fat, 4 g saturated fat, 15 mg cholesterol, 114 mg sodium, 1 g carbohydrates, 2 g protein, 46 mg calcium, 0 g fiber

shrimp with pepper-cilantro dip

A cilantro pesto and bell pepper puree spice up that popular party-starter, shrimp. Rely on purchased cooked shrimp to speed up the prep time in the kitchen. Pictured on page 283.

Prep time: 15 minutes • Broiling time: 8 to 10 minutes

- **1** medium plum tomato, cored and halved
- **3** tablespoons pine nuts (pignoli), divided
- **½** cup prepared roasted red bell peppers
- **1** tablespoon olive oil
- **½** teaspoon salt
- **¼** teaspoon freshly ground pepper

CILANTRO PESTO:
- **1** cup fresh cilantro leaves
- **3** tablespoons olive oil
- **¼** cup freshly grated Parmesan cheese
- **1** large clove garlic
- **¼** teaspoon salt

- **1** pound cooked, shelled and deveined large shrimp

1. Heat broiler. Line a broiler pan with foil. Place tomato, cut sides down, on prepared pan. Broil tomato 8 to 10 minutes, until evenly charred.

2. Meanwhile, toast pine nuts in a small skillet over medium heat, stirring, until golden, 5 minutes. Puree tomato in food processor with half the nuts, the bell peppers, oil, salt and pepper, until smooth. Transfer to serving bowl.

3. *Make cilantro pesto:* Clean processor bowl. Puree all pesto ingredients and remaining pine nuts, scraping down sides of bowl. Spoon dollops of cilantro pesto onto pepper puree and swirl with a knife. Serve with shrimp. Makes 8 servings.

Per 1 shrimp with 1 tablespoon dip: 50 calories, 3 g total fat, 0.5 g saturated fat, 38 mg cholesterol, 134 mg sodium, 1 g carbohydrates, 5 g protein, 23 mg calcium, 0 g fiber

golden onion and bacon tartlets

Mini phyllo pastry shells are filled with sweet onion, Gruyère cheese and bacon for a delicious bite-size starter. Pictured on page 281.

Prep time: 20 minutes • Baking time: 9 to 11 minutes

- **1½** tablespoons butter
- **2** cups thinly sliced sweet onions
- **¼** teaspoon salt
- **¾** cup shredded Gruyère or Swiss cheese
- **¼** cup heavy or whipping cream
- **¼** teaspoon minced fresh rosemary or
  - **⅛** teaspoon dried rosemary
- **¼** teaspoon freshly ground pepper
- **4** slices pancetta (Italian unsmoked bacon) or bacon, finely chopped
- **24** mini phyllo pastry shells*
  - Fresh rosemary sprigs, for garnish (optional)

1. Heat oven to 350°F. Melt butter in a large nonstick skillet over medium-low heat. Add onions and cook 15 minutes, stirring occasionally, until lightly browned and tender. Sprinkle with salt and cook 3 to 5 minutes more, until very tender and deep golden brown. Remove from heat; stir in cheese, cream, rosemary and pepper.

2. Meanwhile, cook pancetta in a medium skillet over medium heat, 2 to 3 minutes, until crisp. Drain on paper towels.

3. Arrange phyllo shells on a cookie sheet. Divide and spoon onion mixture into shells. Sprinkle tops evenly with pancetta. Bake 9 to 11 minutes, until golden brown. Garnish with rosemary, if desired. Serve immediately. Makes 24 tartlets.

*Note: Can be found in the frozen food section of supermarkets or through mail-order sources.

Per tartlet: 75 calories, 6 g total fat, 2.5 g saturated fat, 12 mg cholesterol, 93 mg sodium, 4 g carbohydrates, 2 g protein, 42 mg calcium, 0 g fiber

pâté in savory puffs

This is a simply scrumptious starter that's sure to impress your guests. Prepared pâté can be purchased from specialty markets for easy prep. Pictured on page 281.

Prep time: 20 minutes • Baking time: 30 to 33 minutes
Microwave used

- ¾ cup water
- 5 tablespoons butter or margarine
- ¼ teaspoon salt
- ¾ cup all-purpose flour
- 3 large eggs, at room temperature
- ⅓ pound duck, goose or vegetable pâté
- 3 tablespoons red currant jelly, melted and cooled
- 1 teaspoon balsamic vinegar
  Lemon leaves, for garnish (optional)

1. Heat oven to 400°F. Grease a large cookie sheet with vegetable shortening.

2. Bring the water, butter and salt to boil in a medium saucepan; reduce heat to medium and add flour all at once. Stir until dough pulls away from side of pan. Continue stirring, 1 to 2 minutes more to dry. Transfer mixture to a food processor. Add eggs, one at a time, pulsing until blended after each addition. Drop dough by teaspoonfuls into 3½ dozen balls about 1 inch apart onto prepared sheet. Bake 30 to 33 minutes, until deep golden brown; turn oven off and let puffs stand in oven 5 minutes more. Transfer puffs to wire racks and cool completely.

3. Cut a slit on one side of each puff; fill with 1 level teaspoon of pâté. Combine currant jelly and vinegar in a cup; spoon a small amount over puffs. Garnish with lemon leaves, if desired. Serve immediately. Makes 3½ dozen puffs.

Per puff: 45 calories, 3.5 g total fat, 1.5 g saturated fat, 24 mg cholesterol, 57 mg sodium, 3 g carbohydrates, 1 g protein, 5 mg calcium, 0 g fiber

---

menu

open house

PÂTÉ IN SAVORY PUFFS
left

GOLDEN ONION AND BACON TARTLETS
page 290

CHEESE PLATE
see tip, page 21

CHAMPAGNE COCKTAILS
page 289

---

oysters in gruyère sauce

Serve these gems to oyster lovers. Pictured on page 281.

Prep time: 15 minutes • Broiling time: 4 to 6 minutes

- 24 oysters on the half shell
- 1 teaspoon cornstarch
- ¾ cup heavy or whipping cream
- 1 tablespoon unsalted butter (no substitutions)
- ½ cup plus ⅓ cup coarsely shredded Gruyère or Swiss cheese, divided
- 1 tablespoon Pernod (anise-flavored liqueur)
  Fresh chervil or parsley sprigs (optional)

Heat broiler. Arrange oysters on a large broiler pan. Whisk cornstarch into cream in a small saucepan. Add butter and bring to boil, whisking; boil 1 minute. Remove from heat; stir in ½ cup of the cheese and the Pernod until cheese melts. Divide sauce over oysters. Divide and top with remaining ⅓ cup cheese. Broil oysters 4 inches from heat, 4 to 6 minutes, until golden and oysters are cooked through. Transfer to serving plates. Garnish with chervil, if desired. Serve immediately. Serves 8.

Per serving: 175 calories, 14.5 g total fat, 8.5 g saturated fat, 71 mg cholesterol, 96 mg sodium, 3 g carbohydrates, 7 g protein, 153 mg calcium, 0 g fiber

salmon and caviar crepes

Here's an elegant appetizer for your next gathering—delicate crepes filled with smoked salmon slices, caviar and crème fraîche (a thick, rich cream). Pictured on page 282.

Total prep time: 35 minutes

- ½ cup water
- ½ cup milk
- 1 teaspoon butter or margarine, melted
- ¾ cup all-purpose flour
- ¼ teaspoon salt
- ½ cup crème fraîche (see tip, page 219) or sour cream
- ¼ pound thinly sliced Nova or cured salmon, cut crosswise into ½-inch strips
- 1 jar (1 oz.) caviar, such as osetra
- 3 tablespoons finely chopped fresh dill
  Fresh dill sprigs, for garnish (optional)

1. Process the water, milk and butter in a food processor; add flour and salt and process until smooth. Transfer to a glass measure; skim off foam.

2. Lightly coat a 7-inch nonstick skillet with vegetable cooking spray; heat over medium-high heat 1 minute. Fill a ¼-cup measure halfway with batter. Add batter to skillet, tilting to cover bottom. Cook 1 minute; loosen edge with a small spatula and turn out onto a plate (crepe should be just lightly colored; if any darker, reduce heat slightly). Repeat making 11 more crepes, stacking crepes onto plate.

3. Place one crepe on a flat surface; spread 1 rounded teaspoon crème fraîche down center. Top with 2 strips salmon, ¼ teaspoon each of the caviar and dill. Fold in sides and roll up. Cut in half diagonally. Repeat. *(Can be made ahead. Cover with plastic wrap and refrigerate up to 1 hour.)* Garnish with dill sprigs, if desired. Makes 24.

Per appetizer: 45 calories, 2.5 g total fat, 1.5 g saturated fat, 13 mg cholesterol, 144 mg sodium, 3 g carbohydrates, 2 g protein, 17 mg calcium, 0 g fiber

exotic mushroom soup

Exotic mushrooms make this soup rich and flavorful.

Prep time: 25 minutes • Cooking time: 50 to 63 minutes

- 3 tablespoons butter, divided (no substitutions)
- 1 cup chopped onions
- ¼ cup chopped shallots
- 2 celery ribs, peeled and chopped
- 1 carrot, chopped
- 2 pounds assorted mushrooms (such as shiitake, cremini, portobello or white mushrooms), stemmed and sliced
- ¼ cup white wine
- 1 teaspoon fresh thyme leaves or ½ teaspoon dried thyme
- 3 cans (14½ oz. each) chicken broth
  Salt
- ½ pound chanterelle or trumpet mushrooms, stemmed and sliced
- ¼ cup chopped fresh parsley
  Freshly ground pepper

1. Melt 2 tablespoons of the butter in a large saucepan over medium heat. Add onions, shallots, celery and carrot. Cook until vegetables soften, 5 to 8 minutes. Stir in assorted mushrooms, wine and thyme. Cook 10 to 15 minutes, until mushrooms soften and are lightly browned. Stir in broth and ½ teaspoon salt. Bring to boil. Reduce heat; simmer until mushrooms are very soft, 35 to 40 minutes.

2. Puree one-third of mushroom mixture in a blender; transfer to a bowl. Repeat with remaining mixture, then return to saucepan and reheat.

3. Meanwhile, melt remaining 1 tablespoon butter in a large nonstick skillet over medium-high heat. Add chanterelles; increase heat to high and cook, stirring often, until edges are golden brown, 8 to 10 minutes. Sprinkle with salt.

4. Divide soup among 8 serving bowls. Sprinkle top of each serving with chanterelles, parsley and pepper. Makes 8 appetizer servings.

Per serving: 110 calories, 6 g total fat, 3 g saturated fat, 12 mg cholesterol, 820 mg sodium, 12 g carbohydrates, 5 g protein, 22 mg calcium, 3 g fiber

turnip and turnip greens soup

For a starter course to our Thanksgiving feast, Alice Waters—American restaurateur, cookbook author and tastemaker extraordinaire—offered this fresh take on turnips. Pictured on page 283.

Prep time: 40 minutes • Cooking time: 50 to 54 minutes

- **1 tablespoon olive oil**
- **1 tablespoon butter**
- **1 tablespoon water**
- **1 medium yellow onion, thinly sliced**
- **1 medium clove garlic, thinly sliced**
- **2 bunches (2½ lbs.) young turnips with greens or 1 pound turnips and 1½ pounds fresh spinach, trimmed**
- **7 cups chicken broth**
- **1 (1-inch) square piece prosciutto or ½ slice bacon, chopped**
- **½ teaspoon chopped fresh thyme**
- **1 bay leaf**
- **¼ teaspoon freshly ground pepper**
  Freshly shaved Parmesan cheese (optional)

1. Heat oil, butter and water in a large stainless-steel pot over medium heat until butter is melted. Add onion and garlic. Reduce heat to medium-low; cover and cook until onion softens, 7 to 8 minutes.

2. Meanwhile, cut greens from turnips; discard stems and cut greens (or spinach, if using) into ½-inch-wide strips. Set aside.

3. Trim turnip roots. (If turnips are very young and tender, do not peel.) Thinly slice turnips; add to pot and cook 3 to 4 minutes, until softened. Stir in broth, prosciutto, thyme, bay leaf and pepper. Bring to boil. Reduce heat to low; cover and simmer 30 minutes, until turnips are tender; discard bay leaf. *(Can be made ahead. Cool. Transfer broth and turnips to a large container.*

Cover. Wrap greens. Refrigerate soup and greens up to 24 hours. Return to boil before continuing recipe.) Stir greens into soup. Simmer 10 to 12 minutes more (4 minutes for spinach), until greens are tender. Serve with Parmesan, if desired. Makes 8 cups.

Per 1 cup: 95 calories, 5.5 g fat, 1.5 g saturated fat, 7 mg cholesterol, 1,011 mg sodium, 9 g carbohydrates, 4 g protein, 134 mg calcium, 3 g fiber

watercress salad with belgian endive (EASY)

This recipe, also from Alice Waters, will bring her hallmark fresh, seasonal appeal to your holiday table. Pictured on page 282.

Total prep time: 25 minutes

- **3 bunches (1 lb.) watercress, tough stems removed**
- **2 Belgian endive, cut into thin strips**
- **1 apple (such as Granny Smith), peeled, quartered and thinly sliced**
- **2 tablespoons fresh lemon juice**
- **1½ teaspoons champagne or white wine vinegar**
- **1 tablespoon Dijon mustard**
- **2 tablespoons olive oil**
- **¼ teaspoon salt**
- **⅛ teaspoon freshly ground pepper**
- **2 tablespoons heavy cream**

Combine watercress, endive and apple in a large bowl. For dressing, whisk together lemon juice, vinegar, mustard, oil, salt and pepper in a small bowl. Toss greens with dressing; add cream and toss again. Makes 8 servings.

Per serving: 65 calories, 5 g fat, 1.5 g saturated fat, 5 mg cholesterol, 140 mg sodium, 4 g carbohydrates, 1 g protein, 66 mg calcium, 2 g fiber

Alice Waters' recipes adapted from *Chez Panisse Vegetables* (Harper-Collins, 1996).

roast like a pro

A few of our tips for a top holiday turkey:

ROAST the turkey on a flat or V-shaped adjustable rack in a heavy-duty, shallow open pan that's at least $2\frac{1}{2}$ inches deep.

IF A DEEPER PAN IS USED, the roasting time will be longer than for a shallow pan, so check for doneness in the thighs using a meat thermometer (the breast will probably be done sooner than the thighs).

IF USING A DISPOSABLE large foil roaster, the pan size should be approximately $16\frac{1}{2}\times12\times2\frac{1}{2}$ inches. To be sure the turkey gets enough support, use 2 disposable pans, or place in a single pan on a large cookie sheet.

lhj's classic thanksgiving turkey with gravy

Our step-by-step roasting instructions cook up a magnificent golden, juicy bird and a foolproof pan gravy. Pictured on pages 284 and 285. To gild the lily, try the Brined Turkey variation, page 295, from Alice Waters.

Prep time: 10 minutes plus standing
Roasting time: 3 hours 45 minutes to 4 hours 30 minutes

	Corn Bread Stuffing (see recipe, page 298)
1	whole turkey (10 to 18 lbs.), thawed if frozen
2	tablespoons butter, melted
2	teaspoons salt
$\frac{1}{2}$	teaspoon freshly ground pepper

PAN GRAVY:

$\frac{1}{4}$	cup all-purpose flour
	Chicken or turkey broth
	Salt and freshly ground pepper

1. Prepare Corn Bread Stuffing as directed.

2. Heat oven to 325°F. Remove neck and giblets from body and neck cavities of turkey. Rinse turkey and drain; pat dry. Loosely fill neck and body cavities with stuffing. Fold neck skin over back of turkey and fasten with skewers or toothpicks. Tie legs together with kitchen string.

3. Place stuffed turkey, breast side up, on a rack in a shallow roasting pan. Brush skin with melted butter and sprinkle with the salt and pepper.

4. Roast turkey $3\frac{3}{4}$ to $4\frac{1}{2}$ hours. When skin is golden brown, about two-thirds done ($2\frac{1}{2}$ to 3 hours), shield breast loosely with foil to prevent overbrowning.

5. Start testing for doneness one-half hour before end times. Insert metal stem section of an instant-read thermometer at least 2 inches into the inner thigh of the bird. Let stand 15 to 20 seconds, until temperature reaches 180°F. To test the stuffing for doneness, insert thermometer into the center part of stuffing and let stand 15 to 20 seconds, until the temperature is between 160°F. and 165°F. (If turkey needs more roasting, remove the thermometer before returning the bird to the oven, thoroughly washing the stem section in hot, soapy water after each use. Even if your turkey has a pop-up temperature device, the USDA recommends double-checking with another thermometer to be sure the turkey reached 180°F. for safety and doneness.)

6. Transfer turkey to a serving platter; cover loosely and let stand 20 minutes.

7. *Make pan gravy:* Scrape drippings from roasting pan into a glass measure. Let stand 5 minutes, until fat rises to the top. Skim off fat, reserving $\frac{1}{4}$ cup fat. (Note: Reserve any remaining fat if you want to make extra gravy.) Return reserved fat to pan. Stir in $\frac{1}{4}$ cup flour and cook over medium heat, stirring, 2 minutes. Add skimmed pan drippings plus enough chicken or turkey broth to equal 3 cups. Bring to boil and cook, stirring, 3 minutes. Season with salt and pepper to taste. (If you want extra gravy, double the recipe.)

8. Remove and discard skewers or toothpicks. Carve turkey. Serve with Corn Bread Stuffing and pan gravy. Makes 10 to 14 servings.

Per 3-oz. serving without stuffing: 690 calories, 34.5 g fat, 10.5 g saturated fat, 257 mg cholesterol, 924 mg sodium, 2 g carbohydrates, 86 g protein, 83 mg calcium, 0 g fiber

ALICE WATERS' BRINED TURKEY:

Prepare turkey as directed *except* do not stuff; place in a large stainless-steel pot. Add *2½ gallons cold water; 1²/3 cups kosher salt; 1 cup sugar; 5 sprigs each thyme and flat-leaf parsley; 5 allspice berries, crushed; 4 juniper berries, crushed; 1 teaspoon peppercorns, crushed; and a pinch red pepper flakes (see tip, page 95).* (There should be enough liquid to cover the turkey.) Brine turkey in the refrigerator 8 to 15 hours. Drain turkey well; stuff and roast as directed.

spiced cranberry- fruit sauce EASY

A heavenly condiment. Pictured on page 285.

Prep time: 10 minutes • Cooking time: 10 minutes

- 1   bag (12 oz.) fresh or frozen cranberries
- 1   Bartlett or Bosc pear, peeled, cored and diced
- 1   Granny Smith apple, peeled, cored and diced
- ¾   cup sugar
- 2   tablespoons water
- 2   tablespoons raspberry vinegar
- 1   tablespoon chopped crystallized ginger
-     Pinch anise seed
-     Pinch freshly ground pepper

Bring all ingredients to boil in a medium saucepan. Reduce heat and gently boil mixture 5 to 6 minutes, until thick and cranberries have popped but still have some shape. Cool completely. *(Can be made ahead. Transfer to an airtight container. Cover and refrigerate up to 1 week.)* Makes about 3 cups.

Per ¼ cup: 80 calories, 0 g fat, 0 g saturated fat, 0 mg cholesterol, 1 mg sodium, 21 g carbohydrates, 0 g protein, 5 mg calcium, 2 g fiber

pot roast with roasted vegetables

Fully cooked pot roasts have been popping up at the supermarket lately. On one of those hectic nights around the holidays, team the product with this easy recipe. You'll have a quick, comforting supper in less than an hour.

Prep time: 15 minutes • Roasting time: 35 to 37 minutes
Microwave used

- 2 **tablespoons butter or margarine**
- 2 **turnips (8 oz. each), peeled, halved and sliced ½ inch thick**
- 2 **medium potatoes (8 oz. each), peeled, halved and sliced ½ inch thick**
- 1 **(1½ lbs.) small butternut squash, peeled, cut in half lengthwise and sliced ½ inch thick**
- 1 **package fully cooked beef pot roast**
- 1 **teaspoon minced fresh thyme or parsley**
- ½ **teaspoon salt**
- ¼ **teaspoon freshly ground pepper**
   Cooked broccoli (optional)
   Fresh thyme sprigs, for garnish (optional)

1. Adjust oven racks to divide oven into thirds. Heat oven to 450°F. Divide butter into 2 equal pieces. Add one piece to each of 2 large jelly-roll or broiler pans; place pans in oven for 1 minute, until butter melts. Divide turnips between pans, toss with butter and spread in a single layer; roast 5 to 7 minutes. Divide potatoes and squash between pans; roast 30 minutes more, switching pans between racks halfway through roasting, until vegetables are tender.

2. Meanwhile, after 20 minutes, begin to heat pot roast in microwave as directed on package. Toss vegetables with thyme, salt and pepper. Slice beef and transfer to a serving platter. Spoon gravy over top. Serve with vegetables and, if desired, broccoli. Garnish with thyme, if desired. Makes 4 servings.

Per serving (figured with a 2-lb roast): 530 calories, 15.5 g total fat, 7.5 g saturated fat, 144 mg cholesterol, 1,125 mg sodium, 44 g carbohydrates, 54 g protein, 105 mg calcium, 6 g fiber

herb-roasted rack of pork

This savory pork roast is a delicious way to deviate from the holiday ham, turkey or roast beef. Ask the butcher to trim the fat and tie up the meat for you to make your prep work easier.

Prep time: 55 minutes plus standing
Roasting time: 1 hour to 1 hour 25 minutes

- 1 **rack of pork (11 ribs) with back bone removed (4½ to 5 lbs.)**
- 1 **teaspoon olive oil**
- 1½ **teaspoons salt**
- 1 **teaspoon cracked pepper**
- 4 **large sprigs fresh rosemary**
- 4 **large sprigs fresh thyme**
- 6 **bay leaves**
- 1 **can (14½ oz.) chicken broth**
- 2 **tablespoons cider vinegar**

1. Arrange oven rack in center of oven. Heat oven to 350°F. Cut rack of pork in half; trim excess fat from pork loin and trim rib bones of all extra meat. Tie the two halves together with kitchen string, intertwining the ribs. Cover rib bones with foil. Brush pork with oil and sprinkle with salt and pepper. On sides of loin, weave rosemary and thyme under string.

2. Arrange bay leaves in bottom of a shallow roasting pan; place pork in pan, rib-side up. Roast 1 hour to 1 hour 25 minutes, until meat thermometer inserted in center of loin registers 155°F. Transfer pork to a serving platter; cover with foil and let stand 10 minutes. Discard bay leaves.

3. Add chicken broth to roasting pan with drippings and cook over medium-high heat, scraping brown bits with wooden spoon, 5 minutes. Stir in vinegar and cook 3 minutes more. Transfer to a glass measure; spoon off fat.

4. Untie string from loin and remove foil from ribs. Slice pork between ribs and serve with pan drippings. Makes 8 servings.

Per serving: 320 calories, 15.5 g total fat, 5 g saturated fat, 104 mg cholesterol, 753 mg sodium, 1 g carbohydrate, 42 g protein, 19 mg calcium, 0 g fiber

the perfect prime rib roast *EASY*

This king of roasts will make a commanding centerpiece to your holiday dinner. Selecting the proper grade of meat is essential. Look for a USDA choice grade rib roast.

Prep time: 15 minutes
Roasting time: 2 hours 15 to 30 minutes plus standing

PRIME RIB:
- 1 (4-rib) beef rib roast with chine bone removed (about 7½ lbs.)
- 1 teaspoon kosher salt
- ½ teaspoon freshly ground pepper
- ½ teaspoon dried thyme

HORSERADISH CREAM:
- ½ cup sour cream
- 2 tablespoons grated fresh horseradish root or prepared horseradish
- 2 teaspoons chopped shallots
- 1 teaspoon white balsamic or white wine vinegar

1. Arrange oven rack in lower third of oven. Heat oven to 325°F. Trim beef rib roast of excess fat, leaving a thin layer.

2. Rub the roast with salt, pepper and thyme. Arrange roast, rib bones down, in a large shallow roasting pan. (Do not add water or cover pan.) Insert an ovenproof-dial meat thermometer so tip is centered in thickest part of rib roast, not resting in fat or touching the bone. (This thermometer will remain in the roast during the entire roasting time.)

3. Roast 2 hours 15 minutes to 2 hours and 30 minutes or until the meat thermometer's

temperature reaches 140°F. (If you're using an instant-read thermometer, insert the metal shaft into the thickest part of the roast, at least 2 inches into the meat. Let stand 20 seconds.)

4. Transfer roast to a carving board, and tent loosely with foil. Let stand 15 minutes. (Temperature will continue to rise 5 degrees to reach 145°F.) Carve roast. Makes 10 servings.

5. *Make horseradish cream:* Meanwhile, combine all horseradish cream ingredients in a small bowl. Refrigerate.

Per serving: 645 calories, 52.5 g total fat, 21.5 g saturated fat, 150 mg cholesterol, 262 mg sodium, 1 g carbohydrates, 39 g protein, 37 mg calcium, 0 g fiber

---

m e n u

holiday dinner for eight

BLUE CHEESE-WALNUT DIP WITH ASSORTED CRUDITÉS
page 289

OYSTERS IN GRUYÈRE SAUCE
page 291

EXOTIC MUSHROOM SOUP
page 292

THE PERFECT PRIME RIB ROAST
left

BLUE MASHED POTATOES
page 300

PEAS PARISIENNE
page 301

THE PERFECT PUMPKIN PIE
page 304

corn bread stuffing

Alice Waters' traditional corn bread stuffing recipe makes just the right amount to stuff an 8- to 10-pound turkey, but if you want some for leftovers, double the recipe. Pictured on pages 284 and 285.

Total prep time: 55 minutes plus standing

CORN BREAD:

- 1¼ cups yellow cornmeal
- ¾ cup all-purpose flour
- 1½ teaspoons baking powder
- 1½ tablespoons sugar
- 1 teaspoon salt
- 1 cup milk
- ½ cup plus 1 tablespoon butter, divided
- 1 large egg, beaten

- 2 tablespoons butter
- 1 cup chopped onions
- ½ cup diced carrot
- ½ cup diced celery
- 2 teaspoons fresh thyme leaves
- 1 bay leaf
- ¼ teaspoon salt
- ¼ teaspoon freshly ground pepper
- ½ cup chicken broth
- ¼ cup heavy or whipping cream

1. *Make corn bread:* Place an 8- or 9-inch cast-iron skillet in oven. Heat oven to 400°F.

2. Meanwhile, combine cornmeal, flour, baking powder, sugar and salt in a large bowl.

3. Heat milk and ½ cup of the butter in a saucepan over medium heat until butter melts. Whisk warm milk-butter mixture and egg in a bowl. Make a well in cornmeal-flour mixture; pour liquid mixture into well and stir just until combined. Remove hot skillet from oven. Add remaining 1 tablespoon butter to pan, swirling to evenly coat bottom of skillet. Pour in batter. Bake until a toothpick inserted in center of bread comes out clean, 12 to

16 minutes. Cool. Invert bread onto a cookie sheet; crumble into large pieces. Loosely cover and let stand overnight to dry.

4. Melt butter in a large skillet over medium heat. Stir in onions, carrot, celery, thyme, bay leaf, salt and pepper. Cook until vegetables soften. Transfer vegetables to bowl; discard bay leaf. Stir in crumbled corn bread, broth and cream. *(Can be made ahead. Cover and refrigerate up to 24 hours.)* Makes 5½ cups. Stuff into turkey as directed on page 294.

Per ½ cup: 195 calories, 12 g fat, 7 g saturated fat, 48 mg cholesterol, 409 mg sodium, 19 g carbohydrates, 3 g protein, 65 mg calcium, 1 g fiber

sautéed brussels sprouts EASY

"Brussels sprouts taste best when cooked quickly," says Alice Waters. "All they need is a quick wilting in butter or olive oil." So instead of boiling the sprouts whole, she slices them for this speedy skillet sauté. Pictured on page 285.

Prep time: 15 minutes • Cooking time: 12 to 17 minutes

- 2 tablespoons olive oil
- 1¼ pounds fresh Brussels sprouts, thinly sliced
- ½ cup chicken broth
- 2 tablespoons chopped parsley
- 2 teaspoons fresh lemon juice
- ½ teaspoon salt
- ¼ teaspoon freshly ground pepper

Heat oil in a large skillet over medium heat; add Brussels sprouts and broth. Cook, stirring, until tender, 10 to 15 minutes. Add parsley, lemon juice, salt and pepper; cook, stirring, 2 minutes more. *(Can be made ahead. Transfer vegetables to a medium microwaveproof bowl; cover and refrigerate up to 3 hours. Microwave on High until heated through, 5 to 6 minutes.)* Makes 4 cups.

Per ½ cup: 60 calories, 4 g fat, 0.5 g saturated fat, 0 mg cholesterol, 227 mg sodium, 7 g carbohydrates, 3 g protein, 31 mg calcium, 4 g fiber

celery root and potato puree

Leave it to Alice Waters to transform ordinary mashed potatoes into something special. Pictured on page 285.

Prep time: 25 minutes • Cooking time: 40 to 45 minutes

- 2   pounds medium celery root, peeled and cut into 1-inch chunks
- 1½ cups water
- ¾   cup butter (no substitutions)
- 4½ pounds yellow Finn, Yukon gold or red potatoes, peeled and cut into 1½-inch chunks
- 3   teaspoons salt, divided
- 6   tablespoons heavy cream
- 6   tablespoons milk
- ½   teaspoon white wine vinegar
- ¼   teaspoon freshly ground pepper

1. Bring celery root, the water and butter to boil in a large saucepan. Reduce heat; cover and gently boil 20 minutes. Uncover and gently boil 20 minutes more, until very tender and liquid is reduced to about ⅔ cup. Reserve cooking liquid.

2. Meanwhile, bring potatoes, enough cold water to cover and 1½ teaspoons of the salt to boil in a saucepot. Cover and boil until very tender, 20 minutes; drain. Working in batches, press potatoes and celery root with reserved liquid through a ricer into a bowl or use a potato masher.

3. Heat cream and milk in saucepan until warm. Beat cream mixture, remaining 1½ teaspoons salt, the vinegar and pepper into potatoes and celery root; mash with a wooden spoon. *(Can be made ahead. Cool. Transfer to a microwaveproof bowl; cover and refrigerate up to 24 hours. Let stand at room temperature 1½ hours. Microwave on High for 4 minutes, stirring once halfway through, until heated.)* Transfer mixture to a serving bowl. Makes 10½ cups.

Per ½ cup: 160 calories, 8.5 g fat, 5 g saturated fat, 24 mg cholesterol, 445 mg sodium, 19 g carbohydrates, 2 g protein, 25 mg calcium, 1 g fiber

winter squash with sage butter (EASY)

Winter squashes are often served when in season at Chez Panisse, Alice Waters' renowned restaurant in Berkeley, California. Pictured on page 284.

Prep time: 20 minutes plus standing
Baking time: 45 minutes

- 4½ to 5 pounds winter squash (such as butternut, acorn, hubbard or kabocha)
- 2   tablespoons olive oil
- 1½ teaspoons salt, divided
- ½   teaspoon freshly ground pepper
- 3   tablespoons butter
- ⅓   cup sliced shallots
- 2   tablespoons chopped fresh sage leaves or 1 teaspoon dried sage

1. Arrange oven rack in lower third of oven. Heat oven to 400°F. Line a large jelly-roll pan with foil; set aside. Cut squash into 2-inch-thick pieces; transfer to a large bowl. Add oil, ½ teaspoon of the salt and the pepper; toss. Arrange squash, skin side down, on prepared pan. Bake 30 minutes. Turn pieces over and bake until squash can easily be pierced with a knife, 15 minutes more. Let stand until cool enough to handle. Remove skin with a small paring knife; transfer squash to a large bowl and gently stir with a spoon until coarsely mashed.

2. Meanwhile, melt butter in a small skillet over medium heat. Add shallots; cook until they soften and just begin to color, 5 minutes. Stir in sage and cook 2 minutes more. Add sage-butter mixture and remaining 1 teaspoon salt to squash. *(Can be made ahead. Transfer squash to a medium microwaveproof bowl; cover. Cover and refrigerate up to 24 hours. Microwave on High until heated through, 4 to 5 minutes.)* Makes 8 servings.

Per ½ cup: 145 calories, 8 g fat, 3 g saturated fat, 12 mg cholesterol, 488 mg sodium, 18 g carbohydrates, 3 g protein, 65 mg calcium, 4 g fiber

Alice Waters' recipes adapted from *Chez Panisse Vegetables* (Harper-Collins, 1996).

what a spud!

To bring something unexpected to your holiday spread, check out the two potato recipes on these pages. They call for popular potato varieties popping up in markets all over, including:

YUKON GOLD: gold flesh, firm texture.

ROUND RED: thin skinned with firm, moist and waxy texture.

BLUE: blue skin and blue flesh; moist texture.

FINGERLING VARIETIES include Austrian Crescent, with light brown skin and light yellow flesh; Rosevale, with red and yellow flesh; and Ruby Crescent, with tawny skin and yellow flesh.

blue mashed potatoes

We added plenty of butter and shallots to purple-blue spuds, and a dollop of sour cream to keep them extra creamy. A mash of a different color—yes, they're definitely blue—but definitely delicious, too!

Prep time: 15 minutes • Cooking time: 20 to 22 minutes

2½	pounds blue or red-skinned potatoes, peeled and quartered
1½	teaspoons salt, divided
5	tablespoons butter or margarine, divided
¼	cup chopped shallots
½	cup milk
½	cup sour cream
¼	teaspoon freshly ground pepper

1. Bring potatoes, 1 teaspoon of the salt and enough cold water to cover by 2 inches to boil in a large saucepan. Reduce heat and simmer, covered, 18 to 20 minutes, until potatoes are fork-tender.

2. Meanwhile, melt 4 tablespoons of the butter in a small skillet over medium heat. Add shallots; cook until shallots are lightly golden and softened, about 5 minutes. Set aside.

3. Drain potatoes. Return to saucepan and cook 1 to 2 minutes over low heat to dry. Coarsely mash potatoes with a potato masher or large wooden spoon. Stir in shallot mixture, milk, sour cream, remaining ½ teaspoon salt and the pepper, mashing over low heat until well combined and heated through. Cut up remaining 1 tablespoon butter and swirl into potatoes. Transfer to a serving bowl. Makes 5 cups.

Per ½ cup: 170 calories, 9 g total fat, 5.5 g saturated fat, 23 mg cholesterol, 369 mg sodium, 20 g carbohydrates, 3 g protein, 32 mg calcium, 2 g fiber

roasted fingerlings

Roasting intensifies the richness of potatoes, especially sweet fingerlings, named for their shape and size.

Prep time: 5 minutes • Roasting time: 30 to 35 minutes

2	pounds fingerling potatoes (Rosevale, Ruby Crescent, Austrian Crescent), scrubbed, or Yukon Gold or red potatoes, scrubbed and cut into quarters
2	tablespoons olive oil
1	tablespoon chopped fresh rosemary leaves
½	teaspoon kosher salt
¼	teaspoon freshly ground pepper

Heat oven to 425°F. Pat potatoes dry with paper towels. Transfer to a jelly-roll pan and toss with oil and rosemary. Roast until golden and tender when pierced with tip of knife, 30 to 35 minutes. Transfer to a serving bowl and sprinkle with salt and pepper. Serve immediately. Makes 4 to 6 servings.

Per serving: 195 calories, 5.5 g total fat, 1 g saturated fat, 0 mg cholesterol, 161 mg sodium, 33 g carbohydrates, 3.5 g protein, 2 mg calcium, 3 g fiber

peas parisienne

For our holiday chapter, we couldn't resist including this delicious vegetable dish from France. It's a lovely combination of sweet peas (we use frozen for ease), chopped romaine lettuce, garlic and thyme. Pictured on page 284.

Prep time: 10 minutes • Cooking time: 12 to 18 minutes

- 2 **tablespoons butter**
- 1 **cup finely chopped onions**
- 1 **tablespoon finely chopped garlic**
- 1 **teaspoon fresh thyme leaves or**
  - ¼ **teaspoon dried thyme**
- 1 **package (16 oz.) frozen peas**
- ¼ **teaspoon freshly ground pepper**
  - **Pinch nutmeg**
- 1 **cup chicken broth**
- 2½ **cups chopped romaine lettuce**

1. Melt butter in a small Dutch oven over medium heat. Stir in onions, garlic and thyme. Cook until onions soften and begin to color slightly, 5 to 8 minutes.

2. Stir in peas, pepper and nutmeg, gently breaking up peas with a wooden spoon. Add broth and bring to boil. Simmer peas until heated through, 5 to 8 minutes. Add lettuce and cook until lettuce is wilted, 2 minutes more. *(Can be made ahead. Transfer to a microwaveproof bowl; cover and refrigerate up to 3 hours. Microwave on High until heated through, 4 to 5 minutes.)* Transfer to a serving bowl. Makes 4 cups.

Per ½ cup: 85 calories, 3.5 g fat, 2 g saturated fat, 8 mg cholesterol, 223 mg sodium, 10 g carbohydrates, 4 g protein, 25 mg calcium, 3 g fiber

turkey and white bean stew

No holiday chapter would be complete without a great idea for leftover turkey.

Prep time: 20 minutes • Cooking time: 49 minutes

- 3 **slices thick-cut bacon**
- 1 **tablespoon olive oil**
- ½ **cup chopped onion**
- 1 **tablespoon chopped garlic**
- 1 **teaspoon chopped jalapeño chile with seeds**
  - **(see tip, page 95)**
- ½ **cup chopped carrots**
- ½ **cup chopped celery with leaves**
- ¾ **teaspoon salt**
- 1 **can (19 oz.) cannellini beans, drained and rinsed**
- ½ **cup chopped canned tomatoes**
- 2 **cans (14½ oz. each) chicken broth**
- 2 **cups cooked turkey cut into ½-inch pieces**
- ¼ **pound green beans, cut diagonally into 1-inch pieces**
- 1 **potato (7 oz.), peeled and shredded**
- 2 **cups chopped escarole or spinach**

1. Cook bacon in a small Dutch oven until crisp; drain. Crumble and set aside. Discard fat.

2. Heat oil over medium heat in Dutch oven. Add onion, garlic and jalapeño; cook until onion softens. Add carrots, celery and salt; cook until softened slightly, 5 minutes. Stir in cannellini beans and tomatoes; cook until mixture thickens slightly and tomatoes are heated through, 3 to 5 minutes. Add broth and turkey; bring mixture to boil. Reduce heat; cover and simmer 20 minutes. Add green beans and potato; simmer uncovered, 10 minutes. Add escarole and cook until tender, 3 to 4 minutes more. (If using spinach, cook 1 minute.)

3. Divide stew into 4 shallow bowls. Sprinkle the top of each with reserved bacon. Serves 4.

Per serving: 380 calories, 13 g fat, 3.5 g saturated fat, 61 mg cholesterol, 1,735 mg sodium, 31 g carbohydrates, 34 g protein, 101 mg calcium, 8 g fiber

kahlúa pot de crème

French for "pot of cream," this custard dessert makes for an elegant finish to a holiday dinner party for eight.

Prep time: 10 minutes plus standing and chilling
Baking time: 25 to 27 minutes

- 1⅔ **cups milk**
- ½ **cinnamon stick**
- 4 **large egg yolks**
- ⅓ **cup sugar**
- ¼ **cup Kahlúa (coffee-flavored liqueur)**
  Grated bittersweet chocolate, for garnish (optional)
  Fresh berries, for garnish (optional)

1. Heat oven to 325°F. Bring milk and cinnamon to boil over medium heat in a saucepan. Remove from heat. Cover and let stand 20 minutes. Strain mixture through a sieve into a 4-cup glass measure. Discard cinnamon.

2. Arrange eight ovenproof espresso or 4-ounce cups in a roasting pan. Beat yolks and sugar in a mixer bowl on medium speed, until mixture is pale yellow and thick, 3 to 5 minutes. Add Kahlúa; beat until well combined. Gradually stir in milk with a rubber spatula, until mixture is completely smooth.

3. Strain milk mixture through a sieve into a glass measure. Discard foam. Divide mixture into each cup (spoon off any remaining foam). Add enough hot water to roasting pan to reach halfway up the sides of cups. Loosely cover pan with foil.

4. Bake until the edge of the custards are set, 25 to 27 minutes (the centers will be jiggly). Remove cups from the water and cool to room temperature on a wire rack, 15 to 20 minutes. Cover and refrigerate overnight. *(Can be made ahead. Refrigerate up to 2 days.)* Sprinkle tops with grated chocolate and serve with berries, if desired. Makes 8 servings.

Per serving: 100 calories, 4 g total fat, 2 g saturated fat, 113 mg cholesterol, 29 mg sodium, 13 g carbohydrates, 3 g protein, 73 mg calcium, 0 g fiber

poached pears in red wine

The quintessential autumn and winter fruit makes for a light but elegant finish to a holiday happening when simmered in our vanilla-infused wine sauce.

Prep time: 15 minutes plus standing and chilling
Cooking time: 25 minutes

- 6 **pears (2½ lbs.) (such as Bartlett or Anjou), peeled with stems intact**
- 1 **bottle (750 ml) Beaujolais wine**
- ½ **cup crème de cassis (black currant-flavored liqueur)**
- ½ **cup sugar**
- 3 **tablespoons fresh lemon juice**
- 1 **vanilla bean, split lengthwise or 2 teaspoons vanilla extract**
- 12 **whole black peppercorns**
- 1 **sprig fresh thyme**
  Fresh thyme sprigs, for garnish (optional)

1. Combine pears, wine, crème de cassis, sugar, lemon juice, vanilla bean, peppercorns and the 1 sprig thyme in a Dutch oven that's large enough to almost cover the pears with liquid. Bring liquid to boil. Reduce heat and simmer pears until tender, turning occasionally, about 25 minutes.

2. Let pears cool in liquid. Transfer pears and liquid to a large bowl; cover and refrigerate overnight. Using a slotted spoon, arrange pears, stem end up, in shallow dessert bowls. Spoon liquid over fruit. Garnish with thyme sprigs, if desired. Makes 6 servings.

Per serving: 131 calories, 0.5 g fat, 0 g saturated fat, 0 mg cholesterol, 7 mg sodium, 31 g carbohydrates, 1 g protein, 16 mg calcium, 4 g fiber

free-form apple pie

For our Thanksgiving dessert spread, Maida Heatter lent us this recipe for a gorgeous dessert that's every bit as delicious as a standard double-crust apple pie—but easier to make. For more great recipes from this dessert diva, see pages 306 and 307.

Prep time: 30 minutes plus chilling
Baking time: 45 minutes

PASTRY:
- 1¼ cups all-purpose flour
- 1 tablespoon sugar
- ½ teaspoon salt
- ½ cup cold butter, cut up (no substitutions)
- 3 to 4 tablespoons ice water

FILLING:
- ¼ cup butter (no substitutions)
- ¾ cup sugar
- 1 tablespoon brandy, cognac or water
- 3 to 3½ pounds (6 to 7 large) Granny Smith apples, peeled, cored and cut into eighths
- ⅓ cup raisins
- ½ cup toasted walnuts, coarsely chopped

GLAZE:
- ½ cup apricot preserves

1. *Make pastry:* Combine flour, sugar and salt in a bowl. Cut in butter until mixture resembles coarse crumbs. Add water, tossing with a fork, until pastry holds together. Shape pastry into a ball and flatten into a thick disk. Wrap and refrigerate 1 hour. *(Can be made ahead. Refrigerate up to 24 hours.)*

2. *Make filling:* Melt butter in a 12-inch skillet over medium heat. Increase heat to high; add sugar and brandy. Stir in apples; cover and cook 3 minutes, stirring apples twice. Uncover; add raisins. Cook apples, stirring, until tender and liquid evaporates, about 6 minutes more. Cool apples completely. Stir in nuts.

3. Heat oven to 425°F. Meanwhile, on a lightly floured surface, roll out pastry into a 14-inch circle. Transfer pastry to a large cookie sheet. Arrange apple mixture on pastry, leaving a 2- to 2½-inch border around the edge. Fold edge of pastry over apple mixture. (The pie should be about 9 inches in diameter.) Bake 15 minutes. Reduce oven temperature to 400°F. and bake 30 minutes more, until crust is golden brown.

4. *Make glaze:* Melt preserves in a small saucepan over medium heat. Strain preserves through a sieve into a cup; drizzle over filling. Cool on cookie sheet. Transfer to a serving platter when cool. *(Can be made ahead. Transfer pie to a foil-lined baking sheet. Freeze 1 hour until firm, then wrap well and freeze up to 1 week. Unwrap pie. Thaw at room temperature 1¼ hours. Reheat in a 350°F. oven 20 minutes.)* Serve pie warm. Makes 6 to 8 servings.

Per serving: 580 calories, 26 g fat, 13 g saturated fat, 53 mg cholesterol, 378 mg sodium, 88 g carbohydrates, 4 g protein, 33 mg calcium, 5 g fiber

Adapted from *Maida Heatter's Best Dessert Book Ever* (Random House, 1990).

---

test kitchen tip

flour power

Bleached flour or unbleached? Sift or stir? Here are some hints:

BLEACHED FLOUR is, as the name suggests, whiter in color than unbleached flour because it's been chemically whitened. Though both bleached and unbleached can be used whenever all-purpose flour is called for, some cookie bakers prefer bleached all-purpose flour because it makes baked goods more tender. It also contains a dough conditioner that eases rolling.

FOR MORE ACCURATE MEASURING choose pre-sifted all-purpose flour. Stir flour to aerate while it is still in the canister or package, then spoon into a nested plastic or metal cup. Level off excess with a metal spatula or knife.

the perfect
pumpkin pie

*What makes ours the ultimate pumpkin pie? We've
made the traditional filling even more luscious by using
heavy cream, so that each bite has a smooth, custard-like
texture. In addition to nostalgic hints of nutmeg and
cinnamon, there's a pinch of black pepper for extra
pizzazz. Pictured on page 286.*

Prep time: 20 minutes plus chilling and freezing
Baking time: 45 minutes

PASTRY:

- 1¼   **cups all-purpose flour**
- 1   **tablespoon sugar**
- ¼   **teaspoon salt**
- 5   **tablespoons cold butter or margarine, cut up**
- 3   **tablespoons cold vegetable shortening, cut up**
- 3   **to 4 tablespoons ice water**

FILLING:

- 3   **large eggs**
- ¾   **cup sugar**
- 1   **teaspoon vanilla extract**
- 1   **can (16 oz.) solid-pack pumpkin**
- 1   **teaspoon cinnamon**
- 1   **teaspoon ginger**
- ¼   **teaspoon salt**
- ¼   **teaspoon freshly ground pepper**
-    **Pinch nutmeg**
-    **Pinch ground cloves**
- 1   **cup heavy or whipping cream**

-    **Whipped cream and cinnamon, for garnish
     (optional)**

1. *Make pastry:* Pulse flour, sugar and salt in a food
processor to combine. Add butter and shortening;
pulse until mixture resembles coarse crumbs. Add ice
water, 1 tablespoon at a time, through feed tube,
pulsing until mixture just begins to hold together.
Shape pastry into a ball and flatten into a thick disk.
Wrap in plastic wrap and refrigerate 40 minutes.
*(Can be made ahead. Refrigerate up to 2 days.
Let stand at room temperature 10 minutes before
rolling out.)*

2. Arrange rack in bottom third of oven. Heat oven
to 425°F. On a lightly floured surface, roll pastry
into a 12-inch circle. Fit into a 9-inch pie plate.
Trim edge and flute. Place in freezer for 15 minutes.

3. *Make filling:* Whisk together eggs, sugar and
vanilla in a large bowl until well combined; gently
whisk in pumpkin, cinnamon, ginger, salt, pepper,
nutmeg and cloves until smooth. Stir in heavy
cream with a rubber spatula. Pour into prepared
crust. Bake 15 minutes. Reduce oven temperature
to 350°F. Bake until filling is set, 30 minutes. If
pastry edge gets too dark, cover edge with foil.
Cool on a wire rack. *(Can be made ahead. Cover
and refrigerate up to 24 hours. Let stand at room
temperature 4 hours before serving.)* Garnish with
whipped cream and cinnamon, if desired. Serves 8.

Per serving: 410 calories, 25 g total fat, 13 g saturated fat,
140 mg cholesterol, 255 mg sodium, 41 g carbohydrates,
6 g protein, 53 mg calcium, 2 g fiber

mixed nut strudel

*Our filling combines four kinds of rich nuts, all wrapped
up in thin, flaky phyllo dough. Pictured on page 286.*

Prep time: 40 minutes plus freezing
Baking time: 25 to 30 minutes

FILLING:

- ¾   **cup walnuts**
- ¾   **cup pecans**
- ¾   **cup whole blanched almonds**
- ¾   **cup hazelnuts**
- ½   **cup light corn syrup**
- 1   **large egg yolk**
- 1   **tablespoon butter, melted (no substitutions)**
- 2   **teaspoons vanilla extract**
- 1   **teaspoon cardamom**
- 3   **large egg whites, at room temperature**

- 6   **tablespoons sugar**
- ¼   **teaspoon cinnamon**
- 8   **sheets phyllo**
- ½   **cup butter, melted (no substitutions)**
- 1   **tablespoon butter, melted (no substitutions)**

1 large egg yolk, lightly beaten
Orange Custard Sauce (recipe follows)

1. *Make filling:* Heat oven to 350°F. Spread walnuts, pecans and almonds in a single layer on a large jelly-roll pan, and spread hazelnuts on a small jelly-roll pan or cookie sheet. Bake nuts 10 minutes, until toasted (hazelnut skins should be crackly). Wrap hazelnuts in a clean kitchen towel and let stand 5 minutes; rub nuts in towel to remove skin. Cool all the nuts completely.

2. Process half of the nuts, the corn syrup, egg yolk, butter, vanilla and cardamom in a food processor until most nuts are finely chopped and mixture holds together (some larger pieces of nuts should still be visible). Beat the egg whites in a medium bowl on medium speed, just to stiff peaks. Fold into nut mixture. Place filling in freezer 30 to 40 minutes, until stiff but not frozen. Coarsely chop remaining nuts. Remove 2 tablespoons and chop slightly smaller for topping. Set both aside.

3. Combine sugar and cinnamon in a small bowl; set aside 2 teaspoons in a cup for topping. Arrange phyllo on a flat surface. Remove 1 sheet phyllo and place with long side facing you (keep remaining phyllo covered with a sheet of plastic wrap). Brush phyllo with some of the melted ½ cup butter; sprinkle with scant 1 tablespoon cinnamon-sugar. Repeat three more times, laying phyllo sheets on top of each other. Spoon half the nut filling 1 inch from long edge of phyllo facing you and shape into a 2½-inch-wide log, leaving a 1-inch border on short ends. Sprinkle filling with half the reserved coarsely chopped nuts. Fold in short ends, then carefully roll up. Repeat process to make a second roll with remaining phyllo, butter, cinnamon-sugar, filling and coarsely chopped nuts. Arrange rolls 4 inches apart on a large ungreased cookie sheet. Brush tops of rolls with the 1 tablespoon butter, then with beaten yolk. For topping, sprinkle with reserved 2 tablespoons chopped nuts, then reserved 2 teaspoons cinnamon-sugar.

4. Bake rolls 25 to 30 minutes, until golden. Cool on pan on a wire rack. *(Can be made ahead. Wrap well and store at room temperature overnight.*

Unwrap and reheat in a 350°F. oven 10 minutes.) Cut each roll crosswise into ten 1¼-inch-thick slices. Serve warm or at room temperature with Orange Custard Sauce. Makes 20 servings.

Per serving without custard sauce: 235 calories, 17.5 g total fat, 4.5 g saturated fat, 37 mg cholesterol, 115 mg sodium, 17 g carbohydrates, 4 g protein, 33 mg calcium, 1 g fiber

orange custard sauce

Here's our luscious choice for topping the above recipe.

Prep time: 10 minutes • Cooking time: 6 minutes

1 cup heavy or whipping cream
1 cup milk
1 (2-inch) strip orange peel
5 large egg yolks
⅓ cup sugar
⅛ teaspoon cinnamon

1. Heat cream, milk and orange peel in a medium saucepan until small bubbles appear around edge of pan. Remove peel and set peel and mixture aside.

2. Meanwhile, beat yolks and sugar in a large mixer bowl until thick and light-colored, about 3 minutes.

3. Gradually beat the hot cream mixture into yolk mixture; beat in cinnamon. Return to saucepan with orange peel. Cook over medium heat, stirring, until mixture thickens and temperature registers 170°F. on an instant-read thermometer, about 2 minutes. (Mixture should be slightly thicker than heavy cream.) Immediately pour custard through a fine sieve set over a medium bowl. Cool completely. *(Can be made ahead. Transfer to an airtight container and refrigerate up to 24 hours.)* Makes 3 cups.

Per 2 tablespoons: 75 calories, 6 g total fat, 3.5 g saturated fat, 71 mg cholesterol, 12 mg sodium, 4 g carbohydrates, 1 g protein, 28 mg calcium, 0 g fiber

kentucky pound cake

Sure to become a holiday favorite, this big brown-sugar pound cake comes to us from Maida Heatter, author of seven best-selling cookbooks. Serve the bourbon-infused cake in thin slices. Pictured on page 287.

Prep time: 20 minutes • Baking time: 1 hour 20 to 25 minutes

CAKE:

- **3¼ cups all-purpose flour**
- **1½ teaspoons baking powder**
- **1½ cups butter, softened (no substitutions)**
- **1 tablespoon vanilla extract**
- **½ teaspoon mace or nutmeg**
- **3¼ cups firmly packed brown sugar**
- **5 large eggs**
- **¾ cup milk**
- **¼ cup bourbon**

GLAZE:

- **⅓ cup granulated sugar**
- **¼ cup bourbon**

1. Adjust oven rack to lower third of oven. Heat oven to 350°F. Grease a 10×4-inch tube pan. Sprinkle pan with flour, tapping out excess.

2. Sift together flour and baking powder in a medium bowl. Beat butter, vanilla and mace in a large mixer bowl on medium-high speed, until smooth. At low speed, beat in brown sugar until blended. Increase speed to medium-high and beat mixture 3 to 4 minutes until creamy, scraping sides of bowl. Add eggs, one at a time, beating well after each addition.

3. Combine milk and bourbon in a glass measure. At low speed, beat in milk mixture, alternately with flour mixture, beginning and ending with flour mixture, scraping bowl twice, until batter is smooth.

4. Pour batter evenly into prepared pan. Bake 1 hour and 20 to 25 minutes, until a toothpick inserted in center of cake comes out clean. Cool cake in pan on a wire rack 15 minutes. Run a knife around edge of pan and invert cake onto rack, then invert cake again, right side up.

5. *Make glaze:* Meanwhile, combine sugar and bourbon in a small saucepan. Cook until sugar dissolves. Brush warm glaze over warm cake. Cool. *(Can be made ahead. Wrap well and freeze up to 2 weeks. Unwrap and let stand at room temperature 4 to 5 hours before serving.)* Makes 16 servings.

Per serving: 475 calories, 20 g fat, 11.5 g saturated fat, 115 mg cholesterol, 265 mg sodium, 68 g carbohydrates, 5 g protein, 94 mg calcium, 1 g fiber

Adapted from *Maida Heatter's Book of Great Desserts* (Andrews McMeel Publishing, 1999).

carrot cake

This recipe is also from Maida Heatter, who loves to serve carrot cake at Thanksgiving. Try it once, and it may become a regular feature on your holiday table. Pictured on page 287.

Prep time: 40 minutes plus freezing
Baking time: 35 to 40 minutes

CAKE:

- **1 cup raisins**
- **2 cups minus 2 tablespoons all-purpose flour**
- **1 tablespoon unsweetened cocoa**
- **2 teaspoons baking powder**
- **2 teaspoons cinnamon**
- **1 teaspoon baking soda**
- **1 teaspoon salt**
- **4 large eggs**
- **2 teaspoons vanilla extract**
- **1 cup granulated sugar**
- **1 cup firmly packed dark brown sugar**
- **1¼ cups corn or vegetable oil**
- **4 cups firmly packed grated carrots (1½ lbs.)**
- **1½ cups chopped walnuts**

FROSTING:

- **2 packages (8 oz. each) cream cheese, softened**
- **¼ cup butter, softened (no substitutions)**
- **1 teaspoon vanilla extract**
- **2 cups sifted confectioners' sugar**

1. Adjust oven racks to center and upper third of oven. Heat oven to 350°F. Grease three 9-inch round cake pans. Line bottoms with waxed paper; grease paper. Sprinkle paper lightly with flour, shaking out excess. Set aside.

2. *Make cake:* Place raisins in a strainer set over shallow water in a medium saucepan. Cover and bring water to boil; steam raisins 10 minutes. Set raisins aside. Combine flour, cocoa, baking powder, cinnamon, baking soda and salt in a bowl. Beat eggs in a large mixer bowl on medium speed, until blended. Beat in vanilla, both sugars and oil until well combined. At low speed, add flour mixture and beat just until blended. Stir in raisins, carrots and nuts. Divide and spoon batter into prepared pans. Place 2 pans on 1 oven rack and 1 pan in the center of the other rack. Bake until tops of cakes spring back and edges begin to pull away from sides of pans, 35 to 40 minutes. Cool in pans on wire racks 10 minutes. Invert and remove pans; peel off paper. Invert cakes again, right side up, on racks and cool completely. Place layers in freezer 1 hour, until firm.

3. *Make frosting:* Beat cream cheese and butter in a mixer bowl on medium-high speed until smooth. At low speed, beat in vanilla and confectioners' sugar, until well combined. Increase speed to high and beat until mixture is smooth. Transfer 1 layer to a large serving plate; spread top with one-third of the frosting. Repeat with remaining layers and frosting. *(Can be made ahead. Freeze cake uncovered 1 hour, until frosting is firm, then wrap well and freeze up to 2 weeks. Thaw in refrigerator overnight. Let stand at room temperature 4 to 5 hours before serving.)* Makes 12 servings.

Per serving: 835 calories, 52 g fat, 15 g saturated fat, 123 mg cholesterol, 584 mg sodium, 87 g carbohydrates, 10 g protein, 144 mg calcium, 4 g fiber

Adapted from *Maida Heatter's Cakes* (Andrews McMeel Publishing, 1998).

cornmeal cat's tongues

These dainty, crunchy cornmeal cookies are a favorite of Maida Heatter's—she calls them the cat's meow! Pictured on page 287.

Prep time: 30 minutes
Baking time: 14 to 15 minutes per batch

1¾	**cups all-purpose flour**
⅔	**cup yellow cornmeal**
¾	**cup plus 2 tablespoons butter, softened**
¾	**cup sugar**
1	**teaspoon vanilla extract**
½	**teaspoon salt**
2	**large eggs**

1. Arrange oven racks on upper and lower third of oven. Heat oven to 350°F. Line 2 cookie sheets with parchment paper. Sift flour three times into a large bowl; stir in cornmeal. Set aside.

2. Beat butter, sugar, vanilla and salt in a large mixer bowl on medium-high speed, until well combined. Add eggs, one at a time, beating well after each addition. Scrape bowl with a rubber spatula and beat mixture until blended. At low speed, slowly add flour mixture; scrape sides of bowl again with rubber spatula and beat mixture until just blended.

3. Spoon one-third of dough into a large pastry bag fitted with a ³/₈-inch plain round tip. Pipe dough into 3×½-inch sticks, 1 inch apart, on prepared sheets. Bake 7 minutes; switch cookie sheets between racks and bake 7 to 8 minutes more, until cookies have golden edges. Transfer cookies to wire racks and cool. Repeat with remaining dough. *(Can be made ahead. Transfer cookies to an airtight container and freeze up to 1 month. Thaw at room temperature 2 hours.)* Makes about 10 dozen.

Per cookie: 25 calories, 1.5 g fat, 1 g saturated fat, 7 mg cholesterol, 24 mg sodium, 3 g carbohydrates, 0 g protein, 1 mg calcium, 0 g fiber

Adapted from *Maida Heatter's Book of Great Desserts* (Andrews McMeel Publishing, 1999).

the perfect
holiday
coffeecake

One recipe makes two cakes, so enjoy one at Christmas and enjoy the other after the festivities have subsided.

Prep time: 20 minutes plus rising
Baking time: 25 to 28 minutes

DOUGH:

2	packages rapid-rise yeast
	Pinch sugar
½	cup warm water (105°F. to 115°F.)
5¾	to 6⅓ cups all-purpose flour, divided
½	cup sugar
1½	teaspoons salt
1	teaspoon cardamom
½	cup butter or margarine
1	cup lukewarm milk
2	large eggs, at room temperature
1	large egg yolk, at room temperature

CHEESE FILLING:

1½	cups mascarpone; or 1½ cups (12 oz.) cream cheese, softened, plus 2 tablespoons sour cream
¼	cup sugar
2	large egg yolks
2	tablespoons all-purpose flour
1	teaspoon grated orange peel
2	cans (15¼ to 16½ oz. each) apricot halves, pitted sweet cherries or plum halves in syrup, drained and patted dry
1	large egg, lightly beaten
1	tablespoon melted butter or margarine
2	to 3 tablespoons crystallized sugar

1. *Make dough:* Sprinkle yeast and sugar over warm water in a measuring cup. Stir. Let stand just until foamy, 2 to 3 minutes. Meanwhile, whisk together 2 cups of the flour, the sugar, salt and cardamom in a large bowl. With a pastry blender or 2 knives cut butter into flour mixture, until mixture resembles coarse crumbs. Whisk together lukewarm milk, the 2 eggs and egg yolk in a medium bowl until blended; whisk in yeast mixture. Stir milk mixture into flour mixture with a wooden spoon until combined. Gradually stir in 3¾ to 4 cups flour, until dough begins to pull away from sides of bowl. On a lightly floured surface, knead dough, adding ⅓ cup flour as needed until smooth and elastic, 7 to 10 minutes. Generously butter a large bowl. Add dough and turn to coat. Cover and let rise in a warm, draft-free place, until doubled in bulk, 50 to 60 minutes.

2. *Make cheese filling:* Meanwhile, beat all cheese filling ingredients in a small bowl until smooth. Cover and refrigerate.

3. Transfer dough to a lightly floured surface; cut in half and let stand 10 minutes. Lightly grease two large cookie sheets and line with parchment. Cut a ½-cup piece of dough from each half of dough; set aside. Transfer each remaining piece of dough to a prepared sheet. Press each piece into a 16×9-inch rectangle. Divide and spread cheese filling into a lengthwise strip 4 inches wide down center of each rectangle, leaving a 1-inch border at each short end. Divide and arrange fruit in a single layer on cheese filling. With a sharp knife cut twelve slits in dough on a 30-degree angle along each side of filling, forming strips about 1 inch wide. Leaving 2 parallel strips on top and bottom of dough flat, gently stretch remaining strips across filling, alternating from side to side and pressing gently; then fold short ends over filling and tuck ends underneath.

4. Cut one reserved piece of dough in half. Roll each half into a 16-inch-long rope. Pinch together one end of each rope and twist ropes together. Repeat with remaining reserved dough. Arrange each twisted rope down center of each loaf; pinch lightly on each end to seal. Cover loaves and let rise until almost doubled in bulk, 50 to 60 minutes.

5. Meanwhile, arrange oven racks in middle and lower third of oven; heat oven to 350°F. Uncover loaves. Brush beaten egg over loaves (avoid egg dripping onto parchment), then brush with melted butter. Sprinkle tops with crystallized sugar. Bake

15 minutes; switch pans between racks. Bake 10 to 13 minutes more, until deep golden brown. Cool on pans on wire racks 20 minutes. Transfer to a serving platter or board. Serve warm or cool completely. *(Can be made ahead. Wrap loaves tightly in foil and freeze up to 1 week. Let stand at room temperature 3 hours. Bake in a 350°F. oven 10 minutes. Open foil to expose tops of loaves and bake 10 minutes more, until heated through.)* Makes 10 to 12 servings per loaf.

Per serving: 320 calories, 14 g fat, 8.5 g saturated fat, 86 mg cholesterol, 232 mg sodium, 42 g carbohydrates, 7 g protein, 65 mg calcium, 1 g fiber

french macaroons

Be sure to beat the egg whites to very stiff peaks—use a standing mixer for best results.

Prep time: 55 minutes plus decorating and standing
Baking time: 5 to 7 minutes per batch

1	**cup whole blanched almonds**
2	**tablespoons firmly packed brown sugar**
1¾	**cups confectioners' sugar, divided**
¾	**teaspoon vanilla extract, divided**
⅛	**teaspoon almond extract**
3	**large egg whites**
¼	**teaspoon cream of tartar**
⅛	**teaspoon green paste food color**
¼	**cup butter, softened (no substitutions)**
3	**ounces semisweet chocolate squares, melted (see tip, page 265) and cooled**

1. Adjust oven rack to center of oven. Heat oven to 450°F. Line three large cookie sheets with foil; grease foil with vegetable shortening. Process almonds, brown sugar and ½ cup of the confectioners' sugar in a food processor until almonds are ground to a powder. Sift almond powder through a coarse sieve into a large bowl, pressing with a wooden spoon to sift as much nut mixture through the sieve as possible. (If there are any almond pieces in sieve, set aside in bowl for buttercream. You may have about 2 tablespoons.) Sift ½ cup confectioners' sugar into almond powder; stir until well blended. Add ¼ cup almond mixture to reserved almond pieces in bowl for buttercream.

2. Combine ½ teaspoon of the vanilla and the almond extract in a cup; set aside. Beat egg whites in a large bowl of a heavy-duty standing mixer on low speed until foamy. Add cream of tartar; beat at medium-high speed until stiff. Gradually beat in remaining ¾ cup confectioners' sugar. Add food color and vanilla-almond extract mixture; beat 2 to 3 minutes more until stiff, scraping bowl once with a rubber spatula.

3. Fold egg whites into almond mixture until well blended and mixture looks shiny. Spoon into a large pastry bag fitted with a ½-inch round tip. Pipe 1¼-inch rounds 1½ inches apart onto one prepared cookie sheet. Dip fingertip into water and press to smooth any peaks. Bake 1 minute. Reduce oven temperature to 375°F. Open oven door and leave door slightly ajar. Bake cookies 4 to 6 minutes more, until they're firm and look dry. Slide foil onto a wire rack to cool completely. Repeat with remaining almond mixture, increasing the oven temperature to 450°F., then reducing the oven temperature after 1 minute to 375°F. as directed before baking each batch.

4. For buttercream, beat butter in a small mixer bowl on low speed until light and fluffy. Beat in remaining ¼ teaspoon vanilla, reserved ¼ cup almond mixture with any almond pieces until blended. *(Can be made ahead. Cover and freeze buttercream and store macaroons in an airtight container up to 2 weeks. Thaw buttercream in refrigerator overnight before using.)*

5. Line a cookie sheet with waxed paper. Slide small, thin spatula under cookies to remove from foil. Spread buttercream on bottom side of half of the cookies. Top with remaining cookies. Dip half of each cookie into cooled chocolate; transfer to prepared sheet. Let stand 30 minutes, until chocolate is set. Makes 2 dozen cookies.

Per cookie: 115 calories, 6.5 g fat, 2 g saturated fat, 5 mg cholesterol, 28 mg sodium, 13 g carbohydrates, 2 g protein, 18 mg calcium, 1 g fiber

almond pears

These exquisite shape-and-bake cookies are courtesy of contributing editor Kelly Staikopoulos, whose mother Mary taught her the fine art of Greek pastries. Pictured on page 288.

Prep time: 1 hour plus standing and decorating
Baking time: 20 to 22 minutes

DOUGH:

- 2 **cups whole blanched almonds**
- ¾ **cup confectioners' sugar**
- 2 **large egg whites**
- ¾ **teaspoon grated lemon peel**
- 2 **drops almond extract**

FILLING:

- 6 **dried Calimyrna figs (4 oz.), stems removed**
- 1 **tablespoon honey**
- 1 **teaspoon orange juice**
- ½ **teaspoon cinnamon**
- 1 **drop almond extract**
- 2 **tablespoons granulated sugar**
  Softened butter
- 36 **whole cloves**

MARZIPAN LEAVES (OPTIONAL):

- ¼ **cup almond paste**
  Green paste food color

1. *Make dough:* Process almonds and confectioners' sugar in a food processor until almonds are finely ground. Add egg whites, lemon peel and almond extract; process until mixture forms a ball. Transfer dough to a bowl.

2. *Make filling:* Pulse figs in food processor until finely chopped; add remaining filling ingredients and pulse until blended. Transfer to another bowl. Cover dough and filling and let stand 15 minutes.

3. Meanwhile, heat oven to 325°F. Grease 2 large cookie sheets with vegetable shortening. Spread granulated sugar on a plate. Coat hands with about 1 teaspoon softened butter. Roll dough into 1-inch balls. Place in palm of hand and press in center to make an indentation. Spoon ½ teaspoon filling into

indentation and press dough around filling to cover. Re-roll dough into a ball and form into a pear shape. Insert a clove into top to make a stem, rounded side down. Gently roll pear in granulated sugar. Place, stem side up, 2 inches apart on prepared cookie sheets. Repeat with remaining dough and filling.

4. Bake 15 minutes. Lay a sheet of foil loosely over cookies and bake 5 to 7 minutes more, until golden. Cool on wire rack. Transfer to an airtight container and let stand overnight. Makes 3 dozen cookies.

5. *Make marzipan leaves (if desired):* Dab green paste color into almond paste with toothpick. Mix until well blended, gradually adding dabs of paste if necessary for desired color. Roll ⅛-inch thick; shape into ½-inch leaves. Attach one leaf to each cookie.

Per cookie: 75 calories, 5 g fat, 0.5 g saturated fat, 1 mg cholesterol, 9 mg sodium, 7 g carbohydrates, 2 g protein, 26 mg calcium, 1 g fiber

fruit-filled biscotti

Prep time: 45 minutes plus freezing and standing
Baking time: 50 minutes

- 1¾ **cups all-purpose flour**
- ½ **teaspoon salt**
- ¼ **teaspoon baking powder**
- ½ **cup butter or margarine, softened**
- 1½ **cups sugar**
- 2 **teaspoons grated lemon peel**
- 2 **teaspoons vanilla extract**
- ½ **teaspoon anise seeds, finely chopped**
- 4 **large eggs**
- 1 **cup sliced natural almonds**
- ½ **cup red candied cherries, coarsely chopped**
- ½ **cup diced candied pineapple**
- ½ **cup dried cranberries, coarsely chopped**
- ½ **cup shelled unsalted pistachios, chopped**
- ⅓ **cup candied orange peel, chopped**

1. Heat oven to 350°F. Line two 9-inch square baking pans with foil, leaving a 1-inch overhang. Lightly grease foil with vegetable shortening.

2. Combine flour, salt and baking powder in a bowl; set aside. Beat butter in a large mixer bowl until creamy. Beat in sugar, lemon peel, vanilla and anise. Beat in eggs, one at a time, until well blended. Beat in flour mixture. Stir in almonds, candied cherries, pineapple, cranberries, pistachios and orange peel. Divide batter between pans, spreading evenly. Bake 30 minutes, or until a toothpick inserted in center comes out clean.

3. Cover pans tightly with foil and let cool completely on a wire rack. Using the foil overhang, lift each cookie square out of the pan; wrap and place in freezer until firm, 1 hour or overnight.

4. Adjust oven racks to divide oven into thirds. Heat oven to 300°F. Unwrap cookie squares and let stand at room temperature 10 minutes. Place 1 cookie square, top side up, on a cutting board. With a long serrated knife, cut square in half; then, using a sawing motion, cut each half crosswise into twenty $^3/_8$-inch-thick slices. Arrange slices $^3/_4$ inch apart on an ungreased cookie sheet. Repeat with remaining cookie square. Bake 10 minutes. Switch sheets between oven racks and bake 10 minutes more, until pale golden. Cool on wire racks. Makes 6½ dozen.

Per cookie: 65 calories, 2.5 g fat, 1 g saturated fat, 14 mg cholesterol, 32 mg sodium, 9 g carbohydrates, 1 g protein, 9 mg calcium, 0 g fiber

pepparkakor

We made star shapes of these classic Swedish molasses spice cookies, but they make great gingerbread people too! If the dough becomes too soft to transfer the cutouts to sheet, freeze 5 minutes until it becomes firm.

Prep time: 1 hour plus chilling, standing and decorating
Baking time: 8 to 10 minutes per batch

- **3 cups all-purpose flour**
- **2 teaspoons baking soda**
- **2 teaspoons cinnamon**
- **½ teaspoon ginger**
- **½ teaspoon cardamom**
- **1 cup butter, softened (no substitutions)**

---

test kitchen tip

make a wish

Next time you share Pepparkakor with friends, partake in this Swedish tradition: Hold a cookie in your palm, then, while making a wish, tap it in the middle with the knuckle of your pointer finger. If the cookie breaks in three pieces, lucky you—your wish will come true.

- **1½ cups sugar**
- **1 large egg**
- **2 teaspoons grated orange peel**
- **2 tablespoons dark molasses**
- **Decorative Icing (see tip, page 317)**
- **Pearl dusting (optional)***

1. Combine flour, baking soda, cinnamon, ginger and cardamom in a bowl. Beat butter and sugar in a large mixer bowl until light and fluffy. Beat in egg, orange peel and molasses. At low speed, beat in flour mixture until blended. Shape dough into a ball; divide into quarters, then flatten into disks. Wrap and refrigerate 4 hours or overnight.

2. Heat oven to 350°F. Let dough stand at room temperature 15 minutes. On lightly floured surface, with a floured rolling pin, roll 1 disk $^1/_8$ inch thick. Cut out with 3-inch snowflake- or star-shaped cookie cutter. Transfer cutouts with a spatula and arrange $^1/_2$ inch apart on 2 large ungreased cookie sheets. Bake 8 to 10 minutes, until set. Cool on wire racks. Repeat with remaining dough, rerolling and cutting scraps. Decorate as desired. Makes 5 dozen.

* *Note:* To decorate cookies with pearl dusting: Combine *$^1/_4$ teaspoon pearl dust powder* (available from specialty baking mail-order sources) and *1 to 2 teaspoons pure lemon or almond extract* until spreadable. Paint on cooled cookies with a brush; let dry. Repeat if necessary.

Per cookie: 105 calories, 3 g fat, 2 g saturated fat, 12 mg cholesterol, 76 mg sodium, 18 g carbohydrates, 1 g protein, 13 mg calcium, 0 g fiber

vanilla wreaths

These sugar-glazed wreaths (which are really sophisticated butter cookies) would make any baker proud. Pictured on page 286.

Prep time: 30 minutes plus standing and decorating
Baking time: 10 to 12 minutes per batch

- 2⅔ cups all-purpose flour
- ½ teaspoon baking powder
- ¼ teaspoon salt
- 1 large vanilla bean or 2 teaspoons vanilla extract
- 1 cup butter, softened (no substitutions)
- ¾ cup granulated sugar
- 1 large egg
- 2 cups confectioners' sugar
- 4 to 5 tablespoons hot water
  Decorative Icing (see tip, page 317)

1. Heat oven to 350°F. Combine flour, baking powder and salt in a bowl. Cut vanilla bean in half lengthwise, then cut each piece in half crosswise. With tip of a small knife, scrape out seeds from the bean. (Discard vanilla pod.)

2. Beat butter, sugar and vanilla seeds (or vanilla extract, if using) in a large mixer bowl at medium-high speed until light and fluffy. Beat in egg until smooth. At low speed, beat in flour mixture until blended. Spoon dough into a large pastry bag fitted with a #4 star tip. Pipe dough into circles 2½ inches in diameter 1 inch apart on 2 ungreased cookie sheets. Bake 10 to 12 minutes, until cookies are browned at edges.

3. Meanwhile, whisk confectioners' sugar and 4 tablespoons hot water, adding remaining 1 tablespoon water if necessary, to make a thin glaze. Transfer cookies to a wire rack set over a piece of waxed paper. Immediately brush hot cookies with glaze to cover. Let stand 30 minutes until glaze sets. Decorate as desired. Makes about 2 dozen cookies.

Per cookie: 220 calories, 7 g fat, 4 g saturated fat, 25 mg cholesterol, 102 mg sodium, 39 g carbohydrates, 2 g protein, 18 mg calcium, 0 g fiber

maple butter cookies

Great for mailing, because the baked-on glaze won't smudge. Order maple sugar through specialty baking catalogs.

Prep time: 45 minutes plus chilling and decorating
Baking time: 10 to 12 minutes per batch

- 1¼ cups butter, softened (no substitutions)
- ¾ cup granulated sugar
- ½ cup maple sugar
- 1 large egg
- 2 teaspoons vanilla extract
- 3 cups all-purpose flour

EGG PAINT:

- 1 large egg
- 1 to 2 drops *each* red and green food color

1. Beat butter and sugars at medium speed until fluffy. Beat in egg and vanilla. At low speed, beat in flour just until blended. Gather dough into a ball and divide into four pieces. Roll each piece ⅛ inch thick between two sheets of waxed paper. Refrigerate until firm, about 1 hour. Grease 2 large cookie sheets with vegetable shortening.

2. *Make egg paint:* Meanwhile, beat egg with a fork in a cup, making sure yolk and white are well blended. Transfer half the beaten egg to another cup. Tint half the egg red, the other half green.

3. Working with 1 piece of rolled-out dough at a time, uncover and cut out with a 3-inch leaf-shaped cookie cutter. Transfer cookies with a spatula 1 inch apart onto prepared cookie sheets. Decoratively brush cookies lightly with red and green egg paint, making sure it doesn't spill over edges. Refrigerate 30 minutes. Heat oven to 350°F. Lightly brush cutouts again with egg paint. With a toothpick, trace lines to resemble veins of a leaf. Bake 10 to 12 minutes, until golden brown. Cool on wire racks. Repeat with remaining dough, decorating and rerolling scraps. Makes 5½ dozen cookies.

Per cookie: 70 calories, 4 g fat, 2 g saturated fat, 16 mg cholesterol, 38 mg sodium, 8 g carbohydrates, 1 g protein, 3 mg calcium, 0 g fiber

festive fortune cookies

Fill fortune cookies with your own festive holiday greetings! Thin vanilla wafers are shaped into fortunes while hot and pliable, so you'll need to work quickly. If the wafers become too firm on the cookie sheet, return them to the oven for a few seconds to soften.

Prep time: 1 hour 15 minutes plus decorating
Baking time: 4 to 5 minutes per batch

- **2 large egg whites, at room temperature**
- **½ cup superfine sugar**
- **½ cup all-purpose flour**
- **1 tablespoon butter (no substitutions)**
- **¼ teaspoon salt**
- **¼ teaspoon vanilla extract**
- **¼ teaspoon almond extract**
- **Nontoxic paper**
- **Nontoxic pens**
- **3 ounces semisweet chocolate squares, melted (see tip, page 265) and cooled**
- **3 ounces white chocolate squares, melted (see tip, page 265) and cooled**

1. Grease 2 large nonstick cookie sheets with vegetable shortening. Vigorously whisk egg whites, sugar, flour, butter, salt, vanilla and almond extract in a medium bowl until smooth. Let stand 10 minutes.

2. Meanwhile, heat oven to 400°F. Cut nontoxic paper into twenty-four 3×¹/₂-inch strips. Write fortunes on strips with nontoxic pens.

3. *To bake 2 cookies per sheet:* Dip the top edge of a 3¹/₄-inch wide glass into the batter. Gently press onto prepared cookie sheet to trace a circle onto the sheet. Repeat tracing another circle 5 inches apart. Spoon 1 heaping measuring teaspoonful of batter into the center of each circle, scraping out batter from teaspoon with a rubber spatula. Fill each circle by spreading the batter with the back of the spoon

as evenly as possible. Repeat process with second cookie sheet.

4. Bake one cookie sheet at a time, 4 to 5 minutes, until cookies have a ¹/₂-inch brown rim around the edges. (If they brown unevenly, that's OK.)

5. Transfer cookie sheet to a rack. Working very quickly, remove one cookie with a thin, flexible spatula, and place, bottom side up, on work surface. Place a fortune on the cookie in the center of the cookie so the paper extends from only one side. Fold cookie in half and place the folded edge down on the rim of a glass measure. Press the ends down, holding the cookie in place for about 10 seconds, until it starts to harden and will hold its shape. Repeat with the second cookie (if it becomes too hard to shape, return to oven for a few seconds to soften). Cool cookies on wire rack. Repeat with remaining batter, cleaning, drying and greasing sheets between each batch.

6. Using 12 cookies, dip one quarter of each cookie from the edge of the cookie without the fortune extending from it in melted semisweet chocolate. Transfer to wire racks. Repeat with remaining cookies and melted white chocolate. Let cookies stand 1 hour or until set. Makes about 2 dozen cookies.

Per cookie: 70 calories, 3 g fat, 2 g saturated fat, 3 mg cholesterol, 36 mg sodium, 10 g carbohydrates, 1 g protein, 6 mg calcium, 0 g fiber

---

test kitchen tip
do the dough ahead

If you don't have a full day to bake your holiday cookies, remember that many cookie doughs can be made ahead then refrigerated or frozen. (Exceptions in this chapter include the Fortune Cookies, left, and French Macaroons, page 309). Pack dough in an airtight container, and store in the refrigerator up to 2 days or freeze up to 3 months. Thaw dough in the refrigerator until just soft enough to use.

shortbread cookies

Add a batch of these colorful shortbread squares to your holiday cookie platter. Look for decorative cookie stamps in a wide range of shapes and patterns in specialty kitchenware shops. Pictured on page 288.

Prep time: 20 minutes plus chilling and decorating
Baking time: 28 to 30 minutes

- **1 cup unsalted butter, softened (no substitutions)**
- **¼ cup confectioners' sugar**
- **¼ cup granulated sugar**
- **2¼ cups all-purpose flour**
- **BAKED-ON ICING:**
- **⅔ cup butter, softened (no substitutions)**
- **¼ cup confectioners' sugar**
- **⅔ cup all-purpose flour**
- **3 drops *each* red food color, green food color blue food color and yellow food color**
- **4 teaspoons water**
- **2 teaspoons unsweetened cocoa**

1. Heat oven to 300°F. Beat butter, confectioners' sugar and granulated sugar in a large mixer bowl until blended. At low speed, beat in flour until combined.

2. Gather dough into a ball and divide in half. On a lightly floured surface with a floured rolling pin, roll one half into a 7½-inch square, ⅜ inch thick. Trim edges of square. With a small, sharp knife, lightly score nine 2¼-inch squares. Press center of each square with a 2-inch cookie stamp. Cut into squares and transfer to an ungreased cookie sheet. Repeat with remaining dough. Refrigerate 20 minutes.

3. *Make baked-on icing:* Meanwhile, beat butter, sugar and flour in a small mixer bowl until smooth. Divide icing into 4 bowls; tint each bowl with red, green, blue and yellow food color. Transfer half of each color to 4 pastry bags fitted with #2 round tips.

4. Combine water and cocoa in another bowl until smooth. Brush cookies with cocoa mixture or brush or pipe with baked-on icing as desired. (If brushing on baked-on icing, add enough water to make spreadable). Bake 28 to 30 minutes or until pale golden. Cool on wire racks. Makes 1½ dozen cookies.

Per cookie: 290 calories, 20.5 g fat, 13 g saturated fat, 55 mg cholesterol, 106 mg sodium, 24 g carbohydrates, 3 g protein, 9 mg calcium, 1 g fiber

chocolate chip drops

How to improve on the classic? Give it a holiday twist! Here, sweet dried cherries, toasted pecans and three kinds of chocolate make these delights festive indeed. Pictured on page 286.

Prep time: 35 minutes plus standing and decorating
Baking time: 10 to 12 minutes per batch

- **2¼ cups all-purpose flour**
- **1 teaspoon baking soda**
- **½ teaspoon salt**
- **½ cup butter or margarine, softened**
- **½ cup vegetable shortening**
- **¾ cup granulated sugar**
- **¾ cup firmly packed brown sugar**
- **1 tablespoon vanilla extract**
- **3 ounces unsweetened chocolate squares, melted (see tip, page 265) and cooled**
- **2 large eggs**
- **1 cup white chocolate chips**
- **1 cup semisweet chocolate chunks**
- **1 cup pecan halves, toasted and chopped**
- **½ cup dried tart cherries, chopped**
- **CHOCOLATE DRIZZLE:**
- **½ cup white chocolate chips, melted (see tip, page 265) and cooled**
- **2 ounces semisweet chocolate squares, melted (see tip, page 265) and cooled**

1. Heat oven to 375°F. Combine flour, baking soda and salt in a bowl. Beat butter, shortening, sugars and vanilla in a large mixer bowl until light and fluffy. Beat in cooled unsweetened chocolate. Add eggs, one at a time, beating well after each addition. At low speed, beat in flour mixture until blended. Stir in white chocolate chips, semisweet chocolate chunks, pecans and cherries. For each batch of cookies, drop dough by tablespoonfuls 2 inches apart onto 2 ungreased cookie sheets. Bake 10 to 12 minutes, until cookies feel firm. Cool on wire racks. Repeat with remaining dough.

2. *Make chocolate drizzle:* Place cooled white chocolate chips in a heavy-duty plastic storage bag. Place cooled semisweet chocolate chunks in another heavy-duty plastic storage bag. Cut a very small hole in one corner of each bag. Drizzle or dot chocolates over tops of cookies. Let stand 1 hour until set. Makes about 5½ dozen cookies.

Per cookie: 130 calories, 7.5 g fat, 3.5 g saturated fat, 10 mg cholesterol, 60 mg sodium, 15 g carbohydrates, 1 g protein, 14 mg calcium, 1 g fiber

chocolate-walnut meringue bars

This yummy bar has a buttery shortbread base, a thin layer of currant jelly and a fudgy chocolate-nut meringue topping. Tip: If freezing these cookies ahead of time, don't cut them prior to freezing—just wrap them up in the foil they were baked in. Pictured on page 286.

Prep time: 1 hour plus chilling · Baking time: 38 minutes

CRUST:
- 1½ cups all-purpose flour
- ¾ cup butter or margarine, softened
- ¼ cup confectioners' sugar

TOPPING:
- ⅔ cup granulated sugar
- 1½ cups walnut halves
- 3 large egg whites
- ¼ teaspoon salt
- ¼ cup currant jelly

- 2 ounces semisweet chocolate squares, melted (see tip, page 265) and cooled
- 1 ounce unsweetened chocolate square, melted (see tip, page 265) and cooled
- Confectioners' sugar

1. *Make crust:* Heat oven to 350°F. Line a 13×9-inch baking pan with foil. Beat flour, butter and confectioners' sugar in a large mixer bowl on low speed until mixture begins to form a dough (mixture will be crumbly). Pat dough evenly into bottom of prepared pan. Bake 18 minutes, until golden brown. Cool on a wire rack while making topping.

2. *Make topping:* Transfer 1 tablespoon of the granulated sugar to a food processor. Set remaining sugar aside. Process walnuts and the sugar until ground; transfer to a large bowl. (If there are larger pieces of walnuts, that's OK.) Set aside ¼ cup of the nut mixture.

3. Beat egg whites in a large mixer bowl until foamy; add salt and beat to soft peaks. Gradually beat in remaining granulated sugar, 2 tablespoons at a time, until mixture is stiff.

4. Spread jelly over crust, leaving a ¼-inch border. Fold beaten whites and cooled chocolates into walnut mixture just until blended; spread evenly over crust. Sprinkle top with reserved ¼ cup walnut mixture. Bake 20 minutes, until topping is puffed and dry on top. Cool on a wire rack. Refrigerate 2 hours, until cold. Lift out of pan with foil; dust lightly with confectioners' sugar. Cut into 2-inch squares, then cut each square into 2 triangles. Makes 4 dozen bars.

Per bar: 90 calories, 5.5 g fat, 2.5 g saturated fat, 8 mg cholesterol, 46 mg sodium, 9 g carbohydrates, 1 g protein, 5 mg calcium, 0 g fiber

baking with butter and margarine

Whether you're a butter-only purist, or prefer margarine, here are some tips to remember about these essential baking ingredients:

USE ONLY butter or margarine that comes in sticks—no whipped, reduced-fat or tub products. Read the label to make sure that the product contains at least 80% vegetable oil or fat, as products with less fat contain more water, and are not recommended for baking.

RECIPES for more delicate cookies may call for butter, with no margarine substitutions.

UNSALTED BUTTER can be used interchangeably with salted butter, though if you use unsalted butter, you may want to increase the amount of salt in the recipe.

rugelach

These crescent-shaped cinnamon nut cookies from Israel are definitely worth the time and effort. The addition of yeast makes this dough easier to handle than the traditional cream cheese version. Substitute pecans for the walnuts, if preferred. Pictured on page 286.

Prep time: 1 hour 15 minutes plus chilling
Baking time: 18 to 20 minutes per batch

DOUGH:

- 1 package active dry yeast
- 2 tablespoons granulated sugar
- ½ cup warm water (105°F. to 115°F.)
- 3 cups all-purpose flour
- ½ teaspoon salt
- 3 large egg yolks
- ½ cup heavy or whipping cream
- 1 teaspoon vanilla extract
- 1 cup butter or margarine, softened

FILLING:

- 1 cup pecans or walnuts, chopped
- ½ cup raisins
- ½ cup chopped dried tart cherries or cranberries
- ¼ cup firmly packed brown sugar
- ¾ cup granulated sugar
- 4 teaspoons cinnamon
- ½ cup apricot preserves
- ½ cup crystallized sugar (optional)

1. *Make dough:* Dissolve yeast and granulated sugar in the water in a bowl. Combine flour and salt in a large mixer bowl of a heavy-duty mixer. At low speed, beat dissolved yeast, egg yolks, cream and vanilla into flour mixture, or beat with a large spoon until smooth and well blended. Beat in butter, 2 tablespoons at a time, until blended. Gather dough into a ball; divide into 8 equal pieces. Shape each piece into a ball; wrap and refrigerate 4 hours or overnight.

2. *Make filling:* Combine pecans, raisins, cherries and brown sugar in a medium bowl.

3. Combine granulated sugar and cinnamon in a small bowl. Heat oven to 350°F. Line two cookie sheets with foil; grease foil with vegetable shortening. Sprinkle 1 tablespoon cinnamon-sugar on work surface. Working with one ball of dough at a time (keep remaining balls refrigerated), roll each ball into an 8-inch circle, turning circle over a few times to coat both sides with cinnamon-sugar. Spread top with 1 tablespoon preserves, then sprinkle with heaping ¼ cup nut filling, leaving a ½-inch border around edge. Sprinkle with 1 teaspoon cinnamon-sugar. Cut circle into 8 wedges; roll wedges up from outer edge. Transfer onto prepared cookie sheets, 1 inch apart, curving into crescent shapes. Sprinkle tops with crystallized sugar, if desired. Repeat process with remaining dough, preserves, filling and crystallized sugar. Bake 18 to 20 minutes, until lightly browned. Cool on wire racks. Makes 64 cookies.

Per cookie: 95 calories, 5 g fat, 2.5 g saturated fat, 20 mg cholesterol, 50 mg sodium, 12 g carbohydrates, 1 g protein, 8 mg calcium, 0 g fiber

german sandwich cookies

Love the rich, sweet flavor of hazelnuts but haven't baked with them before? Here's how to toast the nuts: Spread on a cookie sheet. Bake at 350°F. until lightly browned and skins are crackly, 12 to 15 minutes. Wrap the nuts in a clean kitchen towel; let stand 5 minutes. Rub nuts in the towel to remove their skins, then cool completely. Pictured on page 286.

Prep time: 45 minutes plus chilling and decorating
Baking time: 8 minutes per batch

- ¾ **cup toasted, skinned hazelnuts**
- 12 **tablespoons granulated sugar, divided**
- 1 **cup butter, softened (no substitutions)**
- 1 **large egg yolk**
- 1 **teaspoon vanilla extract**
- ¼ **teaspoon cinnamon**
- 2½ **cups all-purpose flour**
- 1 **cup plus 2 tablespoons raspberry jelly**
  Decorative icing (see tip, right)
  Confectioners' sugar

1. Heat oven to 350°F. Grease two large cookie sheets with vegetable shortening. Process nuts and 2 tablespoons of the granulated sugar in a food processor until finely ground.

2. Beat remaining 10 tablespoons sugar and the butter in a large mixer bowl on medium speed until light and fluffy. Beat in egg yolk, vanilla and cinnamon. At low speed, beat in nut mixture and flour until blended.

3. Gather dough into a ball and divide into 4 equal pieces. Roll each piece ¹/₈ inch thick between 2 sheets of waxed paper. Refrigerate 30 minutes, until firm. Working with one piece of dough at a time, uncover and cut out with a 3- or 4-inch tree-shaped cookie cutter. (Keep remaining dough refrigerated.) Transfer cutouts with a spatula to prepared cookie sheets. With ³/₈-inch round pastry tip or a drinking straw, cut out three circles from half the cutouts. Remove circles and reserve scraps. (If cutouts become too soft, refrigerate for a few

minutes until firm.) Bake 8 minutes, until pale golden. Cool on wire racks. Repeat with remaining dough, rerolling and cutting scraps.

4. Spread ¹/₂ teaspoon jelly on top of each cookie without holes; top each with cookies with holes. Decorate as desired; then dust with confectioners' sugar. Makes about 3¹/₂ dozen cookies.

Per cookie: 160 calories, 6 g fat, 3 g saturated fat, 17 mg cholesterol, 50 mg sodium, 27 g carbohydrates, 1 g protein, 13 mg calcium, 0 g fiber

---

test kitchen tip

decorative icing

Many of our holiday cookie recipes call on this icing to jazz them up. Fortunately, the recipe is as simple as it gets. Rely on it for all your holiday and special-occasion sweets.

- 1 **box (1 lb.) confectioners' sugar**
- 3 **tablespoons meringue powder***
- 6 **to 7 tablespoons cold water**
  Assorted paste food colors (optional)

COMBINE all ingredients except food colors in a mixer bowl. Beat at medium speed until smooth. Increase speed to high and beat 5 minutes, until thick and smooth, adding up to 1 tablespoon more cold water for piping consistency, if necessary. Ices about 5¹/₂ dozen cookies.

TO TINT: Paste colors provide the most vibrant hues, and because they are concentrated, you won't need to use much. Divide frosting into separate bowls for each color. Dab paste into icing with toothpick. Mix with a spoon until well blended, gradually adding dabs of paste, if necessary, for desired color.

Note: Can be found in supermarkets, specialty baking stores and through baking mail-order sources.

festive 'n' fiery chile blends

Whip up your own custom spice blends for hot gifts your friends will love. Each is a terrific rub for meat or chicken, or copy our recipe for Sour Cream Spice Dip onto a decorative card or label. Each recipe makes about 1 cup, unless specified; present in small decorative jars.

HABANERO: Stir together 5$\frac{1}{2}$ tablespoons onion powder; 3 tablespoons salt; 4 teaspoons *each* dried oregano, dry mustard and sugar; and 2 teaspoons *each* Habanero powder,* garlic powder and cumin in a bowl.

CHIPOTLE: Stir together 5$\frac{1}{2}$ tablespoons onion powder; 3 tablespoons salt; 4 teaspoons *each* smoked jalapeño flakes,* sugar, cumin and dried thyme; and 2 teaspoons coriander.

JALAPEÑO: Stir together 5$\frac{1}{2}$ tablespoons onion powder, 3 tablespoons salt, 4 teaspoons *each* sugar and jalapeño flakes,* 2 teaspoons *each* coriander and dried oregano in a bowl. Makes about $\frac{3}{4}$ cup.

CURRY: Stir together 5$\frac{1}{2}$ tablespoons onion powder; 3 tablespoons *each* salt, curry and cumin; 4 teaspoons dried thyme; and 2 teaspoons freshly ground black pepper.

SOUR CREAM SPICE DIP: Stir together 1 tablespoon of your choice of any of the Festive 'n' Fiery Chile Blends, 1 container (8 oz.) sour cream and 2 tablespoons mayonnaise in a bowl. Makes about 1 cup.

Per tablespoon spice dip: 35 calories, 3.5 g fat, 1.5 g saturated fat, 6 mg cholesterol, 62 mg sodium, 1 g carbohydrates, 0 g protein, 14 mg calcium, 0 g fiber

Note: Can be found in Spanish or Latino specialty stores.

holiday party nuts EASY

Treat your friends to a bag of these crunchy munchies!

Prep time: 15 minutes • Baking time: 38 to 43 minutes

- ½ cup light corn syrup
- 6 tablespoons butter or margarine
- ⅓ cup firmly packed brown sugar
- 2 tablespoons curry powder
- 1¼ teaspoons salt
- ¼ teaspoon ground red pepper
- 1 can (12 oz.) unsalted cocktail peanuts
- 1 cup unsalted shelled pistachios
- 1 cup shelled pumpkin seeds
- 1 bag (8 oz.) whole blanched almonds
- 1 bag (7 oz.) pretzel nuggets

1. Heat oven to 300°F. Grease the bottom of a broiler pan or large roasting pan with vegetable shortening.

2. Combine corn syrup, butter, brown sugar, curry powder, salt and red pepper in a medium saucepan. Heat over medium heat, stirring occasionally, until butter is melted and sugar is dissolved, 3 minutes.

3. Meanwhile, toss together remaining ingredients on the prepared pan with a large spoon. Pour syrup mixture over nut mixture and toss again to coat. Bake 38 to 43 minutes, stirring once halfway through, until mixture is a deep golden brown.

4. Arrange a 30-inch long piece of foil on a smooth work surface (this will avoid staining your counter from the curry powder). Cover foil with a 30-inch long piece of waxed paper.

5. Scrape nut mixture onto waxed paper with an oiled rubber spatula, then spread to evenly cover the sheets. Cool completely. Break up into small chunks and store in an airtight container at room temperature up to 1 month. Makes 36 servings.

Per serving: 195 calories, 14 g fat, 3 g saturated fat, 5 mg cholesterol, 203 mg sodium, 14 g carbohydrates, 6 g protein, 28 mg calcium, 3 g fiber

cranberry-spiced mulled wine or apple cider

There's nothing quite like the aroma of warm spices during the holidays. Wrap up our fragrant fruit-and-spice mixture into decorative cellophane bags (available from specialty food shops) or make bags from Christmas-colored fabric. Then, present a bag attached to a bottle of wine for a real "housewarming" gift. Be sure to include instructions on how to mull the wine.

Prep time: 10 minutes • Cooking time: 30 to 35 minutes

CRANBERRY-SPICE BAGS:
- 2 cups dried cranberries, divided
- 16 cinnamon sticks, divided
- 16 candied orange peel strips, divided
- 1 cup crystallized ginger, divided

MULLED WINE (PER BATCH):
- 1 bottle (1 liter) fruity red wine (such as Beaujolais); or ½ gallon apple cider or unfiltered natural apple juice
- 2 tablespoons sugar

1. *Make cranberry-spice bags:* Arrange ¼ cup of the cranberries, 2 of the cinnamon sticks, 2 of the candied orange peel strips and 2 tablespoons of the crystallized ginger in each of eight decorative bags. Seal. *(Can be made ahead. Store at room temperature up to 1 month.)*

2. *To make mulled wine:* Empty the contents of 1 bag of spices and the wine into a saucepan. Bring to a simmer over medium heat. Reduce heat to low and barely simmer 30 minutes, until flavor is infused into wine; stir in sugar until dissolved. Strain and pour into wine glasses; discard solids. Makes 6 servings. (Or, for mulled apple cider or juice, prepare as directed above, except omit the sugar and increase the cooking time to 35 minutes. Strain mixture; discard solids.) Makes 8 servings.

Per serving with wine: 205 calories, 0 g fat, 0 g saturated fat, 0 mg cholesterol, 17 mg sodium, 25 g carbohydrates, 0 g protein, 24 mg calcium, 1 g fiber

chipotle pesto

Everyone on your gift list will love this Southwestern take on classic basil pesto. Insert a card indicating that it can be tossed with pasta, spread on crackers or used as a dip for vegetables and chips. Be sure to include the storage instructions (below).

Prep time: 25 minutes • Baking time: 38 minutes

- 4 plum tomatoes, cored and halved
- 2 red bell peppers, seeded and halved
- ½ cup raw shelled pumpkin seeds (pepitas)
- 4 chipotle chiles in adobo sauce, seeds removed (see tip, page 95)
- 1 cup olive oil
- 1 cup fresh cilantro leaves
- 2 teaspoons minced garlic
- ½ cup freshly grated Parmesan cheese
- 1 teaspoon salt
- ½ teaspoon freshly ground pepper

1. Heat oven to 425°F. Place tomato halves, cut side up, and pepper halves, cut side down, on a large jelly-roll pan. Bake 30 minutes, until tomato and pepper skins blister and are evenly charred. Cool.

2. Reduce oven temperature to 350°F. Spread pumpkin seeds on a cookie sheet. Bake 8 minutes, until toasted. Cool. Meanwhile, discard skin from peppers; transfer peppers to a cutting board; coarsely chop.

3. Chop pumpkin seeds in a food processor and set aside. Add chipotles and oil to processor and process until smooth. Add tomato halves and chopped bell peppers and process, pulsing, until mixture is blended but still chunky. Return pumpkin seeds to processor with cilantro, garlic, Parmesan, salt and pepper and process until blended. *(Can be made ahead. Transfer pesto to an airtight container. Cover and refrigerate up to 1 week or freeze up to 1 month.)* Makes about 3¼ cups.

Per ¼ cup: 265 calories, 26.5 g fat, 4.5 g saturated fat, 4 mg cholesterol, 378 mg sodium, 4 g carbohydrates, 4 g protein, 80 mg calcium, 2 g fiber

mini citrus sweet breads

A perfect bread for holiday time, these loaves are baked in small disposable cake pans, perfect for gift-giving or to keep in the freezer for unexpected guests.

Prep time: 30 minutes plus rising
Baking time: 16 minutes

1 **package active dry yeast**
   Pinch sugar
½ **cup warm water (105°F. to 115°F.)**
3 **to 3½ cups all-purpose flour, divided**
¼ **cup sugar**
3 **large eggs, at room temperature**
⅓ **cup olive oil**
1½ **teaspoons grated orange peel**
1 **teaspoon salt**
¾ **cup golden raisins**
¼ **cup chopped candied orange peel**

1. Sprinkle yeast and pinch of sugar over the warm water in a large bowl. Let mixture stand until foamy, about 5 minutes. Beat in 2 cups of the flour, the ¼ cup sugar, the eggs, oil, grated peel and salt with a wooden spoon until smooth. Stir in raisins, candied peel and enough of the remaining flour (about 1¼ cups) to make a soft dough.

2. On a lightly floured surface, knead dough until smooth and elastic, dusting with remaining ¼ cup flour, as needed, to keep dough from sticking, 6 to 8 minutes. Transfer dough to a lightly oiled bowl; turn to oil top. Cover bowl with plastic wrap and let dough rise in a warm, draft-free place until doubled in bulk, 1½ hours.

3. Punch dough down; cover and let rest for 10 minutes.

4. Brush four 15-ounce miniature loaf pans with oil. Divide dough into four portions; shape each piece into an oval and place in prepared pans. With a small, sharp knife, make 2 slashes across the top of each loaf. Transfer pans to a jelly-roll pan; cover with plastic wrap and let loaves rise until doubled in bulk, 45 minutes.

5. Heat oven to 375°F. Bake loaves on jelly-roll pan until golden brown, 16 minutes. Transfer pans to wire racks and cool 5 minutes. Unmold loaves and cool completely. Return cooled breads to baking pans for gift-giving. *(Can be made ahead. Wrap well and freeze up to 1 month. Thaw at room temperature 2 hours before serving.)* Makes 4 mini breads (4 slices per bread).

Per slice: 190 calories, 5.5 g fat, 1 g saturated fat, 40 mg cholesterol, 159 mg sodium, 31 g carbohydrates, 4 g protein, 13 mg calcium, 1 g fiber

white chocolate candies

Start with a bag of white chocolate chips, melted and poured into fancy cups, and presto—you've got dainty confection candies and a wonderful gift. They're sophisticated and not too sweet, since each treat is sprinkled with a colorful assortment of dried fruits and nuts. Pictured on page 288.

Total prep time: 20 minutes plus chilling

1 **package (12 oz.) white chocolate chips,**
   melted according to package directions
½ **cup assorted coarsely chopped dried fruits**
   (such as apricots, cranberries and golden
   raisins) and nuts (such as walnuts, pecans,
   almonds and pistachios)

Divide and pour melted chocolate into thirty-six 1⅜-inch miniature foil candy cups. Immediately sprinkle tops with chopped dried fruits and nuts. Refrigerate until firm, 30 minutes. Makes 36 candies.

Per 2 candies: 58 calories, 3.5 g fat, 1.5 g saturated fat, 0 mg cholesterol, 8 mg sodium, 7 g carbohydrates, 1 g protein, 20 mg calcium, 0 g fiber

nutrition information

To help you plan well-balanced meals, calorie and nutrient analyses appear at the end of each of our recipes.

how we analyze

- When a recipe gives a choice of ingredients, such as butter or margarine, we use the first ingredient mentioned when figuring the analysis.

- When the recipe gives a range in the amount of an ingredient, we average the two amounts. For example, if a recipe calls for $1/2$ to 1 lb. of boneless beef top loin steak, we use $3/4$ pound when figuring the analysis.

- The analysis does not include optional ingredients.

- When there is a range in the amount of servings a recipe yields, the nutrition analysis is based on the average of the two numbers. For example, if a recipe serves 4 to 6, the analysis is based on 5 servings.

- When milk is a recipe ingredient, the analysis is calculated using 2-percent (reduced-fat) milk.

- Nutrition values are rounded to the nearest whole number, with the exception of calories, which are rounded to the nearest 5 calories, and total fat and saturated fat, which are rounded to the nearest .5 grams.

daily goal

The dietary guidelines below are nutrient levels suggested for moderately active adults. While there's no harm in occasionally going over or under these guidelines, maintaining a balanced diet can help you maintain good health.

	WOMEN	MEN
Calories	2,000	2,500
Total fat	60 g or less	70 g or less
Saturated fat	20 g or less	23 g or less
Cholesterol	300 mg or less	300 mg or less
Sodium	2,400 mg or less	2,400 mg or less
Carbohydrates	250 g or more	250 g or more
Protein	55 g to 90 g	55 g to 90 g
Calcium	1,000 mg	1,000 mg
Fiber	20 g to 35 g	20 g to 35 g

low-fat recipes

In planning a healthy diet, it's a good idea to try to keep the percentage of calories from fat to no more than 30 percent. To help you choose recipes that are low in fat, some of our recipes have been flagged with a low-fat symbol. This means that one serving of the recipe contains less than 3 grams of fat per 100 calories.

substitutions in a pinch

No surprise—it's always best to use the exact ingredients a recipe calls for, but when you absolutely can't get out to shop, or your supermarket doesn't have what you need, the following substitutions will do the trick:

ANDOUILLE SAUSAGE
Use equal amount garlic sausage

BASMATI RICE
Use equal amount regular long-grain rice or Texmati rice

BOK CHOY
Use equal amount spinach or white cabbage

BREADCRUMBS, PLAIN DRY
For 1 cup: Use $^3/_4$ cup cracker crumbs

BROTH, BEEF OR CHICKEN
For 1 cup: Use 1 bouillon cube or 1 teaspoon granules mixed with 1 cup boiling water

BUTTERMILK
For 1 cup: Use 1 tablespoon lemon juice or vinegar plus enough milk to make 1 cup (let stand 5 minutes before using); or 1 cup plain yogurt

CAKE FLOUR
For 1 cup: Use 1 cup minus 2 tablespoons all-purpose flour

CANADIAN BACON
Use equal amount smoked lean ham slices

CAPERS
Use equal amount chopped pitted green olives

CONFECTIONERS' SUGAR
For 1 cup: Blend 1 cup granulated sugar and 1 tablespoon cornstarch in a food processor until powdery

CORNSTARCH
For 1 tablespoon: Use 2 tablespoons all-purpose flour

CURRANTS (DRIED)
Use equal amount dark seedless raisins

DARK CORN SYRUP
For 1 cup: Use $^3/_4$ cup light corn syrup plus $^1/_4$ cup molasses or cane syrup

ENOKI MUSHROOMS
Use equal amount bean sprouts

ESPRESSO POWDER
Use equal amount instant coffee crystals

FIVE-SPICE POWDER
Combine 4 teaspoons black peppercorns (preferably Szechuan), 1 tablespoon cinnamon, 2 teaspoons fennel seeds, 2 teaspoons anise or 6 star anise and $^1/_2$ teaspoon cloves. Blend in a spice or coffee grinder until powdery. Measure amount needed.

HERBS
For 1 tablespoon snipped fresh herb: Use $^1/_2$ to 1 teaspoon dried herb, crushed

GARLIC
For 1 small clove: Use $^1/_8$ teaspoon garlic powder

FRESH GINGER (GINGERROOT)
For 1 teaspoon grated fresh ginger (gingerroot): Use $^1/_4$ teaspoon ground ginger

GOUDA CHEESE
Use equal amount Edam or mild Cheddar cheese

GRAHAM CRACKER CRUMBS
Use equal amount vanilla wafer crumbs

GRUYÈRE CHEESE
Use equal amount Swiss cheese

substitutions in a pinch

HALF-AND-HALF OR LIGHT CREAM
For 1 cup use 1 tablespoon melted butter or margarine plus enough whole milk to make 1 cup

HALIBUT
Use equal amount cod

HAZELNUTS
Use equal amount blanched almonds

HOISIN SAUCE
For $\frac{1}{4}$ cup: Combine $\frac{1}{4}$ cup (generous) apricot preserves, strained; 1 teaspoon cider vinegar; $1\frac{1}{2}$ teaspoons soy sauce; pinch red pepper; and 1 small clove garlic, minced

KALAMATA OLIVES
Use equal amount other brine-cured olives

LEMON JUICE
For 1 teaspoon: Use $\frac{1}{2}$ teaspoon vinegar

LEMON OR ORANGE PEEL, GRATED
Use a few drops lemon or orange extract

LENTILS
Use equal amount green split peas; cook longer

LOBSTER
For each $1\frac{1}{4}$-pound lobster: Use $\frac{1}{4}$ pound shrimp and $\frac{1}{4}$ pound monkfish

MAPLE SYRUP
For 1 cup: Use 1 cup brown sugar syrup or dark corn syrup and a few drops maple extract

MASCARPONE CHEESE
Use equal amount whipped cream cheese

NUTMEG
Use equal amount mace

ORANGE ROUGHY
Use equal amount flounder or tilapia

PAPAYA
Use equal amount mango or peach

POLENTA
Use equal amount cornmeal

RIGATONI
Use equal amount penne, ziti or other tube-shaped pasta

ROMANO CHEESE
Use equal amount Parmesan cheese

SWISS CHARD
Use equal amount fresh spinach

TERIYAKI SAUCE
For $\frac{1}{4}$ cup: Use $\frac{1}{4}$ cup soy sauce plus 1 tablespoon brown sugar

WATERCRESS
Use equal amount arugula or chicory

WESTPHALIAN HAM
Use equal amount Italian prosciutto, Black Forest Ham or Virginia ham

WORCESTERSHIRE SAUCE
Use equal amount steak sauce

YELLOW SQUASH
Use equal amount zucchini

h-k

l-m

t-u